When the Innocent are Punished

Palgrave Studies in Prisons and Penology

Edited by: **Ben Crewe**, University of Cambridge, **Yvonne Jewkes**, University of Leicester and **Thomas Ugelvik**, University of Oslo

This is a unique and innovative series, the first of its kind dedicated entirely to prison scholarship. At a historical point in which the prison population has reached an all-time high, the series seeks to analyse the form, nature and consequences of incarceration and related forms of punishment. *Palgrave Studies in Prisons and Penology* provides an important forum for burgeoning prison research across the world.

Series editors:

BEN CREWE is Deputy Director of the Prisons Research Centre at the Institute of Criminology, University of Cambridge, UK and co-author of 'The Prisoner'.

YVONNE JEWKES is Professor of Criminology, Leicester University, UK. She has authored numerous books and articles on the subject and is editor of the *Handbook on Prisons*.

THOMAS UGELVIK is Senior Research Fellow in the Department of Criminology at the University of Oslo, Norway and editor of *Penal Exceptionalism? Nordic Prison Policy and Practice*.

Advisory Board:

Anna Eriksson, Monash University, Australia

Andrew M. Jefferson, Rehabilitation and Research Centre for Torture Victims, Denmark

Shadd Maruna, Queen's University Belfast, Northern Ireland

Jonathon Simon, UC Berkeley, California, US

Michael Welch, Rutgers University, New Jersey, US

Titles include:

Vincenzo Ruggiero and Mick Ryan
PUNISHMENT IN EUROPE
A Critical Anatomy of Penal Systems

Peter Scharff Smith
WHEN THE INNOCENT ARE PUNISHED
The Children of Imprisoned Parents

Phil Scraton and Linda Moore
THE INCARCERATION OF WOMEN
Punishing Bodies, Breaking Spirits

Palgrave Studies in Prisons and Penology
Series Standing Order ISBN 978–1–137–27090–0 (Hardback)

You can receive future titles in this series as they are published by placing a standing order. Please contact your bookseller or, in case of difficulty, write to us at the address below with your name and address, the title of the series and the ISBN quoted above.

Customer Services Department, Macmillan Distribution Ltd, Houndmills, Basingstoke, Hampshire RG21 6XS, England

When the Innocent are Punished

The Children of Imprisoned Parents

Peter Scharff Smith
Senior Research Fellow, Danish Institute for Human Rights, Denmark

© Peter Scharff Smith 2014
Chapters 7 and 10 © Peter Scharff Smith and Janne Jakobsen 2014
Softcover reprint of the hardcover 1st edition 2014 978-1-137-41428-1

All rights reserved. No reproduction, copy or transmission of this
publication may be made without written permission.

No portion of this publication may be reproduced, copied or transmitted
save with written permission or in accordance with the provisions of the
Copyright, Designs and Patents Act 1988, or under the terms of any licence
permitting limited copying issued by the Copyright Licensing Agency,
Saffron House, 6–10 Kirby Street, LondonEC1N 8TS.

Any person who does any unauthorized act in relation to this publication
may be liable to criminal prosecution and civil claims for damages.

The authors have asserted their rights to be identified as the authors of this work
in accordance with the Copyright, Designs and Patents Act 1988.

First published 2014 by
PALGRAVE MACMILLAN

Palgrave Macmillan in the UK is an imprint of Macmillan Publishers Limited,
registered in England, company number 785998, of Houndmills, Basingstoke,
Hampshire RG21 6XS.

Palgrave Macmillan in the US is a division of St Martin's Press LLC,
175 Fifth Avenue, New York, NY10010.

Palgrave Macmillan is the global academic imprint of the above companies
and has companies and representatives throughout the world.

Palgrave® and Macmillan® are registered trademarks in the United States,
the United Kingdom, Europe and other countries

ISBN 978-1-349-49020-2   ISBN 978-1-137-41429-8 (eBook)
DOI 10.1057/9781137414298

A catalogue record for this book is available from the British Library.

A catalog record for this book is available from the Library of Congress.

Transferred to Digital Printing in 2014

Contents

Acknowledgements ... vii

Part I Prison, Society and Prisoners' Children

1. Scenes from Family Life ... 3
2. When the Innocent are Punished ... 7
3. Prison and Society ... 21

Part II Children of Imprisoned Parents: Their Numbers, Problems and Human Rights

4. Children of Imprisoned Parents in Numbers ... 43
5. The Problems and Reactions of Prisoners' Children: A Review of Research ... 48
6. Children of Imprisoned Parents and Their Human Rights ... 82

Part III Prisoners' Children: From Arrest to Release of Their Imprisoned Parents

7. The Arrest of Parents through the Eyes of Children, Police and Social Services ... 115
   Peter Scharff Smith and Janne Jakobsen
8. Remand Imprisonment: A Stressful Phase of Transition ... 133
9. After the Sentence: The Family's Way of Dealing with the Children and the Surroundings ... 138
10. Visiting in Prisons: Staff, Children, Conditions and Practice ... 144
    Peter Scharff Smith and Janne Jakobsen
11. Home Leave and Other Ways of Maintaining Contact ... 170
12. When Visits Do Not Take Place: Opting Out of Visits and Discontinuing Contact ... 180
13. When Contact is Undesirable ... 187
14. When Dad or Mum Returns: Re-entry and Release ... 194

15	With Mum or Dad in Prison: Children Who Live with Their Imprisoned Parent	202
16	Penal Populism and Children of Imprisoned Parents	214

Part IV Conclusion

17	When the Innocent are Punished: Prison, Society and the Effects of Imprisonment	227

Appendix: Prison Visits, Interviews and National Surveys	234
Notes	240
Bibliography	280
Index	293

Acknowledgements

In 2005, I began doing research on children of imprisoned parents and I have since then been involved in several studies and reform projects on the subject. Throughout these years, far too many people and organizations have played a role in my research for me to be able to thank them all individually here. These people include prison staff, prisoners, children's NGOs, police officers, social workers, prison chaplains, politicians, government officials, former prisoners, fellow researchers from different countries, human rights workers and all those engaged in work with prisoners' relatives, whom I have met and sometimes worked with in different European countries. I sincerely thank all these people who have given me some of their time and often spoken with great conviction about something very important and sometimes very personal to them. And then, of course, there are all the studies, interviews and accounts done by others, which I have read without personally knowing the people involved. I would especially like to thank those who have interviewed prisoners' children and either written about it or allowed me to use their often unpublished material, which has proven invaluable to this study (see Appendix).

The world of the prison and the ways in which it affects so many people is generally not an uplifting story to tell, but one of the great blessings of working in this area has been meeting so many people – both inside and outside the system – whose work and dedication I have come to greatly respect and often admire. I have seen organizations and individuals join forces to improve the conditions for prisoners' children, and it has been an incredible experience to play a part in this. With regard to Denmark and for cooperation, inspiration and advice since 2006, I would especially like to thank Line Dahl Krabsen (SAVN) and Brian Lund Andreasen (formerly SAVN), Søren Gade Hansen from the Children's Council (Børnerådet) and Hannah Hagerup from the Danish prison service. Special thanks also to the children's officers who participated in our project from 2010–2011. They grasped the opportunity, were dedicated and came up with many novel ideas.

I would also like to mention and thank the partners in our Scandinavian network, which, in addition to the Danish members mentioned above, include the Norwegian association for prisoner's relatives (FFP), their Swedish counterpart Bryggan and participants from the Norwegian and

Swedish prison services and Children's Ombudsmen. I especially want to thank FFP for inviting me to their 20th anniversary conference in June 2013, which proved to be a unique and very inspirational day for all who are interested in improving conditions for children of imprisoned parents.

One person in particular has been important in connection with my research on children and imprisoned parents, and that is my colleague Janne Jakobsen. We have worked together on several projects at the Danish Institute for Human Rights, and Janne has also co-authored two chapters in this book. It has been hard work, but it has certainly also been inspiring, fun and incredibly productive to work together on this topic for such a long time.

I have also had the pleasure of working with several other colleagues from the Danish Institute for Human Rights on Danish and European projects on prisoners' children and would like to thank Stephanie Lagoutte, Sisse Stræde Bang Olsen, Lone Groth-Rasmussen, Jes Ellehauge Schwartz-Hansen and not least Lise Garkier Hendriksen, who brought home our children's officers project with great professionalism. Thanks also to Kristoffer Marslev for working with me on the bibliography and index for this book.

Many others have given me valuable feedback over the years on articles, previous book manuscripts and conference talks on prisoners' children and related topics. For commenting on previous versions of this particular manuscript, I would very much like to thank Stephanie Lagoutte, Manfred Nowak, Marie Hutton and Janne Jakobsen, as well as my editors, Julia Willan and Harriet Barker, and the anonymous Palgrave Macmillan peer reviewer. Thanks also to the series editors on the Palgrave Studies in Prisons and Penology: Ben Crewe, Yvonne Jewkes and Thomas Ugelvik.

Finally, I have to thank my family, especially my three children: Siri, August and Vera. I cannot help but think of you when I finish a major project or a book. You are a constant motivation and somehow seem to help me both enjoy life and get my work done!

Part I
Prison, Society and Prisoners' Children

1
Scenes from Family Life

One Saturday night in Denmark, Malene, Carina and Tenna's father was arrested. Carina explained that her little sister had hardly woken up before a police officer ordered a dog to jump up onto the bed to sniff out drugs: "My little sister screamed as loud as she could. We had to leave the room so the officer could check it for drugs. When we were on the way out of the room, he opened my drawers and began throwing my underwear and other things all over the place. It was so insulting, I felt like I was the criminal." The father was arrested, and the girls (who were 18, 16 and 14 years old, respectively) were left behind – apparently without the police having contacted any family members or the social authorities, or even asking if the girls had somewhere to go. Seven days later, the eldest girl visited their father in prison. Tenna, the youngest, didn't want to go along. She was still very upset and mostly stayed in bed for the two months following the arrest. After three and a half months in remand custody, the girls' father was sentenced to three years. Malene and Carina had a poor relationship with their mother and her boyfriend, so they continued living in their father's house. They worked as much as they could after school and studying, but despite their efforts, the house was put on a foreclosure auction after six months. The girls then moved into an apartment, and Carina applied to the municipality for financial assistance. She received half of the rent for three months.[1]

Alicia was a 15-year-old girl living with her mother in Sweden. One night she was home alone when the police came and searched the apartment. Later her mom came and made her dinner. The police returned: "I remember that I just stayed in kitchen. It was as if I tried to forget that someone else was there. I just stood there and ate my dinner. My mom came out into the kitchen and told me that she had to go but that she would be back in an hour. But she did not return within the hour. I didn't get to talk with her for a month. I had no one, I was completely alone in the apartment. I didn't know what to do. The police did not contact me, nor did the social authorities or anyone else. It was difficult because I did not have any good contact with my Dad either."[2]

A Norwegian boy remembers the time his mother told him about his father's sentence: "I remember extremely well when dad got his sentence for 13 years." The boy was on his way to an after-school activity: "Then my mother tells me that dad has been sent to prison for 13 years. I began to cry. I remember I ran out of the car and hid myself behind a trash bin. That's when I had really needed someone to talk to."[3]

A Danish police officer remember an experience that still haunts him 30 years later:

> Once, many years ago, I had to carry out an arrest of a female drunk driver together with another officer. Unfortunately, she managed to get into her apartment before we could get hold of her. When we rang the doorbell, she opened the door and was clearly very intoxicated. Her husband, who didn't appear to be under the influence, stood behind her with their almost 5-year-old son. We asked the husband to go into another room with the child and explained: "We just need to chat with your wife and take her down to the station for a blood test. It won't take that long". But he refused and remained standing where he was. The woman certainly did not want to go to the station and began kicking and fighting. She was a very heavy-built and strong lady and very infuriated, so we couldn't get her to come with us just like that. We continued to urge the husband to leave with the child, but he refused. The situation with the woman developed and it all ended very unfortunately by us having to get her to lie down with two officers almost sitting on top of her out in the stairwell. And if that wasn't enough, the husband wouldn't go away with the boy; he didn't even have a proper hold on him. Suddenly, the boy attacked me and beat furiously on my back while shouting, "Get away from my mother! Get away from my mother!" I will never forget the boy's eyes and I often wonder where he is today, how it has affected him and what he thinks about the police and about the episode. It's almost 28 years ago, so he is an adult man now.[4]

Ten-year-old Jonas lived with his father and little brother in Denmark. When his father went on a two-week sailing trip, Jonas and his brother moved in with their cousin. But his father didn't come home after the voyage. For a week Jonas feared that the ship had sunk and his father had perished. Then the police phoned and said his father was remanded in custody. It took three months before the boys were allowed to visit their father, a visit Jonas was looking forward to. The cell was "small and gross", and a police officer supervised the visit. "When it was time for us to leave we cried and clung to his legs.... It was so sickening to drive away from the prison knowing that your father was in there." Sixteen months went by before the case went before the court. This was a trying time for Jonas. He constantly thought about his father, began bullying his classmates and had difficulty keeping up in class. The case ended with an acquittal and DKK 150,000 in compensation. Nine years later, Jonas was still marked by the whole process and very scared of losing his father.[5]

According to a social worker employed with the Danish social services, "it is not widely recognized that one can have a severe social problem" when you "have a man who is in prison, who might also be the father of your child.... I can think back on at least ten times where I haven't thought of the fact that both a child and an adult need help. We (the social services) have failed especially with regard to the perspective of the child. If the prisoner is a parent, there is also a child who practically has lost a mom or dad. We as social workers are usually not afraid to act on this. However, in this situation, it is just not customary".[6]

A Danish boy with several younger siblings was 12 years old when both parents were imprisoned on the same day: "Our father was arrested in the afternoon.... At that time my mother became ill, she fainted and was taken to the hospital.... She came home and was with us in the evening. Then the police arrived; they came in several cars with the blue lights flashing. They were there to arrest our mother and us kids were put in another car and driven to the children's home. We were told that they were arrested because of drugs.... So we were put in the children's home... 1½ months passed before we were able to see our mother and 2½ months before we saw our father.... The children's home was organised in a way so you lived in groups according to ages; so we didn't live together but we spent all day together.... I told the little ones that our mother and father were on holiday. I didn't know what to tell them, but I thought that if I said they were on holiday, then the little ones would know that our mother and father would come back again."[7]

A Danish prison officer remembers a time she was working in the prison visiting area and "praised a little girl's dress. The girl became very happy and the mother got tears in her eyes just because I was nice. Imagine that so little can mean so much".[8]

As a 12 year old, the Danish boy Kristian recounts how as a 7 year old he waited to hear what his father's sentence would be: "Mum explained that I had to prepare myself that my father would probably be imprisoned. It was sort of like waiting for something that you know will be unpleasant, but you don't know how bad it will be.... And it was also as if every time we thought that now we were sure we would be told something, we would have to wait even longer." Kristian's father was in remand custody for ten months and then sentenced to 14 years; Kristian has visited his father many times. He clearly remembers his first visit to the prison. The visit was supervised: "An officer had to stand there and listen to what we talked about. We sat in such a small room and it felt as if you were completely surrounded by people you didn't know." Today, Kristian quite enjoys visiting his father in prison, but "just not when some of those hard-core types are at work. Then it's just stupid because, well, you're allowed to take a drawing in with you one time, and then you're not the next time. You can't take a gift inside one time and then you're allowed to take something along anyway another time and it's just really annoying. It changes all the time." When Kristian is asked about the most difficult aspect of having a father in prison, he responds very promptly: "The most difficult thing is that I can't play football with him. Or do anything else. When he's in prison, I can hardly do anything together with him."[9]

According to a Danish police officer, "it always makes a strong impression when there are children involved, as they are always the losers in all of this. They have under no circumstances chosen the situation they are in, which makes it all distressingly hard."[10]

2
When the Innocent are Punished

Prisoners' children

When a person commits a crime and is punished with imprisonment, it can be a very tough ordeal for the relatives. This is certainly the case when parents are imprisoned and one or more children are left behind. In a sense, the short glimpses of the various "family scenes" in the previous chapter and the children's own stories and emotional reactions tell us almost everything. The naked, straightforward and almost archetypical accounts of loss, fear and anxiety clearly illustrate how imprisonment can affect *some* prisoners' children particularly hard and have extensive negative repercussions on their daily life, well-being and future.

But how shall the state and society approach such an issue when we cannot refrain from prosecuting and punishing persons who commit crimes simply because they are parents? This is certainly not an easy question to answer, and in some ways the issue of prisoners' children seems to be one of the major Gordian knots facing our modern system of punishment and imprisonment This can seem strange given the fact that there have been prisoners' children for as long as there have been prisons. We are dealing with a problem that has existed for centuries but has only recently begun to attract serious attention.

Today we know quite a bit about the problems prisoners' children face. Yet many questions regarding the scope of various problems and the degree to which parental imprisonment causes or perhaps exacerbates these issues are still unanswered. We do know from qualitative research how individual children can experience parental imprisonment as a major life crisis, and we know from quantitative research that parental imprisonment is a risk factor for a number of problems, including anti-social behaviour, offending and possibly mental health problems, drug abuse, school failure and unemployment.[1] From the rising number of research studies and qualitative accounts it is clear that, while the physical removal of a parent can be positive for some children, parental imprisonment certainly affect many children's lives in negative ways, which can include stigmatisation, psychological distress, behavioural changes and economic problems.[2]

Unfortunately, there are millions of children experiencing parental imprisonment all over the world right now. There are no official statistics on the number of children of imprisoned parents in any country, but several attempts have been made to calculate and investigate this in various ways and the resulting numbers are striking. In the United States in 2007, approximately 810,000 imprisoned fathers and mothers had more than 1.7 million children under the age of 18. One third of those would turn 18 while their parents were still in prison.[3] In England, 2007 estimates indicated that 127,000 children experienced parental imprisonment every year.[4] In 2006, it was further estimated that on a single day there were 88,000 children of prisoners in England and Wales.[5] A more recent estimate based on a study of 3,849 prisoners in England and Wales produced the striking result that approximately 200,000 children had a parent in prison at some point during 2009 – 90.000 on a single day by the end of June that year.[6]

By looking at the average number of children per prisoner and the prison populations in Europe, the international NGO Eurochips has calculated that around 800,000 children in the European Union are separated from an imprisoned parent on a given day each year. Estimates from several countries in fact indicate that there are typically more children of prisoners than there are prisoners.[7] But while prisons and prisoners have been the object of serious research since the latter half of the 19th century, the same thing can by no means be said about the millions of children experiencing parental imprisonment.

Prison and society

Historians normally agree that prisons have existed since the 16th century as institutions specifically constructed to incarcerate a significant number of people for prolonged periods of time.[8] In much of this time, and especially during the last 200 years, the effects of imprisonment have been discussed intensively. These many discussions have typically focused on either the effects on the individual prisoner (individual deterrence and rehabilitation) or the possible preventive effect on society at large (general deterrence). The question of how imprisonment has otherwise affected society, particularly the relatives and children of those imprisoned, has by comparison gained sparse attention during the last two centuries.[9] One could say that a critical philosophical and sociological literature on prisons and their relation to society appeared during the 1970s – inspired not least by Foucault's *Discipline and Punish* – but these writings have generally explored prisons as symbols of modern society and modern technologies of power rather than analysing how prisons and society interrelate on a more practical level.[10] In other words, prisons have been studied as a reflection of society and modernity. This "Foucauldian" discourse and other critical interpretations have produced an interesting theoretical literature on power technologies, "governmentality" and so on – and theories of punishment in general – but have certainly not led to any focus on prisoners' relatives and children.

Bearing in mind that we have had prisons for more than four centuries, it might seem rather strange, or even bewildering, that children of imprisoned parents have received so relatively little – and until recently almost no – attention. It is after all a rather logical proposition that the imprisonment of a parent can have a significant negative impact on the lives of the children, in terms of both their current and future well-being, as well as in the context of crime prevention. Yet, as late as 2005, Alison Liebling and Shadd Maruna concluded in *The Effects of Imprisonment* that "there is little research emphasis on the effects of imprisonment on prisoners' families" and that "the impact of imprisonment upon the children of prisoners has been slow to appear in the literature on the effects of imprisonment".[11]

But why are children of imprisoned parents a "new" area of research, with only a recent academic literature? How can this be the case? How can such a seemingly obvious product of any use of imprisonment go more or less unnoticed and untouched for so long? It is difficult to imagine, for example, a political discussion and public debate on a planned new highway that focuses only on how fast one can get from A to B, while completely ignoring such a project's possible effects on nature in aesthetical and environmental terms. The debate on such an issue would involve discussing the impact not only on those driving along the roads but also society and the environment more broadly. It would simply seem absurd not to include these concerns in a discussion on modern-day transportation. But, unfortunately, the recent international trend of rising prison populations in many parts of the world clearly illustrates how penal politics, prison constructions and the use of imprisonment have generally not been "troubled" – or even informed – by political interest in the secondary effects and "collateral damage" that these institutions cause.[12]

The last 10–15 years have, however, witnessed a gradually rising interest in and research on the broader societal effects of imprisonment – thanks to the alarming rise in prison populations. In the United States, the phenomenon of "mass imprisonment" has driven the incarceration rate to hitherto unknown levels, which makes the societal impact of imprisonment obvious in many different ways and therefore impossible to hide. The more than two million people currently incarcerated in the United States make Foucault's so-called great confinement of the 17th century look like a bump in the road.[13] In several other places, Europe for example, prison populations have also expanded significantly over the last couple of decades. This trend also means that an increasing number of children experience parental imprisonment and that families and relationships are challenged and broken up on a massive scale. That millions of children each year become separated from their parents looks, at first glance, more like something caused by war or perhaps natural disaster than a product of a carefully planned and well-thought-out policy on crime and imprisonment in a modern democratic nation.

Prisoners' children and children's rights

But regardless of whether or not a given prison population counts thousands or millions of prisoners, the impact on their children is often significant and help is typically scarce. These issues can be addressed from different perspectives and be framed as questions of child welfare, criminal policy, social problems, welfare state policy and so on. In this sense, we are clearly dealing with a problem that will benefit from a cross-disciplinary approach. Another important point is that these children not only have problems, they also have rights. Rights that are – or rather ought to be – legally enforceable. In fact, the whole question of children's rights makes for an interesting approach to this issue as a human rights case study of the problems surrounding actual implementation of children's rights and as a reform tool that can be used to empower these children.

It is therefore arguably necessary to study not only the problems these children face but also their rights and how the latter can be both enforced and strengthened. According to the United Nations Convention on the Rights of the Child, children can claim several rights of obvious importance for children experiencing parental imprisonment. They include the right to maintain contact with parents, the right to be heard and the right to have their best interest taken into account as a primary concern "in all actions concerning children, whether undertaken by public or private social welfare institutions, courts of law, administrative authorities or legislative bodies" (article 3). These are potentially far-reaching rights to hold for a child – but what do they mean in practice for children experiencing parental imprisonment?

When I began my research in this field in 2005, I had to start almost from scratch when looking at children of imprisoned parents from a human rights perspective. At that time few would question that these children had rights – in fact no other human rights convention has the same international support as the Convention on the Rights of the Child – but what it meant in practice for this particular group of children in the concrete situations they faced was unclear, to say the least. This had simply not been discussed in any great detail, neither by researchers, national lawmakers nor international human rights mechanisms.

One reason is that the broader field of prisons and human rights has almost exclusively focused on balancing the relationship between the rights of the imprisoned on the one hand and society's legitimate use of power on the other hand. So while judgements from various national courts and the European Court of Human Rights in Strasbourg have secured and enforced the rights of prisoners in several ways (and confirmed the state's right to wield considerable power), there has generally been little attention given to rights holders outside of prison and the question of how the use of imprisonment influence their lives and human rights. This is especially obvious in the case of prisoners' children, compared to prisoners' spouses, since children have very limited personal access to legal remedies and their cases are typically not taken to court. It is therefore highly relevant to examine and define the rights of these children in the context of the many practical problems they experience.

The background of this study – research, dialogue and reforms

In 2005, my former director at the Danish Institute for Human Rights, Morten Kjærum, approached me with the question: "Shouldn't we do something on prisons in Denmark?" I suggested a number of possible areas of intervention – prisoners' children being one of them. This particular area appealed to both of us for three basic reasons. It was clearly an important area, as it involved a lot of vulnerable and more or less forgotten children. Secondly, it was a new area – both in terms of researching these children's situations and the treatment they received but also in terms of discussing and analysing their human rights. Furthermore, it was an area where it seemed plausible that we had a relatively good chance of making an impact in terms of implementing human rights and producing an actual, substantial difference for a large group of children.

At that time the Danish political agenda was very "tough on crime" and, as in so many other countries, heavily influenced by penal populism.[14] The former Danish minister of justice Lene Espersen explained when taking office in 2002 that she wanted to govern with her "inner sense of justice", which she claimed to share with "ordinary citizens". She clearly regarded criminological advice and research as less important. What this meant was that she wanted to introduce tougher sentencing policies in a number of areas and seldom missed a chance to appear "tough" and talk about "zero tolerance".[15] How this attitude could harm prisoners' children became apparent on several occasions. For example in 2005, Espersen published a bill, which called for three months' home leave suspension for all prisoners who appeared late for their commitment to prison. Espersen claimed that it would have "a pedagogical effect if you cannot visit your family for three months or participate in your child's birthday".[16] The problems and harm that this would (obviously one should think) cause prisoners' children was never mentioned in the bill and did not become a political issue. At the same time, new "tough-on-crime" legislation caused a rise in the Danish prison population and thereby in the number of prisoners' children – as it had been the case in several European countries from the 1990s and onwards.

The general influence of penal populism meant that it was difficult to discuss a lot of issues involving prisons, punishment and police work. But perhaps serious research on prisoners' children would produce a different result? What, for example, would happen if the ever present public opinion and sense of justice was informed about these children, their situation and their sense of justice?

I decided to focus on the perspective of these children and on the rights of the child and began doing some initial research. After publishing an article in a Danish journal, Morten Kjærum and I wanted to see what a dialogue among the involved actors could bring to the arena. Accordingly, on 9 February and 9 October 2006, I arranged two meetings, which took place at the Danish Institute for Human Rights. Present at these meetings were, among others, representatives of the Danish Prison and Probation Service, the National Council for Children, the police, the social authorities, the Danish Red Cross, associations for prisoners' relatives, inmate spokespersons and previously imprisoned parents. The meetings were arranged as round-table discussions where all parties met each other eye to eye, on neutral ground and with the same rights and speaking time. The topic was prisoners' children and the idea was to have an informal discussion about what could possibly be done to help these children.

In many ways, the participants' points of departure were very different. Experiences were shared and accounts were given from prison staff, prisoners' parents, relatives, researchers and others who in one way or another were involved with children of imprisoned parents. For some of the parties, this was the first time they met in this way. There were some heated arguments, and it was clear that not everyone agreed on everything. This was in no way surprising. However, it was striking that after both meetings, despite the very different points of departure, all participants were willing to do something for children who experienced parental imprisonment. It was furthermore clear that there was an abundance of ideas on how things could be done better and how to improve the conditions for these children. It was also quite apparent that the majority of those present – regardless of whether they were from the Danish Prison and Probation Service or an NGO, or someone who had personal experience as an imprisoned parent or relative – left the meeting uplifted with a sense of having a common goal and a feeling that innovative thinking was both possible and necessary. We felt this way, and subsequent talks with several of the participants confirmed this interpretation. This seemed quite remarkable and whetted our appetites for continuing the work.

Equivalent meetings on similarly relevant human rights problems, which have given rise to criticism of the authorities, will generally not result in finding such common ground. If you work with prisons and human rights, the Danish use of solitary confinement is an excellent example of a topic that has often given rise to conflicting and irreconcilable views between state representatives and various NGOs and, not least, prisoners themselves. A round-table meeting about such a topic would hardly have resulted in the same optimism and reformatory zeal of the participants.

The basis for the round-table meetings was dialogue and cooperation as methods and tools in a reform process. But from the outset, the goal was that this dialogue should have a well-developed foundation in research. My colleague Janne Jakobsen and I therefore drew up a research based project and we applied for funding. Since then I have secured funding for and participated in three different substantial projects on children of imprisoned parents. This research forms the background for this book.

Denmark and Europe: perspectives, data and methodology in three projects

The first research project was carried out from 2007–2010 and consisted of data collection and analysis of children of imprisoned parents in Denmark. Focus was on how these children were met and treated by the state representatives they encountered throughout the whole process from their parents' arrest to their imprisonment and release – especially the police, prison service and social services. A sociological/criminological and legal analysis of the situation was carried out. Data collection consisted of interviews with more than 80 practitioners and representatives from various institutions and NGOs, and numerous prison visits primarily in Denmark, but also in Italy, the United Kingdom and Sweden. Furthermore, a countrywide survey with comprehensive questionnaires was also sent to all prisons, police districts and local social services in Denmark.[17] We had a response from 28 remand prisons (which corresponds to a response rate of 68.3%), 17 prisons for sentenced prisoners (response rate: 94.4%) and 6 halfway houses (response rate: 75%), as well as 34 police districts (response rate: 47.2%) and 28 municipal social services (response rate: 40.8%).

Parallel to the data collection, a survey of the relevant human rights laws and Danish legal conditions was also carried out. This survey was initially conducted by lawyers at the Danish Institute for Human Rights and then an external legal consultant and I expanded the work. The largest group of interviewees has or has had affiliation to the Danish Prison and Probation Service – the majority as employees and some as prisoners or former prisoners – while the remainder of interviewees came from the police, social services, various NGOs, the Swedish Prison Service and other organisations. We were also in contact with relatives and relatives' associations throughout the project.

In other words, we chose to focus on the most important state actors – in this context the prison service, the police and the social authorities – instead of conducting a large, systematic survey of prisoners' children. Others had already interviewed the children thoroughly, and we knew from the outset that we were able to gather these children's stories and statements from many other sources. This will also be apparent in the current study, which quotes many Danish children, as well as children from other countries (see appendix).

But while we had access to numerous interviews with prisoner's children from different sources, almost no interviews with the relevant state actors could be found. No one else had conducted systematic interviews with prison officers, the police or social workers for the purpose of studying how they approached, perceived and treated issues related to children of imprisoned parents. This was certainly not the case in Denmark and, as far as I can see, neither has this been done yet on a similar scale elsewhere. But by consciously focusing on the relevant state actors – including their working methods, culture and the legal frameworks within which they take action – we hoped to produce research that could be used in practice. The idea was that dialogue and research should go hand in hand with practical exploratory proposals for reforms. This is also a principal and methodological starting point for the book you are now reading. If one wants to propose better conditions for prisoners' children, it is in my opinion necessary to carefully study to the work and working conditions of the prison service, the police and the social welfare system, and combine such knowledge with what we know about the children's problems, situations and needs.

Such an approach does not mean that I want to remove the responsibility from parents who have put themselves in a position such that their children experience parental imprisonment. These parents are, of course, ultimately responsible and the immediate cause of the problems. But this does not relieve state and society of responsibility. On the contrary, it is painfully obvious that a lot can still be done in this area in any country with parents in prison.

The second substantial project on children of imprisoned parents that I secured funding for, initiated and participated in at the Danish Institute of Human Rights was an EU project based on the model of our first Danish study.[18] The idea was, once again, to combine academic research with knowledge and information drawn from all relevant professionals and NGOs working in the field – including prison staff in prison visiting areas, police officers doing arrests, social workers involved with prisoners' families, prison education workers and psychologists, as well as prisoners' relatives and children.[19] The primary project partners were the University of Ulster, the Italian NGO Bambinisenzabarre, the European NGO Eurochips and the Danish Institute for Human Rights.

Four studies of varying scale and scope were conducted on the treatment of children of imprisoned parents in Northern Ireland, Denmark, Italy and Poland, and a separate analysis of the relevant human rights instruments and standards was carried out by my colleague Stephanie Lagoutte. In Northern Ireland, Linda Moore, Una Convery and Phil

Scraton produced a thorough qualitative study on prisoners' children, and two valuable contributions were made by Bambinisenzabarre in Italy and by Eurochips in Poland. In all countries, research, dialogue, fieldwork and knowledge drawn from the expertise of those conducting the studies was combined in order to produce not only theoretical but also practical recommendations based on examples of good practice and grounded in children's rights. The research uncovered many issues, problems and good practices and basically demonstrated that although prison conditions and economic and legal situations vary substantially in the chosen countries, prisoners' children face many of the same problems and challenges no matter where they live.[20]

The third project constituted a very concrete attempt to implement children's rights and alleviate some of the problems that children of imprisoned parents face. The project was to introduce children's officers in Danish remand prisons as well as open and closed prisons. Janne Jakobsen and I initiated the project, which was later managed by our colleague Lise Garkier Hendriksen and carried out together with the Danish Prison and Probation Service. The funding came from Ole Kirks Foundation, which belongs to the toy manufacturer Lego. The purpose was to train selected prison staff, primarily prison officers, as children's officers who should work in their respective institutions to firmly anchor the child's perspective in the individual prisons. The project ran for two years (2010–2011) in two remand prisons, one open prison and one closed prison. We focused on introducing simple and reliable measures to improve children's contact with their parents as well as their experience when visiting in prison. Activities conducted by the children's officers included improving visiting facilities and visiting procedures, arranging child-friendly events, introducing different measures to help imprisoned parents deal with parenthood (parenting study groups, individual talks, running "bedtime stories" projects, etc.) and disseminating information to colleagues on how to welcome and handle children visiting the institution. We also collected information and knowledge about other relevant initiatives in the prison service, interviewed staff and conducted a small survey among imprisoned parents.[21] When the project was over and the funding spent, the Danish Prison and Probation Service continued the activities in the four institutions. In November 2012, the Danish government and parliament decided to implement the children's officers scheme on a national basis beginning in 2013. All Danish prisons (for remand and sentenced prisoners) now have children's officers as a result of this project.[22]

Initiating and running the children's officer project gave valuable insight into the many dilemmas and concrete practical issues faced by staff, prisoners, relatives and prisoners' children. Every step of the project – each meeting, training session, prison visit, interview, survey, evaluation, etc. – generated new knowledge and empirical data that could be used in the present study. Working with the children's officers also provided my colleagues and me with a sense of having achieved some very concrete and practical results, results that mattered to the children and their imprisoned parents. It was very uplifting to see how the work also mattered to the children's officers, who put an amazing amount of time, energy and purpose into the project – sometimes while facing scepticism or criticism from colleagues. In that sense, the children's officer project was also about prison culture and reform in a broader sense, which – in my opinion – constituted an effort to decrease the barriers between prisoners and prison officers, as well as between prisons and the surrounding society.

Working with such a practical and normative endeavour as the children's officer project can have implications for the way one works and writes as a researcher – simply because one gets involved in the institutions and issues in a different way. To me this accentuates some of the theoretical and methodological issues inherent in studying more or less vulnerable and marginalised groups in society, that is, questions concerning bias, personal sympathies, research perspectives and ultimately the relationship between values and social science. To put it in other words, one question that often emerges when researching prisons and prison staff is "Whose side are we on?" – and how is that reflected in, or influenced by, the way we approach and conduct our work?[23] Alison Liebling highlight some of the important issues in that regard by asking: "Does acquiring sympathy for those whose worlds we study undermine our professional integrity? And does it matter which social groups draw these feelings from us?"[24] The short answer is yes, of course it matters, and it is therefore important to try to balance "different or competing perspectives" when designing and carrying out research studies, unless one believes in either complete objectivity or "epistemological relativism" as possible avenues.[25]

I believe that working with both prisoners relatives organisations and childrens NGOs on the one hand, and the prison service and the police on the other hand – both as research subjects, dialogue partners and even implementation partners – has helped inform my work with these different and competing perspectives. At the same time, I have undoubtedly also become submerged in the field in different ways. I have come to respect and like people representing these different perspectives, and I appreciate the conditions under which they work, live and act. All this has influenced my values, my research and what I write.

Still, there is no doubt that one perspective has been given priority over others, and that is the perspective of the situation and rights of the child. Not that this is less normative or less informed by different and competing agendas than other research objects and perspectives. On the contrary, it is more a declaration of a basic normative foundation upon which a hopefully thorough and scientific research effort rests.

The aim of this study

In this book I have attempted to gather in one place the knowledge, data and experience on children of imprisoned parents from all my previous work in this area, including what I have learned from the above-mentioned work and research in Denmark and the European Union, as well as the many other concrete practical projects, dialogues, conferences and meetings that I have participated in with prison staff, police officers, prisoner relatives NGOs and children's ombudsmen in Denmark, Sweden and Norway during the last eight or so years. I have also visited nearly 20 prisons and remand prisons in Denmark (as well as a number of prisons in Sweden, Norway, Italy, Poland and the United Kingdom) to observe visiting conditions and child-friendly initiatives.

More specifically, I hope to achieve the following in this book:

1. I want to map all the major problems that prisoners' children face and the way that they are likely to be treated by the authorities they encounter throughout the whole process from a parent's arrest through remand imprisonment and imprisonment following a sentence, until release. I also want to tell the story of these children and their situation as seen and perceived not only by themselves but also by these authorities – especially the police, prison officers and involved social workers. This includes describing and analysing situations, and asking questions such as: What happens when children witness the arrest of a parent? What happens when parents are arrested without their children's knowledge? How do the police treat children during the arrest of a parent? Why and how are many children of imprisoned parents lied to? When, for how long and under what circumstances can the children visit their imprisoned parents? What happens during a prison visit, and how do children react? What are some of the major obstacles for parent-child contact during imprisonment? How

exactly can children and incarcerated parents keep in contact? What happens when young children are incarcerated with their parents? What happens when parents are released from prison?
2. I want to explore, discuss and define what children's rights should mean for this particular group of children throughout the various steps of the process from arrest to release. What does – or rather, what should – children's rights mean in the very concrete situations listed above? What rights, for example, does a child witnessing the arrest of a parent have? And what rights can a child wanting to visit an imprisoned parent claim? Analysing these issues involves acknowledging children's rights according to both international and regional conventions and law in the form of both existing jurisprudence and soft law. As will become apparent, children's rights have up until recently rarely been used or mentioned in the context of children of imprisoned parents. The United Nations has taken important steps in that regard during recent years. By incorporating the most recent human rights developments in the area this study constitutes an attempt to analyse what the principles in the Convention on the Rights of Child and other relevant international and regional human rights covenants and instruments ought to mean for children of imprisoned parents, that is, how our systems of punishment should be shaped to increasingly consider the rights of these children. Such an approach can hopefully strengthen children's rights internationally and overcome the paradox that while there is broad support for children's rights throughout most of the world, children are still a group of citizens who are often not heard, have poor complaint options and are, in practice, easy victims of human rights violations.
3. I also look at children of imprisoned parents as a case study, which is part of a broader discussion of how prisons influence and relate to the surrounding society. This includes adopting a historical perspective on the question of "prison and society" and asking the question of to what degree the barriers and the level of interaction between the world of the prison and society at large have changed (or perhaps will, or should change).
4. Though my empirical data is primarily Danish, I also draw on findings from several other European countries and the United States, highlighting similarities and differences in the various societies and penal systems. This does not turn the present study into a true piece of comparative criminology, but it should help make this work internationally relevant and hopefully useful as a source for comparative criminological research.

5. Finally, I highlight various reform initiatives throughout the text to promote good practice, which can make an impact for children of imprisoned parents. I also want to draw attention to the question of how research and empirical data can help inform and even create a process towards reforming state institutions and practices in the area of penal policy and practice – at least implicitly by using my own work, data and experience in this field.

To accomplish these various goals, it has been necessary to adopt a cross-disciplinary approach drawing upon research from, and to some extent combining, disciplines such as sociology, law, criminology, history and human rights. I have been able to do that because I have had the great benefit of working with many different experts, researchers and practitioners from many different fields. Several of them have been participants and/or employed as consultants in the various projects (lawyers, criminologists, psychologists, family therapists, etc.). By adopting such a multidisciplinary approach and by including the voices of prison staff, police officers, prisoners and the children themselves, I hope to have achieved a fair, facts-based and broad societal perspective on a very problematic and still often neglected side effect of the use of imprisonment.

Millions of prisoners' children are still the innocent victims of our system of punishment. This book is about these children, their problems, their human rights and the way in which they are treated.

3
Prison and Society

A historical perspective

If we want to look at the relationship between prisons and the surrounding society today, and thereby the possible interrelations between prisoners and their families, it makes sense to take a step backwards in time to when the modern prison system broke through in the Western world and created the foundation for our current system of imprisonment. How did it all start; how were prisons used and constructed; and what did that mean for prisoners, their families and children?

While the history of the prison – as an institution used for punishment – dates back to the 16th century, it was not until the late 18th century and especially the 19th century that imprisonment came to play the central role it does today as a state tool in the fight against crime and deviance. Accordingly, it was in the 19th century that prisons were constructed on a large scale throughout Europe and North America. These prisons shaped our prison practices in both an ideological and physical sense which is important even today. Many 19th-century European prisons are still in use and, although refurbished to a greater or lesser extent, their original architectural design and appearance still influence the way imprisonment is practiced.

In the early prisons – the "tuchthuisen", bridewells, etc., which came before the modern penitentiaries – punishment was often both corporal and draconian, and living conditions were horrible. But the regimes in these premodern prisons could also be relatively liberal when it came to allowing prisoners contact with both each other and the outside world. In the premodern Danish prisons, for example, which were constructed more or less along the lines of the Dutch "tuchthuis" model, the conditions and regimes allowed practices and cultures during the 18th and well into the 19th century that would become entirely unthinkable in the modern penitentiaries just decades later. In the premodern prisons it was, for example, common practice that large numbers of prisoners slept together in large dormitories. Sexual relations between prisoners, as well as between guards and female prisoners, were not uncommon and sometimes resulted in births in prison. Another familiar early practice, which was later totally banned, was alcohol consumption. In the Danish "tuchthuis" in Odense, the regulations clearly described how smoking and alcohol consumption were forbidden outside the allowed times, unless they took place within sight of the doorman.[1]

These liberal cultures changed dramatically with the coming of the 19th-century modern penitentiary, and the freedom of the individual prisoner was minimised. The new prisons rested on a system of isolation, through which almost all prisoner contact with his or her family and the outside world was cut off.

The birth of the modern prison – isolating prisoners from family and society

"Day after day, with no companion but his thoughts, the convict is compelled to listen to the reproofs of conscience. He is led to dwell upon past errors, and to cherish whatever better feelings he may at any time have imbibed…. The mind becomes open to the best impressions and prepared for the reception of those truths and consolations which Christianity can alone impart."[2]

From the 1770s until the middle of the 19th century, the ideology of the modern penitentiary was established. The construction of the so-called Auburn and Pennsylvania prison models in the United States in the 1820s confirmed that the aim of this system was to rehabilitate criminals through the use of isolation. The Auburn system (developed in the Auburn prison in New York) permitted the inmates to work together during the day, but under a regime of total silence. In Pennsylvania-model institutions (developed in Philadelphia in the "Cherry Hill" prison) there was no compromise with the ideal of isolation: the prisoners spent almost all their time in their cells, where they worked and slept. At Cherry Hill, the prisoner was supposed to turn his thoughts inward, to meet God, to repent of his crimes and eventually to return to society as a morally cleansed Christian citizen.[3]

This philosophy was expressed very precisely by the English prison inspection, which, for example, explained in 1838 that the Pennsylvania model should "produce that self-communion, that introversion of mind, which is most favourable to the reception of every useful and serious admonition". The convict should experience "that all the mitigation of which his state of mind is capable, must proceed alone from within himself", and thus would "be led to feel no pain but that which is inflicted by remorse".[4] According to the famous Danish fairy-tale author Hans Christian Andersen, who visited a Swedish Pennsylvania-model prison, "a silence deep as the grave" rested over the institution and its isolation cells: "It is as though no one lived there or it was an abandoned house in time of plague.... It is all a well-built machine, a nightmare for the spirit...."[5]

The ideology of the modern penitentiary had an enormous impact all over the Western world. In the United States, the Auburn model became the most popular, but a number of Pennsylvania-model prisons were also constructed. In Europe, on the other hand, the Pennsylvania system was favoured. Pennsylvania-model prisons, or variants, were constructed in many nations, including England, France, Germany, Belgium, Holland, Norway, Sweden, Denmark, Chile, New Zealand and the United States.[6] The exact construction, regime and routines in these institutions varied from country to country and from prison to prison, but they all shared common traits, often to a remarkable degree. In general terms, the regime in Pennsylvania-model institutions consisted of around 23 hours in-cell, where the prisoners worked, slept, ate and washed. Out-of-cell time in these prisons typically consisted of one half hour to one hour yard time in isolation and, depending on the prison, of a weekly visit to the prison church or perhaps a prison school. Many of these prison churches and even some prison schools were constructed panoptically with isolation booths for individual prisoners. Thus, surveillance and solitary confinement were maintained even at these times. The wearing of a prison mask was also a regular feature of Pennsylvania-model prisons. Inmates were required to conceal their faces during transport around the prison and in any of the other few situations where they might encounter fellow prisoners.[7]

In Denmark, solitary confinement was implemented on a large scale beginning in 1859, when Vridsløselille Penitentiary, based on the Pennsylvania system, opened. During the early 1860s, however, it became apparent that serious health problems had arisen in the prison. It quickly became normal procedure to transfer a number of the worst prisoners (who became more or less uncontrollable) to insane asylums in different parts of the country, and the prison authorities fought a constant battle to avoid a general state of mental health chaos.[8] In fact, mental health problems seemed to arise in all Pennsylvania-model prisons regardless of which country and jurisdiction employed the practice.[9]

A natural, but often ignored or simply overlooked consequence of the breakthrough of the modern penitentiary and its ideology of rehabilitation through isolation, was that almost all contact between the prisoner and his or her family was cut off. In Denmark, for example, prisoners in a modern penitentiary of the 1860s were not allowed any visits at all during the first three months of their incarceration and were allowed to write one letter in that period. If prisoners behaved well, they were thereafter allowed to write a letter and receive a visit every second month. At a later stage, after at least 21 months of imprisonment, one visit and correspondence could be allowed on a monthly basis.[10]

Unfortunately, the 19th-century system of solitary confinement was very persistent. While the Pennsylvania model solitary confinement was abandoned relatively quickly in several US states, it continued in several places in Europe. In Holland, Belgium, Sweden, Norway and Denmark, the model continued well into the 20th century.[11] In the United Kingdom, isolation regimes were also very persistent and a relatively large-scale use of solitary confinement also survived into the 20th century. Although the belief in reformation through isolation gradually disappeared in the United Kingdom and a very harsh and punitive prison practice was adopted from the 1860s onwards, this did not put an end to solitary confinement. Isolation was perceived as a contribution to a punitive and deterrent prison system.[12]

A personal description from a prisoner who experienced the Pennsylvania model regime at Denmark's Vridsløselille penitentiary during 1918 and 1919, when it was still being conducted according to the original plan, can tell us something about the how the relationship between a prisoner and the surrounding society actually played out under such conditions. Niels Johnsen, convicted of writing apparently "revolutionary" political articles, began serving his eight-month sentence in Vridsløselille in 1918. Johnsen was an able writer and, as such, a relatively unusual guest in the prison system. Luckily he later produced a brief written recollection of his prison experience, upon which the following is based.[13]

According to Johnsen, an ordinary day at Vridsløselille began at six in the morning and consisted of solitary work in one's cell until half past seven in the evening. Carving toy horses became Johnsen's occupation. There were three daily breaks for eating – two hours in all – which also took place in the cell. Half an hour of fresh air (if the weather permitted) was also allowed each inmate, but time in the yard also took the form of solitary confinement. The prisoner's mask, worn while being moved around the prison, was also still in operation in 1918. Nor did the occasional visits to the prison church and the prison school allow prisoners any social contact (unless the regulations were broken). In Johnsen's time the church and school were still designed panoptically, with isolation booths for each visitor. Visits and correspondence with one's family were also severely restricted. Each prisoner was allowed a 15-minute visit every third month, which – according to Johnsen – was awaited with great excitement not only days but weeks ahead. Correspondence was limited to receiving and sending one letter a month.

All things considered, Johnsen unsurprisingly saw the isolation to be the dominating feature of the prison system. In his view, a need for social relatedness is intrinsic to human nature, and in solitary confinement one is "instantly overpowered" by a "depressing" and "poignant solitude". As one who had experienced it himself, Johnsen knew "what it meant to measure out the cell with tiny footsteps hour after hour, while over and over again a perpetual emptiness grinds away and throws the prisoner into a condition which borders on insanity".[14]

Prisons and the deprivation of liberty – a practice suited to destroying families?

It must have been completely impossible to uphold a meaningful relationship with one's children, family and friends under such conditions. It is quite striking, to say the least, how effectively this system cut off the prisoner's important social relations and thereby often harmed all the people on the other end of these relations – prisoners' spouses, children, parents and friends. The modern penitentiary was thereby ideally suited to crippling and even destroying families and family life – and this damaging capability was a central feature of the prison system established in the 19th century, the foundation and starting point for the system we still employ today. But why construct a mode of punishment that has the capacity to ruin families, which are otherwise considered one of the most important pillars of society? As expressed, for example, in the 1948 Universal Declaration of Human Rights, "the family is the natural and fundamental group unit of society and is entitled to protection by society and the State" (Article 16.3). Many 19th-century observers would undoubtedly have agreed to this. It is indeed striking – and in my opinion surprisingly neglected in criminological and historical research – that our modern societies chose a method of punishing criminals that disrupted the basic life and functionality of all those families that became swept up in the system of punishment. In that particular sense, prisons and prisoners certainly became removed from rather than integrated into society.

During the 20th century, prison visiting regimes changed (across the world, presumably) and prisoners were gradually allowed more visiting time than as described in the Danish example above. The practices surrounding visits also changed and different systems were created in different places. The history of how visiting regimes actually evolved has to my knowledge not been written. The Swedish history of prison reform seems to indicate that in some places it was not until after World War II that visiting regimes began to change significantly. The 19th-century isolation regimes were basically in force in Swedish prisons well into the 20th century, and it was not until the prison reform of 1945 that a more wide-ranging break with this practice emerged (at least when it came to the treatment of sentenced prisoners – remand prisoners have to a large degree remained in isolation).[15] This meant, for example, that the importance of the prisoner's social contacts and more liberal visiting regulations began to be discussed.[16]

In any case, we can see today how different trajectories developed with regard to visiting regimes within the boundaries of Europe. Although the starting point in the shape of the 19th-century modern penitentiary was strikingly uniform, there are still important differences in visiting systems from country to country. Perhaps the most striking difference is between systems allowing private visits – often referred to as conjugal visits – and the UK model, for example, which strictly disallows such practice in closed prisons. Instead, visits take place in big common rooms, and prisoners are ordered to sit on a specific chair without being allowed extended physical contact with visitors, even their children. Somewhere in between these models are systems where visits take place in common rooms but more physical contact and freedom of movement are allowed, sometimes also in outside areas.

I have seen the latter model in operation in a closed prison in Italy. Prisoners and their families were allowed outside in a large, garden-like area, which seemed to create a relatively liberal and natural visiting situation – although private "conjugal" visits like those in Scandinavia arguably allow for the most "normal" visiting situation. Seen from a child's point of view, the basic UK model is perhaps likely to be the most problematic. As children experiencing visits in closed prisons in England explained: "When you went to that prison, she couldn't move she just had to sit there." "It just felt weird because at the tables...you couldn't like get up and give her a hug and it just felt like you were there but you felt like really distant from her."[17] How bizarre such a practice must seem to a child is illustrated by one 5-year-old's reasonable question to his imprisoned mother during visiting: "Mummy why are you not moving?"[18]

But there are also important similarities between the different visiting systems. For example visiting can only take place for one or a few hours each week and visiting conditions in many prisons are not especially well suited for children. Admittedly, the differences within this spectrum can be significant for prisoners and their family. For example, being able to visit for three hours weekly in a low-security prison with access to outside areas is of course vastly different from having one hour in a small cell-like environment. But the typical visiting situation in the European prisons I have observed (in Denmark, Sweden, Norway, Italy, Poland and the United Kingdom) generally entails short visits (one or a few hours) once a week or less frequently, inside prisons. One can argue that it is still possible to see how the institution of prison visits has evolved from a more or less common starting point, provided by the modern penitentiary and its isolation regimes in the 19th century. The resulting limited contact between prisoners and their family is apparently ingrained in the modern prison institution to an extent that prison staff and prisoners – and even external parties such as NGOs, relatives and researchers – simply accept this practice as more or less natural.

The philosophy behind the modern prisons of the 19th century was *social* and *sociological* in the sense that it rested upon a belief that prisoners had a free will and that their social relations, situations, values and states of mind could be influenced in order to make them choose a career without crime.[19] During the latter part of the 19th century, this view began to change as biology and psychiatry influenced the emerging field of criminology as well as discussions on the use and effects of imprisonment. This, however, did not have a positive influence on the way researchers, prison administrators and policymakers viewed the relationship between prisoners and their families. On the contrary, the turn towards biology and heredity had a profound negative effect on the stigmatisation of prisoners' relatives.

Biology, heredity and stigmatisation of prisoners and their families

The debate over the last two centuries on imprisonment's effects has typically focused on how the prisoner is personally impacted by incarceration. Already in the 19th century, this topic gave rise to scientific dissertations in which prisoners' health and reactions to the new isolation regimes were studied and discussed. In the later decades of the 19th century, a number of psychiatrists and other professionals were inclined to attribute a large part of the responsibility for human nature and behaviour – including the actions of criminals and prisoners – to the biological constitution of the individual. Thus, for example, some psychiatrists found that the psychological problems and cases of mental illness diagnosed among the thousands of prisoners exposed to solitary confinement in the 19th century were caused by bad hereditary genes. This was allegedly characteristic of many criminals. For example, in 1871, a Danish psychiatrist found that the brains of criminals were, from birth, already "weighted with pathological Genes as Inherited from a degenerate Family".[20]

Some of these ideas, including the conception of the criminal person's character and genes, were put together in the so-called degeneration theory. In such a context, there was no discussion about whether and to what degree imprisonment could have a negative effect on the prisoner's family and children. On the contrary, from the theory of the *criminal man* followed that a criminal's family was also morally tarnished and equipped with a degenerate biology.

During the middle of the 19th century, the psychiatric science leaned towards a somatic understanding of mental illness, according to which the cause of mental disorders was localised in the form of defects in the brain.[21] This tendency was reinforced throughout the last half of the 19th century and in the wake of Charles Darwin's famous evolution theory, focus was placed on how hereditary biology influenced human behaviour – which included psychological disorders.[22] Among other things, this was expressed in the so-called degeneration theories on "hereditarily determined abnormality".[23] This was biological determinism, that is, the theory that heredity, in a large number of cases, was responsible for the individual's personality and actions.

The famous Italian scientist Cesare Lombroso believed that he was able to separate a number of physiological and anatomical traits of criminal individuals through his criminological and anthropological research.[24] Like many of his peers in the last decades of the 19th century, Lombroso found that criminal behaviour could be hereditary.[25] According to the Italian researcher, this applied particularly to the so-called criminal man, who was simply born criminal.[26] Enrico Ferri contributed to the further development of Lombroso's work and around the turn of the century (1900); he made himself the spokesperson for two possible ways in which to treat born criminals: either isolate and imprison them for an indefinite period, or use lifelong deportation.[27]

It is clear that such a categorical attitude to an allegedly biological and hereditary problem could give the "criminal man's" family problems. This was certainly the case if the so-called born criminals were isolated or deported, thus separated from their families. Apart from that, the suspicion of being a "criminal man" would quickly fall on the other family members. A natural continuation of Lombroso's theories implies that the state must take a sceptical view of the criminal's family and perhaps find it necessary to impose preventive measures. This could take place along eugenic lines by limiting the criminals and their families' possibilities of bringing children into the world.

One of the many researchers who worked according to such a biological understanding of the human intelligence and behaviour was the American H. H. Goddard, who invented the term "moron" and identified a larger group of citizens as hereditary idiots.[28] It did not take long before Goddard basically labelled all forms of deviates as belonging to this group and in 1914, he bluntly stated: "We know what feeble-mindedness is, and we have come to suspect all persons who are incapable of adapting themselves to their environment and living up to the conventions of society or acting sensibly, of being feeble-minded."[29] In this way, he succeeded, in principle, in defining everyone who did not live up to society's social conventions and norms as being unintelligent and genetically feebleminded. At the same time, this built on a doctrine, which many of Goddard's peers also asserted and which prescribed that there was a natural connection between intelligence and morality. Therefore, since they gave the impression of being deviants and morally depraved, criminals, alcoholics and prostitutes almost automatically fell within the category of hereditarily tainted morons.[30] When society captured these dangerous individuals, the interest therefore quickly had to be directed towards their family members and their possibilities of starting new families. In relation to the latter, according to Goddard, such people should simply not be allowed to get married and have children. This could be ensured by imprisoning or sterilising the persons concerned.[31]

Eugenic theories continued to influence social and penal policy way into the 20th century and have had a renaissance during recent decades. During the 1920s and 30s, such practices were in some ways spearheaded by the emerging Scandinavian welfare states. Denmark was in 1929 the first European nation to adopt a eugenic law on sterilisation of citizens whose possible future children were unwanted by the state. This took place within a scientific discourse widely supportive of eugenics, and in a political climate shaped by the rising power of the social democratic party, which embraced eugenics as a natural part of their new national social and health policies. As the later Danish minister of social affairs and father of the 1933 national social reform, K. K. Steincke, stated in

1920: "Any human being has a right to the happiest possible life and is entitled to ward and protection if need be. Society has to be on its guard in only one regard: When it comes to reproduction." Accordingly, all people with bad genetic material should not be allowed to reproduce and thereby "perpetuate and multiply" the evil.[32]

The Swedish eugenic movement also became swept up in the social policies of the emerging welfare state. This was evident in the writings of Gunnar and Alva Myrdal, perhaps the period's most influential proponents of social reform, who declared that the ambition of preventive social policies simply was to create "a better human material".[33] With regard to penal policies and prison practices, this meant that as late as 1943. the Swedish State Institute for Racial Hygiene (eugenics) was assigned to study rates of recidivism among certain groups of prisoners. On a broader note, the prison reform of 1945 and attempts to individualise treatment of offenders reflected biological theories and criminal anthropology in several ways with regard to views and policies on, for example, homosexuality, castration and mental health.[34]

Within the field of criminology and crime prevention, the major force of opposition to eugenic policies and individualised treatment of prisoners based on biological theories came from the sociological school, whose proponents had argued in favour of an understanding of crime that focused more on the social causes and social context of criminality. Throughout the 20th century, the more or less opposing views of biology and sociology influenced penal policies in various ways. One can hardly say that all the resulting discussions have since been settled, but there is today general agreement that criminals cannot simply be labelled as hereditary tarnished morons and that the use of imprisonment can affect both prisoners and their families negatively.

But theories about "the criminal man", the degeneration theories, Goddard's 19th-century reports on criminal families and eugenic policies in the 20th century are, however, still interesting. Not just as historical background but also as a reminder of the obvious stigmatisation a prisoner's family will often experience even today (see Chapter 5). The family ties to an offender can still be experienced as a source of moral contagion. Even today, relatives of offenders are often "perceived to be tainted or polluted either through association or through a genetic or biological connection", and the families of prisoners can find themselves caught up in a "web of shame".[35] Biological theories and explanations of human behaviour have once again gained increasing support and psychiatric treatment and risk assessments seem to be on the rise in prisons.[36] So in that sense both discussions about prisoners' genetic qualities and stigmatisation of prisoners and their families are still topical issues indeed, that can affect the future lives and well-being of prisoners and their relatives.

The effects of imprisonment on the prisoner – from the 19th century until today

It was clear to many in the 19th century that prison could have a significant negative effect on a prisoner's life and health. Following the breakthrough of the above-mentioned biological theories, more and more people were inclined to blame mental illness and instability on individual hereditary defects instead of the situation and the environment surrounding the prisoner. At the same time, this meant that mental illness and deviant patterns of behaviour, which arose in the prison, were to a great extent explained biologically. This was a tendency that had a strong position well into the 20th century.

In 1913, the Danish psychiatrist George E. Schrøder concluded, for example, that it could be established, "as is also apparent from my own Studies that a disposition is present in some of those individuals who develop a psychosis as a result of their imprisonment…. The majority of authors call it simply Degeneration."[37] In an interpretation of an actual medical case history, Schrøder reveals how he was trapped within the boundaries of biological determinism, just like many of his peers. A 36-year-old imprisoned man and his story were described as follows: "Very drunken family; Father also shuns human society and is brutal. Nervous and anxious from childhood, still lacks courage to ride a bicycle or drive a carriage. Arrested one month ago for fraud. Convinced of his innocence. Was weeping in prison, unsettled, poor sleep, saw his wife and child (for whom he cares a great deal) and also believed that once someone touched him. He makes an intelligent impression, has good skills. Significant tenderness with pressure on cardia."[38] The patient was given the diagnosis "Degenerate Psychopathic Hysteria", and on the stated basis, thus deemed to be a hysteric. The described hallucinations in the prison were given a biological reason and the imprisonment itself (i.e., solitary confinement) was acquitted – as was the seemingly obvious psychological distress associated with being separated from his wife and child.

However, not all doctors and psychiatrists proceeded so narrow-mindedly. The well-known Danish doctor Harald Selmer also touched briefly on the problem in his 1879 statistical reports from the institution for the mentally ill in Aarhus. In these reports, he distinguished between mentally ill criminals and criminals who became mentally ill during imprisonment. Thus, Selmer acknowledged that the prison could have detrimental effects on previously healthy individuals. He noted that "the conditions in the remand prisons probably often, perhaps relatively more often than in the prisons, favour the development of mental illnesses since, as a rule, there is hardly the same care given to the detainees' activities during solitary confinement, which naturally can be necessary, but which according to the formulation of our Administration of Justice also regularly stretches over a very long period. They find themselves under conditions that are well-suited to the development of hallucinations that are not always noticed in time."[39] Enrico Ferri, who wholeheartedly supported the theory on the criminal man, also found that imprisonment could have a deteriorating and even criminality-creating effect on a number of individuals.[40] In this way, the prison never succeeded in being completely exonerated, even during the heyday of biological determinism.

In the course of the 20th century, sociology and psychology began to make a crucial impact within prison research. The sociological perspective gained strength at the end of the 19th century when leading French sociologists, in opposition to Lombroso's school of thought, argued that criminality should be studied as a social phenomenon rather than as a physiological and anatomical problem.[41] From the middle of the 1950s and onwards, sociology increasingly influenced discussions on the effects of imprisonment and has since then, as part of the criminological research, been concerned in various ways with "the pains of imprisonment".[42] From the 1970s to the 1980s, however, psychological research began to challenge the sociological prison research and some believed that there was no scientific evidence for several of the allegations about the detrimental effects of prisons. Instead, these researchers argued that the prison was, at the most, a kind of "deep freezer" where development almost came to a standstill but without violent detrimental effects on the inmate.[43] As late as 1995, two Canadian researchers maintained, for example, that "careful empirical evaluations...have failed to uncover these pervasive negative effects of incarceration that so many have assumed".[44]

However, there is good reason to believe that this disagreement has, to a great extent, been about the choice of research method. It can be difficult to prove all of the conclusions of the sociological school of thought through quantitative positivistic studies. Studies of the last mentioned type have provided results which do not fit directly into the sociological tradition. Danish studies have revealed that, measured via quantitative medicinal and psychiatric health tests, some remand prisoners get better in the course of the initial period of imprisonment.[45] In this way, it has been possible to prove, for example, how a number of very disadvantaged criminals – for example, drug abusers – can actually improve their health condition during the initial part of their imprisonment simply because they receive treatment. The same can apply to mentally ill prisoners, who perhaps have not been properly cared for within the community mental health-care system. This does not mean that the sociological studies are incorrect, just that different sides of the effects of imprisonment have been studied. For example, many prison researchers today agree that a number of the psychological studies from the 1970s–1980s were not at all designed to measure "the pains of imprisonment". Later studies made this possible.[46]

There is no doubt, from a research perspective, that the prison as an institution has detrimental effects that far exceed the detrimental effects of the majority of other institutions which are not equally inclined to control and negatively affect the individuals they accommodate. As formulated by Hans Toch, "few environments are more damaging than prisons, and few are more painful to their residents".[47] One problem is that prisons have a tendency to create a breeding ground for a problematic treatment of prisoners even though this is not the intention. This is precisely why securing prisoner rights is so important. As described by Craig Haney:

> Prison environments are themselves powerful and potentially damaging situations, whose negative psychological effects must be taken seriously, carefully evaluated, purposefully regulated and controlled, and, when appropriate, changed or eliminated. This fact argues in favour of creating and enforcing more realistic and effective legal limits to the nature and amount of prison pain that is dispensed inside these institutions.[48]

This of course also means that imprisoned parents can be damaged, which can potentially affect their parenting capabilities and thereby influence the well-being of their children. A Swedish psychiatric study also indicates that imprisoned parents as a group might actually be more vulnerable compared to other prisoners, simply because they have children. In the study, remand prisoners with children were at greater risk of negative health effects while imprisoned compared to those without children.[49] British and American research on mothers in prison has also studied the stress and pain associated with being a parent in prison.[50] Imprisoned mothers, for example, have been found to experience a reduction in parenting confidence, which can be alleviated somewhat through frequent contact between the incarcerated mother and her child(ren).[51] It seems likely that some imprisoned parents simply experience a greater loss through their confinement because they are removed from their children.

With regard to male prisoners in the United States, it has furthermore been found that "formerly incarcerated men are more likely to be abusive, have higher rates of addiction, and poorer self-control than other fathers".[52] It must therefore obviously be considered to what extent imprisoned parents can become worse parents by being imprisoned. This will be discussed in more detail in Chapter 5.

Mass imprisonment and the prison's effect on the surrounding society

As already described, the prison impacts not only the prisoners themselves but also the surrounding society in many different ways. This influence is evident not just at a purely practical and immediate level, but perhaps also at a more abstract level in relation to how we perceive criminality and how we relate to terms such as normality, deviance, exclusion and inclusion.

Within recent years, the general societal significance of the prison has become the object of more debate and research as a natural consequence of the fact that the use of imprisonment and remand imprisonment has dramatically increased in a number of nations. In a country like the United States, a regular wave of "mass imprisonment" has taken place and it is now quite obvious that its use can have radical secondary repercussions, which stretch far beyond the effect on the individual criminal. In a number of American urban societies, for example, this massive use of imprisonment has decimated entire areas.[53] In the United States, the prison population was 2,239,751 in 2011, which corresponds to 716 people per 100,000 inhabitants.[54] In relative numbers, only Russia has been in the vicinity of the American imprisonment rate, although the rate of imprisonment has dropped in recent years. On 1 November 2013, 681,050 were imprisoned in Russia, which corresponds to 475 people per 100,000 inhabitants.[55] This means that on the list of world rates of imprisonment, a number of countries such as Cuba and Rwanda have placed themselves in between the United States and Russia with rates around 500 prisoners per 100,000 inhabitants. When imprisonment is used on such a large scale it is no longer a phenomenon that can only be associated with a minority of persons in society. In the words of David

Garland, "imprisonment becomes mass imprisonment when it ceases to be the incarceration of individual offenders and becomes the systematic imprisonment of whole groups of the population".[56]

The social and ethnic distortion alone, which mass imprisonment in the United States has led to, must be described as an extraordinarily wide-ranging societal problem. Around the turn of the millennium, one out of three African American men between the ages of 20–29 was in prison or under surveillance by a prison authority. In the long term, this could mean that 30% of all African American men born around the turn of the millennium will spend part of their lives in prison (as opposed to 4% of all white men). A term in prison will thus be quite a normal element of an African American man's socialising and upbringing, in the same way that, for example, attending college would be for so many others. As the Norwegian criminologist Nils Christie dryly commented, this is "an ironic situation. Slavery was abolished. The African Americans were free to move. So they do – and end in prisons".[57]

It is almost impossible to predict what influence this large-scale use of imprisonment will have on future generations, not least on African Americans. An obvious product of this policy is enormous state funds for the prison industry rather than other public purposes. "Prisons dot the American landscape, often opened and operated at the expense of schools, roads and social services", explains Robert Johnson.[58]

But in European countries where the rate of imprisonment is lower, this institution still has far-reaching societal consequences. It is naturally of significant societal importance whether the prison creates more criminals. Here, research points in an unfortunate direction. Recidivism is very high in the majority of countries, including Denmark and the rest of Europe (although relapse rates vary significantly), and the use of imprisonment has to take some of the blame. In Denmark, research has illustrated how difficult it can be for someone to return to the labour market after serving a sentence, not least because of the many secondary – more or less informal – conditions that follow after imprisonment.[59] Ex-prisoners typically experience a decrease in their income after their release (compared to before their imprisonment, which can influence their family situations and thus their children.[60]

One of the prison's most striking effects in relation to the rest of society is perhaps the way in which the rest of us – the so-called normal and well-functioning citizens who live outside prison walls – have created a negative mirror image, by which we can have our apparent normality constantly confirmed. By excluding and imprisoning a group of people and calling them criminals, we can thus maintain a self-understanding according to which we, the non-imprisoned, must be reasonably good citizens by default. This conclusion must simply follow from the practice we have established: those who deviate from normality and society's fundamental code of morality are imprisoned either as criminals or as mentally ill. The mere presence of prisons and psychiatric institutions confirms free citizens in their self-perceived mental and moral health.[61] As the use of imprisonment and penal populism have been on the rise in many countries for the last couple of decades and crime control has "become central to political discourse", this mechanism has arguably been strengthened and the "respectable classes" have been further reassured of "their difference from the 'criminal class'".[62]

One of the problems with this function of the prison as an institution is that it very easily leads to a punitive way of thinking whereby everything criminal is connected to something that is outside of the healthy person's sphere. David Garland calls it a "criminology of the other", a deeply anti-liberal philosophy according to which a large number of criminals are simply evil.[63] The malice becomes located within the individual and is not a question of context, social situation and conditions, et cetera. But this alleged malice can easily become associated with the family and stigmatise relatives and children. A related consequence of the prison functioning as a kind of negative reflection of "the good society" and "the good citizens" is that anyone affected by imprisonment is branded by both its real and symbolic power. This means that the family of an imprisoned person can fall under the shadow of imprisonment and experience the resulting stigmatisation and exclusion.

The effect of imprisonment on the family

For some families, imprisonment of a parent can no doubt be a benefit. Such could be the case if a severely abusive parent is imprisoned, and the imprisonment thus leads to more stable conditions in the family. It could also be the case in instances of violence and abuse in the home.[64] In cases where there has been a reasonably functioning family relationship, however, an imprisonment will have a negative effect. In 1991, a report from the British Ministry of Internal Affairs thus summarised the following main points about the effects of imprisonment:

> [Prison] breaks up families. It is hard for prisoners to retain or subsequently secure law-abiding jobs. Imprisonment can lessen people's sense of responsibility for their actions and reduce their self-respect, both of which are fundamental to law abiding citizenship. Some,

often the young and less experienced, acquire in prisons a wider knowledge of criminal activity. Imprisonment is costly for the individual, for the prisoner's family and for the community.[65]

Despite this knowledge, the effect of imprisonment on the prisoner's family remains one of the less studied fields within criminology (although this is changing at an increasing pace). During recent years, we have gained important empirical knowledge in this area, and many of our fears regarding the possible effects of incarceration upon families have been confirmed. As a recent article concludes with regard to the United States:

> Imprisonment diminishes the earnings of adult men, compromises their health, reduces familial resources, and contributes to family breakup. It also adds to the deficits of poor children, thus ensuring that the effects of imprisonment on inequality are transferred intergenerationally. Perversely, incarceration has its most corrosive effects on families whose fathers were involved in neither domestic violence nor violent crime before being imprisoned.[66]

A British study has identified four main areas in which families affected by imprisonment can have problems: (1) damaged relationship between the inmate and his/her spouse and children, (2) financial hardship, (3) stigmatisation of family members and (4) worsened prospects for prisoner' children.[67] An American criminologist reached a similar conclusion when summarising and categorising research on the effects of parental imprisonment in four areas: (1) insecure attachment, (2) economic strain, (3) stigma and (4) social learning.[68] Some of these areas, including the question of stigmatisation, have already been touched on. Chapter 5 thoroughly addresses a large number of issues regarding prisoners' children.

It is clear that family cohesion can be severely exposed and challenged when a parent is imprisoned. In order to ascertain how many families and children this impacts, one must look at whether or not a prisoner has close family contacts at all. A 2002 British survey found that more than half of male prisoners and a third of female prisoners were married or had a cohabiting partner at the time of imprisonment.[69] In comparison, a more recent Danish survey found that slightly more than a third of Danish prisoners are either married or cohabited with someone at the time of imprisonment. The study also showed that slightly more than half of the imprisoned parents lived together with their children at the time of imprisonment, which indicates (but does not prove) that a more or less "ordinary" family relationship existed immediately prior to imprisonment.[70] A recent report from the Danish prison service based on register data shows lower rates, with 15% of all sentenced prisoners and 16% of all remand prisoners living with a partner prior to imprisonment.[71] According to these register data, 11% of all sentenced prisoners and 16% of all remand prisoners were living together with children prior to their imprisonment and around one third of all prisoners had biological children.[72] These figures and other data from the report indicate that between a third and a half of imprisoned parents were living together with their children prior to the imprisonment. In many cases, there will also be a more or less well-functioning contact between the prisoner and his or her family even though they were not cohabiting. Still, these figures acknowledge the possibility that a large group of prisoners' children has no or very little contact with their imprisoned parents.

Family relationships are typically stressed in connection with a partner's or parent's imprisonment. The high risk of a marriage ending during an imprisonment is one example. In the United Kingdom, a study showed that approximately one fifth of all married prisoners get either divorced or separated during the imprisonment.[73] British research further indicates that between 25 and 40% of all fathers, who move from their child/children and partner for various reasons, have completely lost contact with their child/children after a five-year period.[74]

At the same time, it is a fact that prisoners with a functioning association to a family are in many ways in a far better position than prisoners without family ties. Several studies have shown that meaningful contact with family during and after imprisonment can reduce recidivism and strengthen the possibility of reintegration into the community.[75] For example, married men seem to handle the transition from prison to freedom better than bachelors, and men who move back with their wives and children generally cope better than those who live alone or with a parent after release.[76] In other words, it is very important – not only for the sake of the children but also from an ordinary socioeconomic perspective – to take care of the relationship with the family, which is tested to the limits in an imprisonment situation.

Under all circumstances, there is reason to fear that the longer the imprisonment lasts, the greater the risk that the relationships to the family and children are damaged. A qualitative and interview-based British study of long-term prisoners illustrated, for example, that family relations could break down and that the relationship between the imprisoned parent, the partner and the children could not function after the release. First and foremost, the feeling of nearness was gone. One released father stated that the family seemed to be "strangers in the same household…. It's very sad to say it, but I can relate better to strangers than to members of my own family. We sit together for hours and we hardly talk."[77] Several partners admitted that the time during the imprisonment was easier than the time after the release, and the returning person often even wished to be back in prison.[78] A Danish prison chaplain touches on the same problem, describing how the "rift between children and parents becomes deep after just a short time behind bars". This problem is made visible after release and possible return home to the family: "The prisoners hope, of course, that the whole family will get together and have a nice time when they get out. But they can rarely cope with coming home because they have lived in the manageable prison world."[79] Once again, statistics from the United States seem to illustrate both the fragile character of prisoners' families and the immense damaging power of prisons with regard to families. Accordingly, in 2007, "more than half of parents in state correctional facilities (and 84% in federal facilities) were housed more than 100 miles from their residence at the time of arrest" and "by 2004, more than half of the parents housed in state correctional facilities reported never having a personal visit from their child(ren)".[80]

It is self-evident that these issues can be of extremely great importance to prisoners' children. But before we take a closer look at this and all the existing research on the problems and reactions of these children, let's look into the question of how many children actually experience parental imprisonment.

Part II

Children of Imprisoned Parents: Their Numbers, Problems and Human Rights

4
Children of Imprisoned Parents in Numbers

It is difficult to say precisely how many children actually experience having a parent in prison. The explanation is simply that this is typically not registered in any official statistic and I have so far failed to find a country that releases yearly updates or any kind of regular official estimate of the number of prisoners' children. This is one indication that these children and their problems have, as a rule, been outside of the authorities' and, for many years, the media's spotlight.[1]

It would not be difficult to produce such statistics, however. This could be done simply by writing down how many children a prisoner has when he or she arrives in prison. In Denmark, for example, a social worker would normally interview an arriving prisoner about a lot of personal issues. The question of children could easily be added to the checklist as a mandatory question. It is possible that some prisoners would not reveal this information, because they might fear interference from the social authorities. Such information could, however, be verified by checking the official registry. In Norway, the Association for Prisoners' Relatives (FFP) has proposed to the Ministry of Justice that the state ensure central registration of the number of prisoners' children, and the Danish Institute for Human Rights has recommended a similar procedure in Denmark.[2]

In Sweden, on the basis of the children's ombudsman's proposal in the 2004 report "Don't Punish the Child!" ("Straffa inta Barnet!"), prisoners are now asked a number of questions, including if they have children, whether or not they have parental custody, and if they live together with the children. These questions are for internal use in the specific institutions. No central registration or statistical material has yet been produced as a result.[3]

Since no precise figures exist on how many children actually experience having a parent in prison, one has to produce estimates in various ways. One approach is to identify the average number of children per prisoner and multiply this by the total number of prisoners in a given nation.

Estimating the number of prisoners' children

The high number of children who, according to estimates, experience having a parent imprisoned comes as a surprise to many. As previously mentioned, the most recent estimate from the United States claims that in 2007 approximately 810,000 imprisoned fathers and mothers had more than 1.7 million children under the age of 18, one-third of whom would turn 18 while their parents were still in prison.[4] The 1.7 million corresponds to 2.3% of all children in the United States.[5] It has also been estimated that more than ten million children in the United States have had imprisoned parents at some point during their lives.[6] American surveys have furthermore found that 64% of all imprisoned men had children, while approximately 80% of all imprisoned women are mothers.[7]

In England it has been estimated, based on a study of 3,849 prisoners in England and Wales, that 200,000 children had a parent in prison at some point during 2009, and that 90,000 children had a parent in prison at a single point in time at the end of June 2009.[8] A total of 54% of 1,433 prisoners reported having children under the age of 18 at the time they went to prison. These prisoners had an average of 2.1 children, which makes for an overall average of 1.14 children per prisoner.[9]

The FFP, working in cooperation with the Norwegian State Statistical Bureau (Statistisk Sentralbyrå), estimated that between six and nine thousand children annually in Norway experience having a parent in prison.[10] In Sweden, it was estimated that eight thousand children had a parent in prison in 1997, but the figure is almost certainly significantly higher.[11] A more recent estimate can be found on the home page of the Swedish prison service, which claims that 30,000 children in Sweden have at least one parent either in prison or under penal supervision.[12] As far as the whole European Union is concerned, it has been estimated that more than 800,000 children annually experience having an imprisoned parent.[13] As previously explained, estimates from several European countries generally indicate that there are more children of prisoners than there are prisoners. In other words, the average prisoner has more than one child.[14]

Based on figures from Statistics Denmark, the Council of Crime Prevention (Det Kriminalpræventive Råd) estimated in 2005 that there were constantly between four and seven thousand children in Denmark who have at least one parent in prison. Approximately two-thirds of these children were under 6 years old, according to this calculation.[15] The most reliable Danish estimates, however, stem from later research based on data obtained directly from the imprisoned parents as well as Danish register data.[16] In one study, 803 sentenced and remand prisoners in Danish prisons responded to a detailed questionnaire in which they noted, among other things, whether they had children and how many. According to the survey, 402 prisoners – 50% of participants – had children, and they had 909 children in total.[17] Based on these figures, a Danish inmate has 1.13 children on average. This is very close to the English rate of 1.14 children per prisoner and fairly close to other European calculations that estimate 1.3 children for every prisoner.[18] Danish register data, however, show that 32% of all remand prisoners and 34% of all sentenced prisoners have registered biological children under 18.[19] This indicates that if the quotient of 1.13 children is more or less right, then quite a few of these children are not biological children or they are more than 18 years old.

A small Danish interview survey also confirms a "children per prisoner" rate in that vicinity. Here, 59 inmates were interviewed (representative of the entire prison population), 64% of whom had children. This group had an average of 1.9 children per person, which corresponds to all prisoners having approximately 1.2 children on average.[20]

With a quotient of 1.13 children per prisoner applied to the average occupancy in Danish prisons in 2010, 2011 and 2012, we see that there are constantly around 4,500 children in Denmark who are experiencing parental imprisonment. Based on the same quotient and the number of prisoners who passed through the Danish prison system throughout 2010, there were 14,500 children who experienced parental imprisonment at some point that year.[21] Recent Danish research based on register data regarding Danish children born from 1980–1985 shows that between 6.10% and 6.82% of all children born over that period have in fact experienced parental imprisonment.[22]

The relationship between prisoner and child – the family situation and prison visits

Naturally, not all prisoners' children have a close relationship with their imprisoned parent. The scope of the problem will therefore depend on the specific family situation, and in a number of cases it would not be in the child's interests to maintain contact. There is a gap between observers who seem to take for granted "that offenders are bad people, lousy spouses [and] deadbeat parents" and serious research that tells us "offenders typically have complex relationships with their families and communities", are often "primary sources of income for their households" and "play an important role in child rearing".[23] The finer points of this discussion will have to wait until the next chapter, which reviews the available research on the effects of parental imprisonment. Below I will simply present some of the few available data on the basic family situations of prisoners' children and on whether or not they visit their incarcerated parents.

We know, for example, from Statistics Denmark that in the Danish case there "are fewer children who live together with both their parents when the father or mother is convicted for an offence. This is particularly true in cases concerning more serious forms of crime such as violent crimes, sexual assaults, and property crimes. While 79% of the children live together with both their parents when their fathers are not convicted of any offence, only 27% live with both parents when the father has been convicted of a violent crime."[24]

The above-mentioned report from the United Kingdom tells us that out of 1,432 prisoners, 24% lived with a partner and a further 8% were married at the time of imprisonment. But they did not necessarily all have children – and furthermore, around half of those who stated that they were parents did not live together with a partner. In fact, 49% of the imprisoned parents reported they were single and a further 8% were divorced, separated or widowed. These figures, along with other research, suggest that "around half of imprisoned mothers and fathers lived with their children before imprisonment" both in the United States and in the United Kingdom.[25] An American survey revealed that 53% of all imprisoned fathers and 70% of all imprisoned mothers lived together with their children at the time of imprisonment.[26] Data from the United Kingdom give percentages of around 43–45% for imprisoned fathers and 58–62% for imprisoned mothers.[27]

The situation seems to be rather similar in Denmark. In the above-mentioned Danish survey, 402 of the 803 participating inmates had children. Of these 402 parents, 215 lived together at the time of imprisonment with their own or their partner's children, although Danish register data as mentioned provide significantly lower numbers both regarding the number of children (but only biological children were accounted for) and whether they lived with the incarcerated parent or not.[28]

Taken together these data make this cautious estimate seem reasonable: in around half (or more) of all cases of parental imprisonment, the children have significant contact with the imprisoned parent. Such contact can be of varying quality and both good and bad for the children involved. But the fact that the parent and the child (or children) lived together prior to the imprisonment in a significant proportion of cases certainly indicates a certain level of closeness. This is indirectly supported by the frequency of visits in Danish prisons. Approximately two-thirds of the imprisoned parents report that they receive visits from their children during imprisonment.[29] It is furthermore likely that several more of the parents in prison keep contact with their children by other means, typically by phone or written correspondence – and through home leave, which is very important (in a Scandinavian context). A US study reported that "more than three fourths of all state and federal prisoners make an effort to stay in contact with their children".[30]

Another question, of course, is if the imprisoned parent will move back with the child (children) after release. Many couples are divorced and separated during imprisonment.[31] Furthermore, children might end up in some sort of foster care when their parent is imprisoned. Although women constitute a relatively small percentage of most national prison populations, their rate of incarceration has in some places risen more dramatically than that of their male counterparts. The significant rise in the female incarceration rate in the United States actually "explain 30% of the increase in foster care caseloads between 1985 and 2000".[32]

Whichever way we look at it, the fact is that there are a staggering number of children with a parent in prison all over the world, and many seem to have close contact with that parent prior to the imprisonment. The family situation of these children will often be affected significantly – especially if the parent lived at home – and the changed family situation can persist after release, as in cases of divorce, parental separation or placement in foster care. But it would certainly be preferable to have reliable figures and official data on these issues – both on the actual number of prisoners' children and with regard to their specific family situation. This could be obtained relatively easily if standardised procedures were introduced in prison systems around the world.

5
The Problems and Reactions of Prisoners' Children: A Review of Research

A person's arrest and imprisonment often has a serious impact on the lives of several other people. In the case of close family – especially children – this impact can be very serious indeed and these individuals can suffer emotional, economic and psychological consequences. As already explained, imprisonment is wrought with taboos and stigmatisation, which will often affect children on top of all the other problems that follow from having a father or mother in prison. Taken together, the many and far-reaching ways in which imprisonment can affect close relatives has been termed an experience of "secondary prisonization".[1]

After being a more or less neglected subject for decades, how imprisonment affects a prisoner's family and children has been studied with increasing frequency in recent years. The character and scope of this research varies widely, and the studies are often based on different kinds of empirical data. In addition, it is generally very difficult to disentangle the complex factors, which will sometimes influence the situation. Take the question of how pre-imprisonment background affects problems experienced by prisoners' children. Such factors much include criminal behaviour among parents, low income and low levels of education in the family, poor living conditions, culture and lifestyle in poor neighbourhoods, frequency of mental health problems and drug abuse and the level of social welfare in the country/state in question.

This chapter is structured according to a number of themes, which I hope will capture the many different problems prisoners' children can become exposed to and the varied reactions these problems can lead to. I also address some general questions concerning research methodology and to what degree we can compare results and findings across jurisdictions. The following issues are therefore discussed below:

1. Research on prisoners' children – general trends and methodological issues
2. Children of imprisoned parents – individuals with different experiences
3. Background factors – family situation, marital status, risk factors, etc.
4. The effects of parental imprisonment on the relationship between child and parent
5. Financial problems in families with an imprisoned parent
6. Taboos, bullying and stigmatisation
7. Secrecy, lies and children's imaginings
8. Ambivalent emotions, guilt and shame
9. Behavioural changes and mental health problems
10. Antisocial and criminal behaviour
11. The effects of imprisonment on the parent – does a prisoner become a worse parent?
12. Problematic contact with the imprisoned parent – the importance of prison conditions
13. The penal system "upside down" – social and administrative exclusion

These themes cannot describe or explain the situation of all children of imprisoned parents. Neither will all these children be affected within all the above categories; rather, they are likely to experience problems related to a few or many of them. For some children, it can furthermore be an advantage to be separated from a parent. This depends entirely on the specific situation but can be the case with, for example, violent, antisocial or abusive dads living at home.[2] The circumstances and reactions can vary significantly from child to child depending on a number of factors but many children experience similar problems.

Research on prisoners' children – general trends and methodological issues

It is quite remarkable that research on children of imprisoned parents was virtually non-existent 30 years ago. Given that the prison as an institution of punishment stretches more than 400 years back in time and that imprisonment has been a key sanction in Western penal practice in the last two centuries, this fact becomes even more astounding.

From the 1970s–1990s, a few studies of a mainly qualitative character did appear. They described the situation of prisoners' children in various ways. This research was important but limited in scope, and as late as 1999, two researchers concluded that the effect of parental imprisonment on children "may be the least understood and most consequential implication of the high reliance on incarceration".[3] In the same year, Else Christensen completed a small qualitative study of imprisoned parents in Denmark, a study she described as innovative compared to existing research, since she allowed "families and children to personally express their problems and their experiences and wishes for help".[4] Alison Liebling and Shadd Maruna took the same position six years later when they concluded in 2005 that "there is little research emphasis on the effects of imprisonment on prisoner's families".[5]

As this chapter discusses, more research on prisoners' children has now been produced, especially during the last five years or so. Importantly, this research has been not only qualitative but also quantitative and includes studies and reviews which attempt to measure and assess some of the possible effects of parental imprisonment. On a general note, this research has confirmed that parental imprisonment is a risk factor in different ways and that we are dealing with a very vulnerable group of children.

For example, a 2008 review by Murray and Farrington concluded that parental imprisonment is a risk factor in relation to a number of problems, including "child anti-social behaviour, offending, mental health problems, drug abuse, school failure, and unemployment".[6] This was later confirmed by a so-called Campbell Review (co-authored by the same criminologists).[7] On a similar note, Wildeman and Western have found that imprisonment reduces "family resources and contributes to family breakup" and that incarceration "is linked to increases in children's aggression, behavioural problems, and social marginalisation".[8] A recent review concluded "that parental incarceration predicts increased risk for children's antisocial behavior" but was, in contrast to previous reviews, unable to find the same strong prediction of risk with regard to mental health problems, drug use and poor educational performance.[9] In contradiction to this, the multinational EU COPING Project has recently listed as one of its main results that children "with imprisoned parents as a group are at a significantly greater risk of suffering mental health difficulties than children who do not have parents in prison".[10]

One of the big questions is to what degree parental imprisonment might cause or influence these and other negative outcomes. In 2008, Murray and Farrington concluded that we still know very little about whether "parental imprisonment causes these problems".[11] Like their English counterparts, Wakefield and Wildeman concluded in 2011 that it "remains unclear whether and to what extent the incarceration of parents *causes* poor outcomes for their children".[12]

The problem here is that it can be very difficult to differentiate between risk factors and causality. When are these children's problems caused directly by parental imprisonment, and when are they a result of other factors in the children's lives? Or, to put it differently but perhaps more realistically: to what degree are these problems the result of a combination of parental imprisonment and other factors? Various studies indicate that, compared to children in general, prisoners' children are more likely to have parents with abuse problems, mental health problems and limited education.[13] Moreover, the reactions of prisoners' children may stem from their parents' criminal lifestyle or mental health problems, or other possible problematic issues that existed before the parents went to prison. Therefore, it is important to study whether or not these children's problems are caused by these background factors or by the parental imprisonment itself.[14]

A number of quantitative studies have attempted to account for various circumstances, such as the parents' abuse problems, mental health problems and lack of education. This entails working with large volumes of data concerning many children, comparing prisoners' children with control groups containing other children and studying the development over time. For example, data from "The Cambridge Study in Delinquent Development" has been used to show that "parental imprisonment predicted antisocial-delinquent behaviour through the life course with an average odds ratio of 5.7 and predicted violence with an odds ratio of 3.4" and that "prisoners' sons had significantly more convictions (mean = 3.17) than sons whose parents were convicted but not imprisoned".[15] But outside of England and the United States, the evidence is mixed. By comparing Swedish, Dutch and British data, it has been found that while parental imprisonment appears as a likely causal factor (not only a risk factor) in England, a similar effect has not been identified in the Swedish and Dutch material (where parents' criminal habits rather than their imprisonment seem to be the explaining factor).[16]

Recent Danish research has put an interesting twist on this particular issue. By analysing large samples of Danish register data and controlling for various background factors it has been found that parental imprisonment "is not an independent predictor of children's number of convictions in early adulthood", which supports the results in the Swedish and Dutch cases.[17] But by analysing different types of serious crime, it was also found "that offspring of imprisoned parents are indeed more likely to engage in criminal activities such as crime against property as young adults", which suggests that there are long-term causal effects of parental imprisonment in Denmark as well.[18] Similarly, Danish register data have also been used to show that parental imprisonment has an impact on social stratification in Denmark by contributing to inequality as measured by economy and education. The data thus show that among the group of imprisoned parents there is a rising overrepresentation of dad's in the lowest income group and a rising overrepresentation of parents with the lowest registered level of education.[19]

In the United States, quantitative research has also brought important new insights. Based on extensive data from the "Project on Human Development in Chicago Neighbourhoods" and from the "Fragile Families and Child Wellbeing Study", it has been shown that there are "substantial and statistically significant harmful effects of parental incarceration on children". These effects include increasing levels of aggression and behavioural problems among this group of children.[20] In a recent book Wakefield and Wildeman conclude with regard to the United States prison boom that "the incarceration of parents has profound consequences for their children" and that imprisonment of fathers is "associated with substantial increases in children's behavioural problems" as well as "with a significant and substantial increase in the risk of infant mortality".[21]

Regardless, it would be a serious mistake to look only at the quantitative data in this regard. Qualitative research can have unique strengths, which can help us disentangle the jungle of questions about imprisonment's effects. An example of qualitative research contributing to understanding how prison experiences can impact family life is an ethnographic study of the entrance to California's San Quentin prison visiting area. The author presents the thesis that cohabitants of imprisoned men experience "secondary prisonization": they suffer from the imprisonment, though to a lesser degree than their imprisoned partner.[22] Similarly, Else Christensen shows through qualitative interviews in Denmark how profound an impact parental imprisonment can have on children's lives. Christensen demonstrates that, for younger children, a very important element in the first visit with the imprisoned parent is simply the opportunity to establish that dad or mum is still alive.[23] Such research does not provide statistics on a large scale but can get us close to the affected families' situations, problems and feelings. When this is done researchers are able to show clearly how parental imprisonment can cause or exacerbate serious problems for the involved children.[24] In a previous study, my colleague Janne Jakobsen and I explored how children in Denmark experience parental imprisonment by looking at the various stages of the process – from arrest to release – and the concrete problems prisoners' children encountered. We found that many issues were direct results of the arrest and imprisonment of a father or mother.[25] Taken together, the available qualitative research clearly demonstrates that parental imprisonment can have serious negative effects on children in several different ways – in connection with the arrest of a parent, during the imprisonment, and after release. Much of the available qualitative research can certainly also be used to actually *prove* something about the problems experienced by prisoners' children and their causes – although we cannot know exactly how many children are affected in exactly what ways, and it is difficult to say something about long-term consequences.

One cannot rely solely on the existing quantitative control-group studies because they also have several limitations. Take for example a thorough recent review, which claims to summarise "the most rigorous evidence to date" and on that basis finds that parental imprisonment predicts risk for antisocial behaviour but not for mental health problems, drug use or poor educational performance.[26] The review – as far as I can see – is state of the art within the genre, but one nevertheless must be careful when interpreting these types of quantitative studies because they are often unable to take numerous important elements into account. One particular problem is that such reviews are often unable to single out and study those particular groups of prisoners' children in which one would expect to observe effects of parental imprisonment. As the authors of the above-mentioned review state, they were unable to test for variables such as "whether parents and children were living together before the incarceration, the quality of prior and ongoing family relationships, what children are told about the event, the offence for which parents are incarcerated, the length of parental incarceration, types of incarceration (jail or prison, and types of prison), levels of social support, family income, and neighborhood context".[27] So while much of the available quantitative research in this area is groundbreaking and clearly establishes how prisoners' children generally belong to a group at risk for negative life outcomes, a lot of very important – and sometimes crucial – factors are missing from the analysis. In my opinion, these shortcomings are not always reflected adequately in the way the conclusions are drawn.

To highlight one particularly important issue: it is quite relevant to ask how much we actually learn about the problems parental imprisonment might create if we include in the data set and statistical analysis children who had minimal or no contact with their parent before the incarceration.[28] And what if we know nothing about the length and type of incarceration? To put it differently, if one wanted to study the possible negative effects parental imprisonment can have on children, it would make sense to look only at those children who had meaningful contact with the parent before imprisonment. There is, for example, no reason to believe that a child who does not know his or her biological father will be affected by his imprisonment, and similarly, children with a very limited contact should generally not be expected to be severely harmed on that account. As already described, research suggests that around half of the imprisoned parents in Denmark, the United Kingdom and the United States lived with their children before the incarceration.[29] If we looked at this group and then weeded out all short-term sentences, and if we were also able to account for the prison regime (remand, closed, open), that would make a lot of sense. But by including children with no meaningful contact with the imprisoned parent, as well as all short-term sentences, we gain limited knowledge. The group of children who had limited or no contact with their parents before imprisonment is potentially very big – anything from a few per cent to a third or more of all prisoners' children. There is a huge dark number in much of the quantitative research in this area, which the literature in question does not thoroughly address.

If we single out the question of the length of time a parent has spent in prison, we find that we are dealing with a very important factor, which we really need to account for if we want to seriously discuss the possible impact of parental incarceration. Take Denmark, for example. The Danish system frequently uses short sentences, even to a miniscule seven days of imprisonment. This means that in the Danish register data used for effect studies one will find that traffic violators who serve a week or two and then go home to their families are mixed together with drug addicts who have robbed a bank and serve several years. This is certainly problematic. There is no reason to expect that such short sentences will have a serious impact on the children involved. Furthermore, if we look at the possible impact of the various types of prison regimes, there is in Denmark a huge difference between being isolated in a remand prison and doing time in an open prison – especially in terms of the concrete possibilities for interacting with family and children. Likewise, doing time in a supermax prison in the United States is an altogether different story compared to being placed in a lower-tier security facility. But by conducting qualitative, in-depth research into the varying situations and conditions that prisoners and their children experience, we can learn much about the concrete problems faced by the children involved, as well as how various contexts are likely to create different results.

It makes a lot of sense, in other words, to utilise and combine both quantitative and qualitative research. By doing so we can conclude that prisoners' children constitute a very vulnerable group, which will often run into numerous problems related to parental imprisonment. For some children, many of these problems are directly linked to the fact that they have a parent in prison.

Another important question is to what degree research on children of imprisoned parents and the negative effects they experience translates across countries and jurisdictions. Societies, cultures, penal law, prison practices and social security are certainly different from place to place and must have an impact on the degree and kinds of problems children experience. Obviously, the phenomenon of mass imprisonment in the United States, for example, has some very different consequences compared to the way that relatively low levels of imprisonment influence society in Scandinavian welfare states.[30] What is nevertheless striking is the many and obvious similarities between the experiences described by prisoners' children across jurisdictions. This seems to tell us that there are some very basic problems, emotions and experiences inherent to the phenomenon of parental imprisonment. But there are also differences, and some of them will be touched upon in various places throughout this book.

Children of imprisoned parents – individuals with different experiences

All children are different and all children have different experiences. Family situations and children's relationships with imprisoned parents also vary greatly. As a result, it can be difficult to determine which reactions and problems are a result of parental imprisonment and which are a result of other circumstances in children's lives. Therefore, it is not surprising that prisoners' children display different reactions – even within the same family. As an example of the latter, a mother describes the reactions and behaviour of her three daughters whose father went to prison:

> Cecilie has been sulky when we go there [to the prison] and sad when we had to go back home. She's on the verge of tears and is easily hysterical. Amanda has suffered from headaches, stomach aches, and

has had difficulty concentrating on her homework. One day, in frustration, she bit her teacher.... Between five and eight in the evening, Melinda goes around restlessly until the phone rings and then she wants to be the one to answer it and talk to Claus first.[31]

Even more diverse reactions can be expected from children in very different family situations, ranging from no reaction or experience of loss in cases where the child and the imprisoned parent have had no previous contact, to a major crisis in the case of children who are removed from a close relationship and placed in an institutional setting. For some children, the imprisonment of a parent strikes suddenly and comes as a shock, while for other children it is a recurring event. There are also children who experience more or less violent arrests of their parent, while other children do not experience the arrest itself and perhaps are even kept ignorant of the arrest and imprisonment. A few children, move into the institution where the parent – most often the mother – is imprisoned. Usually this concerns very young children, typically in the 0- to 3-year-old age group. But in some countries, like in Norway, this is never allowed.

Children's experiences visiting the remand prison or prison also vary, as do their impressions of whether or not they have someone to talk to about what has happened and about how they feel. There are children who face having to cope without their parent for a very long time, and there are children who are separated from their parent for only a short time. The age of the child can be of significant importance. For example, 2-year-olds have another experience than 14-year-olds. A child's psyche and development are important factors in determining how the child handles parental imprisonment.[32] Furthermore, as already mentioned, for some children it will actually be beneficial to be separated from a parent.

How great an effect parental imprisonment has on a child's life is also very dependent on the nature of the relationship between the parent and the child and the structure of the family prior to the imprisonment. At the time of imprisonment, some children had none or only very limited contact with the parent concerned, while others lived with or saw the parent regularly.

In the following I look at some of these background factors, which are often part of the family context, and can influence the children's experience of parental imprisonment and affect their lives and their future.

Background factors – family situation, marital status et cetera

If we look at the family situation of children of imprisoned parents, it is a fact that many prisoners both come from, and find themselves living in, fragile and problematic family situations. Hence many children of imprisoned parents have difficult family backgrounds.

If we start by looking at some of the problems found in most prison populations, we get a sense of some of the family situations and issues that we are dealing with. One has to keep two basic things in mind when looking at general prison population statistics in this context: (1) all prisoners are not parents, and (2) one can find imprisoned parents who do not have any of the problems discussed. Still, the available figures discussed in Chapter 4 indicate that around half of all prisoners have children.

Prison populations in general are overrepresented in an abundance of unfavourable statistics. A striking example is the prevalence of psychological suffering and mental disorders in prison populations in many countries. In 2002, a review of 62 psychiatric surveys including 22,790 prisoners in 12 different countries concluded that 3.7% of all male prisoners and 4% of all female prisoners had a psychotic illness, while 10% of the male and 12% of the female prisoners suffered from major depression. Personality disorders affected 65% of men and 42% of women. It was concluded "that the risks of having serious psychiatric disorders are substantially higher in prisoners than in the general population".[33]

Another trademark of prison health is the very high prevalence of drug and alcohol abuse or dependence.[34] Alcohol abuse or dependence rates found in 18 studies ranged from 50–66% in one group to much lower frequencies ranging from 9–17%. This substantial difference can be explained by a gradual shift in abuse or dependence patterns away from alcohol towards drugs. Drug abuse or dependence was reported in 18 studies with a prevalence rate of 24–61%, with one Finnish study reporting 6%.[35]

A review of the literature on mental disorders in prison populations in various (primarily Western) countries found a prevalence of psychiatric morbidity ranging from 46–88% among sentenced prisoners in North America, and a prevalence of 37% and 57% in two European studies. In North American remand populations, two studies reported 70% and 94%, while European studies reported 62–76% (these figures counted substance dependence or abuse as disorders).[36]

Research in US prisons generally reveals similar or higher rates than those reported for European prisons.[37] In 2002, the National Commission on Correctional Health Care estimated the prevalence of a number of mental disorders:

> On any given day, between 2.3 and 3.9 percent of inmates in state prisons are estimated to have schizophrenia or other psychotic disorder, between 13.1 and 18.6 percent major depression, and between 2.1 and 4.3 percent bipolar disorder (manic episode). A substantial percentage of inmates exhibit symptoms of other disorders as well, including between 8.4 and 13.4 percent with dysthymia, between 22.0 and 30.1 percent with an anxiety disorder, and between 6.2 and 11.7 percent with posttraumatic stress disorder.[38]

Some studies and data deal with the prevalence of substance abuse and other problems specifically among imprisoned parents. According to the US Bureau of Justice statistics, for example, "four out of five prisoners in state prisons reported some type of past drug use, with the majority stating that they had used drugs the month before their offense and often committed their offense while under the influence of drugs".[39]

Danish research furthermore showed that imprisoned parents primarily come from the lowest rated income group and that most of prisoners' children had parents with only basic schooling (up to 9th grade, i.e., the lowest registered level of education).[40]

We can use these statistics to say that prisoners' children are generally more likely than their peers to find themselves in a problematic (family) situation in which at least one parent has mental health or substance abuse problems, low income or a low level of education. Many of these children, in other words, come from fragile families. It also seems more likely that these families were run by single mothers even before the father went to prison. In addition it is well known that offenders have a greater than normal risk for getting divorced or separated during their time in prison.[41]

An especially vulnerable group of children are those placed in some sort of foster care outside the family – children's homes, for example – by the social authorities. Analysis of Danish register data tells us that many of these children have a parent with a criminal record. In a particular study, 13.1% of 8,743 children from 0–6 years who had previously been in foster care had a father who had received either a prison sentence or a suspended prison sentence, compared to 0.9% of the 2,156,794 children who had not been placed in foster care.[42]

How many of the various risk factors often co-occur and what concrete family situations and experiences they can create for prisoners' children are illustrated in a presentation of the Danish "family house" in the Engelsborg open prison, which features a seemingly unique model of family therapy for prisoners and their families. The families and prisoners who are allowed into the family house have been screened thoroughly and are believed to have the potential to become a more or less well-functioning family. In that sense, the family house does not deal with the very worst cases. Nevertheless, the families there often "have massive social problems that become visible" while they live in the family house.[43] Among the children who have stayed in the family house are those who have cut themselves, have involuntary discharge of faeces, have concentration problems, are violent, suffer from depressions, feel anxiety, are socially isolated, and drink and smoke as 10- to 12-year-olds. Among the parents in the family house are those who abuse alcohol and/or drugs, suffer from anorexia, are paranoid, are violent, are in deep grief, are lonely and isolated, stutter, have (other) children placed in foster care, are long-term unemployed, have debts, lack housekeeping skills, have problems relating to their own children, are immature, suffer from somatic diseases and, of course, are criminal.[44]

This gives a glimpse of what reality can look like in at least some of these families and for some prisoners' children. In a quantitative researcher's terminology, this growing up with parents having one or more of the above issues would be called *co-occurrence of risk factors* or *cumulative disadvantage*.[45] The psychological and social problems observable among these children hint at the kind of reactions such "risk factors" and "background factors" can produce. It is of course often easier to relate to when illustrated by real life stories. I remember, for example, how a family therapist at Engelsborg once told me that many of the children they housed had never been to a classmate's birthday party – because their families simply lacked the financial or social resources to buy a present, get them to the party or keep the time.

Gender is also believed to be a factor in how children handle parental imprisonment, but the available data in this regard is very limited. In Annelie B. Turresson's study of nine Swedish families with imprisoned mothers, she refers to the various ways in which boys and girls handle separation. Here, there is indication that boys are most vulnerable to separation from their parents in early childhood, while girls are most vulnerable in their teenage years.[46] But the research on the latter point is not entirely clear. A child psychiatric study from 1977 showed that boys were particularly affected by separation from their fathers. Shortly after the imprisonment, many boys already showed aggressive and antisocial behaviour. The study also indicated that teenage boys especially had a tendency to develop behavioural problems if their fathers were imprisoned.[47]

That boys have a tendency to react more violently outwards than girls is supported by more general studies of children's gender-specific reactions to coping with trauma. Here, research indicates that boys generally react outwards (by displaying aggressiveness), while girls react inwards (with depression and anxiety). Because boys' reactions are often more visible to the outside world, they get help more easily than girls do. Girls get help when their problems become more serious. Another study shows that girls have an easier time making contact with others and talking about their feelings and experiences than boys.[48]

Research in the United States has similarly found a positive and robust "association between paternal incarceration and boys' physical aggression", while the same was not the case for the girls.[49] British data on the criminality of prisoners' sons have been interpreted the same way: "We found a relationship between parental imprisonment and the offending of sons, not of daughters. This is in line with the possibility that boys and girls react differently to stressful life events, with boys showing externalizing problem behaviour including criminal behaviour while girls have more internalizing problems."[50]

The effects of parental imprisonment on the relationship between child and parent

Imprisonment of a parent can have severe consequences for the future relationship between a child and parent. There are many possible reasons for this, including the massive difficulties associated with parenting while imprisoned, the lack of close contact between parent and child, the possible damaging effects of serving time and the risk of divorce. In the United States, the phenomenon of mass imprisonment has therefore produced a situation where "incarceration has emerged as a primary force in the redefinition of parenthood".[51]

As already mentioned, every case is different. For children who live with or see their parent often before imprisonment, the imprisonment means a dramatic change. For other children, there is no great impact on their daily lives. In all cases where there is some sort of relationship between the parent and child, this relationship changes to some degree due to parental imprisonment. In many cases an obvious result is that the child has to do without the closeness of his imprisoned parent, since there are far fewer possibilities to spend time together and keep in contact. Furthermore, the circumstances surrounding the few hours' contact that can be had weekly or monthly is significantly different from what is possible outside of prison – and even from prison to prison depending on the prison regime (remand, open, closed), as well as local conditions and the culture in the various institutions.

No matter the circumstances, the way children can spend time with their parent changes fundamentally. During the remand imprisonment period, the police can sometimes also influence decisions on a number of issues surrounding visits and the regime employed. A particularly Scandinavian kind of problem during the remand period is the use of pre-trial solitary confinement, which has been an integral part of the system in Norway, Sweden and Denmark for many years.[52] The problem is that solitary confinement for 22–24 hours every day, with minimal access to psychological, meaningful social contact, exposes people to a number of negative effects, including anxiety, depression and possibly mental illness.[53] It is obvious that such consequences can play a significant role in the prisoner's ability to function as a parent. For the children, this means that contact with parents can be extremely difficult.[54]

According to the well-known "attachment theory", which was originally developed by John Bowlby, separation from parents is generally detrimental to children.[55] Based on this theory, it can be established that parental imprisonment and the separation of child and parent will often have a negative effect on children.[56] A Danish child psychologist, who has worked with prisoners' children talks about "the very serious break" between the child and his or her primary caregiver as something that can burden the child severely.[57] The psychological consequences of the separation depend on the character of the relationship between the child and the parent before the break, as well as the child's age and level of development.[58] According to the child psychologist, parental imprisonment can affect young children very severely because they are more dependent on their parents: "Their world turns around dad and mum, who are their safe base in daily life and, moreover, it is difficult for young children to understand what is happening when they are not told about it and can talk about it in the same way as older children."[59]

An 11-year-old British girl recollects how she "used to spend lots of time with Dad" but "see[s] him a lot less now. I don't speak to him so much. I miss that."[60] Naturally, many children miss their imprisoned parents, especially if they are used to living with them or spending a lot of time together. Many people who work with children whose father or mother is in prison point out that this loss of contact is comparable to other major family crises, such as serious illness or bereavement.[61] Swedish research also highlights that prisoners' children can react similarly to children with a parent who is seriously ill or dies.[62] Several researchers also point out that separation as a result of parental imprisonment can be especially detrimental to children because it often comes suddenly, can be violent and is often not explained. Furthermore, prisoners' children experience many restrictions in the contact with their imprisoned parent.[63]

A 1995 study that interviewed 30 families from Cambridgeshire in England indicated that the early stages of the separation process can be particularly difficult for the children, not least when the arrest in itself had been traumatic.[64] For children, witnessing parental arrest is comparable to seeing their parents assaulted or observing violence in the family.[65]

Numerous descriptions confirm that the arrest situation can be painful for children: "At the time they arrived, my sister and I were alone at home. Suddenly we heard noise downstairs and the door was kicked in. There were officers everywhere. Eight in all and dogs that barked. Our little sister was sleeping and she woke up. So my father was there and they put the handcuffs on him and we started crying. There was an officer who said that we should say goodbye. Dad took us aside and gave us 150 Kroner and said that he had done something stupid. He said that he would be back soon. We sobbed like crazy. That was the worst day of my life. Afterwards, all the furniture was overturned. The drawers pulled out and clothes were all over the place."[66]

Such an experience can leave deep marks, especially if the arrest does not take place in an appropriate manner. The child's experience depends on the way in which the apprehended, the relatives and the police handle the situation.[67] When the arrest does not proceed successfully – from a child's point of view – the period surrounding the arrest and remand imprisonment can "be a time of extreme shock, stress, fear, confusion and instability for children, especially if the arrest is witnessed at home".[68] The mothers of a group of children with imprisoned fathers responded to a 1995 survey that it was especially during the remand imprisonment period and immediately after sentencing that they experienced a worsening of their children's behaviour and demeanour.[69]

It has also been suggested that it can be devastating for a child who has not experienced the arrest to suddenly hear about it at a later stage, for example, in school or in the press.[70] On the whole, it seems that the adults' (the parents, police, prison personnel and others) handling of the situation plays an important role in the child's experience and the imprint that is left on the child from the arrest and imprisonment.

Children of imprisoned parents are, not surprisingly, also affected by the parent or the caregivers who remain with them. The parent who remains is often very affected by the situation and experiences tremendous stress, which is likely to be transferred to the children.[71] A consequence of this can be that a great deal is unloaded onto the children and they are treated as little adults. Naturally, this means that the relationship between child and parent – both the imprisoned parent and the caregiver living at home – changes significantly.

In those cases where there has been positive emotional attachment and he child has felt secure in his or her relationship to the parent, the child will experience the separation "as very dramatic and painful".[72] In those instances where there is a loose or ambivalent emotional attachment, the problems will be less serious but still present.[73] According to some, the children in all circumstances will experience the loss of a parent as traumatic.[74] The obvious exceptions are those situations where ceased or minimal contact is in the best interest of the child, as in the case of an antisocial or violent father.[75] This does not necessarily mean that no contact at all is in the best interest of the child in all such cases.

Given the above-mentioned issues, it is not surprising that the relationship between child and parent can be discontinued due to parental imprisonment and that the separation can lead to a permanent break in the relationship.[76] How often this happens against the best interest of the child we do not know.

Many prisoners describe how it can be difficult to have visits and to relate to the outside world and the family they feel they have let down. A former imprisoned father says: "Sometimes I really had to get myself together before visits. I always thought that they would be disappointed. That can be difficult to cope with when you're inside."[77] Another formerly imprisoned father opted out of visits for a period: "We had a lot of money – that's often the attraction with criminality. But when I was in prison, they [the family] were on income support. They probably felt it as a letdown. That dad is gone, the money's gone and all possibilities are gone. That made me withdraw from them because I couldn't cope with being guilty of that as well. It's not nice to think back on that."[78] One father in an interview survey of more than 200 imprisoned fathers in England explains: "It's very hard to be a dad from prison. I'm on the outside of their lives looking in."[79]

It is not strange that many prisoners feel they are placed outside their parental role. They cannot be included in their child's daily life and often do not have much chance of otherwise participating in the child's life. For example, prisoners become frustrated about the limits on telephonic contact: "After applying, I have been allowed to call once a week…. It's difficult since my mother, my son and my daughter need contact. Every week I have to decide who I should get on the line. When I can call and the length of the call depends on who's on duty."[80] Restrictions on what may be brought along by visitors can also influence, for example, imprisoned parents' involvement in children's school work. As a mother explained in 2007: "If Kristian wanted to take a reading book in, we had to go to the most senior staff and practically beg for permission. He's now in third grade – and he still hasn't been allowed to read one line for his dad."[81]

Financial problems

We know from a number of studies that many prisoners' children experience economic problems.[82] Some of these studies cannot tell us if this was caused by parental imprisonment or if the bad financial situation existed before the imprisonment.[83] It is, however, a likely hypothesis that many children of imprisoned parents experience financial regression, especially in those cases where a family suddenly loses an income, perhaps even the primary income. In addition, many families encounter new expenses such as transport for prison visits and telephone call charges.[84]

Some studies show how imprisonment of a parent can lead to a financial crisis for a family. An American study from 2003, based on 56 families affected by imprisonment, showed that the economic situation of the families worsened after the imprisonment of a family member.[85] Imprisonment can also have long-term financial consequences and can even lead to unemployment and reduced possibility of obtaining an education for ex-prisoners and thus harm their families and children in the long run.[86] A Danish study from 2008 shows that for prisoners with a sentence of six months or longer, a "very serious worsening of their attachment to the labour market occurs…. The difference between 'before and after' prison for this group is so dramatic that it must necessarily be attributed to what they experience in the interim – prison!"[87] The authors conclude that the "informal punishment for criminality is very tough in Denmark in the way that the criminals are marginalised, with great probability, from the labour market".[88] Naturally, this can expose a significant group of prisoners' children to financial problems, and these stretch far beyond the period in which the parent serves the prison sentence.

Taboos, bullying and stigmatisation

Imprisonment is a topic surrounded with taboos, and researchers commonly refer to the resulting stigmatisation as an important element that might create long-term effects of parental imprisonment.[89] For instance, as a 15-year-old Danish boy explains: "I thought it was embarrassing and awkward that my father was in prison, while their parents had a job.... I told some of my friends at the time, some of my really good friends. And one of them told some others, so they all heard about it and I was teased a little."[90]

A 16-year-old boy experienced being stigmatised because of his father's actions: "There were many who said, 'I don't want to be together with him' because they were afraid of becoming involved in something or other. So I said, 'But you won't get involved in anything.' But they weren't convinced. So I also lost a lot of friends."[91]

Christina lost contact with family members when her mother's brother disowned his sister because of her mother's criminality: "He cannot understand that she could do something criminal when she has children. He's disowned her, and that means that I don't get to see that part of the family anymore either. It has destroyed the family.... Before, we always celebrated Christmas together. And birthdays with cake, scones, cacao and lots of chatter and laughter. I was used to big family gatherings, and I loved it. It was really wonderful. Real unity."[92]

The risk of negative social heritage is a well-known phenomenon. Children of alcoholics, for example, face a greater risk of becoming alcoholics themselves compared to other children, and prisoners' children face greater risk of going to prison themselves compared to other children.[93] It is important to bear in mind that risk is not equivalent to causality, and such statistics can be "dangerous" in the sense that they can create prejudice and condemnation of children of imprisoned parents. A high school pupil, who was an intern for a few days at the Danish Institute for Human Rights illustrated this by expressing just such a concern: "Many children ARE, after all, like their parents – well, they often end up the same way as the parents when they grow up themselves. And after all, they're not the types you want to be friends with, the ones who might probably become criminals, even though it's not their fault.... Well, there are many actors whose children also become actors."

There are also children who experience outright bullying because their father or mother is in prison. In a British study, a 7-year-old boy relates: "They bully me, say nasty things. I don't let them know

I care, but sometimes I cry on the way home."[94] Some children react violently to the bullying. In the same study, a mother explains how her 9-year-old boy hurt himself: "He shaved his head and made it bleed so that he wouldn't have to go to school the next day, where he is being bullied."[95]

In a recent EU study, it was prisoners' children in the United Kingdom especially who reported being bullied, while there were few such cases in Sweden and Romania. In Germany, even "less evidence of stigma was found". Where bullying was reported, it "was a result of the shared secondary social stigma which had a 'contaminating' effect on the child".[96]

In some cases, the media can make the situation worse. Ten-year-old Jakob says: "The worst was the time he [father] was pasted on the front page of Ekstra Bladet [a Danish tabloid], so everyone knew it. There was a photo of him and I bunked off school a whole lot afterwards. At one time my teacher said something, and someone joked about it, so I got mad."[97] A British mother describe the effect the media's handling of the situation had on her children aged 9 and 11: "It broke their hearts when their dad went away. The offence was reported in the local papers and as we live in a small village it soon became common knowledge. The children suffered verbal abuse from other children. They were very upset by this and didn't want to go to school. They have been crying a lot and are generally very upset."[98]

There are also children who experience that "everyone knows", but no one says anything. A young woman explained, for example, how after her father's arrest and remand imprisonment, "everyone had read about my father's crime in the newspaper, but no one asked about it. This made it even worse, because it made me even more shameful."[99]

In a situation characterised by taboo and potential stigmatisation, it is not difficult to understand why many children of inmates spend a great deal of time wondering how they should relate to the surroundings. This is especially the case if the children or their families does not want anyone else to know about the imprisonment. As a family therapist from the Danish prison service express it, "the children's inner life can easily become all about the issue that their father or mother is in prison, while on the surface they pretend everything is okay".[100]

It is clearly problematic for prisoners' children that they have to handle these things. It is not surprising that such stigmatisation seems likely to worsen the risk of prisoners' children developing antisocial behaviour and experiencing psychological problems.[101]

Secrecy surrounding the imprisonment and children's imaginations

Since the middle of the 1990s, work has been done at the Danish Social Development Centre (SUS) to develop programmes for children who have parents with serious mental health, physical, or social problems.[102] At SUS, the conclusion is that a common denominator for children, whose parents are mentally ill, have abuse problems or are serving a prison sentence, is that these children "are often isolated and left to their own imaginings of what has happened to their parents".[103] Studies of prisoners' children support this conclusion.

In continuation of the taboo and stigmatisation associated with crime and prison, many parents choose to either keep the imprisonment secret from the child or ask the child to lie to the people around him or her.[104] Two studies document that 33% and 40%, respectively, of the children had not been told why their father or mother was absent.[105] In a study from a prison in Dublin, two-thirds of the imprisoned parents reported that their children were unaware of their imprisonment.[106] In a Danish study, children over 7 years old were told that their parent was in prison, while the younger children had usually been given other explanations of the absence.[107]

Thus, many prisoners' children do not know why their parent is absent. They are either given no explanation or they are told a story that their father is out sailing or that their mother has gotten a job in another country. Nonetheless, many children can sense that things are not as they have been told. A 7-year-old girl, who was told that her father had gone on holiday, explains: "I didn't know where he was, but I knew that he hadn't gone on holiday. Because he would never leave before saying goodbye to me."[108] As a result, many children worry a great deal and have anxious imaginings about what is actually going on, such as whether their parent is ill or perhaps even dead.[109] Ten-year-old Jonas describes how relieved he was when after three weeks during which his father had "disappeared", he was told that his father was not out sailing but had been imprisoned on remand: "It was a huge relief. A huge, huge relief that they had found him. I had been so scared that he was at the bottom of some ocean somewhere."[110]

Psychologist Else Christensen also believes that it is best to tell children the truth because they will often see through the lie. "Regardless of how old the child is, in the majority of cases it would be best to be told the truth. If children are lied to, that their father is travelling, they will start to ask questions: when dad has been out travelling, he usually calls home to say goodnight. They can immediately feel that something is not right. When the mother chooses instead to tell about the situation, the secrecy is over. And suddenly it is much easier to understand that dad will be away for a while."[111] Similarly, the EU COPING study found that prisoner's children "find it much harder to deal with the parent's absence if the truth is concealed: it can increase insecurity and erode trust between parents and children". On the other hand honest disclosure could "help children see the consequences of actions". Even "young children were thought by some to benefit from knowing the sequences of events and what would happen when, particularly as children often subconsciously pick up on what is occurring".[112]

There are also children who visit their parents in prison but are not told the truth about where they are or what their parent is doing in the prison. A family therapist in the Danish Prison Service explains that such situations typically apply to younger children. One mother told her 5-year-old daughter that they were going to visit her father at his new workplace. "When they arrived at the prison and called on the entry phone, a voice said 'Y Prison', and the girl then asked, 'Is this a prison?', to which her mother replied: 'Yes, dad is painting the prison.'"[113] According to the family therapist, even young children usually see through such a lie and are shaken and become uncertain when they discover that their parents have lied to them.

In the reverse situation, when children are well aware that their parent is in prison but have not visited, they can have unpleasant imaginings about what the prison looks like and what it is like to be in prison.[114] Such imaginings can be inspired by the dark dungeons of adventure stories or by American films in which the inmates wear orange prison uniforms and shackles on their wrists and ankles. The Danish Institute for Human Rights asked a fifth-grade class, for instance, what they thought a Danish prison looks like today. The pupils drew pictures and explained. Their answers and drawings varied greatly. Some of the children had a fairly realistic sense of what a Danish prison looks like and how things take place. Others drew something resembling a medieval dungeon or maximum-security prison as represented in American movies. They explained, "the windows are very small and it's dark"; "you wear a blue uniform – or orange"; "you have to do what you're told or otherwise, I don't know what happens, but it's not good"; "the guards are strict because you're a criminal". Else Christensen also found that children who are placed in an institution are put in an especially difficult situation and feel very alone. These children can feel that the arrested parent "cease[s] to exist".[115]

In summary, when parental imprisonment takes place, some children can experience a void that gives free rein to uncertainty and thus the imagination. This situation can worsen when the children are not informed of or lied to about what has happened.[116]

Ambivalent emotions, guilt and shame

Many children grapple with ambivalent emotions in relation to their imprisoned parent and what he or she had done. In a British study, descriptions from prisoners' children and their mothers indicated that on the one hand, the children had strong positive feelings for their imprisoned parent, but on the other hand were very angry with that parent, especially for having let them down and putting the family in a difficult situation.[117] In the children's groups – which the association for prisoners' relatives in Sweden, Bryggan, has established – the experience is that many children have difficulty reconciling the image they have of their father to the image they have of a criminal.[118] This is also a theme in the groups for children of prisoners, which the Danish Red Cross arranges in Denmark.[119]

There are many children who have feelings of guilt because they think that they are partly responsible for their mother or father being in prison.[120] A child psychologist who has experience with prisoners' children explains that children are often very specific in their way of thinking. Children think: "It's probably because I wanted a new Playstation that dad committed a robbery", and "If I had behaved properly, then dad would never have beaten up that man".[121] A young women also explains how her father, who was a drug addict, came to her high school and wanted to borrow money from her. But she did not have any money, and so "he committed an armed robbery in the bank right next to my school and was put in prison. I couldn't stop myself from thinking that if only I had had money for him."[122]

A warden at a children's home describes how she has witnessed that the feeling of guilt appears again and again in many children of prisoners. "Sometimes the child has an explanation perhaps of why it is his or her fault, but often the child cannot really explain why. It's just an emotion or feeling of depression."[123] A Danish study showed that the older children could become doubtful about whether they had been kind and good enough to the imprisoned parent, while the younger children could have the experience of the parent not caring about them anymore.[124]

Other children can react with anger, embarrassment or shame. "I don't know how I can say it, or who I should talk to. I am seriously embarrassed about what he has done. There's no one who knows about it yet", says 17-year-old Trine about her father being in prison.[125] In a Swedish study on children of imprisoned mothers, the author concludes that "shame was the most dominant feeling in the children".[126] The children whose mothers had committed crimes for the first time felt most ashamed, especially if the mothers had committed violent crimes. The children handled the shame in one of two ways, either by being silent about what happened or by becoming attached to friends with similar life situations.[127]

A British study of relatives of serious offenders describes how families became caught in a "web of shame", which has five dimensions. Two of these dimensions were based on "familial contamination", which can also easily affect prisoners' children through simply being *associated* with the offender and thereby perceived as "the same as the offender by virtue of their kin relationship"; and through an alleged *genetic* connection, which can provoke "primitive ideas of bad blood".[128] As explained by a woman whose partner was convicted of homicide: "I think neighbours, the media, friends, often find it difficult to cope with this and therefore the family are treated as though they've done something wrong as well."[129] Another woman, whose husband was also convicted of homicide, explain that this stigmatisation extends to the children as well: "Because you're a wife of a murderer or rapist or whatever you're classed in the same category as them. If you're a son or a daughter of a murderer they paint you the same."[130] All these feelings of shame are of course connected to the previously described stigmatisation, which prisoners' families often experience.

Taken together, these different emotions of ambivalence, guilt and shame can result in ambivalence towards the imprisoned parent. A young child who participated in an interview-based study in the United States responded: "My mom says he's going to come out in a few weeks. Deep in my heart I miss him, but outside of my heart I don't."[131]

Behavioural changes and mental health problems

As already mentioned, quantitative studies show that children of prisoners are at risk of experiencing adverse outcomes, and qualitative research suggests how this, at least in some situations, is likely to be a direct effect of parental imprisonment.

Research describes several reactions and different behaviour among prisoners' children. Some children react by displaying feelings of loss.[132] As a natural consequence of this, some children will experience sadness or despondence.[133] Some children will become insecure and lose self-confidence, some children are prone to crying and some children will have difficulty sleeping properly at night.[134] It is nevertheless difficult to say precisely how many children react in one or several of these ways, and it can be difficult to determine if other factors cause or contribute to creating the reactions.

In a British survey, only 8% of the 127 participating mothers (or others who had responsibility for the children) responded that the parental imprisonment had no effect on the child or children at all, while 22% were of the opinion that the children's behaviour had been negatively affected as a result of the parental imprisonment. Among the reactions and problems the mothers (or others who had responsibility for the children) experienced was that the children withdrew into themselves, displayed violent behaviour and wet their bed.[135]

Other studies have produced more drastic results. In one survey, 80% of the families reported behavioural problems among children as a result of parental imprisonment. For example, mothers of prisoners' children described how their children reacted with regression – that is, a step backwards in their development – and by becoming clingier.[136] Other studies also indicated that many children can have various behavioural problems in connection with parental imprisonment.[137] The behavioural reactions are very different. Some children withdraw into themselves and become more introverted, while others display aggressive behaviour.[138]

A Swedish qualitative interview study showed that the participating children were "negatively affected emotionally by parental imprisonment" and that they expressed "feelings of stigma".[139] The children described having different problems, particularly "sleeping problems, feelings of depression, general sadness and negative physical sensations".[140] In the EU COPING study, sleeping problems and nightmares were reported with a high frequency among prisoners' children in Sweden and the United Kingdom, and "behavioural or psychological problems were observed for two-thirds of the children in Germany".[141]

It has been pointed out how the children's behavioural problems can manifest themselves in a school situation, for example, by truancy. This can have long-range consequences for the individual child. The evidence is nevertheless mixed. On the basis of several studies, it has been concluded that "parental imprisonment strongly predicted school failure".[142] A later review by the same authors, however, found that parental imprisonment did not predict poor educational performance.[143] The EU COPING study found that "children's school attendance could be adversely impacted by parental imprisonment" in the United Kingdom and Sweden. In general, however, the children "continued to perform well at school, although for a minority [in the UK, Sweden and Germany], their school performance 'tailed off'".[144]

One possible reason that some children of imprisoned parents experience problems in school could be that they constantly think about their imprisoned parent and therefore have difficulty concentrating.[145] Seven-year-old Amalie thought so much about her mother that she "couldn't keep up in class".[146] Jesper had the same problem: "It's often in classes when we have time to sit and read or something, then I begin wondering what he [dad] is doing, then everything switches off and I can't do anything at all."[147] A 14-year-old Danish girl described how her father being in prison affected her in school: "But every time I think about him at school or when I'm alone, then I just can't handle it and then everything just goes wrong after I have thought about him. Things I need to do in school don't get done, I don't pull myself together, never go to school, don't know what I'm doing and it all just goes around in a huge, vicious circle."[148]

A family therapist from the Danish Prison Service's Halfway House, Engelsborg, who works with children of prisoners also finds that the majority of these children have great concerns: "I draw a circle and say to the children: try to show me how much time you spent thinking about your father during the day while he was in prison. It's 95% of the time. When they eat their breakfast, they think, 'Wonder if my father is getting breakfast today?' and that's how they relate to their own day throughout the day.... And it's also bad if they have visited him and he's been in a fight and has a black eye, and then they think, 'Wonder if anyone will hit my dad again today?' 'I wonder if he has been awake all night and been scared that someone will come and hit him again?' 'I wonder if his bed could be taken from him in prison?'"[149]

A warden at a Danish children's home explains:

> I once had an experience with a 2–3-year-old boy whose father had been imprisoned. A child psychologist taught me a great deal about how to talk with even young children about something so difficult. She knew that the most important thing for the child was that he was told and that he understands that someone was taking care of his father. You could plainly see how the little boy became more relaxed when she said this to him. It weighed on him because even though he was so young, he was worried about it. It can seem a little trivial, but it is just so important for children to know that someone

is taking care of their father and mother when they're not there. That the prison is not just a place where you "can rot", but that there are people who ensure that there is food and drink and that there's a bed to sleep in. You cannot take the worries away from the children, but you can ease them by explaining.[150]

There are also children who react by becoming "young adults" who take on the care of the family.[151] One 13-year-old British boy explained:

I was very upset and shocked at first. Over three years I have come to terms with it but I had to develop a 'hard streak' and grow up quickly. My brother and I have to help Mum a lot with the chores in the house and garden that my dad would normally do. We do it because she needs us to, but I'd rather I hadn't had to.[152]

Similarly, prisoners' children interviewed in the United States "were keenly aware of their caregiver's stresses and many went to great lengths to alleviate them".[153]

This tendency to behave as young adults is likely to be reinforced in situations where the children become involved in "adult matters", such as the parents' experience of being unfairly treated by prison staff or social authorities, the parents' attempt to have their case reopened or the parent's struggle to keep the household going. "Typically, the father is in prison and the child then becomes involved in the finances, when the bailiff comes, in adult feelings and adult thoughts and all other possible things, which children should not be involved in. And they take so much consideration of the adults that they do not show when they are sad or scared – because they do not want to make their parents even more upset."[154] This was also the motive for a 14-year-old British girl who hid her feelings from her mother: "When he first went to prison I really missed him and used to cry a lot in bed at night. I didn't want my mom to know I cried because that would have just upset her too."[155]

Some children also start to wonder if they risk becoming criminal themselves because of what their parent has done. One young woman described her childhood with her father in prison: "My parents are divorced and my mother sometimes said 'You are so like your father!' So I thought about that phrase, 'the apple doesn't fall far from the tree'".[156] Another study describes how a process can be triggered so a sort of "sense of badness can become a self-fulfilling prophecy and lead children to illegal behaviour and ultimately prison".[157] A psychologist from the Danish Red Cross's dialogue groups for prisoners' children also emphasises that it is very important that the children are told that their parent's criminal actions do not mean that they are in any way "biologically disposed" to committing crime, which some children fear.[158]

Research and personal accounts also suggest that parental imprisonment can affect children's health both in psychological and physical respects – although as previously described it is important to remember that in terms of causality several factors can come into play. A father, for example, describes how his 3-year-old daughter displayed physical as well as psychological reactions in connection with his imprisonment: "She wasn't doing well at all by me being away and began soiling her trousers and hitting other children in kindergarten."[159] According to the Danish NGO for prisoners' relatives, SAVN, children can have reactions to the imprisonment that are demonstrated physically, such as stress, headaches or stomach aches.[160]

There are also examples of prisoners' children displaying depressive reactions.[161] It has furthermore been argued that parental imprisonment is associated with psychological problems when the child becomes an adult, as well as with drug abuse and unemployment – but the evidence is mixed.[162] Other experts maintain that some children can have a more unstable upbringing as a consequence of the parental imprisonment. One reason is that the imprisonment can force the family to move around a lot, or the child to move and live with different people.[163]

Although it has not been demonstrated that parental imprisonment generally *causes* all the above-mentioned problems, it is nevertheless fair to say the quantitative and qualitative research – when looked at together – indicates that parental imprisonment can exacerbate and sometimes cause or contribute to creating the described problems for prisoners' children.

Antisocial and criminal behaviour

A further, particularly undesirable, result of parental imprisonment according to several studies is an increased risk of later antisocial behaviour and criminalisation among the children. International criminological research has found a strong correlation between separation from parents before the age of 10 and conviction up to the age of 32.[164] According to Statistics Denmark and The Danish Council for the Prevention of Crime, the same tendency is evident in Denmark. In 2005, the Council concluded that children with parents who have been in prison have three times the average risk of ending up in prison themselves.[165]

Within recent years, however, new research has been produced in this area in several countries. Some of this research, which has found a clear association between parental incarceration and antisocial behaviour among the children, was discussed in the beginning of this chapter. A review from 2008 concluded that "parental imprisonment (compared with no history of parental imprisonment) approximately trebles the risk for child antisocial-delinquent behaviour of children".[166] In a meta-analysis from 2009, this assessment was diminished slightly and it was estimated "that children of prisoners have about twice the risk for antisocial outcomes...compared with their peers". It was still concluded that "parental imprisonment is quite a strong risk factor for these outcomes".[167] In 2012, another review confirmed "that on average, children with incarcerated parents are at significantly higher risk for antisocial behavior compared with their peers".[168]

As mentioned earlier in this chapter, parental imprisonment was found to be a causal factor in the British data, but this was not the case in Sweden or Holland, where the parents' criminal habits seemed to be the explaining factor rather than their imprisonment.[169] Recently collected Danish data on different types of serious crime has nevertheless documented "that offspring of imprisoned parents are indeed more likely to engage in criminal activities such as crime against property as young adults", which suggests that there are indeed long-term causal effects of parental imprisonment in Denmark.[170]

In the US data from the previously mentioned "Fragile Families" study "suggest that paternal incarceration is associated with increased physical aggression for boys, and that effects are concentrated among boys whose fathers were neither incarcerated for a violent offense nor abusive to the boys' mother".[171]

If we look at it from the perspective of young offenders, we find that prisoners' children are overrepresented in such statistics. Figures from Statistics Denmark, for example, show that children of imprisoned parents are part of a group with increased risk of committing crimes themselves. According to a 2008 calculation, there are 11,000 children in Denmark aged 15–17 who have committed an offence. These children often have parents who have also committed offences. The correlation particularly applies when the parent has been sentenced to imprisonment. Of the 15- to 17-year-olds who have a father who has been sentenced to imprisonment, 12.3% have committed an offence themselves. In comparison, 15- to 17-year-olds with offences constitute 5.5% of all youth in that age group.[172] A major Swedish study found that 25% of the prisoners' children who participated in the study committed a crime between the ages of 19 and 30, compared to only 12% of those children whose parents had not been in prison.[173]

This means two things for prisoners' children: (1) they have a significantly greater risk of adopting antisocial and criminal behaviour compared to other children, and (2) the majority of these children will apparently *not* become criminals.

The second point is important as a reminder that there is no automatic social heritage at work here and that parental incarceration and other risk factors do not simply trigger antisocial behaviour. But the sheer mass in the use of imprisonment and the related social problems is of course crucial, and the phenomenon of mass imprisonment in the United States has created a unique situation with consequences on a different scale. With regard to the United States, the research in this area has been summarised accordingly: "Taken together, results imply that mass imprisonment may contribute to a system of stratification in which crime and incarceration are passed down from fathers to sons (but not daughters)."[174]

The effects of imprisonment on the parent – does one become a worse parent?

As Chapter 3 describes, the question of the effects of imprisonment is an old discussion. What is crucial in this context is whether, and to what degree, a prisoner is socialised into a prison environment – and, as a consequence, loses some of his or her competences as a citizen in a broad sense and as a functioning family member, spouse and parent in a more specific sense. This is not an unlikely hypothesis. As a review on the detrimental effects of imprisonment concludes, "both during incarceration and upon release, the experience of imprisonment does considerable harm to prisoners in obvious and subtle ways. Continuing beyond the prison term, these ongoing harms create significant obstacles to successful community reintegration, extending the harm of imprisonment, and, for most prisoners, diminishing life chances."[175]

Many criminologists emphasise how big the difference is between the prison's closed world and life in freedom. In a sociological typology of different ways of coping with imprisonment, one of the four identified strategies is to "withdraw" and focus upon "little beyond immediate events". A second strategy is called "conformity", which means that prisoners "appear relatively satisfied with their existence in prison".[176] A Danish criminologist has described the overall result of living within a prison regime as one in which "prisoners do not need to take personal responsibility for anything else other than surviving among other prisoners. They are spared from being confronted with the harm and problems they have inflicted on their victims. In this sense, the prison is a place where criminals can hide."[177] As explained by Shadd Maruna, "no institution does a better job of *hindering* the development of generativity than prison, with its unique ability to separate individuals from their social responsibilities and civic duties".[178]

But, if this is correct, one would have to say that hiding, losing conscience and not taking responsibility are not exactly qualities normally perceived as beneficial for a spouse or parent.[179] At the same time one could argue that one of the few areas in which it certainly ought to be possible to take some sort of responsibility in a prison situation is in relation to the parent role, which, legally speaking, would be taken away from the prisoner only in very rare cases. But the practical possibilities of acting as a responsible and caring parent during imprisonment are severely limited. In Denmark, many children and partners have described how frustrating it is that children may not as a rule take either school books or homework into the prison. This makes it impossible for the imprisoned parent to take responsibility, help the child and keep up with the schooling.[180]

The lack of parental agency in prisons also means that "incarceration changes how parents see themselves".[181] According to Else Christensen, the prisoners she interviewed described how they use a great deal of energy thinking and worrying about their family outside of the prison. It torments them that they have no possibilities of action in relation to the family. They have a great desire to have their possibilities of action expanded, for example, in the form of increased possibility for home leave to attend meaningful events in their children's lives or in emergency situations where the partner needs practical relief for the care of the children.[182]

Accordingly, some researchers have tried to measure the effects of imprisonment on parents in particular. In the United States it has been found that "incarceration has both immediate and enduring consequences for major depression among fathers".[183] As already mentioned, a Swedish study has also found that parents in solitary confinement experienced greater psychological health problems compared to prisoners in solitary confinement who did not have children.[184]

Research on mothers in prison has also identified the parental role as an issue causing separate and extraordinary stress – in addition to the other deprivations of prison life. Imprisoned mothers have themselves cited "being separated from their children as the most difficult aspect of incarceration".[185] Other research supports this assertion. Imprisoned mothers have been found to experience a reduction in parenting confidence as well as higher levels of anxiety after six months of imprisonment, when compared to non-mothers also in prison.[186]

The prisonization and adaptation to prison, which some prisoners experience, can also become a very specific problem when a parent is released and has to figure out how to be a parent outside of the prison again. "Parents who return from periods of incarceration...cannot be expected to effectively organise the lives of their children or exercise the initiative and autonomous decision making that parenting requires".[187] Very important factors in that regard are the amount of time spent in prison as well as the prison's conditions and regimes.

In any event, evidence points in the direction that learning to manage in a prison can negatively affect a parent's role and ability to create cohesion in a family.[188] In this way, the use of imprisonment is likely to have far-reaching consequences that can severely impact families and entail major practical and emotional problems for the affected parties – especially the children.

Problematic contact with the imprisoned parent – the importance of prison conditions

Regardless of the impact the prison regime might have on the parent, it will certainly create a new situation in terms of the possibilities for maintaining contact between parent and child. Many prison systems limit this contact and it often takes place under conditions that are not exactly child friendly. Nevertheless, there seems to be a general agreement among researchers that children value whatever contact is available. According to Danish research, children usually react positively to visiting their imprisoned parent in remand prison or prison.[189] Another study showed that the children's concerns for their imprisoned fathers diminished after they had visited them in prison and ensured themselves that the fathers were alright.[190]

Naturally, discontinued contact can be the best option when parental interaction is not beneficial or outright harmful to the children, as in cases concerning violence and abuse in the family. There are also instances of imprisoned parents trying to exploit their children by asking them to smuggle things into the prison or using them to get extra home leave without being sincerely interested in the child in question (see Chapter 13). But generally, Danish as well as international research indicates that maintaining good contact between imprisoned parents and their children is very important.[191] Unfortunately, such contact can be difficult to maintain for several reasons.

First and foremost, many children want to see their imprisoned parents far more often than is typically possible in today's prison systems. Opportunities to visit parents imprisoned on remand are typically very limited, even though the visiting frequency – in the case of Denmark – in some of the prisons exceeds the minimum requirements stipulated in Danish law. In addition, children whose parents are in remand prison or serving a sentence in a closed prison typically cannot communicate with their imprisoned parent in a "normal" way, via frequent personal meetings, telephone calls, text messages or the Internet.[192] For many children, the result is that they do not have well-functioning communication with their imprisoned parents for weeks, months or even many years at a time. In some prison systems, open prisons allow much more "normal" ways of contact: access to outdoor areas during visits, furlough and home visits, and liberal rules regarding phone access.

It is also problematic that the visiting facilities in many prisons are not at all suitable for children's visits. How relatives and children are welcomed in a prison or remand prison depends very much on the staff culture in the institution concerned, and even who is working in the visiting unit on a given day. Children and parents describe how nice it is when staff are friendly and how unpleasant it is when the opposite is the case. Likewise, the visiting situation can be difficult to handle for both the prisoner and the relatives who accompany the child. This of course affects the child's experience. Finally, the transport to the remand prison or prison is sometimes a financial and time-consuming challenge. Later chapters (especially Chapter 10) elaborate on several of these factors.

The penal system upside down – social and administrative exclusion

A possible reason why prisoners' children have not been the objects of political and legal interest for many years is that some of the most basic conceptions of justice and guilt are turned upside down when the talk falls on prisoners' children. For example, this can be a problem in relation to much of the political rhetoric about longer and tougher sentences, which currently characterises the debate in many countries. Within the context of "penal populism", politicians often refer to public opinion and sentiments on justice as an argument for longer sentences as well as harsher and stricter policies towards offenders (see Chapter 16). But this "tough-on-crime" language can lose legitimacy if the perspective of prisoners' children is adopted.

Despite insufficient or opposing documentation, it is often taken for granted that the public wants revenge rather than more lenient sentences and prison practices.[193] This is also the case if we look at Danish prison law – the Danish Sentence Enforcement Act – in which consideration of public sentiments on justice figure only as purely punitive considerations. In other words, when the law requires that public sentiments on justice be taken into account – for example, when the prison service has to approve or reject a release on parole – referring to public sentiments will always weigh against the prisoner and fulfil the role as society's revenge.[194] Strictly speaking, this is absurd, since one can just as well refer to the public sense of justice as an argument for more lenient sentencing and sentence enforcement.[195] But such thoughts have apparently not been on the minds of the legislators. This is just one concrete illustration that a reference to the public sense of justice is often – both politically and legally – the same as arguing for more or tougher punishment.

The point is that this often place prisoners' children – and their sense of justice – in a difficult situation. Put another way, if mum or dad ends up in prison, penal populism and popular political catch phrases such as "zero tolerance" and "tough on crime" will often make poor sense for the children concerned. For many prisoners' children, public and political debate on crime and the current international wave of penal populism can appear decidedly hostile. This arguably produces a risk of reinforcing the "them" and "us" tendency, which can thrive in a situation of parental imprisonment and possible stigmatisation. This can have very concrete results in terms of how prisoners' children view society and society's representatives. A son's recollection of a prison visit with his father illustrates this point. "I remember clearly when the officer said: 'Visiting time is over.' I regarded him as a stupid pig who just enjoyed bothering us."[196] Similarly, a 10-year-old girl's traumatic recollection of her father's arrest meant she "was scared for a long time" every time she saw a police car.[197]

It is not surprising that such impressions come about in these situations, but from a societal point of view, it is essential to control and limit them. Otherwise, we risk the many children of imprisoned parents developing a severely negative impression of the state, society and the public service system. One can argue that the increased risk of antisocial and delinquent behaviour among this group of children is partly an expression of such alienation. To put it differently, prisoners' children experience the penal system not only from beneath – as the weaker part – but also as a kind of upside-down world in which society's official representatives become enemies instead of sources of support and no help can be obtained where one would normally expect help to be found.

In such a context, the police can be experienced as a direct threat against the family and hence the child's well-being. The prison officer who fulfils an important security function in society can take on the role as a "stupid pig" who torments the parent and the child. Municipal social workers can be perceived, first and foremost, in the light of their competence to monitor families and forcibly remove children. The French psychologist Alain Bouregba argues that when a parent is imprisoned, a child's sense of community can be destroyed and the loss replaced by withdrawal, narcissistic tendencies and isolation – which can again result in antipathy towards society.[198]

If this is the case, it is important that representatives of state and society step into the arena on the children's side as well. Otherwise, prisoners' children are likely to develop animosity and lack of loyalty towards society. A former spokesperson for the prisoners in Jyderup State Prison – an open Danish prison – outlined the same problem in the following statement: "It is, in my opinion, in society's short-term and long-term interest to...ensure that children of prisoners do not become defiant towards society, which can be the result when children experience that contact to their parents is hindered and that the contact which does take place, occurs under conditions that do not promote a positive dialogue between child and parent."[199]

What we are dealing with here is a possible process towards social and even administrative exclusion. The social exclusion that prisoners' families, including the children, can experience has to do with several of the already described problems – for example, the taboo and the stigmatisation of imprisonment and the financial problems that families can experience. The term *administrative exclusion* refers to how groups in society can become overlooked by bureaucracies and public policies. Criminologist Murray explains: "Unlike the plight of prisoners themselves, prisoners' children barely appear in official reports, national statistics, Home Office research agendas, or media coverage.... Despite continuing calls from lobby groups, there is still no official monitoring of the number of children who experience parental imprisonment each year in England and Wales.... Hence, prisoners' children are also 'administratively excluded', and have been referred to as 'forgotten victims'...and the 'invisible population'".[200]

6
Children of Imprisoned Parents and Their Human Rights

Traditionally, discussions, research and court judgements within the field of prisons and human rights have almost exclusively been a matter of balancing the state's legitimate use of power and security concerns against the individual prisoners' rights. The question of whether, how and to what degree the use of imprisonment has also affected the rights of people living outside of prison has for many years been left out of consideration. This has certainly been the case with prisoners' children – a group of people whose rights are clearly affected through the use of imprisonment.

Part of the explanation for this is that despite the long history of the prison, it took many years for even prisoners' rights to become an area of serious legal and penal concern. From a historical perspective, prisoners' rights are in fact a relatively new phenomenon. Eighteenth-century Enlightenment brought with it a critique of the corporal system of punishment – including torture, public executions and the death sentence – a process that eventually paved the way for an expanding role for imprisonment. Sparked by the Enlightenment spirit and the accompanying legal reforms, new types of prisons were (as previously explained) constructed in Europe and the United States from the late 18th century and during the 19th century. This did not mean that prisoners were given actual legal rights, however. On the contrary, their well-being was often left at the discretion of prison staff and especially the prison management who – with the help of the isolation regimes of the modern penitentiary – actually gained much tighter control of prisoners than had previously been the case.

The American history of prisoner rights provides an illustrative example. Here, the so-called hands-off doctrine dominated in the courts of law from the late 19th century all the way up to the 1970s. American judges essentially refrained from interfering in prison matters.[1] A judgement from Virginia in 1871 ruled that a sentenced and imprisoned criminal was simply a "slave of the state", and his estate was to be administered like that of a dead man.[2] A prisoner, in other words, had no rights. The hands-off doctrine was enforced for almost a century. In the 1960s and 1970s, a reform process began and prisoners' rights were gradually secured in a number of rulings. This was an international trend, and in many countries it was recognised that ordinary citizens' rights were not automatically suspended when a person passed the prison gate and became a prisoner.[3] As stated by the US Supreme Court in 1974, there "is no iron curtain drawn between the Constitution and the prisons of this country".[4]

Parallel to this development, the human rights conventions, rules and guidelines were created and went into force after World War II and slowly began to influence prison standards. Thus, a principle gradually developed according to which a prisoner upheld his or her basic rights except for those rights that were taken away by necessary implication. This principle was spelled out in a 1969 Canadian judgement according to which "an inmate of an institution continues to enjoy all the civil rights of a person save those that are taken away or interfered with by having been lawfully sentenced to imprisonment".[5]

When looking at the relevant human rights conventions, rules and recommendations, it is clear that this principle was based on the philosophy that all human beings – including the imprisoned – must be treated with respect for their human dignity. Particularly important was the adoption of the International Covenant on Civil and Political Rights (ICCPR) by the United Nations (UN) in 1966 (came into force in 1976) as well as the UN's Convention against Torture and Other Cruel, Inhuman or Degrading Treatment or Punishment from 1984 (came into force in 1987). As explained in article 10 of the ICCPR: "All persons deprived of their liberty shall be treated with humanity and with respect for the inherent dignity of the human person" (10.1). This principle, the very basic starting point for all discussions on prisons and human rights, is related to an understanding of prisons according to which the deprivation of liberty is punishment enough in itself. As famously argued by Alexander Paterson in the 1920s, "men come to prison *as* a punishment, nor *for* punishment".[6]

In 1955, the UN's prison rules (the "Standard Minimum Rules for the Treatment of Prisoners") were also adopted. The document is not legally binding but nonetheless gathered and internationalised a number of fundamental standards on how prisoners should be treated. Numerous other soft-law recommendations have since been produced by the UN as well as by regional human rights mechanisms such as the European Council.

Despite the fact that the human rights principles in the Universal Declaration of Human Rights (adopted in 1948) and the UN's prison rules have strong historical roots in the international prison conferences dating back to the 19th century, there was (and is) still a long way to go to an actual realisation of these principles. At the European level, a binding convention was adopted in 1953 in the form of the European Convention on Human Rights and Fundamental Freedoms (ECHR), which even had an affiliated human rights court where states could be accused and found to have breached individuals' human rights. But in the initial 30 years of the court's existence, only 72 judgements were passed. Approximately 15 of them concerned prisons.[7] In Golder v. United Kingdom, the European Court of Human Rights (ECtHR) nevertheless took one of the first steps in a more progressive direction by establishing that prisoners have the same rights as other citizens except those taken away as a necessary consequence of imprisonment.[8]

Today, the ECtHR has handed out thousands of judgements and helped create a large number of prison standards through numerous verdicts, but these are almost exclusively based on prisoners' rights. Seen from a rights perspective, it is not enough to protect and uphold only prisoners' rights. As long as prisons exist there will also be a large group of people outside of prison whose rights can be challenged and violated due to the imprisonment of others. Prisoners' relatives and perhaps especially prisoners' children fall within this category. The rights of this group are not well developed within the field of prisons and human rights, but there is currently a very interesting development in progress. Reports and recommendations from NGOs, human rights institutions and conference workshop groups have for the last five years or so begun to include and sometimes focus on the rights of this particular group of children. For example, as described by a working group at a human rights conference in Strasbourg in February 2009, states should be "aware of the duty to protect and promote the child's interests when family members are imprisoned".[9] The Quaker United Nations office in Geneva has also done extensive and influential work in this area and has during the last decade produced a long list of reports and briefing papers that address the rights and needs of women in prison and prisoners' children (several of which are referred to in this study).[10]

In 2011, the previously mentioned European report, which analysed the situation of prisoners' children within a human rights framework, identified one overall recommendation:

> Incorporate the UN Convention on the Rights of the Child in relation to children of imprisoned parents into European standards, national laws, and practice so as to ensure that children of imprisoned parents are able to maintain contact with them; are consulted and receive timely information regarding what has happened to their parent; are free from discrimination on the grounds of the acts of their parent; have their views taken into account.[11]

Later the same year, the UN Committee on the Rights of the Child held a landmark event for prisoners' children by dedicating their yearly Day of General Discussion to children of incarcerated parents. The committee produced a detailed set of recommendations, urging, among other things, "that States parties ensure that the rights of children with a parent in prison are taken into account from the moment of the arrest of their parent(s) and by all actors involved in the process and at all its stages, including law enforcement, prison service professionals, and the judiciary".[12]

But before we can look in greater detail at how this can be done – that is, what taking the rights of these children into account means in practical terms – we have to take a step back and look at what basic rights children actually have and to what extent they are relevant and applicable, especially for children of imprisoned parents.

Children's rights

Even though children are not legally responsible or allowed to decide for themselves as adults are, they nevertheless have rights. This includes a special set of rights only for children set down in the UN's Convention of the Rights of the Child (CRC), which has gained broad international support. Since the CRC came into existence in 1989, it took just 10 months for 20 countries to ratify it, at which time it came into force. The development continued at a fast pace and in April 1993, no fewer than 134 countries had ratified the CRC. When states sign a convention they can have several motives, but it is nevertheless difficult not to take the rapid large-scale ratification as an expression of some sort of international support of children's rights. In comparison, it took 10 years for 35 countries to ratify the UN Convention on Civil and Political Rights.[13]

The starting point of the CRC is that the family "as the fundamental unit in society" should be protected, not least to ensure "children's growth and well-being". The convention furthermore "acknowledges that with a view to full and harmonious development of his or her personality, the child should grow up in a family environment, in an atmosphere of happiness, love and understanding". The aim of ensuring the child such upbringing is "that the child should be completely prepared to live his or her own life in society and be brought up in the light of the ideals that are expressed in The Charter of the United Nations and in particular, in an atmosphere of peace, dignity, tolerance, freedom, equality and solidarity".[14]

In order to put such a vision into practice, the convention ensures children's rights in a large number of areas that include civil, financial, social and cultural rights.[15] Children are ensured a fundamental right to food, shelter, health care and – naturally – life. Civil rights are also ratified, such as the right to have an identity and a name, and to be able to achieve citizenship. Children are also ensured a right to development, which includes the right to attend school. The child must also be protected against war, violence and abuse and is ensured a number of rights with regard to living a family life, which includes "as far as possible, the right to know and be cared for by his or her parents".[16] Finally, the child is ensured the right to co-determination, including freedom of speech. As we will see below, several of these rights can have direct relevance to prisoners' children.

Despite the rapid and large-scale support of the CRC, it can be difficult to ensure children's rights in practice, partly because children are not of age and partly because, in the nature of things, they are a weak pressure group. Their well-being is often left to the discretion of their parents, which makes a lot of sense in most cases, but not always. Why, when and how shall the state intervene in what is otherwise traditionally perceived as the parents' area of responsibility? Another question is whether the state always has the necessary tools and knowledge to ensure children's rights in a responsible manner. Sometimes it seems that the children are forgotten simply because it is automatically assumed that their parents take responsibility. Nevertheless, the CRC actually compels member states to undertake all appropriate legislative, administrative and other measures in order to implement the rights set out in the covenant.

Prisoners' children – their fundamental human rights

Looking at the field of prisons and human rights from a perspective of rights holders outside of prison is not common. Court judgements as well as research reports and monographs on prisons and human rights reflect this. The latter tend to deal systematically with prisoners' rights in most areas of prison life, but the question of the rights of others outside of prison seldom arises. When the rights of other parties do come into play, it's most commonly in connection with the prisoner's right to privacy and family life, where the rights of spouses and partners are sometimes taken into account. In a 2012 Danish monograph on prisons and human rights, my co-author and I therefore covered not only the rights of prisoners and prison staff but also dedicated a chapter to the rights of "third persons". This section analysed the rights of crime victims and thoroughly discussed interpreting the rights of children of imprisoned parents under Danish law and human rights law.[17]

Human rights conventions and soft law clearly express the rights to private life, family life and children's rights. All three areas can be of crucial importance to children and relatives of prisoners. The original Universal Declaration of Human Rights from 1948, which paved the way for the later legally binding UN Covenants, contained an article for the protection of family and private life: "No one shall be subjected to arbitrary interference with his privacy, family, home or correspondence, nor to attacks upon his honour and reputation. Everyone has the right to the protection of the law against such interference or attacks" (article 12).

The ICCPR elaborates on these principles and establishes that the "family is the natural and fundamental group unit of society and is entitled to protection by society and the State" (article 23.1). In the same covenant, it is furthermore made clear that children have their own independent rights: "Every child shall have…the right to such measures of protection as are required by his status as a minor, on the part of his family, society and the State" (article 24.1).

The child's rights have since been furthered primarily in the CRC, which went into effect in 1990. It states that participant states "shall take all appropriate measures to ensure that the child is protected against all forms of discrimination or punishment on the basis of the status, activities, expressed opinions, or beliefs of the child's parents, legal guardians, or family members" (article 2.2). The requirement in article 3 is equally fundamental: "In all actions concerning children, whether undertaken by public or private social welfare institutions, courts of law, administrative authorities or legislative bodies, the best interests of the child shall be a primary consideration" (article 3.1).

Family rights expert Stephanie Lagoutte conclude that three principles in the CRC are central for children of imprisoned parents: 1) the protection of the best interest of the child, 2) the right of the child to express his or her view and to be heard in matters affecting the child and 3) the principle of non-discrimination.[18]

Article 3.1 on the best interest of the child potentially demands a great deal of the relevant public authorities – specifically in relation to prisoners' children – and is arguably one of those paragraphs that the social, welfare, health and penal systems of most states can find difficult to support and comply fully with.[19] To give a brief concrete example that relates to prisoners' children: what are the consequences if a child suffers from serious behavioural and/or psychological problems that are exacerbated by lack of contact with the imprisoned parent or parents? Is the best interest of the child always a "primary consideration" when the authorities choose where to place a parent in prison, decide whether or not to grant the imprisoned parent leave, consider alternatives to imprisonment or permit more visiting time?

Article 9 of the CRC addresses situations in which children are separated from their parents. In such cases, the participant states shall "ensure that a child shall not be separated from his or her parents against their will, except when competent authorities subject to judicial review determine, in accordance with applicable law and procedures, that such separation is necessary for the best interests of the child. Such determination may be necessary in a particular case such as one involving abuse or neglect of the child by the parents, or one where the parents are living separately and a decision must be made as to the child's place of residence" (article 9.1).

Article 9 further emphasises – with obvious relevance for prisoners' children – that children have the right to regular and direct contact with parents from whom they are separated: "States Parties shall respect the right of the child who is separated from one or both parents to maintain personal relations and direct contact with both parents on a regular basis, except if it is contrary to the child's best interests" (article 9.3). The same article addresses the right to information about separation in the case of parental imprisonment: "Where such separation results from any action initiated by a participating state, such as the detention, imprisonment, exile, deportation or death (including death arising from any cause while the person is in the custody of the State) of one or both parents or of the child, that State Party shall, upon request, provide the parents, the child or, if appropriate, another member of the family with the essential information concerning the whereabouts of the absent member(s) of the family unless the provision of the information would be detrimental to the well-being of the child" (article 9.4).

Other CRC articles are also relevant to the challenges of parental imprisonment. For example, article 12 focuses on the child's right to be heard "in all matters affecting the child". It is important to remember that if children were "heard" in cases of parental imprisonment, the majority would likely want more frequent and longer visitations with their imprisoned parent.[20] There is no clear jurisprudence on how to define "matters affecting the child", but the Committee for the Rights of the Child supports a broad definition while also acknowledging that this cannot be interpreted as a boundless "general political mandate".[21]

The right to family life

The family is entitled to protection by society and the state according to the Universal Declaration of Human Rights, the ICCPR and the International Covenant on Social, Economic and Cultural Rights. In addition, an individual's private and family life is also protected by human rights conventions. Accordingly, interference in these rights must be both prescribed by law and necessary to protect a certain number of interests (national security, public safety, prevention of disorder or crime) as well as the rights of other persons.[22]

The European Convention on Human Rights is also of importance to prisoners' children, not least article 8, which ensures the right to private life and family life. According to article 8, everyone has the "right to respect for his private and family life, his home and his correspondence" (article 8.1). In the same article, it is further established that "there shall be no interference by a public authority with the exercise of this right except such as is in accordance with the law and is necessary in a democratic society in the interests of national security, public safety or the economic well-being of the country, for the prevention of disorder or crime, for the protection of health or morals, or for the protection of the rights and freedoms of others" (article 8.2).

The rights of prisoners' children in practice

But what does all this mean in practice? Is it, for example, acceptable if more than a month passes before children can visit their imprisoned parents? How much should be expected from the social authorities in terms of taking responsibility for and ensuring the child's best interests in the case of parental imprisonment? Do visits in bare and austere conditions live up to the relevant human rights conventions and the European Prison Rules, when viewed from a children's rights perspective?

Answers to these questions can be sought in official interpretations of the human rights covenants and instruments, but often without immediate success. For instance, in some cases the ECtHR has handled questions involving imprisoned parents and the right to family life, but up until quite recently "the best interests of the child" were rarely "even a consideration in the final decisions on these cases, as compared with other factors such as the interests of national security or the prevention of disorder and crime".[23] However, as previously indicated, a certain development has taken place within the area of prisoners' rights that can also be of importance to their children. Relevant cases from ECtHR will therefore be used and discussed below. But these judgements will only take us some of the way, since the ECtHR, arguably, has often held itself back from focusing on the child's best interests and rights in cases concerning imprisoned parents.

I now take a closer look at what it actually means – or perhaps rather *ought to mean* – in practical terms that prisoners' children have rights. The following specific issues and situations are those where children of imprisoned parents are particularly vulnerable and where the rights of these children are clearly at stake:

1. The arrest of parents
   a. How are the children treated and how do they experience the arrest situation?
   b. Are the children informed about the arrest and the possible separation that subsequent imprisonment will entail?
   c. Are the social authorities notified with a view to assessing the children's situation?
2. Sentencing a parent – meting out the sentence and choosing alternatives to imprisonment
3. During imprisonment
   a. How are the remaining family members and children assured in a financial respect?
   b. How is direct and regular contact maintained between the imprisoned parent and his or her child/children?
   c. Choice of prison and the question of stationing
   d. Living with mum (or dad) in prison – what is in the best interest of the child?

The arrest of parents and the rights of the child

Witnessing or otherwise experiencing the arrest of a parent can have lasting effects (see Chapter 7). Josephine clearly remembers when a large group of police officers stormed into the family's apartment in Denmark. Her father was imprisoned and sentenced to four years. "I didn't tell anyone at school straight away, but I began crying all the time. During classes. In the school yard."[24] Anthony, who lived in the United States with his mother and her boyfriend (who sold drugs) also remembers the day the police came: "Anthony was five years old. The police broke down the door, then smashed through the floorboards looking for drugs. Anthony remembers a lot of things shattered or crushed after that, things that belonged to his grandfather. He remembers an officer putting him in the back of a car. He was frightened, and didn't know where he was being taken."[25]

Chapter 7 discusses the problems that children experience during a parent's arrest from the perspectives of the children, police and involved social workers. This chapter focuses on the relevant legal human rights issues in connection with the arrest of parents.

The arrest situation

The arrest of a parent can become an unpleasant and traumatic experience for children, all depending on how the implicated parties, especially the arrested parent and the police, handle the situation. In connection with the question of whether the children suffer psychological harm from the arrest itself, the human rights regulations are only applicable in a very overall and general respect. It follows from the CRC that "the child must be protected against all forms of discriminatory treatment or punishment due to the child's parents', guardian's or family members' position, occupation, expressed views or faith" (article 2.2). Article 16 can perhaps be applied more directly to the arrest situation, since it states that no "child may be exposed to random or illegal interference in his or her private and family life, his or her home or his or her exchange of letters, or illegal assault on his or her honour or his or her reputation" (article 16.1).

The Committee on the Rights of the Child accordingly "calls upon States parties to identify best practices for arrest procedures that are compliant with human rights and the rights of the child. These should serve as the basis for establishing and implementing a protocol for law enforcement in situations where the arrest of a parent(s) occurs in the presence of their child, and for suitably informing and supporting children not present at the arrest."[26]

The European Commission explained in 1992 how a forceful arrest of a parent can amount to interference with the child's right to respect for private and family life. The Commission found that "the use of force against a mother in the presence of her minor child amounts to a negative experience with considerable repercussions on the child's state of mind. The Commission, having regard to the second applicant's uncontested statement that she watched major parts of her mother's forcible arrest and noting that she considerably suffered from what she had seen, finds that there was also an interference with the second applicant's right to respect for private life."[27] The European Commission determined that the use of force against the mother amounted to a violation of article 3, and the display of violence in front of the child amounted to a violation of article 8. However, the ECHR later found that the facts in the case were not properly established and therefore could not conclude that there was a violation of articles 3 and 8.[28]

A very recent ECtHR ruling from October 2013 shed new light on some of these questions. In *Gutsanovi* v. *Bulgaria*, one of the issues at stake was how the arrest of a parent had affected his two daughters aged 5 and 7 at the time. The exact facts of the case were disputed, but the father was arrested by several policemen, including special agents, in his house early in the morning. According to the court, both his wife and two daughters witnessed armed police wearing balaclava make the actual arrest near the entrance to the bedroom. The court found that the girls were psychologically vulnerable, considering their young age, and accepted a later psychiatric evaluation, which found that the girls had been very strongly affected by the experience. The court also noted that the arrest had been planned without considering the presence of the wife and children. The court ruled, among other things, that the arrest had caused fear and anxiety in the girls and found that they had been subjected to degrading treatment in a breach of article 3 of the ECHR.[29] This is a very interesting ruling indeed, one which clearly establishes that children's rights and well-being matter when a parent is arrested, and that the police and the state can be held accountable for how such arrests are conducted. Although the present case did not involve shootings, beatings or physical violence as such, the way the police were armed and dressed, as well as the fact that the arrest took place in the house and was witnessed by the family, were enough for the court to find that the children had been subjected to degrading treatment.

If we look at the Danish law covering arrests, for example, we find that chapter 69 of the Danish Administration of Justice Act (§ 755 ff.) contains the rules for arrest, but that these are not concerned specifically with whether or not children are present at the arrest. Paragraph 758 establishes, however, that the arrest "must be conducted as gently as circumstances allow", which is also in the interests of children present.[30] The principle of a gentle approach and the principle of proportionality appear to be directed towards the treatment of the detainee, however, not towards children who are present at the arrest. This is a typical case of how the relevant laws are concerned with balancing the state's legitimate use of power against the rights of the particular individuals who the states use of force is directed against, while leaving out reference to other parties like prisoners' children. In that sense, Danish law offers no direct protection of children who witness the arrest of a parent.

The 2011 European study on children of imprisoned parents produced a number of recommendations specifically with regard to the situation of parental arrest. These recommendations included the following:

1. Guidelines should be drawn up regarding how police officers should handle situations where parents are arrested and their children are present.
2. Protocols should be developed for police officers in relation to arresting parents and dealing with children who may be present at the time of the arrest.
3. The arresting officer should be under obligation to identify whether there are children affected by arrest, and a system should be in place to ensure that children are taken care of properly.
4. Procedures should be in place if children are brought to a police station in connection with the arrest of a parent, consistent with children's rights.
5. Procedures should be in place to ensure that the opportunity is given immediately after the arrest for the primary carer to inform their child about what has happened.
6. Children's officers should be established within the police.[31]

Some of these recommendations aim at dealing with the two remaining legal human rights issues involving the arrest of parents, namely, whether or not children are informed about the arrest and social authorities are notified with a view to assessing the child's situation.

Are the children informed about the arrest?

If the children are not present during the arrest of their parent, the question arises whether or not they are informed of the arrest and the later imprisonment (if that takes place). The CRC makes it quite clear that if the child is separated from a parent as "a result of an action initiated by a participant state, such as detention, imprisonment, expulsion, deportation or death (including death by any reason while the person is in the custody of the state) of the one or both parents or of the child, the participant state must, upon request, give the parents, the child and if necessary another member of the family, the essential information of where the absent member or members of the family are located unless giving the information would be damaging to the child's welfare" (article 9.4).

The ECtHR has not processed cases that focus specifically on a detainee's possible contact with his or her child. But in *Sari and Colak* v. *Turkey*, the court made it clear that if a detainee is denied contact to his or her family, this may violate ECHR article 8, which discusses the right to respect of his or her family life. In the case concerned, Sari and Colak had been detained for eight days without any contact with their families. The court found a violation of article 8, as in the given case an effective safeguard had not existed, which gave the detainees the possibility of contacting their families.[32] But the ECtHR was concerned with the rights of the prisoner and not his family.

It is not uncommon in different jurisdictions for involved families to lack information from the police.[33] According to the Danish Administration of Justice Act, a detainee should normally have access to inform the family, employer, lawyer or others personally – or alternatively, through a police officer.[34] The Council of Europe Anti-torture Committee (CPT), however, found cause to criticise Denmark in this area in 2002. During its visit to Denmark, CPT became aware that a number of prisoners had not been allowed to inform their families of their imprisonment, apparently because, in several cases, this had been postponed in order to avoid collusion and protect the police's investigation. This can be done according to Danish law, but the correct procedure had not always been followed The CPT recommended changes to Danish law:

> The CPT recommends that legal provisions be adopted to ensure that all persons detained by the police have a formally recognised right to inform a relative or another third party of their choice of their situation, as from the outset of their detention. Any possibility exceptionally to delay the exercise of this right should be clearly circumscribed in law, made subject to appropriate safeguards (e.g. any delay to be recorded in writing with the reasons therefore, and to require the approval of a senior police officer unconnected with the case at hand or a prosecutor) and strictly limited in time.[35]

The CPT returned to this issue in connection with the committee's next visit to Denmark, which took place in February 2008. In the subsequent report, published in September 2008, the CPT referred the Ministry of Justice's circular dated 12 June 2001 to the police and the prosecuting authority.[36] This circular establishes the rules regarding contact with relatives in connection with an arrest. But these rules were apparently not being followed: "Despite the fact that the circular has been in operation for six and a half years, the findings from the 2008 visit suggest that its instructions are still not being applied systematically by the police and, as a result, the safeguards advocated by the CPT are not wholly effective in practice."[37]

According to the CPT, the Ministry of Justice promised to review the circular, and on this basis, the torture committee recommended that the opportunity should be used to create "a firmer legal basis to the provisions relating to the above-mentioned fundamental safeguards, by integrating them into relevant laws".[38] Specifically, in relation to the question of whether the detainee was allowed to inform relatives of their detention, the CPT noted again that the prisoners they had spoken with had not been allowed to do so. On this basis, the CPT repeated its recommendation from 2002 "that legal provisions be adopted to ensure that all persons detained by the police have a formally recognized right to inform a relative, or another third party of their choice, of their situation, as from the very outset of their detention. Any possibility exceptionally to delay the exercise of this right should be clearly circumscribed in law and made subject to appropriate safeguards (i.e. any delay to be recorded in writing with the reasons therefore, and to require the approval of a senior police officer unconnected with the case at hand or a prosecutor)."[39]

As already described, it is far from certain that the children are informed of their parent's arrest and imprisonment – even though the detained parent or another family member is informed – since many choose not to tell their children the truth. This cannot be considered a violation of the child's rights as the parent/caretaker has the parental authority. Whether or not this is appropriate is another question. Regardless, the remaining parent/caretaker must be informed of the imprisonment as quickly as possible; otherwise, the child cannot get this information at all. The Committee for the Rights of the Child agrees and emphasises in their recommendations "that children have the right to information regardless of whether the child was present at the time of the arrest, and that State Parties have the duty to ensure that a request for information or the sharing of information has no adverse consequences for the person(s) concerned while taking into account the best interests of the child". This means that state parties should "provide the parent or, if appropriate, other members of the family with essential information concerning the whereabouts of the incarcerated parent...as well as details about available support for the children".[40]

Should the social authorities be informed?

One very crucial question is whether the social authorities should be contacted when a parent is arrested and imprisoned. This is a relevant question both with regard to remand imprisonment and imprisonment following a sentence, and public employees often have the duty to inform the social services if they surmise that a child under 18 needs special support. At least this is the case in Denmark, Sweden and Norway. With regard to prisoners' children, it will most often be the police who, in connection with the arrest of a parent or person with parental custody, are in a position to assess if such reporting should take place. If the police choose not to inform social services, there is a great chance that no other public employee will either, simply because they do not come in contact with the children in question or because they are unaware that a child's parent is in prison. The assessment of whether the child needs special support is therefore largely in the hands of the police and a particular police officer's own discretion.

The assessment of whether or not children need such support should in principle be the responsibility of the social authorities (if the parents/caregivers fail) who have – or should have – the professional competence to determine if the child needs special support. As stated in the CRC, the child's best interest should be the first priority "in all provisions regarding the child" (article 3.1). Accordingly, the UN's Children's Committee has recommended that the child's best interest must be subject to an independent and careful assessment by competent professionals for all decisions on arrest and detention.[41]

It should therefore be carefully considered exactly what conditions oblige public employees, including the police, to inform the municipality when a parent or a person with parental custody is arrested or detained. One could argue that such notification is simply necessary in order for the state to live up to its responsibility to vulnerable children in this context – regardless of whether an assessment of a specific notification leads to the authorities choosing not to take action in the case concerned. But without a notification, the social authorities do not have the chance to be proactive and secure the child's best interest. This seems to be the line of thought in the Belfast Declaration, which urges public authorities to produce "a well developed care plan...involving the convicted parent, her/his child(ren) and significant others" in the event of parental imprisonment.[42]

On the other hand, it could be both highly controversial and very expensive to adopt policies that would require notification of social authorities whenever a parent is arrested and imprisoned – expensive because it would require significant resources for the social authorities to actually look into the situation of all these children, and controversial because such policies could potentially violate the rights to privacy and family life by requiring the state to get involved in such a large number of cases.

Sentencing parents and the question of the rights of the child

The principle that the child's best interest should be a primary consideration in "all actions concerning children" (article 3.1) has been interpreted by the Committee on the Rights of the Child in relation to the question of imprisonment and conviction of parents. On this basis, the committee has recommended the following:

> Where the defendant has child-caring responsibilities, the Committee recommends that the principle of the best interests of the child (art. 3) is carefully and independently considered by competent professionals and taken into account in all decisions related to detention, including pre-trial detention and sentencing, and decisions concerning the placement of the child.[43]

This recommendation was originally given to Thailand in 2006 but has recently been expanded and issued as a general recommendation to all states that have signed and ratified the covenant: "The Committee emphasises that in sentencing parent(s) and primary caregivers, non-custodial sentences should, wherever possible, be issued in lieu of custodial sentences, including in the pre-trial and trial phase. Alternatives to detention should be made available and applied on a case-by-case basis, with full consideration of the likely impacts of different sentences on the best interests of the affected child(ren)."[44]

The committee has thus made it clear that alternatives to imprisonment should be considered to ensure the best interest of the child. The African Charter on the Rights and Welfare of Children recommends that "a non-custodial sentence will always be first considered" when sentencing mothers and that alternatives "to institutional confinement" are established and promoted for mothers who have committed a crime.[45] One example of applying such principles in practice – at least to some degree – can be found in Italy, where the so-called Finocchiaro Law has "introduced special house arrest for mothers with children under the age of 10, for sentences of less than four years, provided that there is no identified risk of the offender committing further crimes and that they have served at least one-third of their sentence".[46] Similarly, in Argentina since 2009, "women with children aged under five can be imprisoned at home, enabling them to continue caring for their children outside a prison environment", and judges in Germany can impose a "housewife sentence" allowing certain women to "leave prison during the day to be mothers and return to prison in the evening".[47] Such arrangements are positive from a children's rights perspective, although they are obviously gender biased and should arguably include fathers – when adopted in the best interest of the child.

The Council of Europe's general assembly has also discussed this issue and has urged that the imprisonment of mothers with young children be avoided and alternative forms of sanctions developed. The Council has also recommended that "appropriate guidelines" are developed "for courts whereby they would only consider custodial sentences for pregnant women and nursing mothers when the offence was serious and violent and the woman represented a continuing danger".[48]

In Denmark, the Children's Council has similarly recommended that "the conditions for the upbringing of these children should be a significant factor in the choice of punishment. Here, it would be relevant to prioritise sentences which limit the separation between the child and the parent, for example, a form of punishment where the parent continues to sleep-over in the home."[49]

According to § 80 of the Danish penal code, the offender's situation must be considered when setting the sentence. This can include personal and social circumstances as well as family circumstances.[50] In Danish legislation, consideration of the child's best interests is not in the enumeration of extenuating circumstances in the event of sentencing in § 82 of the penal code – although the list is not exhaustive.[51] One example has been found of a judge considering the best interest of the child when ruling on the question of parental incarceration. The 1985 case concerned a suspended sentence of one year given for the sale of 25 kilograms of cannabis. Normally, imprisonment would have been used for such an offence, but the court focused on "the considerable adverse impacts which the serving of a sentence must be assumed to give rise to". This assessment was based on, among other things, a statement dated 4 December 1984 from the Danish Prison and Probation Service, which stated that the defendant was found suitable to receive a suspended sentence and that the consequences of imprisonment in regard to work, family and housing would be of such character that it would be immensely difficult to get the family on the right track again.[52]

In a study of practice in Northern Ireland, some examples have been found of judges considering "the impact of custodial sentencing on children...resulting in a reduced tariff for the parent".[53] Furthermore, the Northern Ireland Human Rights Commission "has recommended that women should only be detained in custody as 'a measure of last resort and only in serious cases'".[54]

There are more or less similar examples from around the world.[55] In Australia, the case of *Walsh* v. *Department of Social Security* provides an example. Both parents of three children faced prison sentences, and the judge decided upon a conditional release order, arguing that the case had "one unusual feature not present in any of the various cases to which counsel made reference during their submissions. That is, that the sentences, both of which were to be served forthwith, would result in three children, the youngest only just two years of age, being separated from both their parents during the period of their imprisonment."[56]

In South Africa, the Constitutional Court has made two important judgements related to prisoners' children. In 2007, the court established that "all South African courts [must] give specific consideration of the impact on the best interests of the child when sentencing a primary caregiver. If the possible imprisonment will be detrimental to the child, then the scales must tip in favour of a non-custodial sentence, unless the case [is] so serious that that would be entirely inappropriate."[57] In 2011, the court narrowed the scope of this provision, "limiting it to single primary caregivers only".[58]

Imprisonment: remand custody and serving a sentence

There can be significant difference between remand custody and imprisonment as a sentenced prisoner. Even though a person must be considered innocent until the opposite is proven, it is a paradox that the conditions of imprisonment for those in remand custody are sometimes worse than the conditions for the convicted. In the Scandinavian countries a sentenced prisoner often has better access to visits, telephone use, meaningful activities and perhaps rehabilitative programs. Yet in many respects, the fundamental problems are the same for persons in remand custody and imprisoned persons. In general, the problems discussed in the following are relevant to both remand custody and imprisonment.

Financial assurance of the remaining family and children

As already explained, the family's and thus the children's financial situation can change drastically when a parent is imprisoned. One income often disappears, and there can be new expenses, such as transport to and from the prison for visits. In some cases, parental imprisonment has minimal or no importance in this respect. This can be the case when there is no longer contact and financial connection between the involved parties, for example. In other situations, the impact on the family's finances can be quite extensive, especially when a main provider is imprisoned.

The Committee on the Rights of the Child is "aware that incarceration can remove eligibility for State financial and other support, and that this can have negative impacts on the children of those incarcerated", and it therefore recommends to state parties "that the removal of support should occur on an individual basis and that the best interests of the child(ren) should be a primary consideration when making such decisions".[59]

If we look at Danish legislation in this area, we will find that a prisoner has several different legal avenues for getting his family financial support.[60] For example, the rules regulating social security for those imprisoned stipulate the following: "If a prisoner has participated in the actual support of a child prior to the imprisonment and the support is taken over by a person who receives social security, the municipality can provide assistance to the prisoner in order to support the child if a need for this is deemed necessary. At the most, the assistance can comprise an amount corresponding to a standard contribution and it is given on the condition that the prison actually contributes to the support with an amount that at least matches the assistance provided."[61] The same rules also provide that "assistance can be provided to cover expenses in the event of visitation by children under 18 years of age, according to the rules in § 83 in the act on active social policy".[62]

Such rules seem to be a good way of ensuring that prisoner's children – and their families – can get financial help. But the question, of course, is whether and to what degree such rules are actually followed. This is both a question of whether or not contact is established at all between the social services and the families in need, and a question of whether the relevant social workers use the rules. Research suggests that this varies greatly from one municipality to another in Denmark.[63]

Contact between the child and the imprisoned parent

The CRC makes clear that participating states "must respect the right of a child who is separated from one or both parents, to maintain regular personal connection and direct contact with both parents except if this in conflict with the child's best interests" (article 9.3). This is potentially a far-reaching paragraph that can involve many issues, including telephone calls, letters, visits and even home leave, possible sentence interruption, probation and location of prison.

Based on this background, the UN Children's Committee has recommended that the child is supported and counselled so that the child can maintain contact with imprisoned parents as long as this is in the child's best interest.[64] In the committee's 2011 recommendations, it emphasised "that children have the right to regularly visit their parent(s), if this is in their best interests" and made it clear that measures should "be taken to ensure that the visit context is respectful to the child's dignity and right to privacy".[65] It is especially interesting to note how the committee thereby interprets the CRC and children's rights in a manner according to which the visit situation and its frequency have to live up to certain standards.

The committee develops this point further by recommending that state parties "ensure the right of children to regularly visit their incarcerated parent(s)" and that "wherever possible, State parties provide for such visits to occur in a child-friendly environment, including by allowing visits at times that do not negatively interfere with other elements of the child's life, such as schooling, and for durations conducive to building or maintaining strong relationships. Consideration should also be made to permitting visits to take place outside the detention facility, with a view to facilitating necessary emotional bonding between the child and the incarcerated parent(s) in a child-friendly environment."[66]

The 2011 EU report on prisoners' children makes a number of specific recommendations regarding prison visits and contact between parent and child. These include a general recommendation that minimum standards for visiting facilities are created, and that all staff working on visits are "to be trained in understanding the perspective and needs of children visiting their parent in prison"; that "clear, easy to grasp and age-appropriate information" is made available for children and those accompanying on the visits procedures; that an "age appropriate selection of toys & activities for girls and boys (incl teenagers) and the opportunity of being outside during visits" is provided in the visits area; and that every prison appoint "a designated Family/ children's officer".[67]

The international prison rules also set standards regarding visits and contact. The UN's prison rules elaborate on article 9 of the CRC when stating: "Prisoners shall be allowed under necessary supervision to communicate with their family and reputable friends at regular intervals, both by correspondence and by receiving visits".[68] The same principle is upheld and developed in the European Prison Rules from 2006.[69] They establish that prisoners "must have the right to communicate as frequently as possible by letter, telephone or other forms of communication with their families, other persons and with representatives of organisations outside of the prison and to receive visits from these persons" (rule 24.1). Moreover, prison authorities "must assist the inmates in maintaining sufficient contact to the outside world and give them the necessary financial support for this" (rule 24.5).

Of significance as well is the rule that "visiting arrangements must give inmates the possibility of maintaining and developing the relationship to their families in the most normal way possible".[70] Like the recommendations from the Committee on the Rights of the Child, the European Prison Rules aim to set standards for the *quality* of visits. In other words, the prison should not only facilitate contact between a child and an imprisoned parent but must also establish a context for visits that allows *development* of the relationship between the individual child and imprisoned parent.

The ECtHR has accepted that imprisonment entails a natural and legitimate limitation of the right to family life, but has simultaneously established that the prison authorities have a duty to assist prisoners, including those in remand custody, to maintain contact with their immediate family.[71] According to the court, certain control measures in relation to the inmates' contact to the outside world are in accordance with ECHR, but these must have a legal basis, be necessary and be predictable.[72]

In a number of cases, the court has decided if specific control measures constitute a violation of the inmate's right to family life. In *Baginski* v. *Poland*, the court found that an injunction on seeing family for a person in remand violated article 8, since there was no proportionality between the intervention and the desire to solve the case.[73] In *Messina* v. *Italy*, however, the court did not find such a violation. Messina, who was sentenced to 14 years' imprisonment, was placed in a special unit with a number of special restrictions due to his association with the mafia. The restrictions included no access to a telephone and a maximum of one, one-hour visit by family members per month. Only visits by children under 16 could take place without the glass wall between them.[74] In this case, the court chose to weigh Messina's status as a member of the mafia against his right to family life. The ECtHR did not take into consideration the *child*'s possible right to see his or her parent under acceptable circumstances. However, Messina had been given permission for extra visits from his wife and daughter, so it is perhaps doubtful whether such assessment would have made a difference.

The ECtHR has on several occasions accepted that states implement special regimes and control measures when prisoners are believed to pose a particular security risk.[75] In *Ciorap* v. *Moldova*, the court found, however, that a number of conditions and restrictions surrounding visits did violate article 8. In the case of Ciorap, all visits by the family took place with a glass wall between them and all physical contact between the inmate and the visitor was precluded.[76]

Other relevant article 8 issues, which have nothing to do with physical conditions for prison visits, have also been taken to the ECtHR. In the *Ostrovar* v. *Moldova* case, the court found that the legislation regarding a prisoner's contact with family was so unclear that it in itself constituted a violation of the right to family life.[77] The plaintiff in *Estrikh* v. *Latvia* was a father who had been denied prolonged visits by his partner. When the circular which entitled such rejection was never disclosed, the court found once again that this was a violation of the right to family life.[78]

In none of these cases did the court refer to the child's rights. But *Sabou et Pircalab* v. *Romania* did. The case concerned a journalist and father who was sentenced to six months' imprisonment for defamation. Initially, he was given a postponed sentence in consideration of his two children and a third that was on the way. After imprisonment, the journalist complained that he had been denied his parental rights while he was in prison. The Romanian state maintained that the injunction against exercising parental rights must automatically follow from imprisonment due to moral considerations. The ECtHR emphasised, however, that in such cases the best interest of the child must be considered and that the father's imprisonment had nothing to do with insufficient parenting skills. Based on this, the court found a violation of article 8.[79]

In summary, it is noteworthy how the court in Strasbourg in most of the above cases has refrained from considering the child's best interest. This is likely to be a product of the way in which cases regarding prisons and human rights have traditionally focused on prisoners and *their* rights. But there is reason to believe that change is on the way. The development in soft law – most notably the 2011 recommendations from the UN Committee on the Rights of Child – point in that direction, as does a recent judgement from the ECtHR. In *Horych* v. *Poland*, the applicant was detained in a "special high-security prison ward" for dangerous offenders under a regime of solitary confinement.[80] The applicant, who had a wife and three daughters, was allowed a one-hour visit from his family each month and from August 2004–January 2008 (almost three and a half years) he was granted permission to have 32 visits in all (out of which 11 were open visits, the rest closed).[81]

During that period, the applicant was normally visited by his wife and received only two visits from his oldest daughter and one from the two young daughters. He claimed this was due to the visiting conditions, which were not satisfactory "for visits by children or minor persons". According to the applicant, "a visitor, including a child, in order to reach the visiting area in the ward for dangerous detainees had to walk through the entire prison, past prison cells situated on both sides of the corridor. This exposed his daughters to the gaze of prisoners and their reaction to the girls' presence constituted an exceptionally traumatic experience for them. During the meeting, they were separated by a window and bars from their father, which was very stressful for them and made it impossible for them to have any normal contact. For that reason, considering that the conditions in which he was allowed to see his family in prison caused too much distress and suffering for his daughters, the applicant had to give up receiving visits from his daughters."[82]

When making a decision, the ECtHR aimed at striking a fair balance "between the requirements of the applicant's detention under the 'dangerous detainee' regime and his right to respect for his family life".[83] But interestingly, the court explicitly included the applicant's children and their situation in its argument:

> The Court would note that, by the nature of things, visits from children or, more generally, minors in prison require special arrangements and may be subjected to specific conditions depending on their age, possible effects on their emotional state or well-being and on the personal circumstances of the person visited. However, positive obligations of the State under Article 8, in particular an obligation to enable and assist a detainee in maintaining contact with his close family...includes a duty to secure the appropriate, as stress-free for visitors as possible, conditions for receiving visits from his

children, regard being had to the practical consequences of imprisonment. That duty is not discharged properly in situations where, as in the present case, the visits from children are organised in a manner exposing them to the view of prison cells and inmates and, as a result, to an inevitably traumatic, exceptionally stressful experience. The Court agrees that, as the applicant said, the exposure to prison life can be shocking even for an adult and, indeed, it must have caused inordinate distress and emotional suffering for his daughters.... It further notes that, owing to the authorities' failure to make adequate visiting arrangements, the applicant, having seen the deeply adverse effects on his daughters, had to desist from seeing them in prison.[84]

The ECtHR ruled "that the restrictions imposed by the authorities on the applicant's visiting rights, together with their continued and prolonged failure to ensure proper conditions for visits from his daughters, did not strike a fair balance between the requirements of the 'dangerous detainee' regime on the one hand, and the applicant's Convention right to respect for his family life on the other. Accordingly, there has been a violation of Article 8 of the Convention."[85]

The ECtHR has thus begun to set concrete standards with regard to children's contact with their imprisoned parents. Another recent case also indicates that the court in Strasbourg is increasingly aware of how rights holders outside of prison can be affected by the use of imprisonment. In the case of *Salahhov and Islyamova* v. *Ukraine*, the court ruled that a prisoner's mother had been "a victim of inhuman treatment" because she had watched her son suffer and later die in prison.[86] The ECtHR stated that "Article 3 enjoins the authorities to react to the plight of the victim's relatives in an appropriate and humane way" and thereby included the prisoner's relatives in their assessment.[87] The court noted especially the importance of "the parent-child bond" between the mother and her imprisoned son.[88]

But visits are not the only way of maintaining and developing contact, only the most typical. Home leave, as well as phone calls and letters are other ways to stay connected. Such contact is possible in many jurisdictions. In Denmark, some prisoners in open prisons will also have a limited access to the Internet and can correspond with their children by email, and in some cases Facebook, once or a couple of times each week.[89] Such a practice reflects some of the available recommendations in the area.[90]

If we look at the Danish case as an example and focus on the more typical ways of contact – visits, phone calls, etc. – then a remand prisoner in Denmark is normally entitled to a half-hour visit each week and is often granted one hour, while a sentenced prisoner is normally entitled to a weekly one-hour visit and is normally granted more than that.[91] The various visiting conditions, practices and other issues in that regard are discussed in Chapters 10 and 11.

When it comes to home leave we are dealing with a potentially useful method to alleviate the problems that some prisoners' children are experiencing. It has been recommended that "opportunities for Home Leave should be granted with regard to the needs of children of imprisoned parents".[92] There are possibilities under Danish law to do just that. For example, home leave can be granted when the prisoner's child is seriously ill.[93] Moreover, the child's first school day, christening, confirmation and similar events form the basis for granting home leave for important family events.[94] In connection with Christmas and/or New Year, it is furthermore possible to obtain an extended home leave (§ 38, section 6).[95]

Telephone contact and letters can also be important communication channels. Both remand and sentenced prisoners are allowed to write letters in Denmark, but the police will often impose restrictions and control on a remand prisoners' correspondence. Thus, the police can "examine the letters before receipt or forwarding" (§ 772, section 1 of the Administration of Justice Act). Letters can also be withheld in consideration of the investigation or in consideration of "order and security in the remand prison". The question of maintaining the withholding must be submitted to the court for ruling (§ 772, section 1). A remand prisoner in Denmark will normally not be allowed to use the phone at all.[96]

The authorities in Denmark are in other words well equipped for limiting and controlling a remand prisoner's contact with the outside world. The ECtHR is well aware of the fact that authorities can overstep their authority in this respect, and in *Golder* v. *United Kingdom*, the United Kingdom was found to have stopped a prisoner's correspondence wrongfully.[97] This, however, concerned a violation of article 6 and thus the right to a fair trial. It is doubtful how much a remand prisoner's child would have been considered in such a context.

Finally, the massive increase in mobile phone use and Internet communication has created an entirely new situation with regard to children's communication with their parents as well as prisoners' rights in general. Accordingly, the CRC has made it clear that "alternative means of communication" should also be considered as a supplement to visits to "further regular contact between the child and the incarcerated parent(s) through telephone, video-conference and other means of communication".[98]

The rights of children of imprisoned parents cannot be interpreted as minimum standards, requiring that the state allows, for example, Skype or email contact between prisoners and their children. However, the rights of these children to maintain contact with their parents and the way that these rights have been applied to children of imprisoned parents in human rights soft law certainly supports the idea that "states should consider the use of ICTs such as e-mail or video-conference to strengthen the contact between prisoners and their children, in cases where this is in the best interest of the child".[99]

If we look broadly at the question of how a prisoner's communication with the outside world is regulated in Danish law, we must conclude that the best interest of the child is typically not mentioned in the otherwise relevant legal paragraphs and rules regarding visits in prison, telephone contact and letter writing. In Norway, on the other hand, the authorities have taken a very important step in that regard, and the rights of the child have been written directly into the national prison law. Norwegian prison law stipulates that "children's right to contact with their parents shall receive special attention" during the implementation of the imprisonment.[100]

Choice of prison and stationing

According to the European Prison Rules, prisoners must, as far as possible, be placed in a prison close to their homes or near the place where their reintegration into society is supposed to take place (rule 17.1). Furthermore, the prison rules recommend that rulings on placement should generally take the situation of prisoners' children into account.[101] Equally, the Committee for the Rights of the Child recommends that state parties, wherever possible, seek "to situate the incarcerated parent at a facility close to his/her child to facilitate the child's right to visit and contact the parent. Where the incarceration location results in significant distance and/or related travel and subsistence costs, States parties are urged to facilitate and/or subsidise travel and other costs related to the visit."[102]

These human rights guidelines are to a certain extent reflected in the Danish prison law, according to which a prisoner must, as far as practically possible, be placed in the vicinity of his or her residence (§ 23, section 1) and in that connection "consideration must be taken of the prisoner's...family circumstances" (§ 23, section 1). Furthermore, prison sentences of up to three months can, with certain exceptions, be served at the residence under intensive monitoring and control – the so-called electronic tag – provided a number of detailed conditions are fulfilled.[103] If that is not an option, a prisoner in Denmark will normally be placed in an open prison, a closed prison or a remand prison. In practice, an open prison would almost always be preferable, especially from a child's point of view, as the possibilities to maintain contact with his or her imprisoned parent is far better under the conditions that exist here. In a remand prison and in a closed prison, the conditions are typically much more restrictive.

With mum in prison – children who live with their imprisoned parents

A very special situation will arise for those children who end up living in a prison as a result of parental imprisonment. Different countries and prison systems have different rules in this area, but typically a limited number of small children will be allowed to live with their mothers for a few years. It is not known how many children live with their parents in prisons around the world because it is often not registered.[104] In Denmark, for example, there will on an ordinary day be up to five children under the age of 3 living with an imprisoned parent in the Danish prison system.[105] This is out of a prison population of between 4,000 and 4,500 prisoners. At the other end of the spectrum, it has been reported that 2,135 children lived with 1,774 mothers in prison in India in 2008.[106] In Norway, children are never allowed to live with an imprisoned parent. It can also happen that an imprisoned mother is or becomes pregnant and gives birth to a child. This raises the question of whether or not the mother and the child should be allowed to stay together, since according to research, "breaking the maternal-child bond through the practice of at-birth separation can have serious detrimental consequences on the mother as well as on the child".[107]

Children seldom live with their fathers in prison. There is clearly a greater tendency towards women being the single or main provider for their child, and gender roles and cultures often point in that direction. As a result, male prisons simply do not often have facilities for children.[108] An international report mentions that Australia and Denmark are among the countries where children can live with their fathers who are serving a sentence.[109] Similarly, Finland allows both mothers and fathers to bring their children into prison to live with them.[110] But even in countries where children *can* live with their imprisoned fathers, this occurs much less frequently compared to the number of situations where children live with their imprisoned mothers.[111] This applies in Denmark as well, although one will more often find a father living with his child in a halfway house (see Chapter 15).[112]

The human rights guidelines in this area attempt to strike a balance between two seemingly obvious – but opposing – truths: (1) prisons are not suitable places for children to live and (2) separating a young child from its primary caregiver, for example a mother and her infant child, is generally a very bad idea. This is why diversion from imprisonment and the use of other sanctions is often a better solution. This is also the general approach adopted by the European Council, which recommends that the overwhelming majority of female offenders with young children be managed in the community outside of prisons.[113] The European Council thus recognises the "adverse effects of imprisonment of mothers on babies" and that "the development of young babies is retarded by restricted access to varied stimuli in closed prisons", but on the other hand acknowledges that "early maternal separation causes long-term difficulties, including impairment of attachments to others, emotional maladjustment and personality disorders".[114]

When detention of both mothers and babies cannot be avoided, the CPT emphasises that the "governing principle in all cases must be the welfare of the child...Where babies and young children are held in custodial settings, their treatment should be supervised by specialists in social work and child development. The goal should be to produce a child-centred environment, free from the visible trappings of incarceration, such as uniforms and jangling keys."[115]

In a later resolution, the European Council elaborated further on the needs of children living with a mother in prison and recommended that "prison regimes and facilities must be 'flexible enough to meet the requirements of pregnant women, breast-feeding mothers and prisoners whose children are with them'."[116] According to the European Council, children staying in prisons with their mothers should be given access to crèches outside the prison whereby "the detrimental social effects of imprisonment on their personal development" would be alleviated.[117]

The European Prison Rules address the situation with regard to both fathers and mothers and state that "infants may stay in prison with a parent only when it is in the best interest of the infants concerned. They shall not be treated as prisoners" (rule 36.1). Furthermore, "where such infants are allowed to stay in prison with a parent special provision shall be made for a nursery, staffed by qualified persons, where the infants shall be placed when the parent is involved in activities where the infant cannot be present" (rule 36.2) and "special accommodation shall be set aside to protect the welfare of such infants" (rule 36.3).[118] Rule 36 does not set any upper limit for the age of children living with a parent in prison, and the national rules – where such a practice is allowed – vary.

The situation of pregnant female prisoners gives rise to additional issues because of their special situation and vulnerability. According to the British professor in prison studies and former prison governor Andrew Coyle, "pregnant women should only be held in prison in the most extreme circumstances" and if "this is necessary, they should be provided with the same level of health care as is provided in civil society".[119] The UN's prison rules stress that institutions for women prisoners must contain "special accommodation for all necessary pre-natal and post-natal care and treatment".[120] Furthermore, "where nursing infants are allowed to remain in the institution with their mothers, provision shall be made for a nursery staffed by qualified persons, where the infants shall be placed when they are not in the care of their mothers".[121] The UN prison rules can also be interpreted as proscribing that children living in prison with an imprisoned parent should also always be registered in the prison records.[122]

More recently the UN "Bangkok rules" for women prisoners have elaborated on some of these principles and state, for example, that "children living with their mothers in prison shall be provided with ongoing health-care services and their development shall be monitored by specialists, in collaboration with community health services" (rule 51.1). According to these rules "the environment provided for such children's upbringing shall be as close as possible to that of a child outside prison" (rule 51.2).[123]

Naturally, the birth itself represents a particularly sensitive situation. International guidelines recommend that births occur in ordinary hospitals and without the use of handcuffs or other "restraining devices".[124] This is also the practice in the majority of countries, that is, pregnant inmates give birth at hospitals or other "medical facilities" and return to the prison after the birth.[125] But unfortunately, this does not always take place under humane conditions. For example, in 1995, several female prisoners in Holloway Prison told the then head of the British prison inspection, David Ramsbotham, that they had been shackled while they gave birth to their children, and also during toilet visits, at a birth clinic.[126] According to the CPT, such use of shackles or handcuffs is "completely unacceptable, and could certainly be qualified as inhuman and degrading treatment".[127] According to the UN's torture committee, "shackling" of female prisoners in labour still takes place in the United States.[128]

When the birth is over, the question naturally arises of what should be done for the mother and the child. However, there is no consensus on what is appropriate for the newborn and infant children – neither among researchers, legislators or prison authorities – and the rules vary from country to country, although most allow small children to stay with imprisoned parents in at least some cases.[129] In 2002, in connection with the Kleuver case (see below), the ECtHR examined whether a common European standard could be identified with regard to detention centres offering facilities for a mother and a newborn baby to stay together. The court found it difficult to discern a common European standard in this area, and "according to the Court, detention centres offering facilities for mothers and newborn babies to stay together existed mostly in open institutions, but not in closed institutions".[130]

The jurisprudence of the ECtHR reveals that it came close to passing an interesting sentence in the case of *Togher* v. *United Kingdom*. This case concerned a mother, who during remand imprisonment was separated from her newborn daughter and precluded from staying with her child in Holloway Prison's "Mother and Baby Unit". The British government argued that the separation was justified because of the seriousness of the charge and in order to prevent an escape, which was also why the "Mother and Baby" unit was not considered suitable. According to Madeleine Togher, the separation violated her right to family life. The case was regarded as suitable for trial but was subsequently settled and therefore never tried.[131]

In *Kleuver* v. *Norway*, the ECtHR rejected the complaint of a mother who was not allowed to have her newborn daughter with her in prison. The Dutch woman was arrested and imprisoned in Norway for drug smuggling. ECtHR ruled in favour of Norway because the prison's conditions were not suitable for children and because the national authorities had placed the child in a good nearby children's home where the mother visited him often and where the staff ensured that he was given his mother's milk. The court found that the Norwegian authorities had done a great deal to maintain contact between mother and son and therefore the mother did not have a right to demand further special measures to ensure that her son could be in the closed prison with her.[132]

As explained by Stephanie Lagoutte, the argumentation used by the ECtHR in the Kleuver judgement is "quite striking" in the way "that it solely deals with the situation of the parent and her responsibility for the situation she has created. However, the son has no responsibility whatsoever for the fact that his mother was on remand at the time of his birth (and later convicted) – he did not 'know' about the situation before he was born. He is however the one who has to suffer from the separation from his mother."[133] In light of this, it is very positive to recall the ECtHR's somewhat different approach in the cases of *Horych* v. *Poland* and *Gutsanovi* v. *Bulgaria* (discussed earlier). In those cases, the court specifically addressed the situation, problems and needs of the children involved.

When contact is not in the child's best interest

Again, the child's best interest should be the starting point for all discussions regarding the relationship and contact between an imprisoned parent and his or her child. This is the perspective adopted here and by the CRC. Therefore, it goes without saying that if it is not in the child's best interest to maintain contact with an imprisoned parent, then the contact should not take place. There can be numerous reasons for such a situation, but the crucial thing is that the child's best interest is put into the foreground. It is essential that the imprisoned parent's interests are not indulged at the expense of the child's needs.

One of the few ECtHR cases in which the child's best interest is actually seen to be discussed in relation to imprisonment of a parent concerns a situation where contact was denied between a child and an imprisoned parent. The case of *M.C.* v. *Finland* involved a Pakistani man who had killed his wife, after which their daughter was placed in foster care. The Finnish authorities imposed injunction against contact between father and daughter until the daughter was old enough to decide for herself whether she wanted contact. Authorities rejected the father's application to take care of his daughter in prison with reference to the fact that it was not in the child's best interest. The father considered this discrimination due to his gender and ethnicity and complained to the ECtHR. The court ruled in favour of Finland and found that Finnish authorities had placed the daughter in care to her best interest. The father and daughter did not speak the same language and did not have much contact prior to the mother's death. Hence, in this case, the ECtHR decided in favour of what was best for the child.[134]

There are also examples within Danish legal practice of such consideration being taken in relation to a child and an imprisoned parent. In a case of an imprisoned father who wanted his son handed over for visitation against the mother's wish, a Danish court found that the boy's mental health would be exposed to serious danger and rejected the father's wish. This ruling was later upheld by the Danish High Court.[135] The child's best interest was a main consideration for both courts, and the result was that no contact was established between the child and the imprisoned parent.

Part III

Prisoners' Children: From Arrest to Release of Their Imprisoned Parents

7
The Arrest of Parents through the Eyes of Children, Police and Social Services

Peter Scharff Smith and Janne Jakobsen

When children tell their stories, it is easy to understand that the arrest of a parent can leave deep traces. One 18-year-old Danish girl, for example, describes the arrest of her father as the worst day in her life.[1] This chapter discusses some of the few available studies about children's reactions to parental arrests. The chapter is primarily based on Danish empirical data on how police handle the arrests of parents, and how the arrests can be experienced by and affect the arrested parents' children.

International research on the arrest of parents and the experiences of their children

A number of qualitative studies touch upon the personal experiences of children who have witnessed or been told about their parents' arrests, but there is very little research available that focuses specifically on the arrest situation. There is nevertheless general agreement in the literature that the arrest situation can pose a specific problem for the involved children and cause them harm. This conclusion is primarily (although not solely) based on interviews and qualitative studies.

According to a Dutch study, for example, a violent arrest of a parent can leave traces that the child will never forget: "Impressions of the arrest are burned on the child's mind and are likely to return at night: the violence of the police, the yelling and crying of the mother, the faces of curious neighbours and, above all, the way the father was removed in handcuffs or with a bag over his head, are sensations the child will never forget."[2]

In a study of prisoners' children in Northern Ireland, interviewed family members of prisoners discussed "arrests by the police and immigration services taking place in the presence of young children, leaving children with strong images of their parents being taken away".[3] An NGO worker described a specific situation: "I remember going out to see a girl one time and she had seven children and the police came out and arrested her husband at half five tea time with all her kids in the house. All the police cars in the driveway, came out, took him and away they went and she hadn't a clue where he was going, where he was away to. There was hardly any communication. The children were stood out the front in their sock soles while they [the police] searched the house, no support what so ever. She hadn't a clue where he was...and that really affected that whole family."[4]

In a qualitative British study, the relatives of those arrested reported "mixed experiences" with the police. Often the same relatives had both negative and positive experiences ranging from encounters with "very hostile" and "arrogant" police officers to "very good treatment and understanding from the police".[5]

In the United States, it is estimated – based on a national study conducted in 1998 – "that of parents arrested, 67% were handcuffed in front of their children, 27% reported weapons drawn in front of their children, 4.3% reported a physical struggle, and 3.2% reported the use of pepper spray".[6] Such data seem to support the conclusion that arrests will tend towards having a dramatic and violent element, which can be shocking to children, although it might appear routine to police officers. But there are undoubtedly huge differences from country to country when it comes to the frequency of using handcuffs and weapons.

Nevertheless, it has been argued (also in Denmark) that for the children an arrest will always be dramatic: "Adults talk about a 'violent' or a 'peaceful' arrest. But the children will always experience an arrest as dramatic. It is always traumatic that someone comes and removes a parent. It is important that we think in the child's perspective. Children find arrests much more frightening than we can image, because we see it with our adult eyes."[7] Others argue that many prisoners' children are used to a certain level of violence, crime and drama and are therefore not necessarily affected by such experiences. As we shall see, the Danish data support both these conclusions in the sense that the passive reactions of some children could be the result of familiarity with that kind of situation. On the other hand, the data – including information from the police – clearly show that a lot of children are quite affected and upset as a result of parental arrest.

Evidence from a US study also shows that many prisoners' children have previously experienced violence in their homes and even been victims of violence themselves, which could influence their experience of parental arrest.[8] Nevertheless, the same study indicated "that, all else being equal, witnessing the arrest of a household member either alone or in conjunction with the recent arrest of a parent is predictive of elevated posttraumatic symptoms. Approximately 1 in 4 children who witnessed an arrest and also had a recently arrested parent had elevated symptoms of posttraumatic stress."[9] Arrests in other words clearly affect many children negatively, also when they come from disadvantaged homes and have various experiences with violence.

An American interview-based study of imprisoned mothers and their children similarly revealed that "depending on the circumstances of the arrest, the situation that arises can be complicated and frightening for children".[10] In that particular study, more than 60% of the children did not witness their mother's arrest. Many of them reacted with sadness and anxiety "not only about their mother but also about what would happen to them until she returned".[11] Those who witnessed their mother's arrest "reacted with fear and sadness" and were scared by the experience.[12] Some of the worst situations arose for those relatively few children who went from being observers to participants in the arrest – either because they were involved in the incident that led to the arrest or because the police wanted them to help find their mother. This could make the children feel at least partly responsible for their mother's arrest.[13]

The following focuses on the arrest situation and children's related experiences and problems in Denmark and is based primarily on Danish research and empirical data from the national survey covering the role and thoughts of police and social workers (see Appendix).

Arrests where the child is present – as experienced by the children

Children's experiences can vary significantly depending on how and when their parents are arrested. When 10-year-old Cherie's father was arrested, it was an unpleasant experience, but it took place quietly and calmly. Cherie explained afterwards that the two "policewomen" were kind.[14] But other children have had very different experiences.

According to the Danish police, the majority of arrests fortunately progress without drama. As the former head of the police's criminal preventive division in Copenhagen explained: "The majority of the arrests are calm – you chat a little and the man understands to go voluntarily."[15]

It is difficult to evaluate whether this assessment is correct, since there are no available statistical data on how arrests proceed.

In any event, there are – also according to the police – situations where things can become violent: "If we suspect a person of very serious crimes, we don't, for instance, wait for the door to be opened. And if the suspect is armed or has drugs in the house, it can be a very violent experience."[16] A chief superintendent in Copenhagen described how the violent arrests are often those where drugs are involved: "The father perhaps tries to lock himself in the bathroom to flush the drugs down the toilet and the police have to break the door down and handcuff him. This is not nice for the children to see."[17]

The family therapist quoted earlier who works in the Family House in the Danish Prison Service's halfway house, Engelsborg, is in contact with many prisoner's children and several have told her about very violent arrests: "There are children who describe how they were sitting and eating dinner when the door was broken down and six uniformed officers marched in and handcuffed their father. This is not an image that is easy to let go again. It stays with them permanently."[18]

Some of the things the children point out in their accounts are the details of the police's arrival (if the police arrive with sirens wailing, if the door is kicked in, etc.) and the fact that some police officers have dogs with them. A boy described his father's arrest when he was scarcely 7 years old: "So I got home the same time the police arrived. There were four officers from the police with turnout and then I also arrived. So my mother said that she wanted to know why they were there. They said they had caught my father and if she said no to them coming inside, then they would get hold of the neighbours to witness. So they were allowed to come in. Then I met the dogs and I am scared of dogs, 'what's going on?' I said. Then I wasn't allowed to stay at home, I had to go, they said. So I left and played with my mother's friend's daughter... But I have wondered many times why they had dogs with them."[19]

A girl who was 10 when her father was arrested also emphasised that there had been many policemen and a dog: "We drove up and a man was standing next to the road and there was a dog, and the road was full of police cars and we were stopped. They asked if we lived there... And everyone had seen it and asked what was going on... I cried and asked my mother 'Has this something to do with Dad?' It had. Then they went around looking for him."[20]

Eighteen-year-old Charlotte described her experience of her father's arrest this way: "Suddenly we heard noise downstairs and the door was kicked in. There were officers everywhere. Eight in all, and dogs that barked. Our little sister was sleeping and she woke up. So my father was there and they put the handcuffs on him and we started crying. There was an officer who said that we should say goodbye."[21] Charlotte also noted the searching of the house as a terrible experience: "Afterwards, all the furniture was overturned. The drawers pulled out and clothes were all over the place."[22]

It is understandable that the searching of the home, especially the children's own bedrooms, feels very intimidating to witness or to come home to. Carina, who was 16 when her father was arrested, told her story to the daily newspaper, *Information*: "The officer said that we had to leave the room so he could check it for drugs. When we were on the way out of the room, he opened my drawers and began throwing my underwear, among other things, all over the place. It was so insulting I felt as if I was a criminal."[23] After the arrest, Carina and her siblings went home to their mother and their mother's boyfriend. When Carina returned home the next day to clean up in the house, it all came back again: "It looked a lot worse than I thought. Every time I saw a drawer, I remembered how they were pulled out the day before."[24]

The head of The Criminal Prevention Division in Copenhagen Police explained that searches cannot be avoided when looking for evidence. And neither can the children's private possessions be omitted: "We have to search the children's rooms as well. The teddy bear could be a good hiding place."[25]

Naturally, each arrest is different, but regardless of how it progresses and what the children experience, it can be frightening and make a lasting impression A Danish police officer who has many arrests behind him, agree and described it thus: "Children are always anxious, regardless of whether it is a calm or violent arrest. You can always see the anxiety in their eyes."[26]

The children's reactions

The children's own accounts generally seem to match the perceptions of the police. In the Danish Institute for Human Rights' questionnaire survey (distributed to all police districts in Denmark), 53% of police officers responded that they had experienced children who remained passive and calm during parental arrests; 53% had experienced children who behaved as if they did not understand what was happening; 47% had experienced children who cried; and 32% had experienced children who clung to their mother or father.[27]

Some police officers point out that it is difficult to make general observations about children's reactions,[28] as these depend on the situation and the children's ages.[29] Some officers are of the opinion that the younger children are the most passive, perhaps because they understand the least about what is happening and are therefore less afraid.[30] On the other hand, one police officer concluded that "older children become hostile, younger children become scared".[31] One sergeant described how many children do not understand what is going on, elaborating: "I don't believe that they think it's police officers, but just that there are some people who want to take dad/mum with them."[32]

According to the Danish Institute for Human Rights' survey, many police officers experience children who in arrest situations are friendly towards the police (38%) or afraid of the police (44%).[33] That they react by being friendly does not mean, however, that they necessarily "have a good relationship with the police" – in fact, the opposite sentiment would be natural in many situations. Quite a few police officers also find that some children are particularly hostile (18%). In the words of a chief superintendent, it can "be a negative experience for the child to see the police in action".[34]

How the children experience the police is of course connected to how the police handle the situation. It is important that the individual police officer ensures that the arrest takes place in an appropriate and sober manner, so the children do not experience the authorities as dangerous and as the enemy. How the arrested person and other relatives tackle the situation and relate to the police also influences a child's perception of the event. As quoted in Chapter 1, an assistant detective described one particular experience that still affects him many years later. Together with a fellow police officer, he had to arrest a female drunk-driving offender who unfortunately managed to get into her apartment before they could get apprehend her. The episode "ended very unfortunately by us having to get her to lie down and having to sit two officers on top of her out in the stairwell... Suddenly, the boy attacked me and started beating furiously on my back while shouting, 'Get away from my mother! Get away from my mother!' I will never forget the boy's eyes and I often wonder where he is today, how it has affected him and what he thinks about the police and about the episode. It's almost twenty-eight years ago, so he is an adult man now."[35]

Training of the police in handling children and other relatives in arrest situations

Arresting parents in front of their children can be a challenge for the involved police officers, and the officers' behaviour can greatly influence the children's experience. The question of whether or not the social authorities should be contacted is also essential and left to the discretion of individual police officers. The question then arises, how are police officers trained and equipped to handle these issues?

Some states and jurisdictions in the United States have developed and implemented "child-sensitive arrest protocols" that "include detailed guidance for arresting officers to minimize trauma for children who are present". The good practices these protocols promote include "not handcuffing parents in front of their children whenever possible, allowing parents to reassure their children, waiting for a designated caregiver, not using the siren when leaving, and allowing the parent an additional phone call to arrange childcare. They also include guidance for looking for signs of children who may not be present but may be dependent on the arrested person for care and supervision."[36]

Denmark has no such written protocols. One of the instruction leaders at the Danish Police Academy explains that "no two arrests are the same and therefore, you cannot teach according to a clear-cut model. Police training is about equipping the students well so they can generally make sensible decisions in the many different situations they find themselves in as police officers."[37] One could question this line of argument and argue that it would still be a good idea to implement protocols and establish some sort of baseline in a sensitive and important area like this. At the Danish Police Academy, the question of how children and other relatives of the arrested are handled is included in various contexts and in different subjects.[38] In psychology classes work is done on conflict resolution, which addresses those situations where children are present in the home in connection with an arrest.[39]

The tuition at the Police Academy, which involves how to handle prisoners relatives and children, is based on various cases and role-playing games. Arrest scenarios give students practice considering the different aspects police need to handle in such situations, such as safety for themselves and the others involved, complying with various rules and how to handle relatives In these role-playing games, the students themselves as well as the teachers and – in rare cases – actors play the parts. The Police Academy also has positive experiences with involving maladjusted children and youngsters of twelve to sixteen years of age. Younger children do not participate in these role-playing games, so in relation to younger children, the learning is theoretical (e.g., the question is asked: "And what would you do then, if an 8-year-old girl was standing next to the person [you have to arrest]?"[40]

With regard to the police's duty to inform, the Police Academy teaches that the municipality's social services must be notified in all situations where the family circumstances give rise to an assumption that the children may need special support. The police officers are taught what signals might indicate child neglect, violence against the child or that the remaining relatives are for one reason or another unable to take care of the child.[41]

In the Danish Institute for Human Rights' questionnaire survey, however, only 24% of the responding police officers felt that they have received a good education in handling children as relatives in connection with an arrest. Sixty-eight per cent placed a check mark in the option: "Children as relatives played a very small or no role at all in my training." According to the Police Academy, however, there is currently more focus on relatives and especially related children. Several responses did acknowledge that "[the training] has changed since, with more focus on the topic now",[42] and "the new graduates we receive have a pretty good understanding of how children should be treated".[43]

Nevertheless, many responses in the questionnaire survey also reflect that the handling of children is something that is learned best through experience. For example, a deputy assistant commissioner was of the opinion that it is only when "you are in practical training that you learn to handle children as relatives"; it is not "something you learn in school".[44]

The police's handling of arrests when children are present

The police have many tasks in connection with an arrest. They must arrest the suspect(s) and ensure they gather the evidence, but they also need to focus on the safety of themselves and those who are present. Additionally, the police are responsible for how the arrest is handled in relation to any children who are present.

As mentioned earlier, the Danish legislation require that arrests should be "conducted as gently as circumstances allow", but this principle is first and foremost directed towards the arrested person and does not take prisoners' children into account.[45] Some police officers point out that it is difficult to legislate more specifically because circumstances vary significantly "from time to time".[46] Nevertheless, it seems that some police officers agree that a set of guidelines and standards – like the US examples mentioned above – would be a good idea. Otherwise, far too much depends on whether the officers who conduct the arrest focus on and understand how they handle the children who are present. As described by a chief superintendent: "The police can be very focused on the task, by which the attention to the children present depends, to a high degree, on the individual officer's empathy and sense of the situation."[47] A police sergeant suggested that there should be "more focus and reference to 'prisoners' children' from senior management in the police districts. Set procedures that MUST be complied with."[48] This suggestion is in line with international recommendations and the previously mentioned "child-sensitive arrest protocols" being used in parts of the United States.[49]

Many police officers seem aware that the police's handling of parent arrests plays an important role in relation to the experience of the children who are present. Of those asked, 82% responded that they found that the police, generally speaking, have a great deal of focus on the children in connection with the arrest of parents.[50]

In other words, the survey mainly indicates that there is awareness of the arrested person's children on the part of the police. But as previously described, no other surveys exist for comparison, and the above is self-evaluation. If this is taken into account and the self-critical statements (which several police officers have submitted), as well as the accounts from children who have experienced the arrest of a parent are added, a careful assessment points in the direction that while there is a fundamental awareness of the problem – that is, the arrest of a parent when a child/children are present – the Danish police force still needs specific guidelines and a much more standardised approach.

Approaches and practices also vary when it comes to the question of whether police officers check the National Register of Persons before the arrest and how this affects the planning of the arrest. It seems that most police officers, but not all, check the National Register, which lets them know whether or not children can be present.[51]

According to the Danish Institute for Human Rights' survey, it is not standard policy for the police to use this knowledge to conduct a planned arrest at a location or time when children are not present. Of respondents, 26% said that children's possible presence does not play any role in determining where and when the arrest takes place, just as 38% stated that it merely plays a less important role in planning an arrest. Yet many responses indicated that it is best that the arrest take place at a location where the children do not witness it. A deputy assistant commissioner, who responded that children are not part of the considerations, elaborated: "The planning is done according to when it is convenient with regard to deadlines – we may only detain people for 24 hours. When planned – all aspects must come into play equally. Children are not one of the aspects."[52]

It is important to note that considering the presence of children when planning an arrest is not necessarily synonymous with taking the children's best interests into account. A deputy assistant commissioner elaborated that children present in the home during an arrest is positive and something to plan for because it "secures the operation considerably".[53] The children are thus sometimes exploited by the police. How this can work out is explained by a mother who described her husband's arrest in the apartment in front of her and her three children, for whom the experience was quite intense. A concerned neighbour heard the noise and offered to take the children upstairs, but the police would not allow this. The mother explained: "Thirty minutes earlier I was walking with the pram and the twins right past the bushes where it turned out that the policemen were hiding up to the arrest. They could have just kept us back quietly and calmly, and then gone into the apartment to arrest Claus. But instead, they waited until we were all at home."[54]

Police officers also have different attitudes about handcuffing parents in front of the children. There are rules for when the police may use handcuffs, but not for when they may be used in front of children. At the Police Academy, students are taught that using handcuffs in front of children cannot always be avoided, but that they should try to do so.[55] In practice, however, there seems to be considerable differences in how the police relate to this question. In the Danish Institute for Human Rights' survey, only 40% responded that they, as far as possible, did not use handcuffs in front of children.[56]

There are however a number of precautions police generally take when children are present at an arrest. All except one respondent said that they try to conduct the arrest as calmly as possible. Based on the officers' responses, the police are generally aware of the fact that someone must take care of the children during arrests of parents. Of the respondents, 75% said that they try to get another parent or other relatives to leave with the child.[57] Another 63% responded that they ensure that an officer specifically attends to the child and possibly other relatives.[58]

There are officers who emphasised how important it is that the police communicate with the children. A police sergeant pointed out that "cool-headed and calm behaviour is crucial. Speak with the children if possible."[59] Another police officer wrote: "As far as possible, contact can be made with the child subsequently, so the child – in the company of a parent – can have a chat about what has happened. And the child can then re-establish a sensible and safe opinion of the police."[60] A seasoned deputy assistant commissioner described that previously "as a rule, an officer had time to visit the family again to do a little follow-up, but there is no real time for that today. Of course, this depends on the individual officer, but I do not believe that this is something that is practiced to any great extent. It is neither a requirement and nor is it our job. But there are very committed officers who do it."[61]

The police's information to the relatives in connection with arrest

According to the survey, the police's information to the relatives in connection with an arrest comprises verbal information and/or handing out of calling cards. Four of the responding participants wrote in the comment field that they also give information about contact to a social worker. The procedures here are not standardized either.

At the Police Academy they teach that the police can rarely say anything specific to the relatives because the police do not know how long the arrested person will be detained. At best, they can give a rough assessment. Moreover, it is not always possible to give information and instructions because it is sometimes all about "ending the situation and getting the guy to go along".[62]

Only one police officer responded that he or she hands out information material to the relatives in connection with an arrest; the officer did not indicate what kind of information material this is. Another police officer explained that there had supposedly been some information material once but did not think that it is handed out much.[63] There were divided opinions but a predominantly favourable attitude (65%) towards the police handing out the information material to relatives in connection with an arrest.[64]

The parents' and other relatives' handling of the arrest situation

A certain frustration about parents' and other relatives' behaviour in connection with arrests is found among police officers. Many mention that they experience parents who handle the situation very badly in relation to their children. It is clearly the police's experience that the parents play a major role in determining if the arrest takes place quietly and calmly, as well as how the children experience the arrest. An assistant detective explained that the children react based on the adults behaviour: "If the adult is quiet and calm, then the children are as well. Conversely, if the adult reacts violently, then the children react by crying and being fearful of the unknown."[65] A deputy assistant commissioner finds that intoxicated or drugged-up parents tend to dramatise the situation.[66] In line with much research on children of imprisoned parents, one police sergeant explained that the "children often become little 'parents' who have to act like an adult because the adults are unable to".[67]

Another police sergeant told a sad story about a 12-year-old girl who contacted the police: "I had been out and arrested a father – domestic dispute – where I spent a great deal of time on the child. She was the one who called, so her mother thought she was a 'stupid girl'. The mother wouldn't talk to the sobbing kid – 12 years old...I often think about that, even though it's 12 years ago."[68]

An assistant detective and teacher in police theory at the Police Academy also pointed out that the relatives' handling of the situation can be a major problem: "There is something very fundamental, in teaching as well as in practice, that one must try to get the children away when the arrest is made; either together with an officer, a parent or with older siblings. However, it is often quite difficult because a great many parents use the children as shields. They think, and on one level or another they are right, that there is a limit to how much we can 'get at them' – verbally as well as physically – when the children are watching. Therefore, getting the children away is something that is most difficult."[69]

Fortunately, there are examples to the contrary: "I have also experienced several times that the parents are very cooperative and aware of their children. They often have a suggestion to a solution if the ones we suggest don't suffice."[70]

In the wake of the arrest, not all parents have the energy to help their children. In her research, Else Christensen ascertained that some parents who remain behind react by disappearing into a feeling of unreality. At the same time, they face a number of practical problems and often it is all about getting through the immediate situation. It can be a very tough experience for the woman and mother who remains, especially for families with very traditional relationships in which the man manages all the practical things. On top of that, the information available to relatives is often minimal. Not knowing what will happen and what they need to do in the new situation can result in the parents having difficulty handling the child's possible crisis as well.[71] Children who are placed outside the home can find their fear exacerbated by the fact that the surroundings react as if the arrested parent does not exist.[72]

Arrest when the child is not present

What happens when a parent is arrested when the child is not present? Do the police know that they have arrested a mother or father with underage children, and how do the police use this knowledge? Do relatives always get information that the arrest has taken place? This was an area in which the CPT had criticised Denmark, as a number of arrested persons were apparently prevented from informing their relatives.

In the Danish Institute for Human Rights' survey, 62% of the participating police officers responded that they ask if the arrested person has children and, in such case, where they are.[73] Some of the police officers who did not enquire had checked this in the National Register of Persons beforehand.[74] Others elaborated that an arrested person is not always asked if he or she has children because: 1) "not all colleagues are equally aware of possible children",[75] 2) it depends on the situation,[76] or 3) an arrested person will draw attention to the fact if he or she has children.[77]

The police are not required to ask if an arrested person has children, and it does not have to be noted anywhere, just as action is not necessarily required to be taken. A chief superintendent explained that it would be written in the day report if an arrested person has children and that the day report is read by the crime prevention division, which assesses what should occur in that connection and in other situations, a social report is written which is forwarded to the municipality.[78] In the survey, we asked the police officers whether they would contact the social authorities if they can see that children live in the house but the arrested person denies this. Only slightly less than half (47%) responded with a clear yes.[79]

The parents' information to the child about the arrest

The police explained that normally neither the social authorities nor the police inform the child when he or she has not been present during the arrest of the parent. Most often, the parents or other relatives give the child an explanation.[80] But there are situations when the adult relatives are not informed, and thus neither are the children.[81]

In many cases, the children are given stories instead of the truth. This can have a negative consequence, because children can sense that the situation is not what they are being told and they become even more troubled. It can also contribute to distrust of the parents. Diana experienced this in relation to her mother. Her mother told her that her father was in Germany, but Diana was well aware that this was not true: "I cannot blame her for wanting to protect me, but I could just have used the truth for a number of things. Then I wouldn't have to tell lies at school and perhaps it might have been easier to talk about it at home... When she tells me something, I automatically think: Is that really true? I will always have a feeling that she let me down by not answering the questions that were so deep inside me. It was really about my father and not some distant uncle or other."[82]

Involvement of the social authorities

Pursuant to the Danish social service act, as a public authority the police have the duty to report.[83] As already described, it is the attending officer who assesses whether or not the family circumstances warrant that the children need special support and that the social authorities must be notified. In other words, the social authorities are only contacted if the attending officer finds it necessary.

If the police want to inform the social authorities about a child whom they believe needs special support, they can notify the authorities through a social report. If the police determine that the children have an immediate need for special provisions, they can contact the 24-hour social service.[84]

The majority of police officers responded that in those cases where children appear to be neglected, they would either contact the 24-hour social service (76%) or notify the municipality through a social report (likewise 76%).[85] If the home is neglected and disorderly, according to the survey, many police officers would also contact the 24-hour social service (53%) or inform the social authorities through a social report (62%).[86] But the response percentages indicate that there is clearly not general agreement about this.

The vast majority of the officers asked would contact the 24-hour social service in cases where the child would otherwise be left alone because both parents are being arrested (91%), or in cases where the arrested person is alone with his or her child and other relatives cannot be contacted (82%). If the remaining relative is unable to care for the child, 85% of officers would contact the 24-hour social service. This particularly concerns situations in which the remaining relative is under the influence of drugs or alcohol or appears to be mentally unbalanced or ill.[87]

The police must – and should naturally – contact the 24-hour service when a suitable person does not remain behind to take care of the children. But even though the responses indicate that the police do this in the majority of cases, it clearly does *not* happen all the time. As a police sergeant wrote: "Many years ago in Copenhagen in connection with an arrest, I had to entrust the young children to an extremely drunk mother. I cannot remember why the social authorities were not involved."[88]

Neither are the responses consistent as to how often a situation requires the police to contact the 24-hour social service. When asked about the kinds of cases that prompt police officers to contact the 24-hour service, a police superintendent responded, "Many cases actually"[89], while a deputy assistant commissioner wrote: "Rarely. It has to be really bad."[90] This indicates that practice in the area is varied and depends on the individual officer. In any case, it can be argued that the police officers do not necessarily have the professional competence to assess if and when children require special help.

Children who are left on their own

Police officers related that when the 24-hour social service is contacted, it is standard practice that an officer remains at the location until the social authorities arrive. If, this is not possible for one reason or another (e.g., the situation in the home is quite bad or there is no time or possibility for a police officer to wait with the child), the child is taken to the station where the social authorities can collect him or her.[91]

As an alternative or supplement to contacting the social authorities, some police officers stated that they try to contact family members in those cases where both parents are arrested or the arrested parent is alone with the child.[92] In such situations there are, unfortunately, examples of children not being properly taken care of. The family therapist from the Engelsborg halfway house described how a boy was left alone after his mother was arrested. The boy "said 'Mum was frying meatballs when they came and she was given just three minutes to clear it away and then they handcuffed her. She asked: 'But what about Mikkel?' and one of the officers said: 'The 24-hour social service will pick him up.' I didn't know what that was, so I was pretty scared and then I sat all on my own and waited for them to come.'"[93]

There are also instances when older children have been left alone without the police having contacted the social authorities (or family members) at all. Malene, Carina and Tenna (at the time 18, 16 and 14 years old) experienced that the police neither contacted their mother nor the social authorities when their father was arrested. The arrest took place in the home, and the girls were at home. Apparently, the police did not inform them of what would happen and did not even ask if they had somewhere they could go or someone who could come and take care of them. On their own initiative, the three girls took a taxi to their mother's home (30 kilometres away).[94]

This situation is not as unusual as one would like to think. Investigation leader Kenneth Vesth explains: "If there is a 15-year old, it may be that we don't do anything more, but if we see a cot, then of course we make a call."[95] According to the NGO KRIM, children have been left behind many times without the police informing them where their mother or father was going or when they would return.[96] As mentioned, the police are not obligated to ask if an arrested person has children, and only half of the police officers report doing so.

The social authorities as help and support after the arrest

There are critical voices in children's welfare NGOs who find it inappropriate to let the individual police officer assess whether or not the social authorities should be contacted in connection with the arrest of persons who have children. According to Children's Welfare (Børns Vilkår), the police and other public authorities' heightened duty to report is too weakly defined and sends unclear signals. "Myths exist of what neglect is: if the mother is not drunk and if things appear to be clean and the children are nicely dressed, then the assessment is often that everything is alright. A lot of children are lost in this way. There has to be a much closer cooperation between the police and the social authorities, and the social authorities should be responsible for the assessment of which initiatives must be taken in relation to the arrested person's children."[97] The National Council for Children (Børnerådet) has also argued that a set practice should be introduced according to which the social authorities are called on every time a parent is arrested.[98]

The Danish Institute for Human Rights has asked the police if they think that the communication and cooperation between themselves and the social authorities works well when it comes to safeguarding children whose parents are arrested. Most police, 76%, found that the cooperation, generally speaking, works well. Of those participating from the social authorities, only 56% found that the cooperation works well. But more than one-third of each group – 39% of the police officers and 36% of the social workers – would like closer cooperation and better information sharing.[99]

The officers' comments reflect certain differences in their experiences of the social authorities. For example, one police sergeant wrote: "Sometimes it seems as if the municipality thinks: The person concerned is now under the state's (Prison and Probation Service's) organisation and as a municipality we are not interested in helping him/her."[100] On the other hand, a deputy assistant commissioner wrote: "The social services are on their toes as far as children are concerned."[101] The social authorities criticise some of the police for not informing enough. Among other things, they are looking for "more social reports from the police, reports on the parents even though they live in the 'expensive' neighbourhoods".[102] One social worker found that "social reports sometimes arrive with great delays, which makes follow-up difficult".[103]

A mother with young children described the arrest of the children's father: "It would be good if there was someone to talk to (about the arrest). But it is important that there is someone who can explain what will happen. Perhaps it's easier for others, but I knew nothing about arresting and prisons. Everything I know now I have learned through experience. Many times I have developed a headache just from thinking because I couldn't figure it out."[104]

Two factors in particular can keep the social authorities out of the loop. To begin with, the police have a non-disclosure obligation, which they may only breach if they have grounds to report. Secondly, many arrested persons and adult relatives decline the involvement of the social authorities. As one relative explains: "You know very well that the social authorities must not get past your door because you'll never get them out again."[105] At the Police Academy, the problem is also recognised and explains why relatives often request the police to not involve the social authorities.[106] Social workers are also familiar with this attitude. In the survey, 44% said they have experienced families affected by imprisonment who have a preconceived idea that social services is an unpleasant monitoring institution. Likewise, 44% have experienced families affected by imprisonment who fear social services will remove the children from the home.[107]

Taken together, the above issues result in many families and children not receiving the help they need. As a social worker explained: "It is problematic, that we don't know about many of the families who go through this and thus cannot help the children."[108] Of those who are not already known by the social authorities, it is the socio-economically relatively advantaged, according to SAVN, who personally contact the municipality. The more disadvantaged are lost.[109]

Conclusion and summary

Seen from the perspective of prisoners' children, there are a number of potential problems and specific issues associated with the arrest of parents. Not least, this applies to the question of children witnessing the arrest and how, in such case, this progresses. If the children do not witness the arrest, it is crucial that the relatives are informed about the arrest so there is the possibility that the children will be subsequently informed. Next, it is crucial whether – and how – the social authorities are contacted in connection with the arrest of persons who have children.

Police and the social workers confirm that it is often a very problematic and difficult experience for children to experience the arrest of their parent. The police explain that many children do not understand what is going on, and many cry and cling to the arrested parent. This confirms what researchers have claimed, that is, in some cases it can be damaging and even traumatising for children to experience a parent's arrest.

The majority of Danish police officers seem to have a fundamental awareness of the children's situation and exposure in this area, even though the majority of those asked found their training insufficient in this respect. Nevertheless, it seems that police practice varies significantly in several areas, such as if and when the social authorities are contacted. Police officers clearly have different approaches to arresting parents, and some even exploit the presence of children when planning and conducting an arrest.

In any case, in relation to the Convention of the Rights of the Child's rules and to the best interest of the child, it is problematic that the police do not possess the competence of a social service in assessing the child's situation.

8
Remand Imprisonment: A Stressful Phase of Transition

Danish as well as international research indicates that remand custody represents a particularly difficult period for families facing incarceration.[1] It comes as no surprise that the stress usually afflicting the parent remaining at home can also affect the children.[2] For partners who find themselves in this situation for the first time, the rules and their lack of immediately useful experience can be overwhelming.[3] A small British qualitative study found that "the initial process of arrest and remand" was associated with disruption of the family income, disorientation, loss and uncertainty.[4]

There is often a scarcity of information for close kin in connection with detention and remand in custody of their partner/parent. In some cases, the partner does not even know the reason for the remand in custody. Furthermore, many families seem to know little about their rights regarding visitation of those in remand custody or attaining financial support from the social services. Nor can they expect much help about how to deal with the children. Needless to say, the situation becomes particularly absurd if close kin have not even been notified about the detention.[5]

In a US study of women prisoners and their children, Siegel describes how the arrest could trigger "a panicked effort to get someone to care for the children and let the children know what was happening". As described by one mother, she practically had to beg the police: "Please let me...make a phone call to my mother. My son is around the corner waiting on me to pick him up from school."[6]

Research on how remand imprisonment affects prisoners' children is scarce in the sense that most empirical research on children of imprisoned parents does not differentiate between the remand phase and imprisonment following a sentence. This is clearly the case with the available quantitative studies, which record only one category, "imprisonment". This makes it very difficult to track the specific remand issues and their potential impact. But, as described by Rachel Condry with regard to prisoners' families in general: "New responsibilities might emerge at each stage of the criminal justice process. It is important to look at the whole criminal justice process, rather than just focus on the effects of imprisonment on the family; relatives are often very involved with each stage of the investigation and some cases can take years to process from discovery to sentencing."[7]

Waiting in uncertainty

Remand in custody constitutes a transitional period in many ways.[8] The case is investigated; the outcome remains uncertain. Some believe that the individual remanded in custody will be set free, while others anticipate a harsh sentence. The fact that remand custody is often prolonged several times can mean severe tribulation not only for the one in custody but also for close kin. Marie explains the following about when her ex-husband Andreas, the father of her three sons, was remanded:

> After 14 days he was to appear before a judge, who proceeded to prolong his remand for another 14 days. It went on like this for some time; gradually it was prolonged by 4 weeks at a time. Every time I had to explain to Kristian, my son who was then 7, that in "14 days or in a month, a judge will decide whether Daddy has to go to jail or whether he can be released". When it was prolonged time after time, I could do nothing but tell him that it had been extended – yet again. All we did was sit and wait. Andreas was in remand custody for 10 months.[9]

For this boy, it was particularly stressful because his two younger brothers knew nothing and because he and his mother had reached an agreement that if his father received a prison sentence they would have to tell their family, their friends and his school. He was very nervous about this. The boy, who was 12 when interviewed, explained: "My mother did in fact tell me to prepare myself that my father would probably have to go to prison. It was like spending your time waiting for something that you knew was bad, but you did not know how bad it was...every time we thought, now we will be told something, but all that happened was that we had to wait some more."[10]

This situation is quite typical and can be particularly troublesome in cases where children are placed in foster care. For instance, during a visit to a children's home in 2007, staff told about Ali, who at that point had spent half a year in the institution living in uncertainty. Both his parents were in remand custody that was constantly being extended. Nobody therefore knew how long he was going to stay at the home, or how it was all going to end.[11]

A prison chaplain in Vestre Prison in Copenhagen explained that remand prisoners deliberate over whether or not they should tell their children the truth: "There is a great deal of uncertainty as to whether they 'should' say anything because they have not yet been convicted. 'Should I tell them, or should we say that I am in Sweden or out on a sailing trip?'...One woman was thoroughly convinced that she would soon be released because she was innocent, and she did not want to subject her child to having to meet her in a prison setting. The question of whether this is the right thing to do is a difficult one – after all, the real question is whether it is in the child's best interest to reveal anything about it if, say, it is only a question of two weeks before you are free again. But this woman was remanded in custody for seven months before she at last received a visit from her daughter."[12]

As previously mentioned, some kids are lied to about where father or mother has gone. Dennis, a father who did not tell his daughters the truth when he was in prison, explained: "As teenagers they have often asked me why I lied to them. I don't know whether telling them the truth would have been better. Maybe, it is difficult to say. In any case, they are disappointed, and one of them still doesn't entirely trust me."[13]

There are also some parents who admit to the imprisonment but lie with regard to the extent of their criminal activity. A Danish Red Cross employee running discussion groups for children of imprisoned parents remembered a situation that made an impression: "One boy of 12 had been told that his father had stolen a trailer. The father got 12 years in prison. The boy was quite able to realize that this didn't add up."[14] According to research, this kind of subterfuge may spur a fundamental feeling of anxiety and insecurity in the children.[15] An increasing number of international recommendations in the area argue that telling the truth is generally the best option for the children.[16]

"You only have yourself to blame"

As previously described, incarceration is typically associated with shame and stigmatisation. How the involved authorities handle the situation is thus critical. There is reason to believe that many police officers, prison guards and other officials act decently, yet there are also unfortunate stories of families facing incarceration who have not been received and treated in an appropriate manner. Sometimes relatives are met with the attitude that those in custody "only have themselves to blame". This is particularly problematic in the period immediately following the arrest, an insecure time of transition when the family is in dire need of support.

Henrik Mathiasen, who has been a social worker for nearly 30 years and works for the 24-hour youth and family care centre in Aarhus, Denmark, described how it is deemed more acceptable that a family needs help in connection with, say, illness or a death than in the event of incarceration: "When you 'only' have a husband or boyfriend in prison who may also be the father of your child, it is not widely recognized that you may have a serious social problem", he explained. "I can recall the first ten times when I have neglected that here there might be both a child and an adult in need of help. I find that we have especially failed from the child's perspective. If the arrested person is a parent, then there will also be a child who has all but lost his or her mother or father. This is not something that we as social workers as a general rule are afraid to act upon. We just don't have a tradition for doing so in these particular cases."[17]

Moreover, relatives and friends tell SAVN, the Danish NGO for prisoners' relatives, how police and prison officials sometimes meet them with a frustrating "maybe you just need to move on" attitude. "This is precisely what you can't do, what you should not do, and they have no business meddling. The prisoner is not simply a criminal, he or she is also the father or mother of a child or children, and they share all sorts of things together. Therefore it feels degrading."[18]

Visitation during remand in custody

During remand in custody, a number of special restrictions may be enforced, which can seriously hamper contact between the child and the incarcerated parent. This is particularly true if the person in remand custody is subject to control of correspondence and visits, which in Denmark entails that police must supervise visits. All of this is dealt with in a later chapter concerning children's visits to prisons and detention facilities (see Chapter 10).

Remand in custody – a vulnerable period

Remand imprisonment can be a long and difficult time for families, marked by significant uncertainty and many financial and practical problems. It can become a very confusing period, and many do not possess the drive to seek support or just do not know how to go about it. Yet how parents handle the situation will affect the children. During this period, many children find themselves most in need of seeing and experiencing that their father or mother is doing well. But sometimes they are not even told where their parent is. For those children who do get to visit, it is often under very restrictive conditions, as we shall see.

The conditions of prisoners during remand imprisonment are in many ways based on the assumption that remand in custody should be for a short period only. But in practice this is far from always the case. In Denmark, the use of remand imprisonment has risen significantly during recent years. A full one-third of all prisoners in Denmark are currently remand prisoners and the use of "long-term remand", which lasts for more than three months, increased by 45% from 2007–2010.[19] The specific problems related to remand imprisonment therefore affect a growing number of prisoners' children in Denmark. Chapter 10 describes how the restrictive visiting rules and circumstances applied during remand imprisonment in Denmark can affect the children particularly hard.

Unfortunately, the rise in remand imprisonment is not only a Danish phenomenon. Generally speaking, the use of imprisonment (remand and sentenced) has been on the rise on all five continents. On average globally, "one out of every three detainees is awaiting trial and has not been found guilty of a crime".[20] It has furthermore been estimated that "some three million people are in pretrial detention at any given time", and each year "an estimated 10 million people will enter pretrial detention".[21] We are, in other words, dealing with a huge number of remand prisoners, perhaps even more children and certainly many more family members – all of whom are affected by the extensive use of remand imprisonment.

9
After the Sentence: The Family's Way of Dealing with the Children and the Surroundings

The remand prisoner's situation is clarified – for better or worse – after a sentence is passed. An often agonising waiting time is over, and in that sense, it can be a relief when the verdict is passed. But the expectations of the family and the prisoner will of course also shape the family's emotions – were they expecting an acquittal, a short or perhaps a long sentence? And what was the result? For some, the verdict will mean "an end of all hope".[1]

In a British study on how relatives of serious offenders were affected, "the court experience and sentencing were usually the second most significant events [for the relatives] after discovery of the offence".[2] In that particular study, the sentences were serious and long term, which put some relatives into a state of shock. Some even collapsed upon hearing the verdict. Many found the experience of the court "upsetting and frightening".[3]

One clear advantage for many sentenced prisoners and their families is, however, that the remand phase, with its strict rules and conditions, is at an end. In Denmark (as well as in Norway and especially in Sweden), the remand regime is often very strict with high levels of isolation, while the regime for sentenced prisoners – especially those in open prisons – is significantly more liberal. Accordingly, a psychologist in the Danish Prison and Probation Service describes how "the majority of remand prisoners find it an enormous relief to transfer to ordinary conditions for sentenced prisoners because this provides a greater degree of freedom, more social contact, easier access to relatives and networks, better opportunity for a daily structure and better access to activities and education. In addition there is now a time perspective with dates for commencement of home leave processes as well as a release date, which gives peace of mind and a form of certainty that has been absent during the remand period."[4]

For some parents, it is only after the sentencing that they consider how they will tell the children that mum or dad is going to prison and how much the children should be told.[5] This is also when many families make a serious decision about what they will say to the people they deal with on a daily basis.[6]

As previously described, research shows how the taboo and the stigma that surrounds imprisonment can affect the children and how they relate to the outside world. As explained by a child in a Swedish study: "Of course, I could tell my closest friends that she's in prison, but if someone else asks about my mum then I can't tell them anything because it's just so embarrassing."[7] The parent's criminality can also receive publicity, which can reinforce these problems.

Telling the children about the verdict

Marie told her three boys on the day of the verdict that their father would be in prison for 14 years:

> I sat in the court in shock and the only thing I could think about was my children. Subsequently, many people have asked me if I thought about practical things and the finances, but there was simply no room at all in my head at that time. I just sat and talked to myself; how old they would be when Andreas would be released. That consumed all my thoughts. I have spoken with many other mothers in SAVN about it and that's how it was for them too. To begin with, having to tell the children takes a great deal of energy. How, and what should you say?[8]

Marie drove around for a while to gather courage before she went home and told her children the truth. For Kristian, this was a sad ending to 10 months' in suspense. Until that day, the two younger brothers had been told that their father worked as a tattoo artist in the remand prison where they had visited him. Marie remembered: "I wept together with the two eldest boys. The youngest sort of stood at a distance from us and just looked and listened. I don't think he could understand. He had just turned three."[9]

Most parents want to protect their children. Hence, one can assume that the majority of parents who choose to keep the truth from their children, perhaps even when mum or dad has been sentenced to a long imprisonment, do so for such reasons. But to do the opposite – to tell children the truth – can also be motivated by a wish to protect your children. This was the case for Marie when she told her children the truth:

> It had to be something we spoke about at home so they didn't risk being confronted with it by others...Just imagine if there was someone who got wind of it, that it was Andreas who had done it [the crime]. Imagine if there were parents who sat chatting about it and their kids listened and started saying something in school or somewhere else. For me, telling the boys the truth was, to a high degree, about protecting them. They had to know what it was all about and how they could respond if someone said anything.[10]

Telling the children can also have practical motivations; visiting mum or dad in prison requires that at least some of the truth is told. Not giving enough information can certainly create even more confusion for children. A Swedish girl who was 12 years old when her mother was imprisoned explained: "I don't know why she is in prison. Sometimes I want to know, and other times I don't. Everyone says something different, so I don't know what I should believe. So neither do I know who to ask even if I did want to know."[11]

How to handle the surroundings

What you say to the children and the immediate family is one thing. How you relate to the outside world is often another matter. Parents grapple with many questions: How do I handle this so that my children are spared unpleasant reactions as much as possible? How do I guide my children in handling the surroundings? Should I tell teachers and social educators? What about the children's friends? Should the other children in the class be told?[12]

A family therapist explains that it can be a big help for the children if the teachers or day-care staff know that the children's father or mother has been imprisoned. Then they will understand if the children react differently than usual, and they might be able to help.[13] The former Danish association for prisoners' relatives Balance i Frihed (Balance in Freedom) has worked with many children whose parents have told them not to say anything to their teachers or fellow pupils. This placed a huge strain on the children.[14]

Marie chose to tell the adults in Kristian's school and the after-school centre about his father's remand imprisonment:

> Kristian was in the pre-school class at that time and during the remand period we didn't tell the children in the class anything. Kristian was very well aware that the teachers and staff at the after-school centre knew, because I insisted on that. But none of the children knew. I didn't find any reason why they should know that Andreas had been remand imprisoned, if he might be released anyway. But Kristian was also aware that if his father was sentenced, then we'd have to be open about it and tell the truth. We talked a lot about that and he was prepared for it... After the verdict I spoke with Kristian that the time was now, that we had to take a deep breath and keep to the truth. And he agreed to that. The school psychologist had helped me; how I should handle the situation in relation to Kristian during the remand imprisonment, and now I asked her if it would be a good idea for me to write a letter to the parents in Kristian's class. She thought that was a really good idea. So I wrote a letter in which I explained that Andreas had been given a long prison sentence. I wrote that I hoped for some tolerance towards Kristian and that I also hoped very much that no one would hold Kristian accountable for his father's actions.[15]

Kristian's teacher also allowed Marie to come and talk about the situation in class and answer the children's questions, which among other things, were about what clothes Kristian's father had to wear and what he ate in prison.[16] This open approach has apparently been good for Kristian. He says that he has actually never experienced anyone saying or doing something mean because his father is in prison.[17] But there is no easy recipe for handling such situations. Psychologist Else Christensen explains that it is not always an advantage – or it can at least have disadvantages – for teachers at the school to know everything about what's going on:

> It's not always a good thing that the surroundings know that you have a problem. A child risks becoming "a child under observation" if the truth is told. That is, a child who the teachers keep a special eye on. And that's not necessary if she manages well in school. So it's her sanctuary. But... it can certainly also be an advantage that the school knows about the imprisoned father and thus understands the child better.[18]

If the teachers know that the child's parent is in prison, they will – for good or ill – keep a special eye on the child, or the child will probably experience it as such. This might be nice for some children. As Kristian explained: "The good teachers ask you if you want to go outside for a while and chat with them when you're sad. They kind of see it when you're sad."[19] The same observation was apparent among 25 children of imprisoned parents in a British study who felt that the teachers' knowledge of their circumstances was helpful. For example, a 17-year-old girl said: "The head and two of my teachers have been really good, though. I felt embarrassed about it at first but they have made it easy for me to talk to them."[20] For other children, however, teachers and friends knowing about the imprisonment can make the school less of a sanctuary. A 23-year-old boy in the same British study explained how "school helps me forget".[21] The family therapist from Engelsborg similarly emphasised that it can be important for children to have breathing space so they can think about something other than the imprisoned parent.[22] Naturally, a positive outcome depends on the individual child, but it also hinges on how the school and the individual teacher handle the situation.

It may be that parents and children choose a compromise and tell the adults around the child but not the other children in class. Children can certainly be afraid of being bullied, but "secrets, by their nature, create anxiety, tension, shame, guilt and fear within those who keep them".[23] It can be difficult for children to keep something so important to themselves, and it can also mean that children have to lie or come up with all kinds of stories to cover the truth.[24] Secrecy can also lead to even more unpleasant attention than if the truth was told from the outset. A child psychologist explains: "Experience shows that those children who, in one way or another, are involuntarily revealed, if it is not spoken about and if it is not addressed, are exposed to getting nicknames or to bullying."[25]

Again, it is difficult to say what is best. Children have a right to privacy, not everyone has the right to know that their father or mother is in prison and there is no obligation that children's lives be an open book.[26] A psychologist from the Danish Red Cross, who has worked with prisoners' children, believes that the parents must speak with the child and together find a balance both children and parents are comfortable with.[27] The same opinion is shared by a family counsellor from SAVN: "It should not be a secret that mum or dad is in prison, but that does not mean that everyone needs to know."[28]

After the sentence

When a verdict is given and the sentence is imprisonment of a parent, a new situation arises for the family concerned. For some children, this is the first time they hear about the parent's imprisonment; for others, it brings a long period of uncertainty to an end. As a result of this clarification and new certainty, it is natural that the question about the relationship to the surroundings comes up – or reappears – immediately after sentencing. Should the school be involved? What about the social authorities? Should the child's friends be told? Is the imprisonment a family secret? In a number of families, some of these issues have already been clarified in the remand phase, but this is far from always the case, partly because many hope for acquittal.

For the affected children, there can be a certain relief in hearing about the sentence. For some, it is the first time they gain certain knowledge of what has happened and can make sure that their imprisoned parent is alive and well. In some cases, the certainty can concern the fact that an unsuitable, unstable and perhaps violent parent has been removed from the home. In many cases it is after the verdict that the family will decide what to tell others and perhaps to seek help. How the remaining parent tackles these problems can be extremely important for the affected children. Likewise, it can be difficult and painful for the children to handle this situation themselves in relation to their friendships and school or day-care surroundings.

A sentence of imprisonment also means that the parent concerned transfers from remand custody (if remand imprisonment has occurred) to serving the sentence. In Denmark, this typically means more liberal and better arrangements for visits, telephone calls and other contact between prisoners and their children. For those children who knew nothing about the remand imprisonment and are now informed, this can make possible the first visit to the imprisoned parent. How this takes place and what problems the visiting situation gives rise to are addressed in the following chapter.

10
Visiting in Prisons: Staff, Children, Conditions and Practice

Peter Scharff Smith and Janne Jakobsen

Thousands of children visit prisons daily in order to see a parent. But even though the prison, as an institution, has several centuries under its belt, it has generally not tried to adapt to the needs of these children. Fortunately, this is currently changing at least in some prisons in some parts of the world, but it is still difficult to imagine an institution further removed from the idea of a child-friendly place. Under all circumstances, many children *do* visit their imprisoned parents. As this fact gains more attention, it seems increasingly difficult to argue against taking the perspective and needs of these children seriously.

International research on children making prison visits

Several researchers have touched upon the question of how visiting in prison affects prisoners' children, and there is general agreement that while such visits are often very important for the children they can also be problematic, scary and challenging. Much of this research establishes that both prison conditions and the visiting situation are important but often difficult to handle:

> Maintaining contact can be fraught with difficulties such as busy booking lines, inconvenient visiting hours, a lack of transport, and the cost and distance of travel…Exacerbating these problems, prisons are clearly not family friendly places to visit. Poor visiting facilities and hostile attitudes of staff can put families off visiting, especially those with children.[1]

As described by a US researcher, "visiting conditions and restrictions around contact can be seen as contributing or mitigating parental distress, and in this manner connect to parenting".[2]

Contact between the child and the imprisoned parent is often very important, and good visits can have a positive effect on the children.[3] A 1997 British study, for example, concluded that children "developed fantasies and anxieties about their fathers which declined after prison visits had reassured them."[4] Various studies have also shown that the prisoners themselves generally value contact with the family.[5]

The COPING study based on data from Sweden, Germany, Romania and the United Kingdom found that "most children adapted successfully to the experience of visiting prison", but for a "smaller number this proved upsetting". Many of the participating children found it difficult to say goodbye, "and the aftermath of visits painful for some". While "children in the UK and Sweden mainly got used to the prison environment, particularly in less secure establishments", the children "in Germany and Romania found the prison environment more hostile and drab, and lacking facilities for families". Overall, the study concluded that "opportunities to engage in meaningful activities with the imprisoned parent were limited, which was hard for children of all ages".[6]

A small-scale evaluation of a specific visiting facility in a British prison revealed how critical visiting conditions are. The children in the study were very dissatisfied with visits in closed prisons but very appreciative of the special overnight visiting facility in Askham Grange Prison.[7]

Nevertheless, the available studies have generally not focused on the visiting situation as such and therefore not looked in greater detail at all the issues involved. That is what this chapter attempts to do by mapping all the potential problems and relevant questions with regard to children visiting their imprisoned parents. This chapter primarily uses Danish empirical data.

Imprisonment and visits in a Danish context

As in many other countries, the prison population has risen in Denmark during recent years – by around 25% in this century (see Chapter 16 for further information). The rate of imprisonment was 71 per 100,000 citizens in Denmark in May 2010, which is still very low compared to many other countries.[8]

One of the characteristics of the Danish prison system is an extensive use of so-called open prisons, where the regime is relatively liberal as far as prison regimes go. Of the prisons in Denmark, five of them are closed prisons and eight are open prisons. In addition, there are 36 local remand prisons and the "Copenhagen prison" institution, which includes three prison facilities primarily for remand prisoners.

To complicate things further, some of the closed prisons also have remand units – altogether there are 43 remand facilities. Finally, the prison service has eight small halfway houses. Out of the total Danish prison capacity of 4.123 spaces (average during 2012), the open prisons take up around a third (i.e. 1.309 spaces, compared to 1.792 remand and 884 closed facility spaces).[9] The atmosphere in an open prison is certainly very different from the closed prisons (i.e. maximum security). That said, open prisons can still in many ways be similar to low-security prisons in other parts of Europe, and Denmark's closed prisons arguably resemble closed prisons in several Western European countries.[10]

In Denmark, conjugal visits are allowed throughout the prison system and all visits can be carried out in private visiting rooms. The entire Danish prison system features only two visiting rooms in which prisoner and visitor are separated by a screen, and they are used relatively rarely.

One of the basic principles adhered to by the Danish Prison Service is the so-called principle of normalisation. The UN special rapporteur on torture Manfred Nowak, who visited Denmark in 2008, described this principle as a trademark of the Danish prison system,

> meaning that life behind bars reflects life outside to as great an extent as possible. Taken together with an attentive approach to the concerns of prisoners by prison staff, the result is generally a high standard of conditions of detention inside Danish prisons, both in terms of infrastructure and day-to-day living standards.[11]

There are also problems in Danish prisons beyond those that affect all prisons to some extent. Some of the current issues include overcrowding, a rise in the use of long-term remands in custody, a rise in the use of solitary confinement as disciplinary punishment, problems faced by female prisoners imprisoned in mixed-sex units and Greenlanders serving their sentence in Denmark. One particular issue is the use of pre-trial solitary confinement. The official reason for its use is the risk of collusion (i.e. the suspect interfering with the investigation). Since the late 1970s, this practice has been widely criticised within Denmark, and since the 1990s, international criticism (from the CPT and the UN) has been directed at Denmark as well as Norway and Sweden.[12] Legal scholars abroad have termed the practice of pre-trial solitary confinement as a "peculiarly Scandinavian phenomenon".[13] In Sweden it was recently discovered by the children's ombudsman that thousands of Swedish children each year were routinely subjected to solitary confinement in police detention (for up to four days) and more than one hundred children went on to remand prison, where they could stay in solitary confinement for months.[14]

The use of pre-trial solitary confinement has dropped significantly in Denmark during recent years, but what is much less known is the fact that remand imprisonment regimes in Denmark can come quite close to solitary confinement. A normal day for some remand prisoners who are officially not in solitary confinement is thus spent in isolation in the cell for 22–23 hours, with the 1-hour yard time as the only real access to social contact. As described in greater detail below, a significant proportion of remand prisoners are also subjected to a tight regime, including supervised visits. Furthermore, remand prisoners are typically not allowed to use the phone at all. Many are allowed one or two hours' company with another prisoner in the cell on a regular basis, but the defining features of the Danish remand regime are still isolation and strict control. This means that more than one- third of all inmates in Danish prisons likely serve under a regime characterised by isolation and very limited contact with family and friends. As a result, their daily routine is far removed from the principle of normalisation.

Safety considerations, prison culture and child-friendly initiatives in Denmark

When you visit a remand prison or a closed prison for sentenced prisoners, it is clear that the overall focus is on security. This is not surprising. Unfortunately, sometimes this focus is so rigid that there is far too little awareness of the needs of children. The physical settings, security precautions, rules, atmosphere, tone and culture are not exactly child-friendly in many institutions, and this means that it can be unpleasant and unsettling for children to visit their imprisoned parents. This is very undesirable and negatively impacts a group of children who are already suffering from the fact that they have to cope without their parents.

The Danish Prison and Probation Service has recently directed considerably more attention towards the needs of prisoners' children. This positive development began after the 1999 publication of the Danish National Centre for Social Research's report "Parents in Prison" (Forældre i fængsel). Initial efforts quickly trailed off but began again around 2005–2006, when SAVN, the Children's Council and the Danish Institute for Human Rights began working more intensively with the Prison and Probation Service in this particular area.

This chapter takes a closer look at the following issues and problems:

1. What are the children's experiences in connection with visits?
2. How quickly do children have the opportunity to visit their imprisoned parents after imprisonment has taken place?
3. How often and for how long do children have the possibility of visiting their imprisoned parents?
4. Transport problems and inconvenient visiting hours
5. The visiting facilities in the Prison and Probation Service's institutions
6. Certain institutions' special events and initiatives for imprisoned parents and their children
7. The employees' handling of visiting children
8. Security control of children
9. Supervised visits in connection with remand custody
10. Solitary confinement of parents in connection with remand custody.

The children's experiences

The visiting conditions in the Danish Prison Service's institutions have a significant impact on children's experiences of visiting their imprisoned parents. But other factors are equally important. How the visit is experienced depends to a high degree on the individual child's relationship with his or her imprisoned parent. The mood during the visit can also play a major role. A visit will obviously be unpleasant if there is ill feeling between the prisoner and the relative accompanying the child or between the prisoner and the prison staff.

Many children are worried about their imprisoned parents and visiting the prison can help calm the children.[15] A Danish prison officer explains: "Our impression is that children feel safe when coming here when they are within the walls and can see that quite ordinary people are found in here."[16]

Children themselves describe that they are often happy to come and visit because it gives them an opportunity to spend time with their imprisoned parent. Ten-year-old Cherie explains: "It's fun actually, even though you are shut in a teeny, tiny room. But it's still fun to visit him. Just talking with him again – that's really cool. Really cool. I just wish I could talk with him all the time."[17] Kristian agrees: "Visiting is good because I can spend time with my father."[18]

Several Danish children highlight problems when they tell about visits in Danish prisons. One boy explains: "I thought, what on earth are we going to do here? You've asked how things are going and then you sit there and look at your shoes and hope that the time will pass quickly even though you have looked forward to it the whole week."[19] Another child, who rarely visits his father, explains: "There's nothing to do, nothing. What should we do? We just sit and stare."[20] The arrival itself to a prison – with the unfamiliar atmosphere, uniformed staff and strict focus on security – can make the prison a difficult place for children. Some children are frightened by the prisoners, the security check and small visiting rooms. "Those people who work with the scanner are sometimes rude", explains one child.[21] Thirteen-year-old Line has had a similar experience: "I don't like the prison. When I visited him for the first time, I was mostly afraid of the officers."[22]

Children indicate that it is unpleasant to experience that their parent is locked up: "It was sort of very fenced in...The room we were in was very small...It wasn't especially nice...because he was shut in so much."[23] Another child describes the feeling of being imprisoned during the visit: "When he was in [closed prison X], we visited about every 14th day. Once, we had toys with us but the staff said that children had to stay in the room. That wasn't nice. When they closed the door, we were also in prison."[24]

How soon can children visit their imprisoned parent?

There is no legislation in Denmark on how much time may pass after imprisonment before the prisoner (in remand custody or serving a sentence) has a right to see his or her child or when a child has a right to see his or her imprisoned parent. As previously mentioned, a remand prisoner in Denmark has the right to one 30-minute visit per week, while a sentenced prisoner has the right to one 1-hour visit per week. However, it can take some time before a visit permit is granted and the first visit can actually take place. Nevertheless, a child often has an immediate need to see that mum or dad is fine. This applies especially in the case of violent arrest, or if the child has the experience that the parent has disappeared into thin air.

According to the Danish Institute for Human Rights' questionnaire survey, institutions differ in how soon a child is allowed to visit after the remanded or imprisoned parent has requested permission to be visited by his or her child. As far as remand prisoners are concerned, 56% of the participating police officers responded that it is possible for children to visit within one week after the remand prisoner has applied for a visit permit. Still, 14% of the police officers said that up to two weeks can pass. One police officer replied that up to a month can pass after the remand prisoner has applied for a visit permit.

Of the participating employees in the remand prisons, 46% responded that it is possible to have children visit within one week after the remand prisoner has applied for a visit permit, while 29% responded that up to two weeks can pass. Two people said that up to a month can pass, and one wrote that even two months can pass by.[25] Among remand prison staff surveyed, 18% placed a check mark by the option: "No set practice. This depends on whether the police has personnel who can monitor the visit". In the comment field, several prison employees also drew attention to the fact that the decision depends on the police if the remand prisoner has visit and correspondence control.[26] A member of the prison staff also emphasised that it can depend on whether there is room in the visiting facilities.[27] Regarding sentenced prisoners, 53% of the participating prison employees responded that it is possible for children to visit within one week after the prisoner has applied for visits. Thirteen percent responded that up to two weeks can pass.

But it can be much worse than that. A social worker employed by the social authorities wrote that he or she was working on a case where both the mother and father were in remand custody, and the eldest son (17) was also charged with being involved in the case: "As a result of this charge, he has not had the opportunity to visit his parents through the last 7 months."[28]

Overall, the responses from the police and employees in both remand prisons and prisons for sentenced prisoners indicate that the majority of prisoners can have visits within one week. However, a longer time can pass, and there are even a few examples of a really long time passing before the children are able to visit. Different circumstances can come into play, not least in relation to the imprisoned parents. That up to a month can pass must be considered altogether unacceptable – especially when viewed from a child's perspective. As reported by Else Christensen, it is highly problematic that it can take two months before a 2-year-old child can see his mother.[29]

A recent report by the Children's Ombudsman in Sweden revealed how even children deprived of their liberty – in police arrest and during remand imprisonment – are typically put into solitary confinement with special restrictions and often without the possibility of seeing mum or dad for a long time. In one case, a youngster under 18 was not allowed to see his mother for around two and a half months; in another case, a boy had spent 47 days on remand and still not been allowed to receive visits from his parents. Such practices seem to be routine and illustrate how a complete lack of attention to some of the most basic needs of children can thrive in criminal justice systems – and in Scandinavian welfare states that are sometimes highlighted for their (alleged) humanity in these areas.[30]

How often and for how long can children visit their imprisoned parents?

As mentioned in Chapter 6, remand regimes are very strict with regard to visits and maintaining contact. This has a lot to do with the desire to protect the police investigation. The legislation is based on the tension between the need to fight crime and the obligation to protect prisoners' rights, but the question of when a remand prisoner's child has a right to see his or her parent has not been considered. As previously mentioned, legislation in Norway has set new standards in that regard. In Denmark as in most other countries, the child's right to visit in prison is not specified in national law and in practice can only be realised through the prisoner's right to receive visits.

When the remand prisoner is subject to correspondence and visit control or is in solitary confinement, the police approve and monitor the visits. This can affect the visiting possibilities and frequency. There are no official statistics in the Danish system on how often correspondence and visit control are used, but recent figures show that such measures are applied routinely. A count made on 27 May 2013 showed that 70.4% of all remand prisoners in the entire Danish prison system (who were awaiting trial) at that time were subjected to correspondence and visit control.[31] The Prison and Probation Service approves visits for the other remand prisoners.

The Danish Institute for Human Rights' questionnaire survey indicates that there is a significant difference as to how often and for how long visits actually take place. Just under one-third (32%) of prison staff responded that remand prisoners have the possibility of receiving visitors several times per week; 45% said once per week and two staff members said once every two weeks. There is no set practice according to 36%, but this depends on whether or not the police have staff to monitor the visit. In other words, visitation length and frequency vary greatly from one remand prison to another and, by all appearances, from case to case.

When police officers were asked, 82% responded that, in practice, remand prisoners have the possibility for visits once per week. But some police staff also mention lack of resources as a problem, and visits are sometimes "cancelled due to insufficient police staff for supervision of the visit".[32]

When remand prison staff were asked about the length of the visits remand prisoners actually get, 61% responded that they have one hour available, 25% reported one to two hours and 21% said longer than two hours. According to 21%, it also depends on what they and the police have time and resources for.[33]

The majority of the police officers responded that remand prisoners are allowed to have visits for one hour a week, but 12% said that it depends greatly on what they – the police – have time and resources for.[34]

A police sergeant described how visits, which the police must supervise, are in the hands of the individual officer. She described how she sometimes lets a few prisoners have extra visits if she has the time and deems it important, especially if children are involved. On the other hand, in the summer period it is sometimes only possible for visits every 14th day because police officers go on holiday.[35] A prison officer from a remand prison described the same problem: "As a rule, remand prisoners with visiting and correspondence control have one supervised visit per week. This normally also stands in practice, however not during the summer holiday period."[36] Furthermore, as concluded by a police sergeant, there are "different practices from police station to police station".[37]

The actual number of visits a remand prisoner can have – especially if restrictions and supervised visits are in place – is thus not only a question of rights and principles but is highly influenced by the available resources, which can lead to a practice dropping below the legal minimum standards. Seen from a children's perspective, two things can be concluded. First, such variation, uncertainty, and dependence on police time and resources is unreasonable in connection with how many visits a child can have. Secondly, the minimum standard of a half-hour visit, as well as the more "normal" one-hour visit, is too little time.

When it comes to sentenced prisoners, children normally have the possibility of visiting for more than one hour each week. Nearly three-quarters (73%) of prison employees responded that the prisoners can receive visitors several times per week.[38] None of the participating prison employees has responded that the visits last one hour or less, 20% responded that the visits last one to two hours and 33% respond that they last more than two hours. There are several who did not respond to this question but commented that there are longer visiting times.[39]

To summarise, the gathered data indicate that the minimum requirements in Denmark for visits to remand and sentenced prisoners are generally complied with and there is often the possibility of slightly longer and perhaps more frequent visits than the prisoners have a right to. In some cases, the minimum requirements are apparently not complied with at all.

There are other issues besides resources and case-processing times that can have a bearing on how long and how often children can see their imprisoned parent. To begin with, the prisoner and a possible partner or caregiver typically assess whether a child should be included in a visit at all and in such a case, how often. A purely practical problem that can "rob" children of visiting their imprisoned parents arises in families with many children. A mother with four children explained that she has to draw lots between the children when they are to visit, because only a limited number of visitors are allowed.[40] A more common problem is that the prisoner may need to meet and talk about things with an adult relative (often the children's mother) without the children being there. A seasoned prison officer explains: "Often, the 'adults' have one conflict or another and then in their frustration, forget that they have a child with them."[41]

Transport and inconvenient visiting times

"I haven't visited him very often. We have to spend a whole day driving just to be there for two hours."[42]

As previously described, according to the European Prison Rules, prisoners should normally be placed in a prison close to their homes or near the place where their social rehabilitation will take place (rule 17.1). Likewise, the Danish Sentence Enforcement Act states that imprisonment must be carried out in the vicinity of the sentenced prisoner's place of residence when practically possible (§ 23), but for various reasons, this is not always possible. One major problem is that there is a significant shortage of open prison spaces on Zealand and in the Copenhagen area.

The Copenhagen Police chief superintendent reported that they also experience this problem in relation to remand prisoners: "My experience is that, generally, a great deal of consideration is taken so that the arrested person is placed in a remand prison close to his or her home. This is the police's decision. But situations can occur where remand prisons close to the home are too full and the detainee is placed further away."[43]

A prison officer explained that this is often a major problem: "What I experience most is the frustration of the prisoners when they are to serve their sentences in another part of the country than where their children live."[44] A remand prison officer does not find that the prisoners talk a lot about their children, but when they do, "then it's often something about them being far away from home and it's difficult and expensive in regard to transport".[45] The extreme example in the case of Denmark is that of sentenced prisoners from Greenland who are transferred to a closed prison in Denmark (there are currently no closed prison facilities in Greenland, but a prison is under construction). This means that these prisoners are placed several thousand kilometres away from home and relatives – a practice that could be in breach of article 8 of the ECHR.[46]

But even the much shorter distances within Denmark can create huge problems. It is inexpedient if, for example, children have to spend a whole Saturday on transport for a one-hour visit with their imprisoned parent. A treatment consultant in a prison stated that prisoners often "feel that they have no right to insist that the kids must come and see their dad in the prison. Some children travel very far with public modes of transport just to spend time with their father for 1–2 hours."[47] No wonder that the financial aspects of long transportation are also experienced as problematic. Long transportation to a prison can also be very expensive for families. An ordinary return train ticket from Copenhagen on Zealand to Aarhus on Jutland, for example, costs 748 Danish Krone, which corresponds to something like 100 Euro, while going back and forth from Copenhagen to Horsens (also on Jutland) would cost around the half.[48] These are substantial transportation costs for families with low income.

As an example of the long and relatively difficult transport conditions many relatives face, the new Østjylland State Prison (Eastern Jutland) is instructive. In 2006, it replaced the old Horsens State Prison built in 1853. The new prison accounts for the children's perspective in the architecture, the visiting facilities and a number of other areas (which will be discussed later). But the visiting logistics have not been especially well considered. The prison is isolated out in a field, and a bus drives by once every hour to and from the closest bus station. From the bus stop, there is a 1.3-kilometre walk to the prison itself. As a prison staff member explained: "It's a long way in pouring rain, especially for a mother with a pram and two toddlers."[49] The bus timetable does not fit in with the visiting hours, and the visiting hours can be unsuitable for children. For example, in some prisons the visiting hours are on weekday mornings when schoolchildren have to take time off school in order to visit.[50]

The Østjylland State Prison case is a good example of how important issues can easily escape attention, although an effort has been made to take at least some of the needs of prisoners' children into account.

Østjylland has attractive apartments for overnight visits for families, but how these families actually get themselves transported relatively conveniently all the way to the prison is another matter. I remember the same issue surfacing in 2011 when I was a member of an assessment committee that had to look at architectural proposals for a new closed prison on Falster in Denmark. One of the issues we discussed was child-friendly visiting conditions. The director of the Falster municipality was also a member of the committee, and at one point I asked him whether they had good bus lines passing by the prison. He looked at me and said that there were no bus lines at all – and the Prison Service had no thoughts on this matter since it fell outside their responsibility. At the next meeting, the director told me that he had looked into the matter and that it could take several years to establish a new bus line due to the bureaucracy involved. He was glad that I had mentioned the issue. When the prison opens a couple of years from now, they might actually have a bus line.

I also visited the newly established children's officer in Norway's Halden Prison in March 2013. Halden Prison is a closed prison, which opened in 2010 with excellent physical facilities, including an apartment for overnight family visits. But the prison is situated in rural area, and the children's officer told me how, until recently, visiting adults and children had to walk a long distance from the bus stop along a motorway without sidewalks – which could be outright dangerous with small children. She had managed to get the municipality to clear a small forest road where visitors can now walk all the way to the prison.

The visiting facilities in Danish prisons

The visiting facilities and associated possibilities in the Prison and Probation Service's institutions differ greatly, although the standards have risen significantly during the last five years or so. They have also become more similar. Major differences still exist between the closed and the open prisons. The latter, with their far more liberal regimes, can arrange visiting in a different way than closed prisons. For instance, a 2008 survey showed that, in the majority of the so-called open prisons, visits in the rooms and access to play areas, sports halls and outdoor facilities are possible. Many open prisons also allow prisoners and their visitors to make meals together.[51] On the other hand, the remand prisons typically resemble the closed prisons, due to the similar focus on control and security, whereas the small halfway houses are usually even more "open" than the open prisons.

In some of the older remand prisons, in particular, the visiting facilities are quite bad and not at all child friendly. The visiting rooms are small and drab and without room enough for children and parents to play together. In some places, the selection of toys is meagre and worn, with toy cars that do not work, one-eyed dolls and books with torn pages. Moreover, the toys in several institutions are only for really young children. As a rule, children are not permitted to bring along their own toys or, for example, school books.

Many visiting facilities are set up for adults to visit, not children. For the majority of 5 year olds it is unnatural, difficult and boring to sit on a chair and talk with their parents for an hour. But many prisons and some remand prisons have improved their visiting facilities and made family rooms, which look much more inviting and have a better selection of toys. However, in some remand prisons, the visiting rooms still have the character of what was previously termed "screwing rooms", where the defining feature is the access to sheets, condoms and a place to lie down.

Some parents simply do not think that they can invite their children to visit in such surroundings. For instance, a father explained: "The first time I went to prison I didn't tell my children. I just thought the visiting conditions were too miserable."[52] Another father who was in remand custody in a closed Danish prison described a visit by his daughter: "The visiting room was gross. There was a narrow bed with paper on it, a bowl with condoms and a tub for used needles. You simply can't let children come and visit in such a place."[53] A third father also spoke about the visiting rooms:

> Those "screwing rooms" are completely unacceptable. The sofa is full of stains and there's a box with 2½ broken toys, then there's a handful of condoms, paper towels, a clean sheet and a notice to remember to use the sheet.... And then you've got 1–2 hours in there. You cannot even sit and eat there, there's not even a flower, nothing.... The rooms are depressingly bad. There should be a room where you can be with your children and have a nice time. A place that was a little cosy.[54]

Parents also point out that it is gross to go into a visiting room that reeks of smoke and that the visiting rooms are far too small for visits by children.[55]

It is apparent from the Danish Institute for Human Rights' questionnaire survey that several among the prison staff were at that time also dissatisfied with the physical visiting conditions. "The buildings and the way they are constructed is generally a problem", concluded one staff member.[56] Another simply stated that "improvement of the visiting facilities" was in order.[57] A third prison officer asked for "larger visiting rooms";[58] another similarly wanted "more space".[59] Staff also pointed out that there ought to be "a visiting room that is intended for only children's visits",[60] "family visiting rooms"[61] or "special playrooms for children of various age groups".[62]

Some of the above quotes and examples are more than ten years old and many prisons have improved their visiting facilities significantly in recent years. But there are still visiting facilities in the Danish Prison and Probation Service that raise the question of whether they allow prisoners and their children to "maintain and develop family relationships in as normal a manner as possible", as the European Prison Rules prescribe.[63] Some of the visiting conditions described above are not compatible with the Prison and Probation Service's own minimum standards for visiting rooms either. According to the 2004-issued guidelines, visiting rooms must have a "natural, friendly atmosphere" and "bright and friendly rooms".[64]

The different qualities of visiting facilities are noted and felt by the children. Maja, for example, maintained that there is a big difference from prison to prison. In some places she visited her father in a small room where the door was locked, and if you had to use the bathroom, you had to be followed by a guard. Maja felt as if she "was imprisoned herself". However, she has also experienced good visiting facilities in one of the prisons: "It was really nice. There was also a room with pillows, and there were the opportunity to cook together and eat together. And there were many other children, and you could just play together. It was a whole visit department. It was great compared to that little room. Especially when I was younger, it was great to be able to run around a little bit."[65] Such a description fit with the standards in many of the recently established "family visiting rooms".

Among the open prisons, Jyderup deserves to be highlighted as a forerunner. Here, there have been good practices for a number of years when it comes to children visiting. The greater part of the prison area accounts for the visiting facilities in Jyderup State Prison, which creates a relatively normal frame around visitation with the children – as normal as it can be in a prison. For instance, there are green areas and a small church on Jyderup prison's grounds. In the prison itself, there are spaces for making meals and eating together and meeting other prisoners' children under relaxed conditions. The weekend visiting hours are from half past nine in the morning until half past seven at night, which also gives the families the possibility of a more natural visitation where they can do everyday things such as prepare meals, eat together, play and watch TV.[66] Such visiting arrangements clearly live up to the principle of normalisation.[67]

Of the closed prisons, perhaps the most prominent forerunner in this area was Vridsløselille State Prison to which the Egmont Foundation granted funds for a renovation of the visiting area, a project managed by architects Bosch and Fjord. Unfortunately, the visiting rooms have subsequently been affected by dry rot and had to be renovated again.[68] Now the prison, which has been in use from 1859, is slated for closing in a couple of years' time.

When the Østjylland Prison was constructed, two visiting apartments were set up for prisoners and their families to have a longer visitation as well as stay overnight – and the apartments are frequently used.[69] The visiting apartments have an open floor plan, with a small kitchen, a dining room, a living room, two bedrooms and a small terrace.[70] Normally, the space can accommodate two or three children, but an extra bed has been set up occasionally. If a prisoner wants to use the apartment for a visit with family, the prison and the prisoner write to the municipality, which then assesses if it is a good idea for the family concerned to be together in the visiting apartment for 47 hours.[71] Using the visiting apartments is a big plus for the children, but the regime and the conditions governing their use are not entirely unproblematic. First and foremost, the prisoners as well as the adult relatives and children are locked in to the apartments for a period of up to two days. It would be better for the children to have the possibility of going outdoors into a small courtyard area, a playground or something similar.[72] As a treatment consultant from Østjylland Prison explained: "None of us on the outside can imagine being locked in for 47 hours."[73] Recently, the closed prison Herstedvester also opened a visiting apartment, which is very homely and includes access to a small outside area. During my visit to the prison on 27 November 2013, some of the staff, including one of the newly appointed children's officers, told me about some of the practical challenges involved in using the apartment. The challenges included striking a balance between ensuring the children were doing fine and respecting the privacy of the visiting families. For example, staff used to make a number of short unannounced visits, and some prison officers simply opened the door with their keys and hence risked bumping into half-dressed people in the apartment. The practice now agreed upon is to knock on the door, announce the visit and wait a short time before entering.

In any case, the access to overnight visiting rooms resembling normal apartments is a huge improvement and allows for a completely different and more family-like visiting experience. Such apartments have now been set up in three of the closed prisons in Denmark. The new prison on Falster, currently under construction, will have a family apartment as well. Similar arrangements exist in other countries, including England, the United States, Sweden and Norway – although sometimes they are only for use by mothers.[74]

As mentioned, several prisons and remand prisons have upgraded their visiting facilities during recent years, including Vestre Prison – Denmark's largest prison, which primarily holds remand prisoners. One of the biggest concerted efforts to improve visiting facilities has taken place as part of the previously mentioned project on children's officers in Danish prisons and remand prisons. In the four participating prisons and remand prisons, visiting conditions and the associated procedures have been made more child friendly. One of the participating institutions already had a family visiting room, but the other three made such rooms and one remand prison also renovated the entire entrance and security check area to make it more child friendly. The new facilities are very welcoming and live up to the principle of normalisation even when viewed from a children's perspective.[75] The process of improving visiting facilities is set to continue in the coming years as part of the introduction of childrens's officers in all of the Danish prisons and remand prisons.

One of the very general problems surrounding children's visits in the closed prisons is that there are only a few places where you can go outside. The state prison in Ringe has a playground that can be used when prisoners have their children visit. This playground was renovated in 2010 and now sets a high and child-friendly standard. Small courtyards have also been attached to the new visiting facilities in Blegdamsvejens Prison. Allowing visitors to go outdoors is a unique feature for a remand prison like Blegdamsvejen.[76] These initiatives are of great importance, because prisoners' children call for doing physical outdoor activities together with their imprisoned parent.

In summary, the physical visiting facilities in Danish prisons vary significantly and depend partly on the security level of the institution, in addition to local facilities and culture. That standards vary is reflected in the fact that some prison and police staff, as well as some social workers, do not think that visits should take place in the prisons at all – or at the police station for that matter. A prison officer wrote: "I don't think it's okay that the [children] have to go into a remand prison and be locked inside a visiting room. Hear the keys rattle and gates slamming."[77] A social worker suggested that "demands must be made that the child may not visit in the prison or at the police station, but that the visits can be held either in the home or a 'neutral' place".[78] It is conceivable that these responses are coloured by the visiting conditions in local remand prisons, which the person concerned knows about and where visiting conditions have not been improved (or were at the time). If the person were speaking about one of the above mentioned institutions, where significant improvements have taken place, the response would likely have been different.

Nevertheless, it can be a problem when staff in some prisons make their own moral judgements and do not want children visiting. Recently, the Swedish Prison and Probation Service has experienced backlash over its process of making their institutions and visiting practices more child friendly. As the focus on the best interest of the child has increased in recent years in connection with prison visits, some Swedish prisons have interpreted this to mean that children should not visit their imprisoned parents at all.[79]

Special events and initiatives for imprisoned parents and their children

"Last Sunday the chaplain held yet another of those terrific events for relatives. It's fantastic that you can run around and play football with your children."[80] This is how a prisoner described a family event in Vridsløselille State Prison (a closed maximum-security prison). According to the deputy prison governor, Vridsløselille has between four and six family events per year.[81]

Institutions participating in the children's officer project have also held special events for prisoners' children. Other prisons have done that as well. The open state prison in Renbæk, for example, has held Shrovetide celebrations with costumes and the "hitting the barrel" activity for children.[82] Jyderup State Prison has conducted an annual summer trip to Sweden for a number of prisoners and their children.[83] In Jyderup, annual Christmas parties are also held. Prison employees take along their own children, and "no one can see who is who".[84] This is certainly atypical for the typical institutional prison culture, which easily tends towards a "them" and "us" relationship between employees and the prisoners (although this depends on cultures and practices in individual institutions and can change over time).[85] In any case, such events for prisoners and their children are still relatively rare. Of the participating prisons in the Danish Institute for Human Rights' questionnaire survey, only four responded that they had special events for children and their parents.

In Denmark, parent courses or parent groups within the framework of the prison service are not standard, but this is currently changing. As a trial project, the Centre for Family Development held a parent course in the open Jyderup State Prison and a similar course in the closed prison in Vridsløselille, but the latter never gained the needed support from the prisoners and had to be cancelled. Parent study circles and courses have however been carried out successfully in one prison and one remand prison as part of the children's officer project, and in Vestre Prison (remand) in Copenhagen as part of a project called "Dad Behind Bars".[86] The experience gained from this work is currently being assessed by the Danish Prison Service and will hopefully feed into a model of future parental programs or study circles for imprisoned parents.

Prison staff and visiting children

How the prison staff treat children and how they welcome them can be of significant importance. If the children feel – rightly or not – that the employees are stern or condescending, this can ruin the visit from the outset and impact the contact with the parent. The entire staff culture and the mood surrounding visits is thus crucial. However, prison research shows that both staff culture and the general prison culture – which prisoners, staff and the physical context combine to create – can vary greatly from prison to prison. How the prison functions on a daily basis and whether or not prisoners experience fair and respectful treatment is clearly important. With regard to prisons in England, Liebling and Arnold have found that "the relational aspects of a prison's life, and its ethos, were crucial to the prison experience".[87] The entire experience of time in prison was thus "qualitatively different when relationships in general – or individual transactions – were distant or poor".[88] Ultimately, this was mostly about the "attitudes of staff" and if they treated the prisoners fairly and respectfully.[89]

It is clear that the same mechanisms, at least to some extent, must apply in relation to relatives' and children's prison visits.[90] If the local staff culture – in a given prison, or among a specific staff group in an individual prison block or in the visiting block – produces prisoner treatment that is not respectful and dignified, then there is a high probability that this will also rub off on the treatment of visitors. The relatives' association SAVN has found that one of the most important aspects for the relatives – adults as well as children – is the way in which they are received by prison staff: "You can improve the physical frameworks as much as you like, but if the atmosphere is bad and judgmental, then everything else is of no use."[91]

However, there are no fixed rules on how the prison officers should behave towards prisoners' children, or on what the children may or may not take in with them when they visit their imprisoned parent. The management in the various institutions is responsible for these issues. Within the framework of the Sentence Enforcement Act, they have the right to draw up the rules that apply in the prison concerned.

There is no doubt that procedures differ from institution to institution. For example, the rules on what can be brought on a visit vary from prison to prison. Some prisons have their rules written down and supply them to visitors but at the time of the survey less than a third of the institutions had such rules. Children may bring toys on visits according to 64% of the participating remand prison staff and only 28% of the prison staff. A full 75% of the remand prison staff and 39% of the prison staff said a child is allowed to take a drawing in with them. A small percentage of staff – 25% of remand and 11% of prison – responded that it depends on whether they have time to check what the children want to take in with them for the visit. This means that many children do not even get a clear message regarding what they may bring along. Naturally, this can give rise to frustration, as Kristian explained: "So you're allowed to take a drawing in with you, and then you're not the next time. So you can't take a gift inside one time and then you're allowed to take something along another time anyway and it's just really annoying."[92]

In the survey, all the participants who work in a remand prison and 93% of those who work in a prison responded that their institution has no written set of rules on how staff shall treat visiting children. That the welcoming depends a great deal on the individual staff member is something Maria knows a lot about: "I wonder who's working in the prison today? My children chat a lot about that in the car", she says.[93] Marie's son, Kristian, described some of the prison officers as "very kind", and others as "harsh". Marie explained that one time Kristian began to argue with a prison officer because he was not allowed to take a Pokémon card in with him to show his father. Kristian was told that if he could not understand it, then he just was not allowed to go into the prison. For a period following this incident, Kristian began refusing to go on visits because he thought it was idiotic. When the Danish Institute for Human Rights spoke with Marie, she and her children had just had a really good visiting experience: "We went to visit yesterday and two female prison officers were working. They were really nice. I really wanted to say to them afterwards: Listen, it is really, really wonderful that you smile and laugh with us, thank you."[94]

According to the survey, almost none of the prison officers feel well equipped, in terms of training, to handle prisoners' children. In fact, 92% said that relatives play a very small part or no part at all in their training. On the other hand, some institutions and employees try to do something to make the visits more pleasant for the visiting children.

> For Christmas last year, we had applied for some money from the remand prison to get Christmas gifts for the prisoners' children through the Salvation Army. And when the children came to visit up to Christmas, they were given a gift as if it was the prisoners who had bought them for the children. It made a huge impression to see the happy children's lit-up faces.[95]

Besides the importance of the prison staff treating visiting children in an appropriate way, the atmosphere the children experience between their imprisoned parent and the staff in the prison is also very important. A family therapist explained: "The behaviour displayed towards the imprisoned father, by the officers who meet the visitors is, as far as the children are concerned, the gate into understanding how their father is treated when they're not there."[96] A staff member in the central block in Vestre Prison in Copenhagen emphasised that it is also about the language and the tone in the prison world in general. He says that many of the employees use "the prisoners' own language" towards the prisoner; it can be difficult to switch tone when children are visiting.[97]

Security checking of children

Prison staff is in close contact with prisoners' children in connection with the security checking procedure, which the children have to go through when they arrive. In the majority of prisons, this takes place almost like at the airport where you have to walk through a metal detector. But sometimes the control is more extensive.

"Yesterday we found heroin in an 11-year-old child's trousers. So the control and frisking becomes more stringent for a period", explained a supervisor for the visiting block at Vestre Prison.[98] Incidents over which the child has no influence can mean that suddenly the visiting child must endure more thorough security checks. Dogs were also introduced a few years ago as occasional guests in the Danish Prison Service, and visitors – including children – will sometimes be subjected to dog searches. Some of the prisons I visited claim to never subject children to dog searches, but others sometimes do.

It is very important how the prison staff handles the control and particularly the frisking of children. Some children find the meeting with the prison officers and the required security controls unsettling and unpleasant. Kristian described his first visit to his father in the remand prison: "The first time was weird...and sort of...not so comfortable. And the [prison officers] were a little like the police, with uniforms and such. So you didn't want to do anything wrong."[99] Kristian had his shirt pulled up so the prison officer could ensure that he did not have anything stuck to his stomach. "That's not so nice", he says and does not want to talk more about this.[100]

Another boy, Mads, was sometimes allowed to play football with a soft ball inside the prison when he was on a visit. But he did not like being there. He also had a bad experience: "Once I had a gift with me for dad, they destroyed it because they had to see what was inside."[101]

Many prison officers explained that they try to get the children through the control procedure as discreetly and gently as possible, with a bit of playing around, smiles and humour. They try to create a relaxed atmosphere by chit-chatting, crouching down to the child's eye level, showing and explaining: "We take a great deal of consideration when the children are uneasy. Among other things, we crouch down and show them the handheld metal detector and let them hold it because, usually, that's what they are afraid of."[102]

This is, however, not always the image you get from the relatives. Marie thinks that the control sometimes takes place in an unnecessarily harsh way:

> I think it's fine to go through a metal detector, but that you have to spread your arms and legs and put up with prison guards who sneer "Turn around!" I think that's very severe for the children. Sometimes we also have to take our shoes and belts off. The children feel as though they're under suspicion.[103]

Maja described, at the age of 17, how she has had many different experiences with prison guards in many different prisons throughout her childhood: "Some places are really good, and some places are really bad. They [prison staff] could smile a little more, instead of acting like robots...I remember from the time when we were young – if there was something we had made for him at woodwork or art – they had to stand and open it all. It seemed crazy to me. It was humiliating. They almost tore it up and didn't wrap it up again. Well, I just think: They can't be so busy, that they can't do it more nicely – or just say they have to take a small look at it."[104]

Supervised visits in connection with remand custody

A particularly intense security control arises when a remand prisoner only has permission for supervised visits. In such a case, the police are present during the visit in order to ensure that the case is not spoken about. The police officer who supervises the visit can either be the officer who works on the case, a member of a special visiting unit or a "random" officer who is ordered to supervise visits on the day concerned.

Having only one hour or half an hour to visit each week, and only then with a police officer present, can be a very stressful experience and extremely awkward and problematic for visiting children. Unfortunately there are no official Danish statistics on how often supervised visits and correspondence control – which normally go together under the designation "B and B" ("brev- og besøgskontrol") – is imposed on prisoners. From countless visits to remand prisons one gets the impression that while the use of solitary confinement during pre-trial has gone down significantly, there has been an increase in the use of supervised visits and correspondence control. This theory is supported by the few figures available. As already described, a count made on the 27 May 2013 showed that 70.4% of all remand prisoners in the entire Danish prison system at that time were subjected to correspondence and visit control.[105] During two visits to Vestre Prison in 2012 and 2013, the prison governor described how around 60% of all remand prisoners were subjected to supervised visits and correspondence control, which also confirm the commonness of this practice.[106]

These figures, in others words, indicate that more than half and perhaps around two-thirds of all remand prisoners – more than 20% of the entire Danish prison population – are subjected to a very strict regime by which they spend up to 23 hours in their cell daily, are typically not allowed to use the phone, have their letters checked, and have access to only one hour or half-hour visit each week with a police officer present. This is a severe regime, and the Danish Institute for Human Rights is currently conducting a study to get more reliable information on the use of supervised visits and correspondence control, as well as on the remand regime in general. The way that many remand prisons and the police currently conduct supervised visits can have an even more drastic consequence for prisoners' children, namely, that they do not see their imprisoned parents at all or only very rarely. Due to the need for surveillance staff, supervised visits can often only take place Monday to Friday between 10 am and until early afternoon . This is in the middle of an ordinary school day for children, which makes it virtually impossible to visit regularly.

In any case, the police and the prosecutors naturally tend to see such regimes as useful tools. When asked about the use of supervised visits, the majority of police officers find it is an advantage if the officer working on the case is also doing the supervision. "It makes everything go more smoothly", says one officer.[107] "The family can get advice at the same time",[108] says another, and one officer claims that "knowing each other is an advantage".[109] Only 7% of the participating police officers have found that this has given rise to problems, and one officer explains that it can result in "the arrested person spending time on talking/discussing with the officer instead of with the child".[110]

At some police stations and in some remand prisons, specially assigned police officers have an office in the prison and almost always supervise the visits. This may be a specific, appointed person within the police or an older reserve officer in plain clothes. An assistant detective emphasises that at his/her station, "visit friends" are used when the police do not have the time to supervise visits.[111] According to some officers, however, there can be a difference between the younger and the older officers, with the younger ones a little rougher on the edges.

The police and remand prison staff find, on the whole, that the children are happy to come on a visit. They are perhaps a little insecure the first time, but according to the questionnaire responses, this usually passes once they have visited a few times. Some children think it is exciting that the police are present. Others find that the children are, most often, uneasy at visits and/or are afraid of the police. This also depends a great deal on the relationship to the remand imprisoned parent.

It is quite possible that the remand prison staff and perhaps the police in particular (who are especially positive about the visiting situation) are subjective in their responses. In any event, it is remarkable that five social workers who have accompanied children to supervised visits perceive the situation very differently and describe how they have generally found that it affected the children greatly. The children's reactions are described as "insecure", "pressured by the situation", "trapped" and "uncertain". One of the social workers described a child who was very sad after a visit because there was a lot he or she wanted to talk about, but it was difficult to get it out and time was of the essence. Another writes how some children are very embarrassed, some children cry and some children are quiet. Moreover, there are children who are angry and short-tempered towards their parents, and there are children who have difficulty accommodating the fact that the parents are very upset.[112]

A family therapist says that many of the children she has been in contact with at the Engelsborg Family House have told her that it has not been nice to go on visits: "They feel there is a slightly unpleasant atmosphere, and then it's boring. There's nothing to do and in the end, you can't find anything more to talk about. If it's a supervised visit, they become a little shy because they think it's very unpleasant that someone is sitting there and listening to their conversation."[113]

Kristian described such a situation: "The first prison he, [father] was in, it was just like ARGH! An officer had to stand there and hear what we talked about. We sat in such a small room and it felt as if you were completely surrounded by people you didn't know."[114]

Solitary confinement

In connection with remand imprisonment in Denmark, a security level exists beyond correspondence and visit control: pre-trial solitary confinement. If the remand imprisoned parent is in solitary confinement, a particularly difficult situation can arise in relation to contact with the children. As mentioned previously, Denmark – as well as Norway and Sweden – has a special history in this area, and the use of solitary confinement during pre-trial is one of the issues that has received the most international human rights criticism during recent decades. Many other forms of solitary confinement are also used routinely in Scandinavian prisons, including punitive isolation, administrative isolation and so-called voluntary isolation. In Denmark the use of pre-trial solitary confinement (to avoid collusion) has dropped significantly but the use of punitive isolation – that is, solitary confinement as a disciplinary measure – has more than doubled the last decade and was used 2,892 times in 2012.[115]

The fundamental problem is that when you put people into solitary confinement under conditions where they typically remain in their cells for about 22–24 hours every day and have minimal access to psychological, meaningful social contact, they are exposed to a number of potentially negative effects. The effects of solitary confinement has been the object of numerous studies internationally and in Denmark, and such studies clearly show that a significant number of prisoners in solitary confinement will experience negative health effects.[116] Among the possible negative effects are anxiety and depression, but solitary confinement can also cause a number of other psychological and physiological problems as well as outright psychotic behaviour.[117] Accordingly, the CPT concludes that "all forms of solitary confinement without appropriate mental and physical stimulation are likely in the long term to have damaging effects, resulting in deterioration of mental faculties and social abilities".[118]

In connection with remand imprisonment, solitary confinement occurs very suddenly. The person is arrested (on the street, in the home, etc.) and then placed directly in solitary confinement. For the children, this basically means two things: 1) the parent is suddenly extremely restricted in his or her connection with family; and 2) the parent can be harmed by the isolation, which can have a profound indirect effect on the children.

Solitary confinement of a remand prisoner can have the consequence that the contact between the child/children and the parent stops entirely for long periods. However, police officers state that it is normal practice to grant permission for solitary confined prisoners to receive visits from their children.[119] But it is obvious that negative health effects can impact the parent's role and perhaps also result in the lack of will or ability to meet with the children, in which case family relationships can be harmed severely.

Several of the prisoners Else Christensen interviewed for her study had experienced being in solitary confinement in connection with remand imprisonment.[120] The majority had experienced it as an intense strain, and some said that it did affect their contact with their children: "I was in solitary confinement for 7 months and only saw my children after 6 months. For the first 4 months I had a visiting ban...I thought that was unreasonable. I felt really bad about that."[121]

If a traumatic experience of an arrest has come immediately before solitary confinement, the parent's disappearance must constitute an even more shocking event in the child's life. In the long term, solitary confinement and lack of contact can result in young children rejecting the parent at a later stage.[122] How this can happen is illustrated by a mother who experienced being arrested (while her husband was arrested), put into solitary confinement and later released:

> They arrived with police cars and took me into prison...I was told that the children were at an institution. They said they could detain me as long as necessary. I was in solitary confinement for one month, then yet another month where I was allowed visits, but just not from my husband...Then I was told that I was released and that the children

would come home...The youngest, who was 2 at the time, didn't want anything to do with me. In two months he had forgotten me. That felt very cold. He wouldn't come to me. He went to others when he had to go to the toilet or eat. A week went by where he didn't want anything to do with me and only after 1–2 months, would he have contact with me.... When we came home, everything looked like I don't know what. No one had been here since I was arrested.... The flowers had died and everything was just a mess, they had ransacked everything, of course...I just broke down. I couldn't cope with anything. For six months I think, I just sat and cried. Finally, my children said to me that enough was enough; now I had to do something...But I still cry over the smallest thing.[123]

Psychologist Else Christensen explains that the "psychological message is that a person in solitary confinement risks losing himself or herself and disappearing into a non-existence. For the children it means that the contact with the parent is difficult and that the possibility of getting care from the parent is severely limited. In this situation, young children react, like the 2-year old, by rejecting the parent."[124]

11
Home Leave and Other Ways of Maintaining Contact

The possibilities for maintaining contact between the child and the imprisoned parent are far from always satisfactory. A particularly good form of contact, however, can be achieved when imprisoned parents are allowed "home leave" and can stay a day or two at home. In Denmark, home leave can be given to prisoners in connection with work, education or visits with the family. Home leave to see the family is granted more or less routinely for some sentenced prisoners in open prisons. They can go home every third weekend or so, or on special occasions such as birthdays, the first day at school, funerals and so on. Sometimes, depending on the prisoner and the situation, the police or prison staff will escort a prisoner on home leave. This could likely be the case when home leave is granted for a special occasion or to a prisoner in a closed prison or a remand prison (which is rare).

The use of such practices varies greatly from jurisdiction to jurisdiction and from country to country. Generally, however, arrangements for home leave or furlough seem to play a relatively minor role in many penal systems. The fact that the thorough recommendations from the CRC have no mention of home leave and the like could be an indication of this. The European study on prisoners' children, on the other hand, recommends that "Home Leave should be granted with regard to the needs of children of imprisoned parents".[1]

Home leave for imprisoned parents

The rules on home leave in the Danish Sentence Enforcement Act are not written with the child's best interests in mind as such, although several of the regulations do take prisoners' children and families into account.

From the children's accounts, it is apparent that their imprisoned parents' home leave can be of huge importance. This is not surprising, since the form of parental contact that can be achieved through home leave is vastly different from the majority of prison visits.

> He has leave every third week. When we are together we drive to town or just drive around. We have a great time. He says it's terrible to think that he has to go back. But at any rate I am happy to see him. But I would like to see him every second week.[2]
>
> Home leave is far better [than visits in the prison]. Some times we go to the movies, or bowling or to McDonald's.[3]

Since 1965, it has been possible to grant prisoners in Denmark home leave as a normal part of the sentence enforcement. Home leave is only granted for certain purposes and is based on an approved travel plan to an approved residential address.[4] When an assessment is made of whether a prisoner is to have a home leave, importance is placed especially on humanitarian, rehabilitation and security considerations. The humanitarian considerations are particularly relevant to the family and, for example, may result in the prisoner being granted permission to attend special family events.[5]

The account below from a child of a prisoner concerns a home leave, which must have been granted under humanitarian considerations. It is possible that the child's interests have been included in the specific assessment behind the permission. The story shows how home leave can be extremely important for prisoners' children, but it also illustrates that problems can arise depending on how the home leave is handled by all the involved parties.

> My big sister had developed cancer in her head. And he [the imprisoned father] was then allowed to come in and see her after the operation; she was lying in the bed and woke up. There were two officers there and he was in handcuffs and restraints and all that, so he couldn't hug her or give her any water or anything. And she really wanted to, so that was a little stupid…. When he went home, the doctor called the police and said that what they did was despicable and that it was unfair to my father and my sister that they couldn't hug each other after such a serious operation. And then he came again and was allowed to have the handcuffs removed in my sister's room while the officers waited outside.[6]

The child's account was confirmed by the mother, who also said that during the first visit, the father was only able to "gently touch her on the nose with one finger".[7]

Escorting prison or police officers can clearly handle home leaves very differently. Seventeen-year-old Maja described a home leave situation: "She [a female officer, who attended the visit] was really sweet – and was good at making it a nice experience. We made this monster out of a cardboard box and made eyeholes and put hair on it. We played a lot together."[8]

Various forms of home leave currently exist, such as home leave for special purposes or the so-called weekend home leave. Furthermore, in some cases prisoners can obtain "clearance" to attend to a job. Some prisoners can also be "stationed", which typically happens towards the end of a sentence at one of the Prison and Probation Service's halfway houses. At the halfway houses, it is normally possible to stay outside of the institution during the day and evening hours, and permission can be granted to stay overnight with the family on the weekend.[9]

In July 2000, the Danish Prison and Probation Service adopted a set of guidelines, recommending a new "future practice" for imprisoned parents' home leaves. Among other things, it was made clear that prisoners could have home leave to attend the child's first school day as well as for birthdays (up to and including 15 years of age), and some parents with close contact to their child/children could even have a weekend home leave every 14 days. Furthermore, some prisoners could also be released on probation up to one month earlier in consideration of the child.[10] Later it was clarified that only in "special cases" could one deviate from the usual practice of home leave every third week. Thus, the most significant change was arguably that the imprisoned parent gained a possibility to obtain home leave for the child's first school day and on birthdays.[11]

But these initiatives had a limited impact, at least in the beginning. In 2004, the prison chaplain, Lis Poulsen, permitted herself to doubt the effect: "It looks just great on paper, that the requirements have been relaxed. But in reality the prisoners have to obtain one statement after the other."[12] A small random test of the Prison and Probation Service's case processing following the adoption of the new guidelines indicate that this might be true – at least initially. In the period from 11 July to 1 November 2000, 30 enquiries were received from imprisoned parents for home leave every 14th day, which resulted in 9 permits and 21 rejections. The permits were granted when "documentation existed that the child had problems which could be remedied by the imprisoned parent being allowed home leave more frequently" (i.e. statements from day-care centre, school, speech therapist, doctor, social services, etc.). Conversely, "the issue that the child misses the imprisoned parent a great deal and is looking forward to the prisoner coming home...could in itself not justify more frequent home leaves". In a specific case concerning two prisoners who had children together, one of these – the mother – had been granted permission to live with the children in a halfway house. The Prison and Probation Service now argued that the children's needs were met, which is why the other parent – the father – found his request for more frequent home leaves rejected.[13]

A rejection to a request for transfer (stationing) to a halfway house had a similar justification, as the mother took care of the children and apparently did not "need respite".[14] Such case processing shows, on the one hand, that the Prison and Probation Service considered the children at the time but, on the other hand, reveals that this consideration was not always administered quite in line with the recommendations of research and in the spirit of the Convention of the Rights of the Child. An essential point is thus that contact to both parents is important, as is the possibility of maintaining the family's contact on the whole. Of course, there can be other considerations – typically involving security – which, despite the child's needs, can speak against more frequent home leaves or stationing. But seen from the child's perspective, it would, as a rule, be inappropriate – or misunderstood – to refuse increased parent contact with reference to the child having close contact with another parent or that this parent can take care of the child alone.

It is difficult to say how these cases are processed today since there are no statistics on when home leaves are granted because of the children specifically. But according to a treatment consultant in the Prison and Probation Service, they "can easily do a little magic as soon as it has something to do with the child's needs. We just need to have something on paper, e.g. from the social services…. If a school teacher or school psychologist or another relevant person writes to us that, for example, the child is being bullied and that things are not working out at all at home, then it is easier for us to take up the issue that the father should have home leave."[15] This statement is supported by the Directorate for the Prison and Probation Service, which in a report to the parliament's legal committee writes that it would be possible to "grant permission for more frequent weekend home leaves than normal".[16]

Under all circumstances, home leave is quite extensive in the Danish system. In 2010, the Prison and Probation Service granted 15,738 home leaves for prisoners to see family members and 18,466 leaves in connection with education or work. The vast majority of such leaves were granted to prisoners in open prisons.[17]

Nevertheless, a tightening of prison regimes has occurred in Denmark – as in so many other places – due to a so-called zero tolerance policy against narcotics in the prison, which can affect permits for home leave. Since 2004, the normal practice has thus been that prisoners must submit urine samples at regular intervals, even though no specific suspicion exists. If a prisoner is found to have a contaminated urine sample, which reveals misuse of drugs, this can impact whether or not the inmate concerned is granted home leave.[18] As a treatment consultant explained: "More and more are actually being denied home leave as a result of increased testing of urine samples and increased security."[19]

Home leave during remand imprisonment is a separate issue. It is very difficult to get home leave when in remand custody because the case is still being investigated. Furthermore, home leave for a remand prisoner will normally be under escort.[20] As described by two police superintendents: "Remand prisoners are only granted home leave in very special cases, e.g. death in the family."[21]

According to the questionnaire survey, 52% of the participating police officers felt that the child's needs are generally taken into consideration when granting home leave for remand imprisoned parents. Another 24% responded that it depends on whether there is an officer available to accompany the prisoner, while the other 24% responded that they feel children's needs are not considered.[22] There is also difference to what the participating police staff believe entitles home leave. For example, a police superintendent writes: "Not birthdays, but hospital visits for instance."[23] But a police sergeant writes: "Birthdays, school meetings".[24]

Other forms of contact

Children have the possibility of writing to and receiving letters from their imprisoned parents. If the parent is subject to correspondence and visiting control, the letters can be read by the employees in the remand prison or by the police. This form of communication can naturally be important, but one problem is that some prisoners are not used to writing. A survey from 2007 showed, for example, that 11.5% of the prisoners in Danish prisons had not completed an education corresponding to municipal primary and lower secondary school.[25] Another problem is that many of the younger children can neither read nor write. In any event, letter writing is an unfamiliar form of communication today. Telephone calls are a far more ordinary form of contact for many children – depending on age, of course. In a British survey, the children expressed that telephone conversations with their imprisoned father was very important.[26]

That it can be disproportionately expensive to call from prisons is a typical problem. Calls are often made on mounted coin and card telephones, whereas mobile telephones are generally not allowed. Mobile phones are normally allowed in Denmark's open prisons if they are secured to the cell wall with a steel wire. This is not the case in closed prisons, where prisoners can normally only make outgoing calls and often at specific times.[27] In remand prisons, prisoners are normally not allowed to use the phone at all. This can be very frustrating for children, as they cannot contact their parent when they need and want to talk – even in closed prisons the prisoner can actually call now and then. Anne described how she has "often been sad about the whole thing" and that she "cannot just lift the phone and call him...I could be upset and crying all day and then I could only talk with him three days later because that was then he called.... Also because often, a lot of what I was mad or sad about, I actually had a greater need to chat about it with my father than with my mother."[28]

There is a tremendous difference between the conditions in the closed and in the open prisons. Prisoners in closed prisons only have access to telephones following individual approval, and permission may be granted to call four different people outside the prison.[29] This can limit the possibility of maintaining contact to the family.[30] A prisoner explained:

> After applying, I have been allowed to call once every week and I can only call agreed numbers. But it is difficult since my mother, my son and my daughter need contact. Every week I have to decide who I should get on the line. When I can call and for how long depends on who is on duty.[31]

Additionally, a certain difference in practice apparently exists in the various closed prisons. In some places, calls are allowed in the daytime hours,[32] other places limit calls to particular times, such as outside of working hours.[33] A prison section leader explained that in the closed prisons in which he works, the practice is that "the prisoner can ask the staff in the block and if the staff has time and approve, then it is possible."[34]

Naturally, it makes a world of difference if children can call up their parents when they like, and their parents can call as well and speak in privacy from a phone in the cell. The right to make calls can – in both open and closed prisons – be revoked in consideration of order and security, or in consideration of possible victims.[35]

During remand imprisonment, prisoners are even more dependent on staff goodwill. Remand prisoners have no right to use the phone but can in some circumstances be allowed access to a phone. When surveyed in 2008–2009, some remand prison staff claimed that remand prisoners had access to making calls "daily during normal working hours",[36] "in the daytime hours"[37] or "as needed",[38] and others within a certain time period.[39] In other remand prisons, prisoners had – according to staff – normally no possibility or simply "no access" to make calls.[40]

Some of the employees in the remand prisons emphasise that the remand prisoners' telephone access is connected to whether he or she is subject to correspondence and visiting control.[41] In any case, the administrative regulations have recently been tightened and the guidelines from the Directorate of the Danish Prison and Probation Service now emphasise that remand prisoners should normally *not* have access to telephones at all.

In Else Christensen's study, prisoners explained that the limited telephone access was particularly distressing with regard to keeping in contact with the children. The prisoners thus preferred to talk on the telephone instead of writing letters. For some, it was about their children being young and unable to read. A prisoner also explained that he had never been good at writing.[42] That the telephone was simply not accessible during remand imprisonment was therefore a big problem. The prisoner explained that it would have taken a great deal of pressure off the children if it had been possible to call home and say goodnight.[43] Similarly, many children find letter writing an awkward way of communicating: "Many children see writing as a chore, an extension of homework, and far from a fun activity."[44]

Keeping in mind that most children today communicate a great deal via the mobile phone and text messaging, it would be extremely appropriate if possibilities could be established for prisoners' children to communicate with their imprisoned parents via mobile phone. As described by the head of the Prison and Probation Service's Sentence Enforcement Office, "surveys show that Denmark is one of the countries in which text messaging is very popular. That arguably tell us that is has become a very, very integrated part of our society over time." She highlighted security and economic concerns as the main reason that access to mobile phones is not more common.[45]

The prison chaplain at the closed prison Vridsløselille touched on the same issue and explained:

> I have always thought it was strange that prisoners are not allowed to have mobile phones. Perhaps with special numbers they can use to call their wives and children. There are a very few who I think would use a telephone for criminality. And if there is concern about that, well the phones can be tapped or monitored, or whatever. Everything is possible with technological monitoring today. It's important of course, that children can send and receive text messages now and again, or that a child can call and chat with his or her father if, for instance, something happened in school. I think it's quite hysterical that there is so much opposition against this. The prohibition against mobile phones has really been tightened up, so when they are smuggled in today then it probably is for criminal purposes. I don't believe that prohibiting mobile phones puts a stop to potential criminality – if anything, it puts a stop to contact with the family.[46]

But new initiatives have been introduced or are in the pipeline in the Danish prison system. IP telephony has been introduced in all prisons, so it is now cheaper to make calls.[47] Additionally, mobile phones have been introduced in all open prisons, although they are not so "mobile" since they are attached with steel wires to the cell walls. But they can be used for calls and text messages. The situation is therefore vastly different from prison to prison. Children with a parent in an open prison in Denmark have relatively easy access to their imprisoned parent through telephone calls and possibly through texting. The situation in this regard in closed prisons is still very difficult for prisoners' children, and it is almost hopeless in remand prisons, where telephones are normally completely off limits.

Internet access

A third form of communication of great potential relevance is, of course, email and other forms of contact facilitated through the Internet. Politicians and lawmakers – and prison administrators to some extent – tend to be very conservative and fearful of engaging and opening up this area.[48] But there are a number of exceptions, and some of them are to be found in the Nordic countries. In Norway, for example, Verdal

Prison has recently begun to allow prisoners to use Skype as a means of communication with their children who live far from the prison.[49] Skype is currently not being used for such purposes in Denmark, but quite a few prisoners in the open prisons actually have some sort of Internet access. On the other hand, in the closed and remand prisons, the overall picture is still one of either no or highly restricted Internet access.

In open prisons in Denmark, there are three potential ways in which an inmate can achieve Internet access:

1. From a computer in the prison cell
2. From a computer in the prison schoolroom
3. From a computer in a prison "Internet café"[50]

The first model is not widespread and is awarded on an individual basis and then only for educational purposes or work. This type of Internet access is not necessarily restricted and can normally be used for email. The individual prisons arrange and conduct surveillance of this practice. On a specific day in 2009, the Department of Prison and Probation counted 73 prisoners who had attained permission to have a computer with Internet access in their cell.[51] When compared to the average number of prisoners (3,715) on that given day in 2009, the figure corresponds to less than 2%.[52] According to recent information from the Danish prison service, the figures representing prisoners with Internet access have since increased somewhat.[53]

The second model of Internet access in open prisons is only allowed when a prison teacher is attending and only for educational purposes. Electronic communication is normally not allowed. Surveillance of Internet use is conducted by the teacher and log files are controlled on a regular basis. The third model – the Internet café – also includes surveillance, although in this case, electronic communication such as email is allowed.[54] In 2010, six out of the eight open prisons in Denmark had Internet cafés.[55] This means that, unlike the other models of Internet access, the cafés actually allow a significant number of prisoners a relatively free form of access to the Internet. Nevertheless, the access to these cafés is limited and typically restricted. Prisoners are typically allowed to use the cafés "a couple of times each week", and sites about dating, pornography, weapons and so forth are normally blocked. Facebook is also blocked in some prison Internet cafés. Prison staff carry out surveillance, and log files are created and must be checked on a regular basis.[56]

In the closed and remand prisons, prisoners can normally only get Internet access in the schoolroom during classes. Such access is highly restricted and available only for a limited number of prisoners participating in such education. Access is granted through an isolated prison service server system, which allows access to a few pre-selected homepages. Inmates are subjected to periodical surveillance. Furthermore, there are no possibilities for emailing or any other form of digital communication.[57]

It is not known how many prisoners misuse their Internet connection in Danish prisons, but the prison service is only aware of very few such instances. If we, for the sake of comparison, look at the use of home leave from prison, a total of 2.8% of all home leaves granted in 2010 were misused in various ways (prisoner returning too late, in a drunken state, etc.). New criminal activities were recorded in only 0.1% of all cases of prison leave.[58]

12
When Visits Do Not Take Place: Opting Out of Visits and Discontinuing Contact

As described in Chapter 10, children's opportunities for visiting their imprisoned parents and their experience of coming to visit can have a lot to do with the visiting conditions in the prisons. But it goes without saying that the child's relationship to the imprisoned parent or the relationships between the prisoner and other adult relatives who participate in the visit are also crucial. Regardless, there are other factors that can determine whether visits take place at all. Three important issues can be of special importance in that regard:

1. Imprisoned parents and/or families sometimes simply opt out of visits.
2. In some situations, the holder of parental custody does not want the child and the imprisoned parent to have contact.
3. There are situations where the child is placed in foster care, which can make visits difficult.

Any of these factors results in a discontinuation of contact, which can have lasting consequences. Imprisoned parents who opt out of visits with their children possibly think that they can "pick up where they left off" when they have served their sentences, but this is not a good solution. As described by a professor in social work: "The practical issue for fathers, however, is that parenting cannot be put on hold to be taken up 'when I get out of prison'. Children grow up; their memories fade or they create new ones through fantasy and imagination. When there is no contact to support an enduring bond, they begin to experience their parents as strangers. Such situations can lead to permanent rather than temporary severance of family ties."[1]

Imprisoned parents and families who opt out of visits

We have no definite statistics on how many imprisoned parents opt out of visits from their children. A Danish survey cited previously indicates that about two-thirds of the imprisoned parents are visited by their children. In a British study that interviewed 181 imprisoned fathers only 1 out of 12 of those older than 21 did not have visits with their child or children for one reason or another.[2] In the EU COPING study, the visiting frequency among the participating children was also very high – between 75.9% and 92.9% for the four countries involved. But this was a result of the selection process, which primarily identified children with an important connection to the imprisoned parent.[3]

In a US interview sample of imprisoned mothers, however, visits to the prison were "infrequent" simply because the institution was in a rural area far from most of the children's homes.[4] This study – along with many others – illustrates how practical issues concerning transport time, transport costs and visiting hours can severely limit or effectively end contact between children and their imprisoned parents. The specific challenge concerning transport can be especially pronounced in the case of imprisoned mothers, since the relatively small number of female prisoners and the way they are typically separated from male prisoners often result in the upkeep of only a few centralised prisons for this group of inmates.

Many of the employees in the police corps, remand prisons and prisons in Denmark maintain that quite a few prisoners opt out of visits with their children. They suggest that this is often because the prisoners did not have a prior relationship with their children or only had a very peripheral relationship.[5] Other police officers and prison staff suggest that opting out of visits is often due to consideration of the children, as when the prisoner deems it best for the children to be kept in the dark or the parents are simply worried that the remand prison, police station or prison will have a frightening effect on the children.[6]

For example, an employee in a remand prison wrote: "I have a clear feeling that those who opt out of visits by their children, do so in the firm conviction that it is for the sake of the children."[7] A staff member in another remand prison elaborated: "Often the inmate does not want them to come here. It would create too much anxiety for the mother and the child."[8] A treatment consultant in a prison wrote: "We find that especially inmates, who are serving a very long sentence, feel that it is difficult to retain contact with the children and they also often feel that it's difficult to give the children a proper and interesting visit."[9] A police inspector from the Copenhagen Police understands perfectly if parents and relatives would rather not have children visiting in a remand prison: "You look around and think: this is no place for children."[10]

Some imprisoned parents clearly agree and opt out of visits for such reasons. Danish imprisoned fathers have explained that they have chosen not to have their children visit either because they think that the prison is not the place for them or simply because the children have been lied to about the imprisonment itself.[11] Other Danish fathers indicated how stressful visiting situations with their children can be, because it can be difficult to find something meaningful to talk about or do, and because the whole situation is so emotional – which can cause the prisoner to wish for fewer visits and withdraw from important social relations.[12] Furthermore, there is no doubt that children can become unsettled and in some cases scared of the entire visiting situation. A positive staff culture in the prison can be helpful in mitigating visiting children's fears (see Chapter 10).

In a British survey, the prisoners gave reasons for opting out of visits, similar to the Danish examples above. One of the imprisoned fathers explained: "I don't want my son (aged 14 months) to visit. Prison is the wrong environment to bring children into. It's not the right sort of atmosphere to bring children into. I've asked my girlfriend and family not to bring him because it would have a bad psychological effect on him – seeing his father imprisoned."[13] Some of the prisoners explained that changes to the prison procedures could make them choose to have visits from their children.

> If the security searches weren't so intrusive I would let my children visit. The way the officers speak to the visitors and children is not acceptable. I wouldn't want my children to be spoken to like that. There is nothing for them to do if they come. My ex-wife wants to bring them but I don't want them to see me in here. I don't think they could cope with it.[14]

A family therapist from the Danish prison service also finds that there are prisoners who simply give up because the imprisonment makes them despondent. It is too hard and awkward to have their children visit, and they find it difficult to steel themselves for it.[15] This is an interpretation which reflects sociological research on the effects of imprisonment. Sykes's classical study from 1958 describes, among other things, the loss of autonomy an inmate experiences by being subject to an endless string of routines and rules 24 hours a day.[16] A consequence of this loss of autonomy is likely to be a lack of responsibility.

Sometimes it is the children who opt out of visits. As a prison employee put it, there are occasions when "children cry when they arrive and don't want to go in".[17] How often a child opts out of visiting in prisons is not known. The older the children get the more they are likely to be able to make that kind of decision for themselves. A 17-year-old Danish girl whose imprisoned mother has had a long career of crime, drug abuse and prostitution explained: "I have been allowed to see her, but it's too tough. It's too sensitive. It's easier not to do it. If I go there, then I will see how she lives in the prison. I'm afraid of that."[18]

Perhaps that particular girl has concluded that her everyday life is easier without regular contact with her mother? A Norwegian mother with an adult son who has been in prison for many years admitted: "When I sit in the visiting room I try to hide my sorrow...we try to have a cosy time. But the only thing I want to do is to give the tall – and almost as broad man – a proper beating. And thereafter comfort him, hug him – and tell the guards smilingly that today I unfortunately have to take Flemming home with me. Enough is enough – I want to say to the prison guard." And because of all these conflicting emotions – the loss, despair and anger – the mother concluded: "In a way I think I feel better in everyday life when I do not see him. When I get to live my life without thinking about him all the time, as I have otherwise done in many years. When I get some distance."[19]

When the holder of parental custody stops the contact

In the above-mentioned British study, it was the children's mother who prevented imprisoned fathers from keeping contact with their children. One of the prisoners explained:

> When you are in prison there is nothing you can do if your partner suddenly decides to stop bringing the children. I'd love to have regular contact but it's up to my ex when I get to see them. I've seen blokes in here whose wives have refused to let them see the kids and it's nearly driven them over the edge.[20]

The relatives' association SAVN knows this problem is a familiar one, particularly with regard to those cases where the parents are no longer together.[21] In KRIM ("Dansk Kriminalpolitisk forening" – an NGO that gives legal aid to prisoners) they describe how many fathers approach them because their children's mother refuses to let the children visit: "When the parents are divorced, visits to the father depends on the mother's mercy and compassion. A mother holds immensely strong cards when the children's father is in prison."[22]

Of course, this is not a straightforward question of whether or not children should always see their imprisoned parent. There can be many different reasons why the other parent, or the holder of parental custody, finds that it is not a good idea for the child to visit. A child psychologist who has worked with prisoners' children emphasises, however, that most often the child needs to see where the imprisoned parent is. She explains, "In all circumstances it is a good idea that children have the possibility of seeing the prison, so they have a physical image of where dad or mum is. Otherwise, they can imagine all sorts of things.... Therefore, most often it is a good idea to let the child go in and see the prison – even if there is not going to be regular contact and visits."[23] A social worker also highlights as essential that social workers "motivates and creates understanding in the other holder of custody of the importance of visits to the prison so, as a minimum, the physical conditions and surroundings are demystified".[24]

Of course, children can sometimes be "affected" by their mothers who do not think that they should visit their father (or vice versa) and do not support the contact. This problem is reinforced by the fact that many relationships fall apart during the imprisonment, which can increase the chance of the imprisoned parent and the child losing contact.[25] The Danish Red Cross has, for example, observed that many of the prisoners' children they encounter have divorced parents, and the parent outside of prison does not always support the maintenance of contact with the imprisoned parent. Such problems can be further complicated when the children have "two fathers" or "two mothers" and half-siblings. Brian from SAVN described how on some occasions relatives can tend "to use the children as a 'weapon' against the prisoner when a relationship breaks up because of imprisonment".[26]

Situations where the child is placed in foster care

For children placed in foster care or children's homes (whether they are placed prior to the arrest or in connection with the arrest) it can be particularly difficult to establish regular visits. In a Danish study, the children who had an attachment to their father before the imprisonment could not retain contact with their parents when placed in care outside the family. In some cases, they visited their father during remand imprisonment (after tremendous pressure from dad, mum or other relatives), but the placement authorities and the homes or institutions where the children were placed did not take the initiative to continue contact.[27]

Almost ten years ago, the Danish Red Cross had an escort scheme on a trial basis whereby volunteers picked up and brought four siblings to visit their parents in prison. Unfortunately, the project failed because it was difficult to find volunteers and get the municipalities to pay the transport costs.[28]

When contact is discontinued

It is seldom a good solution to put the relationship between children and their imprisoned parent on standby while the parent is remand imprisoned or serving his or her sentence. The prison service in Sweden uses parent courses to inform the imprisoned parents of the importance of keeping contact with their children while they are imprisoned: "It is important to 'remind' the fathers that they have children even though they are serving time. Some of them believe that they can be gone for a couple of years and it will not mean so much to the children in the big picture. We talk about this – and the parent courses can make them aware of what consequences the imprisonment can have for their children and how they can tackle this."[29]

In any case, there is good reason to believe that imprisonment weakens the possibility for life together as a family later on. Many relationships end during imprisonment, and the contact between children and imprisoned parents can be severely tested and sometimes cease altogether. English research indicates that between 25% and 40% of all fathers, who for various reasons (divorce, etc.) move away from their children and partner, have completely lost contact to their children after a five-year period.[30] Such lack of contact is often detrimental for the children.[31]

In the above-mentioned British survey of 181 imprisoned fathers, the overwhelming majority had plans to live together or be in close contact with their children after release. This applied to 85% of the imprisoned fathers over 21 and to 76% of the fathers between 17 and 21.[32] But this often proves difficult in reality, as the time spent incarcerated can change things and breaking contact can suddenly be perceived as the easiest solution. As explained by a Danish prisoner: "I could see that I should not take her as a hostage in all of this. I broke up, which was truly awful. I felt like shit, but I'm happy about it today...I also wanted to spare myself all the problems, which such a situation creates. I can see that by looking at all the others [the other prisoners]."[33]

A significant side effect of supporting the children's contact with the imprisoned parents is that the prisoner, who returns to the family after serving the sentence, has a better chance of keeping away from a life of crime. A released ex-prisoner with a functioning attachment to a family is in many ways in a far better position than those without similar family ties. Several studies have shown that meaningful contact with family during and after imprisonment can reduce recidivism and strengthen the possibility of being (re)integrated into local society.[34] For example, research shows that married men handle the transition from prison to freedom better than bachelors and that released men who move back to their wives and children generally cope better than those who live alone or with a parent after imprisonment.[35]

It thus seems extremely important to support the relationship between the prisoner and his or her family, which can be severely challenged during imprisonment – both from the children's point of view as well as a socio-economic perspective. An even better solution in many cases would be to shorten or avoid the imprisonment altogether There are exceptions to this, of course, as such contact is not always in the best interest of the child.

13
When Contact is Undesirable

Noah's dad was going on home leave from the prison so he could be there for Noah's 12th birthday.

> Well, we assumed that he would be there about eleven o'clock, but when he didn't show, we assumed he would be there around two o'clock and when he didn't show around two o'clock, we just assumed he would be there around five o'clock. We just waited. It was not very nice. My mother had bought a lot of food, because he is a real glutton. And so he let me and [my sister] Ann down. Just because he was out drinking...we kept thinking that he would show up.... If he had to drink, it should just not have been on my day.... But at some point you just need to forgive. You cannot continue to be mad at him for a year. Because he is still my father.[1]

Visits are not always in the child's best interests

In the majority of cases it will be in the child's best interests to maintain some form of contact with an imprisoned parent – assuming there is a meaningful relationship to start with.[2] As psychologist Else Christensen explains based on her own empirical data: "For the child, contact [with the imprisoned parent] means primarily, that the imprisoned parent is still alive. Secondly, the child experiences the contact as an expression that the parent is interested in him/her, that the parent would like to make sure that the child is well, that the parent loves the child. If contact is completely discontinued, children will interpret it as an expression that the imprisoned parent does not care about them anymore."[3]

According to this interpretation it is crucial that prisoners' children always have the *possibility* of establishing and keeping up a meaningful form of contact with their imprisoned parent. For the majority of children, it would also be in their interests to utilise this possibility. For some children, however, this would not be the case. This important issue does typically not receive much attention in the literature.

It is very difficult to say anything general about when contact between an imprisoned parent and his or her children is not in the children's interests. The individual circumstances would be decisive in this respect. But one can attempt to highlight some of the circumstances and conditions which can give rise to *considering* whether it is in the child's best interest to visit and communicate with an imprisoned parent.

Imprisoned parents and problematic families

Prison populations tend to include large proportions of socially and psychologically disadvantaged groups. While this in no way justifies hasty conclusions regarding parental capabilities, it nevertheless illustrates how some prisoners' children have parents who deal with substantial problems that *can* affect their parental capabilities seriously. In any case, committing a serious crime and thereby causing one's removal from the family and from close contact with one's children is obviously a huge parental failure.

If we initially look at the scope of psychological problems and distinct mental illness among prisoners, a dismal picture emerges. As explained in Chapter 5 a review article from 2002 on mental health concluded that among almost 23,000 prisoners in 12 different countries, about 4% were psychotic, between 10% (men) and 12% (women) suffered from severe depression, while 65% of the men and 42% of the women had a personality disorder.[4] A Danish survey showed that among the 8,403 individuals who were in contact with the Prison and Probation Service on 3 November 1992, 29% had previously been admitted to a psychiatric clinic.[5] Later studies have confirmed that there is a very high frequency of mental illness among inmates in Danish prisons.[6] A recent Danish screening study revealed that out of 672 remand prisoners who agreed to be examined by a psychiatrist, 9% were found to be healthy, 8% were diagnosed as mentally ill (insanity) and 83% were diagnosed as suffering from other psychiatric health problems, with a very high frequency of addiction-related problems.[7] The extent of abuse problems is well known from other research. In 18 different studies of prison populations in various countries, it was reported that between 21% and 61% of prisoners were addicted to drugs – with the one exception of a Finnish study in which the frequency of drug addiction was only 6%.[8]

We know nothing about how many of the mentally ill prisoners or prisoners with abuse problems have children. But given that data from different countries indicate that at least half of all prisoners are parents, it is very likely that there is a considerable overlap between these groups. This means that among prisoners with psychological problems and mental illness, there must also be a lot of parents. On a very broad note this indicates that a considerable number of prisoners' children come from problematic family backgrounds. As shown in Chapter 5 this has been confirmed at the Engelsborg Family House, where the resident prisoners and/or their partners have been struggling with alcohol abuse, drug abuse, anorexia and paranoia. Others – all of whom are parents – had previously cut themselves, suffered from involuntary discharge of faeces, experienced concentration problems, suffered from depression or anxiety, were socially isolated, or drank and smoked as 10–12 year olds.[9]

When an imprisoned parent suffers from serious mental health and abuse problems, it can certainly influence the quality and character of the contact between parents and child and in some cases make further contact undesirable. The character of the crime committed by the parent is another relevant consideration. A Danish child psychologist is of the opinion that contact must be questioned in those situations where, for example, the father has killed the mother or the child has been assaulted: "It must be an individual assessment of what the individual child's needs are. Such an assessment should be based on questions such as: What is the child's attachment to the imprisoned parent? What does the child want? What will happen when dad/mum has served the sentence – should the child and the imprisoned parent live together? And how the child has reacted to possible earlier visits in the prison?"[10]

The psychologist further describes how a child sometimes express a desire to see his or her father, out of fear of making the father sad. But if the child has a stomach ache and wets his or her pants, then the adults must step in and consider whether upholding contact is actually the right thing for the child.[11]

> There are in fact cases where the slightly older children decline to go on visits themselves, but where the authorities or the Prison and Probation Service push them and immense pressure is placed on them in order to go on visits. This is deeply problematic and is based on the prisoners' needs and not the child's needs.[12]

In line with previously cited research, the child psychologist emphasises that it is most often a good idea that children visit and have the opportunity to see where their father or mother is so they do not imagine the most awful things. But such visits do not always need to result in continued visits, depending on the specific situation and the relationship between parent and child.[13]

Parents who handle visits very badly

Not all imprisoned parents handle visits well, and some parents sometimes show very little awareness of their children. This can be a result of many things and is sometimes related to drug abuse, frustration and perhaps lack of understanding that certain forms of behaviour harm the children. A prison officer describe that he "unfortunately [had] the impression that many children of imprisoned parents have a really difficult time and are often overlooked. Many of the prisoners (however, far from all), but many prisoners in the closed prison in which I work, have nothing to offer their children since they are often preoccupied with their own problems or simply do not have parental abilities."[14]

A police officer mentioned as an example a "current case where the mother has been remand imprisoned and the 1½-year-old son has been put in foster care. In connection with visits, the mother spends more time complaining about all kinds of things than attending to her son."[15] Another police officer finds that this is a general tendency: "What makes the biggest impression on me are those cases where during visits by a partner plus children, the detainee focus more on himself or herself and the partner than the children. You can clearly see on the children's faces that they are disappointed and have had a bad experience."[16]

A prison officer described that "the worst thing is those fathers who are VERY MUCH under the influence of drugs during and after visits and they have to lean up against the wall to keep themselves upright. And finally, we have fathers who besides using violence on the mother while the children are present, send the children out into the corridor/playroom while loud discussions take place."[17] Naturally, one can only hope that prison staff intervenes in such cases and reports such treatment to the social authorities and the police (in case of violence). Some prison staff members are aware of this duty and do intervene but do not necessarily involve the authorities straight away: "I have experienced that a child sat out in the rain because mum and dad were having sexual intercourse. We spoke with the parents and explained that under no circumstances was this acceptable – and that in recurring instances, we would contact the municipality."[18]

One could question such observations, since prison staff and police officers naturally tend to see things from a perspective shaped by their occupations. But interestingly, these perspectives often differ. I have, for example, noticed that staff in remand prisons sometimes sympathise with prisoners and argue that police put pressure on the prisoners in unfair ways during the investigation. Regardless, the observations regarding bad parenting seem to have more to do with general views on children and parenting than "choosing sides" against prisoners. Some of these accounts are also confirmed by representatives of other occupation groups. For example, a social worker gives the following assessment of the entire situation surrounding contact between children and their imprisoned parents:

> Children gain an unrealistic picture of the imprisonment, since often the prisoner does not admit his or her guilt and the resulting sentence. This means that the children become involved in the prisoner's fight against the systems – they become involved in the prisoner's wishful thinking and anger towards the police, the Prison and Probation Service, the judges, and when they are imprisoned also, most often, their resistance to the support measures the social services initiate due to the imprisonment.[19]

Parents who are only parents when they are imprisoned

Another problem is the way that some imprisoned parents apparently only become aware of their children when they are imprisoned – and perhaps have great difficulty in taking on the parenting role when they return to society. A remand prison officer, who retired in 2008, characterises this phenomenon as "yoyo parents".[20]

These parents live a chaotic life of drug abuse and criminality when outside of prison, while they gain somewhat greater control of their life and perhaps receive therapy and other forms of help in connection with a stay in prison. Such a mechanism is often not satisfactory for the involved children. A former remand prison officer explained that it is not always "in the child's best interest to come to the remand prison and visit his or her father. Perhaps dad shows interest mainly because he is where he is now and is a little bored, and becomes indifferent when he is released again. There are also many of our prisoners who are so addicted to drugs that they are able to keep a little contact with their child while they are here, but they lose touch as soon as they are released. Is it in the child's interest to be disappointed time and again or to experience his or her father's complete collapse?"[21]

In the words of another prison officer, some prisoners are "very interested in their children when they are in prison but...do [not] have the resources for the children when they are out." [22] A third prison officer touches on the same problem but also makes it clear that only a few of the prisoners display such behaviour:

> We often find that prior to imprisonment, they had very poor contact to their children. When they're in here, suddenly the children become very important to them. After the completion of the sentence and when they are later arrested once more, we can then see they have not been able to keep contact with the children and we start all over again. Of course, we also have prisoners who have good contact with their children. They are also able to keep contact themselves during imprisonment. As a rule, they also have a healthy network which supports the children, so our involvement is not necessary.[23]

Parents who use the children to gain something

A third mechanism – one that is extremely problematic – is that of imprisoned parents attempting to exploit their children. This can take place when children are used to smuggle drugs or something else into the prison, but exploitation can take other forms. A prison manager in a remand prison remembers an episode with a "sobbing mother who wanted to have a relationship to her forcibly removed little girl. We did a great deal of work on this and in dialogue with the municipality; a meeting with the foster family was arranged. The foster family was not keen. There were some telephone calls up to the time the mother was to have a § 31 leave and visit the daughter. But the sobbing mother did not show up for the meeting. Neither was she subsequently interested in calling now that she had been on her § 31 leave."[24] Such an event obviously involves the foster family preparing the child for the meeting and sitting and waiting to no avail – a process which can cause anxiety and all sorts of feelings on the part of the child.

One prison officer has experienced several times "that the prisoner would like to see his children even though he has not had any contact with them for perhaps the last couple of years. But when they are imprisoned and have lots of time on their hands, then they are quick to start up a whole lot of things regarding children. Many times I think that perhaps it's not the child's needs that are being considered and many times a possible ex-girlfriend/ex-wife is put in a difficult situation."[25] Another prison officer agree that the "criminals very often use children, whom they otherwise have little time for, as a means to gain a § 31 leave and transfer to a smaller remand prison (with benefits such as more open doors). We often hear tearful stories about their children, but the inmates often forget them when they are released to abuse and the like."[26]

Good and bad parental contact

A checklist that describes precisely when contact is undesirable for the prisoners' children cannot be supplied. Certain circumstances, such as assault in the family, constitute obvious alarm signals. Moreover, it is clear that a number of problematic types of behaviour and neglect in relation to visiting situations and leaves must give rise to serious doubt about whether continued contact is in the child's best interests. Still, many experts advise that maintaining contact is important in the majority of cases. The basic recommendation must therefore be – both in terms of legal rights and prison standards – that prisoners' children always have the *possibility* of maintaining and developing a reasonable form of contact with their imprisoned parents. Arguably, it will for the majority of prisoners' children also be in their interest to utilise this possibility, but for a group of children, this would not be the case. Minimising or ceasing contact can sometimes be the right choice for the involved children.

14
When Dad or Mum Returns: Re-entry and Release

A number of special challenges are associated with release from prison and a parent's return to – or renewed contact with – his or her family and children under more normal terms. The released parent must once again adjust to the parental role outside of the prison, and many children have to get used to having their mother or father home again.

Release, relapse and life after a served sentence

How former prisoners cope when they return to the free world has been the object of serious research for many years. Studies of prisoner release and their return to society have been inspired by the obvious paradox that while the history of imprisonment is rich on ideologies, programs and practices on prisoner rehabilitation, it is nevertheless the case that many former prisoners relapse into a life of crime and return to prison later. This of course depends on local conditions. Another question is how recidivism is calculated, which can vary from one country to another. In Denmark, the authorities look at "how many persons commit new crimes and receive a new sentence of imprisonment or a suspended sentence [with supervision] within two years after they have been released or have finished a suspended sentence".[1] With this definition the rate of recidivism was 27.9 % among those released from Danish prisons in 2010 and those whose suspended sentence with supervision ran out in 2010.[2] If we exclude those with a suspended sentence and look at offenders who finished a sentence of imprisonment in 2010, the rate of recidivism was 37.7%.[3] To give another example, the British Ministry of Internal Affairs stated in 2002 that 59% of all the prisoners who were released in 1999 had committed new crimes within the subsequent two years. Among young offenders, the rate of recidivism was 74%.[4] But "proven re-offending" in

England and Wales is normally "defined as any offence committed in a one year follow-up period and receiving a court conviction, caution, reprimand or warning in the one year follow-up or within a further six month waiting period. This is referred to as a proven re-offence."[5] Measured by this metric, 26.9% of all offenders from July 2010 to June 2011 re-offended within one year. When looking at specific groups, the "proven re-offending rate" for those released from prison was 46.9%; the proven re-offending rate for drug-misusing offenders was 57.2%.[6]

The reasons for the high relapse are many. As explained by Shadd Maruna, "the lethal combination of stigma, social exclusion, social learning, temptation, addiction, lack of social bonds and dangerously low levels of human and social capital (not to mention financial capital) conspires to ensure that over half of all ex-prisoners typically return to prison within a few years of their release".[7]

The informal punishment that follows in the wake of a served sentence – through the associated stigma and exclusion – can be decisive. To give just one example, a long sentence reduces the subsequent "opportunities on the labour market considerably" – even in an expanded and universalist Scandinavian welfare state like Denmark.[8] According to Danish research, the informal punishment for criminality in the country is "very tough". Former prisoners are likely to experience a drop in income and to be "marginalised from the labour market".[9] The authors of this particular study suggest that perhaps the stigmatisation of offenders is in some ways harsher in Denmark than in a country like the United States where it is quite normal in many urban areas to have imprisoned family members.[10] It could be possible that this is an indirect result derived from having a strong welfare state, which rests both on a philosophy that the state takes care of all its citizens and on a strong alliance between citizen and state. One can argue that if in such a society one seriously breaks the pact with the state and becomes marginalised, then it can be even more difficult to be accepted again. On the other hand, one can normally get access to a fairly good financial minimum standard in such a state through the maintenance of an extended social safety net.

In any case, the high rates of recidivism and the underlying causes – stigma, exclusion, informal punishment and so on – sets a very problematic scene for the released prisoner as well as his or her family and children.

When imprisoned parents return

Many researchers are of the opinion that prisoners can become institutionalised by being in prison, and prison adaptation strategies involving psychological withdrawal or conformity are unlikely to help prepare prisoners adequately for release.[11] A significant problem is in other words that much of the behaviour and strategies prisoners often acquire in an attempt to handle prison life better can be directly counterproductive in relation to life outside of the walls.

Equally important in this context is the fact that families and especially children change while dad or mum is in prison. As highlighted by a British study: "On release the families had adapted to living without the men and substantial problems and conflicts could arise when they tried to return to family households. The men related to their children in ways that were appropriate to the age the children had been at the time of arrest."[12]

Another British study found that many families of offenders experience difficulties in connection with the release of a family member, which can include the need to "re-group" as a family and re-negotiate "family responsibilities".[13]

Along the same lines, a Danish child psychologist describes how the family can develop while the prisoners' life has stagnated or perhaps even been pushed back because the imprisonment has made them passive and more antisocial (especially in cases of long sentences).[14] Some prisoners' relatives also find that ex-prisoners can bring the tough, masculine environment back home with them, which is difficult to combine with family life and difficult for the family to handle.[15]

The problems of returning are not necessarily mitigated by the great expectations many prisoners and their families have about the release – expectations that are generally far from being met. SAVN found that both children and parents become very disappointed when the imprisoned parent is released:

> Perhaps the prisoner feels that he is the same, but the family has changed. The children are older, the girlfriend or boyfriend has become more independent and used to managing everything alone. On the other hand, the children have an idea that the family will have a nice time and do fun things all day long.[16]

For many imprisoned parents, the issue of returning to the family is not relevant because they have lost contact during the imprisonment. English data suggest that over two-fifths of all prisoners "lose contact with families or friends in the course of a prison sentence".[17] An unknown but presumably significant number of imprisoned parents, in other words, loses contact with their children during their time spent locked up. But even for those returning to a family the situation does not simply become like "in the old days".

The "new" family

According to a family therapist, "prisoners describe how they experience immense uncertainty about going home. The family has, of course, coped without them and consequently they are uncertain whether there is a need for them at all anymore."[18] A child psychologist also explains that there are cases where the changes and the development that has occurred in the family actually come as a surprise to the prisoner, because he or she has not been able to follow the development at close hand in daily life.[19]

For the children, too, it can be difficult to adapt to the new situation when the imprisoned parent is released. The imprisonment has changed the family dynamics:

> When the father, who has been a 'nice uncle' for five years who played Monopoly and ate cake with them in the prison, now comes and demands that you put away your dolls and you must go to bed, it can be difficult for children to relate to. And when a father, who has been in prison for many years is released to his family where the eldest boy has become a kind of 'new dad' in the family, it is difficult for both the boy and his father to convert to their, all at once new – and simultaneously old – roles.[20]

Release on parole and prisoners' children – the Danish system

As a rule, after a prisoner has served two-thirds of the sentence (although at least two months of imprisonment), a decision is made on whether or not probation should take place.[21] A large number of issues, including the prisoner's behaviour, impact on whether probation is granted. The Danish Probation Service (KIF) functions partly to reduce the risk of re-offending and partly as a support function for the ex-prisoner. In the course of the supervision period, the aim is to create as acceptable a social framework as possible for the individual. KIF works with the starting point in an action plan, which contains 11 bullet points on the released prisoner's circumstances. Unfortunately, children do not take up much space in this action plan, but are just a sub-point under the "family and other networks" bullet.[22]

A social worker from KIF explains that in the action plan, the client – the person on probation – is the focus of attention. Special consideration of children is not made and there are no general rules on how a client's children are to be related to. How this is tackled and how this is prioritised in the supervision depends on the individual social worker. According to two KIF employees, this is not something which generally takes up much time and space in the supervision work.[23] The welfare department head of section emphasises that the ex-prisoners generally do not have their guard up in relation to KIF and are more inclined to open up to receiving assistance compared to the municipal social services: "After all, we have more time to chat and listen than they have at the municipal social service."[24]

Under all circumstances, release on parole is an opportunity to renew and perhaps repair family ties that still exist. Unfortunately, the development in the course of recent decades has gone in the direction of far fewer prisoners being offered release on parole after serving two-thirds of their sentences. From 1976–1984, 6 or 7% of all prisoners were denied probation with referral to it being "inadvisable"; in 2004 this figure had increased to 24% and it is still very high.[25]

Re-entry through the Danish Prison and Probation Service's halfway houses

> One can unlearn everything that has been learned in order to cope in the prison environment – and it takes time. Therefore, re-entry is crucial so that one can slowly find the way back [to] life. My family and my network were also important to me when I was released.[26]

For some prisoners, the last institution they spend time in before release will be one of the Prison and Probation Service's eight halfway houses. Prisoners can apply to serve their sentence or the last part of their sentence in one of these. The sojourn at a halfway house will often be a part of the re-entry into society. According to a Danish psychologist, these institutions are well equipped to prepare a prisoner for release:

> The transition directly from prison to freedom rarely provide good results and therefore, re-entry via the Prison and Probation Service's halfway houses is necessary so that prisoners can be included in the unlearning and learning process that will prepare and help them to navigate in and understand the society they are being released into.[27]

In such institutions, it is arguably easier to "unlearn prison behaviour" and leave that particular identity behind.

The staff at these halfway houses have the task of providing assistance and support to improve the prisoners' social situations.[28] In October 2008, the halfway houses compiled a joint re-entry programme, which unfortunately does not contain one word about children but nevertheless has a bearing on them, as it is focused on giving prisoners "relevant, specific and individual guidelines and support" and supporting prisoners in "building up and maintaining a constructive network".[29]

Some of the halfway houses are particularly aware of prisoners' children. For example, at four of the halfway houses, the prisoners can have their children with them during their stay.[30] All of the halfway houses in the Danish Institute for Human Rights' questionnaire survey responded that they always ask new arrivals if they have children and note this in the person's action plans. Moreover, half of the halfway houses reported that they host special events for children and parents, as well as parent courses, parent conversation groups or similar initiatives for prisoners who are parents.[31] A particularly interesting initiative can be found in the Engelsborg's Family House, which is a relatively new institution where prisoners have been able to live with their families and receive family therapy.[32] The Family House began as a trial project in 2005 but has now become a permanent part of the Danish Prison and Probation Service's re-entry programme. Two family therapists, a social educator and a social worker are associated with the house, in which five families can live at a time.[33]

The family therapist who has been involved at Engelsborg from the outset described how family therapy and the focus on children has been a special characteristic right from the start in 2005:

> Since 1979, it has been possible to serve a sentence in Halfway House Engelsborg with the family, but at that time it was at your own risk and no assistance was available. In the Family House there is 24-hour staff, pedagogical staff and family therapy. The idea here is that development can take place with the family whilst they live here. We can utilise the time they are here to create change.[34]

The Family House has various forms of family therapy, which can be tailored to each family's needs. There are interviews with the parent or parents, interviews alone with the individual child and interviews with the whole family together. The Family House has prisoners who are serving a so-called § 78 sentence (alternative sentence), which for example, could concern a single parent who has been given a three months' sentence and now serves the entire sentence in the Family House with his or her child. The Family House also has prisoners who have served long sentences and have moved into the halfway house, with all or some family members, for the final phase of the sentence.[35] The family therapist reports that many families return for follow-up after a concluded sentence and that follow-up is just as individual as the treatment programmes.

> We also follow up a great deal on the work in the municipalities to ensure ourselves that they follow up on the assistance provisions we have initiated. Of course, we are fortunate to have contact with many good case workers, but I have some totally hopeless municipalities who do not comply with agreements and which just delay things. So the families need us.[36]

According to the family therapist, the Family House re-entry programme provides the prisoner with parenting support and gives the children a pleasant environment in which to reconnect as a family:

> We become involved with all families and create an important, often necessary, "disturbance". We receive some responses from parents who say that the stay has given them more self-confidence in their parent role. I am also pretty sure that we haven't had any children out here who have not thrived. Most of the children are relieved for the clarification that they will now be here and because it's not at all frightening here as it can be in a prison.[37]

Re-entry and release in relation to prisoners' children

It can be very complex and difficult when a prisoner is released and has to return to his or her family or resume the relationship to his or her children outside of the prison walls. The expectations – of the prisoner, the children and any other family members – can be tremendous. The time prior to imprisonment may be remembered as more unproblematic than it was in reality, and often the family has changed. For some, all contact has been lost during the time spent in prison and an unknown number of children thereby simply cease to see their parent.

There is clearly only limited focus on these issues when a prisoner is released from the Danish Prison and Probation Service. Release will often take place without any talk about, or guidance in, relating appropriately to the expectations and problems that can arise during reunion with children. This is likely the case in many other jurisdictions as well. Engelsborg Family House is a reminder that alternative practices that include prisoners' children are possible. But this is a relatively small-scale local initiative within the frameworks of the Danish Prison and Probation Service.[38] Hopefully, the introduction of children's officers and parent groups will mitigate these problems in the future.

15
With Mum or Dad in Prison: Children Who Live with Their Imprisoned Parents

It is one thing be separated from your imprisoned parent and come visit in a prison. It is quite another to move into a prison and live there on a daily basis, even though you have not been sentenced to imprisonment. This is actually a fairly standard practice in many countries around the world and primarily involves underage children. Such a situation can arise when an imprisoned mother is pregnant and gives birth to a child during her sentence. But it is also quite common for some mothers to take their young children with them into prison. The extremely difficult human rights dilemma (see Chapter 6) is how to strike a balance between two competing truths: prisons are not suitable places for children to live, but separating a young child from the primary caregiver is generally a very bad idea.

The typical pragmatic solution to this problem seems to be that some mothers are allowed to bring their small children with them into prison. The following countries have legislation that allows mothers to have children up to a specific age stay with them in prison: England, Canada, Australia, United States, France, Italy, Cambodia, India, Denmark, Finland and Sweden.[1] This list is by no means exhaustive, but it does illustrate that the practice is widespread and not dependent on specific local cultures. On the other hand, Norway completely prohibits children from living in prison with a parent.[2] In Holland, policies have changed over time and while it was not uncommon historically that women brought their children with them into prison, it was apparently disallowed in most of the 20th century. This changed once again towards the end of the 20th century, and in 1993 a trial project allowed female prisoners to bring their children with them to a newly establish maternal unit in a semi-open prison. A new law passed in 1997 provided legal basis for this practice without stipulating a maximum age for the involved children.[3]

Some countries also allow fathers to live with their children in prison. This is the case in Australia, Denmark and Finland.[4] But even in countries where children can live with their imprisoned fathers, it occurs far less frequently compared to children living with their imprisoned mothers.[5] As far as Denmark is concerned, internal statistics from the Prison Service confirm that it is predominantly women who serve sentences together with their children in Danish prisons.[6] In the Prison Service's halfway houses, the picture is somewhat more varied. In the Engelsborg Family House, there are also many fathers who stay with their children.[7]

It is not known how many children live with their parents in prisons around the world, since this not registered in all places.[8] The known figures range from very few (in Denmark, the closed and open prisons on an ordinary day accommodate up to five children in the 0–3 age group, although there are sometimes more children located in the halfway houses) to thousands (more than two thousand in India in 2008).[9] In Denmark, the state prisons in Ringe (closed prison), as well as Møgelkær and Horserød (open prisons), are the institutions that undertake this task.[10] A number of children also stay, normally for a relatively short period, in the halfway houses. In some rare cases, very young children end up living with parents in a remand prison during the investigation, although such institutions are not at all designed to accommodate children.

A national survey in the United States shows both how many prisons have facilities for pregnant women and how many prisons allow underage children to stay with their mothers. The survey covered 999 state correctional facilities for adults in the United States, of which 246 were all-female or co-gender facilities. More than one-fifth of the female prisons offered "special housing for pregnant women", and 6% of the female facilities (i.e. three prisons) and 4% of the co-gender facilities had a nursery, which could "house infants born to incarcerated women". Six per cent of the female facilities and 4% of the co-gender facilities reported "having housing *outside* the facility where mothers can live full time with their children".[11]

The Finnish case illustrate that it is a recent phenomenon to look at such practices systematically from the perspective of children's needs and rights – at least in some jurisdictions. Up until 2010, Finnish legislation thus allowed mothers and, in principle, fathers to bring their children into prison without specifying any maximum age. This practice had existed since 1881 without systematic involvement of child welfare authorities. In 2006 researchers found it very difficult to gather any data on the children who had stayed in Finnish prisons with their mothers even in the beginning of the 2000s. Hence they termed these children "institutionally invisible".[12] It was not until 2010 that it became the duty of the municipal child protection system to assess whether it is in the best interest of the child to enter prison with his or her parent.[13]

It is certainly quite striking that up until a few years ago, children could live in prison in a Nordic welfare state without involvement of the social authorities.

Children in Danish prisons – how many and how old?

There seems to be a general consensus that if children are to be allowed to live in a prison together with their imprisoned parent, then the child must be under a certain age. In Germany, a parent can live with his or her child up until the child is 6 years old. In England, children are allowed to live in the prisons until they are 18 months old.[14] Obviously, the rules vary; some countries have no set age limit, and some countries completely prohibit children in prison with a parent.

In Denmark, parents serving a sentence can have their children with them until the children turn 1 providing that they can take care of their offspring themselves – and they can have children with them until the children turn 3 providing the social authorities and the prison approve that the conditions are suitable for the child.[15] The three-year limit is substantiated thus: "Children who are 3 years old and above have generally reached a development stage where they risk sustaining harm from the prison stay and can therefore not be placed together with one or both parents in a prison."[16] The prison governor in Ringe State Prison – the only closed prison accommodating children of prisoners – find the 3-year age limit important because children over this age begin "to understand a great deal of what is going on around them".[17] According to a member of the Danish parliament, Anne Baastrup (Socialist People's Party), the age limit was raised to 3 years old based on a consideration that "contact between mother and child is terribly important and it is not until the age of 3 that the child forms a personal consciousness".[18]

According to the Prison and Probation Service, the average number of children living in the prisons between 2006 and 2008 fluctuated between two and four.[19] In 2009, the average daily number of children in the open and closed prisons, as well as remand prisons, was 1.65 children.

In 2010 it was 2.79 children.[20] But these figures excluded the halfway houses. We are talking about a very limited group of children and prisoners. The open, closed and remand prisons have no staff with special expertise in the area and provide no special support to the parents.[21]

Children who live with their parents in a prison in Denmark are, as a rule, very young and stay in the prison for six months or up to one year. According to the Prison and Probation Service, these children are often – but not always – those whose parents have shorter sentences.[22] The Danish Institute for Human Rights survey shows that the children are often under 1 year old and confirms that they typically live in the prison for a shorter period.

More often children join their parents when they are serving a sentence in one of the halfway houses. During the last five years, a number of children have lived at the individual halfway houses. Among the halfway houses that participated in the survey, one reported having one child while another had eight children. As previously mentioned, the Engelsborg Family House has had many families and children as residents.[23] From September 2005–June 2008, 47 children between up to 15 years old have lived at Engelsborg for periods of between 20 days to 10 months. Of these children, 15 were under 2 years old, 9 children were 3–6 years old, 20 were 7–12 years old and 3 were 13–15 years old.[24]

In addition to the children who live with their imprisoned parents in a prison or at a halfway house, there are also children who are placed with parents in a remand prison. Children had lived with a parent within the last five years in 7% of the Danish remand prisons that participated in the questionnaire survey (corresponding to two remand prisons or remand units in other prisons). In both cases this concerned a single child in the course of the five years, and both children were under 1 year old and lived in the remand prison for less than six months.

Should children be able to live with their imprisoned parents at all?

> This is not a situation in which there are obvious right and wrong answers: neither separating babies and young children from their mother nor imprisoning them with their mother is desirable.[25]

There is a catch-22 element in the discussion of young children who live with their imprisoned parents. On the one hand, it is quite clear that prisons by no means constitute a desirable place for children stay. Yet it is also obvious that complete separation between young children and a parent who is the sole caregiver can have profound, negative consequences for the child. To the extent that there is an international consensus in the area, most experts and human rights mechanisms recommend that non-custodial measures be implemented whenever possible and that otherwise children should not live with their parents in prisons as a rule. In some cases, it is nevertheless the "least unfavourable" of the possible solutions.[26] In line with this, a Danish psychologist considers that starting life in prison will not necessarily damage a child.[27]

But consensus is not complete, as illustrated by the Norwegian rules and practice. Similarly, a Danish psychologist, who has worked with families of prisoners, does not believe that children should live in prisons: "Prisons are not good for children. There is not enough stimulation...and they are surrounded by a prison atmosphere", which is disseminated through both "the prisoners as well as the employees".[28] She believes that the stress level in many prisons is generally high and that the children's development will be affected. Even infants risk "becoming a 'security blanket' for mum", and it is thus preferable to find an alternate caregiver than to have the child with the prisoner.[29] Neither does a child and youth psychiatrist, who is a member of the central board of the children's NGO Børns Vilkår, believe that children belong in prisons. He is "deeply astonished that in Denmark, it can be assessed as a healthy option for a child to grow up in a prison".[30]

The physical conditions for children who live with their parent while serving a sentence

For the majority of countries in Western Europe and North America, children are only allowed to live in a prison with their mothers if there are special facilities available.[31] In an international report, the British prison service regulations regarding the "Mother and Baby Units" (MBUs) are highlighted as "a good example" of a policy that "ensure[s] respect of the rights of children residing in the prisons".[32] MBUs, however, have also received serious criticism previously.[33]

I visited an MBU in Askham Grange, an open women's prison in the vicinity of York in England. The communal facilities resemble a cosy nursery and were bright and colourful, with soft furniture and toys suitable for children up to 18 months old, the age limit for children who may live in British prisons. There is also access to an outdoor playground. In the daytime, when the imprisoned mothers work or have duties in the prison (from the time their babies are 2 months old), the children are cared for by employed nursery staff.[34] It is interesting – and illustrates the high standard of care – that employees and people from the local community also had their children cared for in Askham Grange's nursery scheme.[35] Unsurprisingly, this particular MBU is described by a "non-governmental prison worker" as "state of the art" and an exceptionally child-friendly unit.[36] Imprisoned mothers in Askham Grange who do not live with their children have access to the Acorn House, a special facility for children's overnight visits.[37]

In Denmark, the Prison Service itself reports that the physical settings in a prison are ordinarily not suitable for children, but that prisoners are allowed to live with their children in selected halfway houses and prisons, which are "specially equipped so children can live there".[38] Efforts are often made so that parents accompanied by their children can serve their sentences in a halfway house.[39] Of the Prison Service's eight halfway houses, children can be brought along in four of them.[40] Security considerations can work against a parent's chances of serving his or her sentence with a child at a halfway house.[41] In such case, the prisoner can apply for permission to have the child with him or her until the child is 3 years old in the closed state prison in Ringe and the open prisons in Møgelkær and Horserød.[42]

In the prison in Møgelkær, a parent with a child would normally live in either a double cell in the women's block or in a 1½ –man cell (cells with cubicles) in a communal block for men and women. In the communal block, there is also the possibility for a married couple to serve together with their child. Horserød has a special family block in which a prisoner can serve with a child. In Ringe, prisoners with children under the age of 3 are placed in the drug-free block, which is a block for prisoners who do not have drug problems and who want to serve their sentences drug free. Parent and child live there in a double cell (two cells, approximately eight square metres).[43]

One couple sentenced to a long imprisonment lived in Ringe with their youngest daughter, Isabella, and were interviewed five years ago about the conditions when their daughter was 18 months old. The prison was described as limiting the girl's possibilities for development, which frustrated her parents. Isabella slept with her mother, and there was little room in the cell for anything other than an adult-sized bed and a crib-sized bed. Isabella's mother arranged a play area around a shelf filled with pink toys in the block's communal room. The mother also had loads of LEGOs donated to the block. There is a small playground outside the visiting block, but apparently the family was not allowed to use this. Isabella instead had a playhouse in the prison courtyard, which she could use when the outside areas were open. Isabella's mother had the playhouse sponsored, and various clothing companies gave Isabella clothes and shoes. The municipality supplemented what the family otherwise lacked.[44] In this case, private initiative clearly played a significant role in relation to the child-friendly standards in the prison. Some things have changed since Isabella's stay. Since 2010, Ringe has employed a children's officer, who has spearheaded changes in the visiting area and elsewhere. The prison playground was renovated and re-built in 2011 and now looks very nice and child friendly.

In the Danish Institute for Human Rights' questionnaire survey, the physical conditions for children who live with their mothers in a prison were also described as being quite diverse. In one prison, "two cells were joined together" to accommodate a father and a child[45]; in another prison, only a single cell was available, but the block had a "playground and playroom".[46] In yet another location, child and parent were "placed at the prison hospital where there is contact to health personnel and the cells are larger than standard cells".[47] In the halfway houses, the physical conditions are described in the following language: "larger room and quieter location", "apartment/double room" and "a Family House, equipped for families".

The Family House

Around the world, a number of special initiatives exist for children who live with their mothers in a prison. Imprisoned mothers and their children in Chile can, for example, be helped by a team of professionals that includes a psychologist and a social worker, who must ensure that the mothers' and children's needs are met.[48] In some countries, children can live partially with their mothers in the prison institution. Canada, for example, allows children up to 12 years old to live with their imprisoned mothers on weekends and holidays in certain minimum- or medium-security prisons.[49] In some prisons in Peru, children may live with their imprisoned mothers during school holidays.[50] In Milan in Italy, the ICAM project has allowed imprisoned mothers to stay with their children age 3 and under in a special institution, which up until 2010 had involved 106 mothers and 144 children.[51] When I visited the institution in 2010, the atmosphere seemed very much like in a kindergarten. Such special initiatives for prisoners and their children are, however, often local and small scale.

In Denmark, the previously mentioned Engelsborg Family House includes five apartments where prisoners can live with their partners and children (up to 15 years old) while they serve their sentence. The Family House staff includes family therapists who focus on helping the prisoners establish better relationships with their children and strengthening the families, thereby improving the possibilities of good and crime-free lives after release.[52]

A family therapist from the Family House described how the families living there vary greatly and how they choose to use the house in different ways: "Some families choose to have the whole family move in, while others, for example, have the mother move so she can serve her sentence with the youngest of the children, while dad stays at home with the older children... We try to arrange individual stays and programmes together so each family gets the help that is best for them. It's all about what suits the individual family best and about the prior history and also about the length of the sentence or re-entry period."[53]

When a prisoner applies to serve his or her sentence in the Family House, he or she must – in the words of the family therapist – be prepared to be "stripped naked" emotionally. To live in the Family House, prisoners must accept that the social authorities, children's schools and other relevant institutions or authorities will be involved. Moreover, a § 50 study is conducted of the children who move in. This is a study that attempts to learn "everything about the child". It includes asking the child's day-care institution, school and doctor if there is anything in the child's life the family therapists should be aware of. This could include reports or concerns in relation to the child's well-being.[54]

An additional requirement of living in the Family House is participation in family therapy. The family therapists have individual interviews with the children, and children's groups are created for the older children: "In the children's groups we talk about the things that preoccupy the children. For instance, we talk about how you can love a father who has committed a crime."[55]

How are the children affected by living in the Prison Service's institutions?

A few studies focus especially on children of imprisoned mothers.[56] But there is no systematic research on how children are affected by living in prison with their mothers – or fathers, for that matter.

Children who live with their parents in Danish prisons, especially remand prisons, are so young that in the majority of cases they cannot tell us how living in the prison institution affects them. On the other hand, there are children all the way up to 15 years old in the halfway houses. A 12-year-old girl, Victoria, described living in the Family House: "It was almost as usual. We just lived in another place."[57] Such as statement reflects that the Family House is a rather unique institution, which cannot be directly compared to other prison solutions in this area. A number of the children who have lived at Engelsborg have clearly liked their stay: "All children should be allowed to come to Engelsborg", believes 9-year-old Emily.[58] "I told my mother everything I already knew – but she didn't know that I knew",[59] says 15-year-old Kenny.[60] These and similar statements from children who have lived in the Family House match the conclusion in an internal 2008 report about the Family House.[61]

But what about the children who live in the ordinary prisons – how do they react? A prison chaplain described how she has had both positive and negative experiences in connection with children living in the open prison where she works: "There are parents who can cope with having their child with them and you think that it's fine that he or she is with the parent. It can also be a good thing for both mother and child to be in the prison. Mum learns to take responsibility for her child and she has the time and tranquillity for the child, which she perhaps might not have outside. There are fixed boundaries here. There is dinner every evening at six o'clock, etc. But for other children, the opposite is the case. You think that those children are being harmed."[62] Such a view seems to match the Finnish experience – at least in the very general sense that prison staff have told Finnish researchers that supporting motherhood in prison can be beneficial, but have also described episodes where children were "being abused by their mothers in prison".[63]

A former treatment consultant who worked in a closed prison in Denmark for many years believes that children do not belong in closed prisons. He believes that they are harmed by the prison environment, all the closed doors and especially by the presence of too many caregivers.[64] This is despite the fact that the Sentence Enforcement Act, § 54, states that the prisoner must be personally responsible for the care of his or her child. A prison governor in the Danish Institute for Human Rights' questionnaire also touches upon this problem:

> It follows from our experience with children living in the prison that the child can have difficulties bonding with the mother/parents because the other prisoners, to a great extent, take care of the child even though the parent is present. In the long term, this problem produces children who do not develop the necessary reservation towards other people and the mother/parent relationship is diluted."[65]

The same prison governor also finds that children normally do fine in the prison, but "at the more general level, there is no knowledge of how such a special environment, which a closed prison is, affects a little child." She further stressed how "the child can witness episodes in the prison, which are not desirable in relation to the child's development".[66] In addition, it can be very complex to administer having parents and their children in prison. What if, for example, a mother living with her child commits a grave disciplinary offence? How should the prison authorities handle that? Putting a mother and her child in solitary confinement is (hopefully) out of the question and imposing other sorts of punishment can also easily affect the child.[67]

A staff member from one of the Danish remand prisons that has housed children for very short periods indicated that it is not an appropriate environment for children: "It is not a place they [the children] can feel at home in. The remand prison accommodates all kinds of prisoners, even those who have abused children, too. We cannot offer or subject them to being locked in a cell for 23 hours a day."[68] This remand prison has had a small child under 1 year stay overnight only twice during five years.

Some of the staff in prisons better suited for accommodating children experience having children living in the institutions as something positive: "The child functions well here and thrives. Many options and good outdoor areas", wrote a social worker from a halfway house, which during the five-year survey period had children living in the halfway house for a period of up to three years.[69] In another halfway house, staff noted that "even though it is different from their [the children's] daily life, they are doing well here".[70] A prison officer observed: "I find it positive. I think it is important that children are with their parents regardless of where they live."[71]

Many of the employees in the Prison Service's halfway houses find that they support the families affected by imprisonment, and many believe that these families need help and support also when they live together on the outside. A social worker explained: "I find that the parental imprisonment can sometimes be beneficial for the children and they can find it difficult to handle when the father is once again part of their everyday life. They can find it difficult to understand their father's boundaries and the father has difficulty setting boundaries."[72] A deputy warden at a halfway house described one such situation:

> The remand imprisonment lasted a very long time and in the meantime, the mother and the child were isolated. Later, the mother

and child served the remaining part of the sentence together [in an open prison]...and were stationed here until the child turned 3. The mother was a very good mother but felt guilty and could therefore not set boundaries for the child. So the child was very single-minded and had hysterical outbursts when boundaries were set. The child bore obvious symptoms of living in a prison. The mother was given support from here and from the Family Centre in [town]...The story ended well though, the mother found the strength to set boundaries and the child became much more satisfied and happy.[73]

Some social workers also criticise letting children live in prison. For example, a social worker wrote: "Generally, children do not thrive in a prison – they experience too much commotion, chaos, etc."[74] A social worker who cooperated with the Prison and Probation Service in connection with two underage children who lived in a prison found that "the younger one was unaffected" but "the older one was wrongfully placed".[75]

Another social worker expressed concern that placing a child with his or her parent in prison is more about the parent's wishes than the best interest of the child. She described a specific case where a mother, whose child was in first grade, had to spend three years in a halfway house.

After a brief, emergency placement process, it was assessed as justifiable that the boy was moved home to his biological father. The parents had been divorced long before the arrest. Despite a parent ability study and statement from the social services against the child staying with the mother in a 24-hour prison system, the Prison and Probation Service worked primarily from the mother's statement only, to find options for mother and child that would require moving the child from his or her immediate environment. It puzzles me that professionals who work with prisoners with children, do not possess sufficient theoretic knowledge and understanding of children and their needs, and do not include what would be best for the child in their assessment. In my experience, their focus is clearly on the prisoner.[76]

A retired prison officer, who had worked in an open prison for many years, described another problem: how older siblings can sometimes find it difficult to understand why they are not allowed to stay with mum or dad if their younger brother or sister is allowed.[77] The older child can feel cheated and perhaps blame his younger sibling. It can be difficult for the two siblings to relate to each other.[78] A British woman who had given birth in prison and already had an older boy described the same problem: "I don't know what effect bringing home the new baby from prison will have on my eldest child. The baby will be a toddler by the time of my release, and I'm worried that my son might not like the baby and will blame him for taking me away. I think it's best if I don't have any more children as I don't want him to think I might leave him again."[79]

The lesser evil

The question of whether children should be able to live with their parents in prison is typically a question of how to cause the children as little suffering as possible. In that sense, the choice is often between two evils: living without the parent versus living in a prison environment. From the child's point of view, the best solution is to avoid both scenarios and take – or create – every possible opportunity for a non-custodial sentence. One alternative, for example, would be to carry out the imprisonment in the prisoner's own home with an electronic tag, although that can raise other problems.

As described a common pragmatic solution is to allow certain mothers and sometimes fathers to bring their underage children with them into prison. This demands a lot in terms of the physical prison standards as well as from the prison staff. The adequacy of many current solutions is questionable when viewed from the perspective of children's needs and rights. But as mentioned above, some praised facilities and special initiatives do exist, which shows that it is possible to create relatively high standards in the area.

As things stand, there is unfortunately reason to believe that many children spend time in prison with their parents without proper focus on the best interest of these children. Such children can easily become more or less "institutionally invisible", and the prison administration and staff will sometimes excuse themselves by saying that they are responsible for the prisoners – not the prisoners' children.[80] The unique situation that these children wind up in nevertheless requires extra and separate attention, so that their interests are taken care of and so that the prison environment will harm them as little as possible. The most important thing is that a professional, individual decision is made for each child based on what would be in that child's best interest.

16
Penal Populism and Children of Imprisoned Parents

Since prisoners' families – perhaps especially prisoners' children – can be severely affected by the use of imprisonment, and since this area has suffered from a remarkable lack of awareness historically, it is obvious to ask whether and to what degree there is currently political focus on prisoners' children. The answer to this question is ambiguous. On the one hand, the amount of research into the effects of parental imprisonment has grown significantly during recent years, and the UN, the human rights system and various NGOs have afforded prisoners' children much more attention. In some countries, the issue has also gained political attention and practical support from reform-oriented prisons and prison services. I argue that this is the case in Norway, Sweden and Denmark. But on the other hand, the general political climate surrounding punishment and crime has become increasingly problematic for prisoners' children in many countries during the last couple of decades. Penal policy internationally has moved towards tougher sentencing, zero-tolerance, harsher prison conditions and growing prison populations. This chapter shows how this penal populism can harm prisoners' children severely, even in a Scandinavian welfare state like Denmark.

Penal populism – the Danish example

Historically speaking, there have always been fluctuations in the way that punishment has been rationalised and legitimised. Retribution has been and continues to be a key rationale for punishment in many jurisdictions. During the last two hundred years, the aim of rehabilitating offenders has also played a prominent role. When the modern prison system broke through in the Western world between the 1820s and the 1860s, for example, rehabilitation, deterrence and retribution figured prominently in the underlying ideology. In England during the latter half of the 19th century, this rationale shifted towards a much more clearly punitive and retributive philosophy. As a result, treadmills were introduced in many prisons. From the 1890s onwards, the focus on rehabilitation once again expanded in England. Historically speaking, fluctuation either towards or away from more or less punitive and retributive prison and punishment practices are well-known phenomena.[1]

There is little doubt that recent years have witnessed an increased focus on retribution and the introduction of more punitive sentencing and penal practices. As discussed in Chapter 2, the United States has inspired and led this international trend for the last three or four decades, and in doing so has reached an unprecedented level of imprisonment. During the early 1990s, this wave of punitive policies reached Europe and prison populations grew significantly in England, Spain and Holland. Criminologists have termed this tendency a new "culture of control", "populist punitiveness" or "penal populism".[2] Contrary to what might be expected by supporters of theories about a possible Nordic or Scandinavian "penal exceptionalism", this punitive tendency has also influenced policies in Denmark.[3]

Penal populism and the new culture of control started to influence Danish penal policy in the 1990s. Under a coalition government led by the Social Democrats, laws introducing longer and stricter sentencing for violent crimes were passed in 1994 and 1997. In 2002 and 2004, under a coalition government led by the liberal party Venstre, sentences for violent crimes were once again lengthened. The arguments behind this legislation, as well as the public and political debate surrounding penal issues and punishment in general, clearly showed that penal populism had gained a foothold in Denmark. The overall political tendency was to constantly refer to and talk about the so-called public sentiments of justice (*retsfølelsen*), while showing increasing willingness to disregard expert advice and criminological knowledge. Here exemplified by the then minister of justice, Lene Espersen, from the Conservative People's Party, who in 2002 declared:

> Crimes committed against people are far more serious than crimes committed against money [sic]. Injustice against another human being is a crime against the most fundamental in our society: the respect for the individual human being. Therefore one of my first deeds as Minister of Justice was to put forward a bill, which contains several distinctive suggestions for tougher sentences against, for

example, violent crimes and rape. By doing that we demonstrate, that society will not tolerate crimes which injure and damage individuals. This legislative initiative is in other words primarily motivated by considerations for the victims and the public sentiments of justice.[4]

In that manner, longer and tougher sentencing policies were introduced despite criminologists and criminological evidence generally advocating diversion and alternatives to imprisonment. Several politicians made it quite clear that they were well aware that they disregarded expert advice and similarly claimed allegiance to so-called public sentiments on crime and justice. Pia Kjærsgaard, the leader of the Danish Folk Party and part of the government's parliamentary majority at the time, concluded in 2003 that Denmark was "a society breaking down", where "gangs of immigrants and bikers" were producing "uncertainty, violence and terror". The solution, according to Kjærsgaard, was to introduce harsher punishment and to help the victims. She made it quite clear, however, that the experts were of no use in these matters, and she warned against their views: "I'm sure that the usual group of criminological experts will soon be badgering us with their statistics – in an attempt to downplay the problems and lull the Minister of Justice to sleep. But many of us began to disregard the statistics a long time ago, we only need to look out of the window, walk the streets or read the papers and watch television in order to realize that things are getting out of hand. It cannot go on for any longer. We will simply not take it anymore."[5] In a more or less similar vein, the then minister of justice coined the critics of much of the new and harsher legislation (on penal issues and antiterrorism) as *hylekoret*, which translates into something like "the whiners" or the "wailing choir".[6]

The public and political debate on penal issues and punishment in Denmark has not been subjected to a large-scale empirical research project but has been the subject of several scholarly articles.[7] It seems that especially during the last decade the debate has shifted more and more towards penal populism, with discussions about zero-tolerance policies, punitive practices, three-strike laws, mandatory minimum sentencing and longer sentences dominating the agenda. As illustrated above, the rationale for these policy suggestions has been emotional rather than rational in a traditional penal sense. Politicians have not primarily argued that they want to rehabilitate criminals or prevent crime, but have simply argued that they base their views and suggestions on the public sentiments on justice. In a 2002 interview, Lene Espersen declared that she governed with her "inner sense of justice", which she claimed to share with "ordinary citizens".[8] The minister clearly regarded criminological advice and research as less important.

In 2008, Brian Mikkelsen (also from the Conservative People's Party) replaced Lene Espersen and immediately speculated that he would probably become known as "Tough Brian" ("Barske Brian") because "I am very tough on crime. And I have been that throughout all my years in politics."[9] In 2010, Mikkelsen was replaced by Lars Barfoed (also from the same party), who stated that he wanted to focus more on crime prevention. This seemed to constitute a significant change of policy, but Barfoed never got around to implementing it. In reality, one of Barfoed's first acts as minister of justice was to get new "tough-on-crime" legislation through parliament. This legislation lowered the minimum age for criminal responsibility in Denmark. Truly populist and punitive, the bill attracted very strong criticism from experts, practitioners, various NGOs, the National Council for Children and the Danish Institute for Human Rights.

Following an election in 2011, a new government took over based on a coalition between Social Democrats, Socialists and Liberals, and the minister of justice became the Social Democrat Morten Bødskov, who attempted to strike more of a balance between tough-on-crime legislation and utilitarian penal policies focusing more on prevention and rehabilitation. In that sense, an era of almost purely punitive political rhetoric seems to have ended. But, like other politicians, Bødskov has been constantly on guard against getting caught wrong footed with regard to the alleged public sentiments on justice. In December 2011, for example, media coverage of a telephone and web-based survey on public attitudes towards prison standards and the possible use of mobile phones in prisons apparently caused Minister Bødskov to cancel a planned project with mobile phones in a closed prison setting. The survey and the debate in the media were ridiculous in the sense that the actual prison conditions and practices were at no point described or discussed. In any case, the mobile phone project was stopped even though it actually had support from the prison officer union.[10]

There is no doubt that Danish politicians from a wide range of political parties have embraced penal populism for more than a decade both in terms of general political rhetoric and promoting and implementing concrete policy changes. It is, I think, also fair to say that the general and politically broad character of this trend has made it more acceptable to propose even very radical tough-on-crime suggestions. One such example was the "three strikes" proposal made in September 2008 by Søren Pind from the liberal Venstre party. In light of gang trouble in

Copenhagen, Mr. Pind suggested legislation according to which gang members sentenced a third time would either be expelled from Denmark (foreigners and immigrants without Danish citizenship) or simply locked up indefinitely until "society could be assured that they were no longer dangerous criminals".[11] Søren Pind was a prominent member of the governing party, and although his radical (even in US terms) third-strike proposal was met with some criticism, it never became a political problem for Pind, who continued moving up the political ladder and later became minister of development cooperation.

The impact of penal populism

But the question remains: how much actual impact has penal populism had in Denmark in terms of concrete legislation, penal policy initiatives and reforms? There is no large-scale empirical research covering this, but penal populism has undoubtedly had concrete and measurable impact. According to the prominent Danish professor of law Vagn Greve, several new pieces of legislation and law amendments from the 1990s and later have violated fundamental principles of criminal law and human rights.[12] One example is the use of Kafkaesque confidential proceedings, whereby the accused is not informed of the accusations.[13] This practice has been introduced as part of antiterrorism legislation, which has enabled PET (The secret service branch of the Danish police) to deny individuals entry to Denmark, deny permits to stay in Denmark and deny citizenship without disclosing a reason.[14] A somewhat similar procedure has been allowed since 2002 in connection with transferring prisoners from an open prison to a closed maximum-security facility. The Prison Service can allege that one prisoner is a risk to other prisoners and remove him or her from an open prison to a much more restrictive environment without producing any evidence and without allowing the prisoner to see any of the relevant proceedings in that regard.[15] As a result, prisoners have also been moved to isolation-type regimes without knowing why.

Several other developments in prisons and prison law in Denmark are equally or more problematic. One interesting example is the way that Danish prisoners' freedom of speech can be limited in order to protect public sentiments of justice.[16] This practice slowly and gradually emerged on an administrative level during the 1980s and 1990s and became law in 2001.[17] A so-called zero-tolerance policy against drugs in prison was also introduced in 2004 according to which the Prison Service must routinely demand urine samples from prisoners whether or not they are suspected of taking drugs.[18] Another important political initiative over this same period was establishing a small prison with extra-high security for the alleged especially difficult and unruly prisoners. Together with the above-mentioned initiatives, these are examples of a lessened focus on the principles of normalisation and prisoner rights. With reference to these and other new prison policies and practices, a Danish prison governor in 2006 claimed that a regular "change of regime" had taken place in Danish prisons during recent years.[19]

Also central to the discussion of penal populism's impact is the fact that the prison population has risen during the last decade as a result of, among other things, legislation introducing longer sentences and a gradual but significant decline in the use of release on parole after serving two-thirds of a sentence. Due to new construction, the prison capacity increased by almost five hundred places during the first years of this millennium. In 2001, the Danish prison population was on average 3,236 inmates (the capacity was 3,563), whereafter the prison population rose to 4,041 in 2005. It dropped slightly in the following years (most likely due to a reform of the court and police system) but then rose again. In 2011, the average prison capacity was 4, 134 and the average prison population was 4, 037.[20] This shows a 25% rise in the prison population from 2001–2011. This increase is certainly significant although limited compared to developments in other European countries since the 1990s (Spain, Holland and England, for example) but it is nevertheless present, and it is at least partly produced by penal populism.

The Danes' sense of justice

A particularly bizarre feature of penal populism is arguably that it runs contrary not only to criminologists' expert advice but apparently also fails to account for ordinary people's actual sense of justice. This certainly seems to be the case when it comes to the Danes' sense of justice, which has been thoroughly researched in a study analysing the Danish population's *general*, *informed* and *specific* senses of justice.

The *general* sense of justice is the general view on punishment and crime, which people exert when they lack relevant background knowledge and facts. The population's *informed* and *specific* senses of justice are, on the other hand, based on knowledge of the crime committed, the circumstances and consequences, as well as what the possible punishments and their consequences.[21] The study researched the *informed* sense of justice by giving the participating individuals the relevant background on a number of specific cases, after which the study participants were asked to choose a sanction/punishment. The *specific* sense of justice was clarified by letting the participants observe and subsequently discuss fictitious – but realistic – video-recorded court cases. The *general* sense of justice was clarified via a telephone interview survey.

The study showed that the population's *general* sense of justice unsurprisingly prescribed longer sentences. Of study participants, 79% wanted far longer sentences for violence. The survey of the *informed* sense of justice revealed, however, that in all of the presented cases, half or more of the participants would give milder sentences than the Danish courts actually gave – both when applied to persons with a prison sentence and to first-time offenders. The participants typically thought they were harsher than the courts when choosing a punishment, although they were in fact milder. The survey of the *specific* sense of justice showed that even though the Danish courts in the cases presented would consistently pass prison sentences, only 17% of the participants would use prison sentences after both presentation of the court case and subsequent voting.[22]

The study shows that Danish politicians feed on the *general* sense of justice, which they have undoubtedly identified correctly at election meetings.[23] The problem, however, is that any thoughtful legal policy should take more seriously the *specific* and *informed* senses of justice –which are based on factual knowledge – and under no circumstances consider only the *general* sense of justice. The latter is simply not related to actual sentencing practice nor to actual levels of crime. Hence it seems to work as an unlimited reservoir of punitive attitudes, while the *informed* and *specific* senses of justice both point towards milder sentencing practices and less use of imprisonment.[24]

Penal populism and prisoners' children

So where does all this leave prisoners' children? Obviously, penal populism is a very unfortunate phenomenon for prisoners' children in the sense that more and more parents are imprisoned. In the United States, where penal populism has helped create a regular "prison boom" with hitherto unseen levels of imprisonment, the wide-ranging intergenerational effects are of frightening proportions.[25] But the tough-on-crime language and the many harsh catchphrases that accompany penal populism can worsen the negative effects of parental imprisonment by reinforcing the element of alienation and stigmatisation that prisoners' children can so easily experience. An all-pervasive punitive language on the part of politicians can help create the experience of an upside-down world, where the state, penal system and elected politicians become enemies of prisoners' children. A world where all talk is about justice, security and punishment in a way which can seem completely backward for this particular group of children, especially those who have meaningful and predominantly positive contact with the imprisoned parent. This is both unfortunate and dangerous and can provoke further alienation and perhaps increase the risk of prisoners' children choosing antisocial and even criminal reactions to their predicament. It is also decidedly unfair both in the sense that these children are innocent, but also in light of the research on the public sentiments on justice in Denmark. Given the relatively mild nature of the *informed* and *specific* sentiments of justice, it is reasonable to believe that prisoners' children and policy initiatives on their behalf will have support in the public sentiments on justice.

But if we take a specific look at a number of Danish penal policy initiatives during recent years, the arrow clearly points in a negative direction. The punitive legislation mandating tougher sentencing and the 25% rise in the Danish prison population since 2001 are obvious examples. While a positive reform-oriented process has begun in the Prison Service (as previously described), the actual number of prisoners' children is likely to have risen 25% during the same period.

Another phenomenon which can also have a considerable negative effect on prisoners' children is the gradual but notable tendency to postpone probation until after two-thirds of the sentence is served. For those children who have significant contact to the imprisoned parent, probation naturally constitutes a possibility to re-establish contact under more normal circumstances. The development, however, speaks for itself: in 1985, 9% of all prisoners were refused probation after two-thirds of the sentence was served; in 1995, this concerned 15%; in 2000, 21% and in 2005 one out of every four prisoners (25%) was denied probation after two-thirds of the sentence was served.[26] This must also have affected many children of imprisoned parents. Probation is clearly a policy area where it makes a lot of sense to consider the needs and rights of prisoners' children.

Just as significant is the issue of home leave. Imprisoned parents' possibility for home leave can be essential for their children and special rules have been introduced in some places to provide the possibility of home leave for the child's birthday or other events. These special schemes are of limited range compared to the general tightening of home leave rules, part of punitive and populist legislation during recent years.[27] For example, the number of unaccompanied weekend home leaves decreased after the new rules were adopted.[28] Moreover, home leave is not granted for the first three months if the person appears late for commitment to prison. In addition, a zero-tolerance policy against narcotics in all prisons entails regular urine sampling of all prisoners. The sanction for a positive sample is often denial of home leave. In 2010, for example, a staggering total of 34,602 urine samples and tests were carried out in Danish prisons.[29] As a result of this policy, the pressure to smuggle drugs into the prisons has apparently increased and in some prisons it has been "necessary to restrict the prisoners and relatives' possibilities of movement during visits".[30] This means that many children of prisoners have less possibility of seeing their parents in connection with home leave, and that the visiting situation at some places has deteriorated. The child-friendly initiatives in this particular area have essentially drowned in punitive and populist efforts and legislation.

Penal policy debates and children of imprisoned parents

Internationally, penal populism has increased the likelihood of harming and creating problems for an increasing number of prisoners' children, most notably by increasing prison populations but arguably also by raising the level of stigmatisation experienced by these children thanks to tough-on-crime rhetoric and lack of focus on rehabilitation and reintegration. In some of the above-mentioned Danish examples, the lack of debate surrounding the consequences for children of imprisoned parents has certainly been remarkable. When Lene Espersen published a bill in 2005, which ordered three months' home leave suspension for prisoners who appeared late for their commitment to prison, she stated: "I think it has a pedagogical effect if you cannot visit your family for three months or participate in your child's birthday."[31] The minister of justice focused exclusively on the prisoner and completely failed to even consider how the children would feel about such legislation. Instead, breaking the contact between children and parents was on the contrary framed as something positive for the state and allegedly reflected the people's sense of justice. On the same occasion, another political party profiled itself by proposing that prisoners who appeared too late for their prison sentence should have a total prohibition on home leave for the duration of their sentence.[32]

But since then, the Danish politicians have fortunately shown some cross-political awareness of the research and debate on prisoners' children. Thus, in December 2008, two motions were presented in the Danish parliament aimed at improving the conditions for prisoners' children, and a further one followed in February 2009. Two of the resolutions were presented by the Social Liberal party and one by the Socialist People's Party. Among other things, the proposals suggested that special visiting plans be made for children of inmates, that parents in remand prison have the same right to visits by their children as other prisoners, that an emergency team be established for prisoners' children, that children's officers are introduced in the Prison and Probation Service's institutions, that more family therapy halfway houses are established, that special visiting facilities be arranged for children, that single providers serve their sentences with electronic tags and that prisoners have access on a trial basis to communicating with their children via mobile phone and emails.[33]

None of the proposals were adopted at the time, but what is interesting is that the debate in the parliament revealed broad support for prisoners' children. Even "Tough Brian" stated: "I agree entirely that we must focus on prisoners' children and the children's visiting possibilities."[34] Vivi Kier from the Conservative People's Party joined in and stated: "To me, as a conservative, children's conditions and possibilities for a safe and good upbringing and good contact to biological parents is incredibly important. Naturally, this also applies to those children whose parents are detained in our prisons."[35] Correspondingly, René Christensen from the Danish People's Party commented: "The desire is to improve the conditions for prisoners' children and we agree in general terms that this is something we have to look at. The visiting conditions have, of course, tremendous impact on how the children experience their contact with their mother, father or a relative."[36] Karen Hækkerup from the Danish Social Democrats elaborated on the problem and stated: "There is no doubt that we must do what we can to help these children. And when you look at the figures and can see the risk that exists for children, whose mother or father is in prison, becoming mentally ill, depressed, excluded, marginalised, then we must say to ourselves: We're not doing it well enough."[37]

While a lot remains to be done, the above political support undoubtedly encouraged the fall 2012 decision to introduce children's officers in all prisons in Denmark (see Chapter 2). Perhaps this is partly due to researchers, NGOs, and others taking advantage of how public sentiments on justice can be utilised to create reforms in this area when these sentiments are *informed* about the situation and problems facing prisoners' children.

Part IV
Conclusion

17
When the Innocent are Punished: Prison, Society and the Effects of Imprisonment

The use of imprisonment carries with it a long list of serious problems, which reach far beyond the question of how the individual prisoner reacts to being deprived of liberty. By looking specifically at prisoners' children – a group of citizens who are likely to be more numerous than the prisoners themselves – we can begin to understand some of the intergenerational effects of imprisonment. Children of imprisoned parents constitute a vulnerable group with heightened risk of adverse outcomes. As shown in this study, the closer we get to the situation and experiences of these children, the more we understand how difficult and devastating it can be to have a parent in prison. The almost countless practical problems and issues that can arise – and which have been described in this book through the experiences and voices of prisoners' children and their families, as well as prison staff, the police and social workers – confirm the serious, complex and far-reaching consequences of parental imprisonment.

Isolating offenders from their families

Historically, the shift in the Western practice of punishment, which took place from the late 17th century until the early 19th century, gradually left a religiously defined system of public shaming and corporal punishment behind but produced a system of extreme isolation that affects not only those punished but also their families and children in hitherto unseen ways. This significant side effect of modern penology was almost completely overlooked for more than a century and has only recently begun to receive serious attention. Today we are used to having prisons in our societies, and few among us question their existence or the basic practice of imprisonment. But the fact remains that we have created and upheld a system of punishment that effectively challenges and threatens family relations on a very large scale without even considering the serious intergenerational and societal consequences.

There are literally millions of children worldwide who have experienced parental imprisonment. Not all these children will be seriously affected, and for some it can even be beneficial to have a parent removed from home. The important issue here is whether or not there has been a significant, close and psychologically meaningful contact between the child and the parent in question – something that much quantitative research on prisoners' children has unfortunately not been able to take into account. The limited data we have on family situations and visiting frequency, however, suggest that a substantial group of prisoners' children are seriously affected. Many children live with their parents when they are imprisoned and many more children want to visit them, but maintaining meaningful contact can be extremely difficult. There are hundreds of issues that can arise and challenge the possibilities for maintaining contact – and even cause it to cease. Even seemingly minor practicalities can have far-reaching consequences. Placing parents in prisons far away from home can make visits too costly and time consuming for families, and having visiting hours only when kids are in school can in itself keep a child from seeing a parent on a regular basis.

From arrest to release – the different stages of the criminal justice process

The arrest of a parent can itself be an unpleasant and perhaps traumatic event for the children who experience it at first hand. This is clearly described not only by children but also by those doing the arrests. Common arrest experiences for Danish police officers include children crying, children who were afraid of or hostile towards the police and children who clung to their mother or father during an arrest. Another very important issue is when and how the social authorities should be contacted – and how states can make sure that remaining children are always taken care of appropriately.

Remand imprisonment often constitute an especially challenging and difficult time characterised by stress and uncertainty for prisoners' families and children. Some parents choose to keep the remand imprisonment secret from even their children, and some include the children but try to keep it a family secret. Some families will begin to experience economic difficulties. Many children also experience shame and guilt in connection with the imprisonment of a parent, and some are bullied. The situation and the surrounding feelings can be especially intense and difficult to handle during the remand phase. The disappearance of the parent will come as a shock to many children, and the remaining parent (if there is one) will often not have sufficient energy to talk about the situation with the individual child.

In some countries, remand imprisonment is also characterized by a very strict regime in order to protect the ongoing police investigation. In Scandinavia, for example, remand prisoners are often subjected to special restrictions on visits and contact with the outside world, which can become a serious problem for prisoners' children. Furthermore, a parent who is exposed to the well-documented detrimental effects of solitary confinement, as sometimes practised during pre-trial in Scandinavia, can find it even more difficult to maintain meaningful contact with his or her child. One would think that it should at least be possible for a child to receive regular phone calls from an imprisoned parent. But in Denmark, remand prisoners are normally not allowed to use the phone at all. From a child's point of view, this seems absurd and once again reminds us that modern penology has neglected to focus on many of the ways prisons interrelate with and affect the outside world.

When a sentence is passed, it can be a relief insofar as the uncertainty comes to an end. However, in many cases, this will be sad news for the child, especially if the parent received a long sentence. Other crucial issues concern the choice of prison – in terms of transport, regime and visiting conditions. Here, and with regard to the choice of sentence in general, it seems obvious that the best interest of the child could play a much more prominent role. Choosing a non-custodial sanction should in some cases clearly be considered an option.

When a parent's imprisonment commences, how and if contact between the child and parent will be able to develop will depend greatly on the conditions in and location of the particular prison. When it comes to visiting conditions and other possibilities for maintaining contact, there are often significant differences in regimes, rules and practises from one jurisdiction to another and from one prison to another. The staff and prison culture in the individual prison, especially in the visiting section, can also be very important. Bad visiting facilities and friendly staff are preferable compared to the opposite combination. Even upholding regular telephone contact can be very difficult during imprisonment. Although modern communications technology offers many possibilities, these are often feared by lawmakers and sometimes prison administrators. The experiences of children, prisoners, prison staff, social workers, researchers, psychologists and other experts tell us that it can often be very difficult to uphold meaningful contact between children and their imprisoned parents – and some fail trying.

If contact is somehow maintained, there will normally come a time when release from prison can bring a parent back to the community and perhaps the family. This process is also fraught with challenges, and success is by no means guaranteed. The families and perhaps the prisoner have changed. Prison can produce withdrawal and loss of agency, which can foster a culture and identity where the responsibilities associated with parenthood are not exactly enhanced. But perhaps most importantly, children change at an incredible pace as a natural part of growing up. Putting a relationship with a child on hold is often impossible and will have long-lasting consequences.

In some cases – for example, when an imprisoned parent has committed family abuse or has seriously harmed his family in another way – it can be best for the child if contact ceases. This naturally applies in all families where a parent does not live up to his or her responsibility as a parent, regardless of whether prisons and crime are involved. Research tells us that contact is often tremendously important for the children, but it is essential to remember, and to take into account, that this is not always the case.

Breaking up families – a neglected paradox of modern punishment

Taken together, the research, data and observations in this book present us with not only a long list of problems experienced by a vulnerable group in our societies but also a major paradox:

> If we hail the family as a fundamental and almost sacred unit in our societies, and if we insist on regarding children as an especially valuable and vulnerable group of citizens, why do we in our modern democratic states break up families on a massive scale on a daily basis and as a result of a conscious, thoroughly planned and generally unquestioned policy of using imprisonment as a key sanction in the repertoire of punishments?

The very basic answer seems to be that the prison has become ingrained in our societies, practices and minds in a way that has created a number of very dangerous blind spots. Part of this explanation is undoubtedly historical. The modern penitentiary presented itself with an impressive force and a convincing ideology at the right time in history. The belief in its possible rehabilitative powers has been hard to overturn, and its power as a tool for revenge – allowing us carry out punishment out of sight of the rest of society – seems to fit our self-understanding as civilised people and nations well. At the same time, the very existence of these institutions indirectly proves the sanity and civilised nature of us who are not imprisoned – or so many seem to think. In addition prisons also "solve" a very real problem of punishing those who break the law. There are several reasons why we continue to use prisons as the cornerstone in our system of punishment. But in my mind, the arguments above only partly explain why we have not seriously considered the paradox of prisoners' children and imprisonment for so many years. There are several other avenues of analysis which need to be opened up empirically if we want to come closer to answering such a question.

One such avenue is the question of how visiting practices have evolved historically in prisons during the 20th century. A specific issue is when, where and how children actually began to visit in prisons in greater numbers. Another interesting area for future research is the question of how we have perceived childhood during the same period and how this has affected the question of visiting parents, not only in prisons but also in hospitals and perhaps other institutions. I remember my own father describing how his parents were not allowed to visit him properly when he was hospitalised as a child; he remembers only seeing his mother waving through a window. I have heard many other similar post-war stories, and now pensioned doctors and nurses have told me that the philosophy was that too many visits would upset the children because they cried after their parents left. This undoubtedly tells us something important about how children and their relationships to adults have been perceived and changed significantly during the last half century or so.

But regardless of how we try to analyse and explain the way prisoners' children have been neglected, there is no doubt that this is currently changing, at least to some degree. It has become more and more clear that the massive secondary effects of imprisonment must be addressed and that children of imprisoned parents stand right in the middle of such a discussion. Nevertheless, many states have in recent decades embarked on a course of penal populism and insisted on increasing the use of imprisonment.

Penal populism, prisoners' children and stigmatisation

Penal populism produce more prisons, more prisoners and more children of imprisoned parents. In addition, the associated political rhetoric demanding tougher sentences and picturing crime as "the evil other" will tend to stigmatise and alienate prisoners' families and children even further. This can have very concrete results in terms of how prisoners' children view society and its representatives, for example, the police or a prison officer. Prisoners' children thereby risk experiencing a sort of upside-down world whereby society's alleged security can become their insecurity and penal populism and its one-sided version of justice can become their injustice.

The fact is that some of our current penal practices may lose legitimacy if we adopt the perspective of prisoners' children. Public sentiments on justice can not only be used to support harsher sentencing; they can also support prisoners' children – illustrated, for example, by the comments of many police and prison officers in this study. This means that we have to take prisoners' children seriously and reform the current practice of punishment and imprisonment. Children's rights are a possible and meaningful starting point for such reforms.

Children's rights and penal reforms

Traditionally, discussions, research and court judgments within the field of prisons and human rights have almost exclusively been a matter of balancing the state's legitimate use of power and security concerns against the individual prisoner's rights. The question of whether, how and to what degree the use of imprisonment has also affected the rights of persons outside of prison has for many years gone unconsidered. This has up until recently certainly been the case with prisoners' children – a group of people whose rights are clearly affected through the use of imprisonment.

As shown in this study, this has gradually begun to change. But there is still a long way towards making sure that children's rights are taken into account where appropriate in this context. We need to make sure that children's rights, when applied to prisoners' children, are not just abstract principles but actual legal rights with practical implications. Such a process should produce concrete national standards with regards to numerous issues such as the child-friendly quality of visiting conditions and practices, as well as basic issues concerning a child's right to visit his or her parent. What, for example, does the child's right to maintain contact with a parent actually mean? How much time can be allowed to pass before a first visit is established? How often does a child actually have the right to visit a parent and for how long? Should a child be allowed to call a parent on the phone now and again? The well-being of prisoners' children is certainly also one good reason, among many, to downscale the use of imprisonment and consider alternative non-custodial sanctions.

Norway has taken an important step towards recognising the rights of prisoners children by legally establishing children's right to contact with their parents as a general principle and requiring that children "shall receive special attention" during the imprisonment. In some countries, children's rights have also been used as a starting point for creating actual reforms and child-friendly changes to prison practice. This has been the case in Denmark, Sweden and Norway – the introduction of children's officers being an important example. But there is a long way to go in terms of securing prisoners' children all the rights set out in the UN Convention on the Rights of the Child.

There are different entry points and levels of reform that must be considered. Within the area of law making and policy children's rights need to be taken into account. Both in terms of considering sentencing and alternatives to imprisonment, but also to make sure that children's rights are considered in prison law and relevant acts on the administration of justice. Another entry point is of course culture and practices in the relevant institutions and among the important actors. This includes the parents themselves – addressing parental skills among imprisoned parents is one example – but it certainly also includes working with and changing cultures in prison and among prison staff and the police.

The very basic challenge is that we need to reform our systems of justice and punishment in order to take innocent children's needs, situations and rights into account. Although we have had prisons and prisoners' children for centuries, this is still a novel and daunting challenge considering the way imprisonment is practised in most nations today.

Appendix: Prison Visits, Interviews and National Surveys

1 Prison visits

Denmark
- Statsfængslet i Vridløselille (closed – has a remand unit as well)
- Statsfængslet Østjylland (closed – has a remand unit as well)
- Statsfængslet i Ringe (closed)
- Statsfængslet i Nyborg (closed)
- Anstalten ved Herstedvester (closed)
- Horsens Statsfængsel (closed). This prison closed down in 2006.
- Vestre fængsel (closed – primarily remand)
- Blegdamsvejens fængsel (closed – primarily remand)
- Politigårdens fængsel (closed)
- Nytorv fængsel (remand)
- Statsfængslet i Jyderup (open – has a remand unit as well)
- Statsfængslet ved Horserød (open – has a remand unit as well)
- Frederikshavn arresthus (remand)
- Helsingør arresthus (remand)
- Hillerød arresthus (remand)
- Vejle arresthus (remand)
- Roskilde arresthus (remand)

Most of the above institutions have been visited on many occasions and some of them more than ten times.

Sweden
- Anstalten Kirseberg (closed)
- Anstalten Fosie (closed)
- Anstalten Tygelsjö (open)

Norway
- Halden Prison (closed)

England
- HMP Askham Grange (closed)
- HMP Wolds (closed)

Italy
- ICAM Prison in Milan (closed)
- Bollate Prison in Milan (closed)
- Trani Male Prison in Puglia (closed)
- Trani Women's Prison in Puglia (closed – situated in a 13th-century convent)

Poland
- Bialoleka Prison in Warsaw (closed – remand)

2 Interviews and other sources

The interviews used in this book have been done by Janne Jakobsen and/or Peter Scharff Smith unless other sources are referred to in the notes.[1]

Prison Service staff

Through interviews and meetings, more than 50 employees and former employees in the Danish, Swedish and Norwegian prison services (more than 40 from the Danish Prison Service, and around 10 from Sweden and Norway) have been cited as verbal sources of information in the notes in this study (many more are cited as written sources through the Danish national survey – see below). This includes staff from the prison service directorate, prison staff and probation officers. These staff members cover a very broad range of positions from prison officers to prison governors, as well as social workers, prison chaplains, prison teachers, mid-level managers and staff from remand prisons, open and closed prisons and the halfway houses.

The names and/or positions of these staff members are mentioned in the notes when appropriate.

The Danish Police

Through interviews and meetings, ten employees and former employees in the Danish Police have been cited as verbal sources of information in the notes in this study (many more are cited as written sources through the Danish national survey – see below). This includes staff and teachers from the Danish police school as well as frontline police officers.

The names and/or positions of these staff members are mentioned in the notes when appropriate.

Prisoners, relatives and children of imprisoned parents

Interviews with and written unpublished statements from prisoners, prisoners' relatives and prisoners' children have been available for this study through a number of different sources. Some of this material has been done or collected directly by the Danish Institute for Human Rights (by Janne Jakobsen, Lise Garkier Hendriksen and Peter Scharff Smith) through interviews, meetings and surveys. Furthermore, a number of non-published sources have been made available for this study through external partners. The interviews and sources used in this study, which have not been published and are not mentioned in the bibliography, include the following Danish material:

- Interviews made by Stine Lindberg with 13 children of imprisoned parents.[2]
- Focus group interviews with 11 children of imprisoned parents on visiting in prison.[3]
- Video interviews by Dorthe Høeg Brask with three children of imprisoned parents.[4]
- Focus group interviews with numerous children of imprisoned parents made by the Danish Red Cross in connection with internal evaluations of their study groups of prisoners' children.
- Interviews with four children of imprisoned parents, their mother and the imprisoned father.[5]
- Written and unpublished data and statements from 33 imprisoned fathers and four imprisoned mothers collected by the Danish Institute for Human Rights as part of a survey made during the evaluation of the project on "children's officers" in Danish prisons. The 37 imprisoned parents had altogether 70 children below the age of 18.[6]
- Interviews by Janne Jakobsen with two former prisoners, two relatives of prisoners (one wife and one ex-wife) and a boy with a father in prison.[7]
- In addition, notes from numerous meetings/interviews with prisoners and imprisoned fathers by Peter Scharff Smith made during or after prison visits as part of different research projects, practical prison projects and prison inspections.
- Unpublished data from the Danish Prison Service on various projects and initiatives collected by Peter Scharff Smith. When such data is referred to in the text, the footnote will describe the specific source of the data.

– Furthermore, Dr. Linda Minke has kindly allowed me to use her survey of 803 prisoners in Danish prisons. Some of the data from this survey is published in her Ph.D. thesis (Minke 2012), but I was allowed to use the entire material from this survey on family issues and children of prisoners.

In addition, a significant number of articles and NGO reports are based on in-depth interviews with prisoners' children. Several of these are from Norway, Sweden and Denmark and not available in English and include interviews with prisoners' relatives in general and prisoners' children in particular. They are mentioned in the bibliography and cited in the footnotes when used in this study.

NGOs

Through interviews and meetings more than 20 people from various NGOs (primarily in Denmark, but also in Sweden and Norway) with relevant knowledge about prisoners' children or surrounding issues have been used as verbal sources of information in this study. This includes members and staff from the following organizations: SAVN, the Danish Red Cross, Børns vilkår, KRIS Danmark, KRIM, FFP and Bryggan.

The names and/or positions of these people are mentioned in the notes when appropriate.

Other sources

Through interviews and meetings, 14 other people with relevant knowledge of prisoners' children or surrounding issues have been used as verbal sources of information. These individuals include researchers, social workers and psychologists.

The names and/or positions of these people are mentioned in the notes when appropriate.

3 National survey on the treatment of prisoners' children

During 2007–2009, a comprehensive country-wide questionnaire survey was sent to all prisons, police districts, and local social services in Denmark. This is referred to in the footnotes in the text as "The Danish Institute for Human Rights Survey". This survey was made and conducted by Janne Jakobsen and Peter Scharff Smith. We had a response from 28 remand prisons (which corresponds to a response rate of 68.3%), 17 prisons for sentenced prisoners (response rate: 94.4%) and 6 halfway houses (response rate: 75%), as well as 34 police districts (response rate: 47.2%) and 28 municipal social services (response rate: 40.8%).

The responses to the questionnaire have been anonymised. Through the system below (mentioning a title and a letter), it is however possible to keep track of the individual responses, so it is clear which title/function the person concerned has when they are cited in the footnotes.

Police:

Deputy Chief Superintendent: S
Police Superintendent: S, T, U, V,W
Deputy Police Superintendent: S, T, U, V, W, X, Y, Z, Æ
Assistant Detective: S, T, U, V, W, X, Y, Z, Æ, Ø, Å
Police Sergeant: S, T, U, V, W, X
Police Officer: S
Supervisor: S

Prisons:

Prison officer: W, X, Y, Z, Æ, Ø, Å
Visitor supervisor: W
Social work consultant: W
Treatment consultant: W, X
Area manager: W
Social worker: W
Prison governor: W
Lack of position designation: W

Remand prisons (and remand units in other prisons):

Prison officer: I, J, K, L, M, N, O, P, Q, R, S, T, U, V, W, X, Y, Z, Æ, Ø, Å
Remand prison supervisor: I, J, K
Remand prison manager: I, J, K
Lack of job designation: I

Halfway Houses:

Deputy governor: Z, Æ, Ø, Å
Social worker: Z, Æ

The social authorities:

Social worker: I, J, K, L, M, N, O, P, Q, R, S, T, U, V, W, X, Y, Z, Æ, Ø, Å
Head of section: I
Children and youth manager: I
Family counsellor: I

Ex-secretary/deputy manager: I
Section leader: I
Children and youth consultant: I
Lack of title: I

Notes

1 Scenes from Family Life

1. These interviews are from "Når uskyldige bliver straffet" (When the Innocent are Punished), *Information*, 2 May 2008.
2. Annelie Björkhagen Tureson, *Mor i fängelse – mödrar och barn berätter. En analys av ungdomars resiliensprocess* (Gothenburg, Sweden: University of Gothenburg, 2009), 11.
3. The quote is taken from interviews with Norwegian children of prisoners made in February 2012 by FFP (Foreningen for Fangers Pårørende) – an NGO for prisoners' relatives. See "Høringsuttalelse fra en gruppe ungdom", FFP, Oslo.
4. Interview with Eiler Larsen, assistant detective, teacher at the Danish Police Academy.
5. The account and quotes are from Marlene Grøftehauge, *Fangebørn (Prisoners' Children)*, Aarhus 2004, 82 ff. It is not apparent from the account who was responsible for the fact that the two boys were only allowed to visit their father after three months.
6. Interview quoted from Janne Jakobsen and Peter Scharff Smith, *Børn af fængslede. En informations- og undervisningsbog [Children of Imprisoned Parents. A Handbook for Relatives and Professionals]* (Frederiksberg: Samfundslitteratur, 2011).
7. The interview quote is from Else Christensen, *Forældre i fængsel – en undersøgelse af børn og forældres erfaringer [Parents in Prison – A Study of Children's and Parents' Experiences]* (Copenhagen: The Danish National Centre for Social Research, 1999), 37 f. It is not apparent who was responsible for 1½ and 2½ months passing by before the visits were established.
8. Interview quoted from Jakobsen and Smith (2011).
9. Interview with "Kristian".
10. Interview quoted from Jakobsen and Smith (2011).

2 When the Innocent are Punished

1. Joseph Murray and David P. Farrington, "Parental Imprisonment: Long-lasting Effects on Boys Internalizing Problems through the Life Course", *Development and Psychopathology* 20, no. 1 (2008), 133. See also Joseph Murray, David P. Farrington et al., *Effects of Imprisonment on Child Antisocial Behaviour and Mental Health: A Systematic Review* (Oslo: Campbel Collaboration, 2009); Christopher Wildeman and Bruce Western, "Incarceration in Fragile Families", *The Future of Children* 20, no. 2 (2010), 157–177; Joseph Murray, David P. Farrington and Ivana Sekol, "Children's Antisocial Behavior, Mental Health, Drug Use, and Educational Performance After Parental Incarceration: A Systematic Review and Meta-Analysis", *Psychological Bulletin* 138, no. 2 (2012); Adele D. Jones

and Agnieszka E. Wainaina-Woźna (eds), *Children of Prisoners. Interventions and Mitigations* (Huddersfield, UK: University of Huddersfield, 2013).
2. See, for example, Murray and Farrington et al., 2009; Wildeman and Western, 2010; Sara Wakefield and Christopher Wildeman, "Mass Imprisonment and Racial Disparities in Childhood Behavioral Problems", *Criminology and Public Policy* 10, no. 3 (2011), 791–817; Peter Scharff Smith and Janne Jakobsen, *Når straffen rammer uskyldige. Børn af fængslede i Danmark* (Copenhagen: Gyldendal, 2010); Peter Scharff Smith and Lucy Gampell (eds), *Children of Imprisoned Parents* (Copenhagen: The Danish Institute for Human Rights, Eurochips and University of Ulster, 2011); Jones and Wainaina-Woźna, 2013.
3. H. C. Hoffmann, A. L. Byrd and A. M. Kightlinger, "Prison Programs and Services for Incarcerated Parents and Their Underage Children: Results from a National Survey of Correctional Facilities", *The Prison Journal* 90, no. 4 (2010), 397.
4. See Murray and Farrington, 2008, 138.
5. See Murray and Farrington, 2008, 137 f.
6. Kim Williams, Vea Papadopoulou and Natalie Booth, "Prisoners' Childhood and Family Backgrounds. Results from the Surveying Prisoner Crime Reduction (SPCR) Longitudinal Cohort Study of Prisoners", Ministry of Justice Research Series 4/12, London, March 2012, iii.
7. See L. Ayre, K. Philbrick and M. Reiss, *Children of Imprisoned Parents: European Perspectives on Good Practice* (Montrouge: Eurochips, 2006), 7.
8. Peter Scharff Smith, *Moralske hospitaler. Det moderne fængselsvæsens gennembrud 1770–1870* (Copenhagen: Forum, 2003), 25. See also, Peter Scharff Smith, "A Religious Technology of the Self – Rationality and Religion in the Rise of the Modern Penitentiary", *Punishment and Society* 6, no. 2 (2004), 195–220.
9. Robert J. Sampson makes a similar point in "The Incarceration Ledger. Toward a New Era in Assessing Societal Consequences", *Criminology & Public Policy* 10, no. 3 (2011), 819.
10. Like many others, I have previously been inspired by Foucault and have written about prisons and technologies of power. See, for example, Peter Scharff Smith, "A Religious Technology of the Self – Rationality and Religion in the Rise of the Modern Penitentiary", *Punishment and Society* 6, no. 2 (2004a), 195–220.
11. Alison Liebling and Shadd Maruna, "Introduction: The Effects of Imprisonment Revisited", in *The Effects of Imprisonment*, ed. A. Liebling and S. Maruna (Cullompton, UK: Willan Publishing, 2005), 16.
12. Using the term *collateral damage* in this context is inspired by Oliver Robertson, *Collateral Convicts: Children of Incarcerated Parents. Recommendations and Good Practice from the UN Committee on the Rights of the Child, Day of General Discussion 2011* (Geneva: United Nations, March 2012).
13. Michel Foucault, *Madness and Civilization. A History of Insanity in the Age of Reason* (New York: Vintage Books, 1988), 38 ff.
14. On penal populism and tough-on-crime policies, see John Pratt, *Penal Populism* (London: Routledge, 2007); David Garland, *The Culture of Control. Crime and Social Order in Contemporary Society* (Oxford: Oxford University Press, 2001); Michael Tonry, *Thinking About Crime: Sense and Sensibility in American Penal Culture* (New York: Oxford University Press, 2004).

15. See Chapter 16. See also Peter Scharff Smith, "A Critical look at Scandinavian Exceptionalism. Welfare State Theories, Penal Populism, and Prison Conditions in Denmark and Scandinavia", in *Nordic Prison Practice and Policy – Exceptional or Not?: Exploring Penal Exceptionalism in the Nordic Context*, ed. Thomas Ugelvik and Jane Dullem (London/New York: Routledge, 2011), 43 ff.
16. See Smith and Jakobsen, 2010, 233 ff. See also Chapter 16.
17. See list of all prison visits in the appendix.
18. Funded by the European Union; the Directorate for Justice, Freedom and Security: Fundamental Rights and Citizenship and by the Danish Egmont Foundation.
19. For a more detailed description of the EU study, see the introduction in Smith and Gampell, 2011, 6 f.
20. The studies and the resulting recommendations are found in Smith and Gampell, 2011.
21. See the final report from the project: Lise Garkier Hendriksen, Janne Jakobsen and Peter Scharff Smith, *Børneansvarlige I Kriminalforsorgen – Fokus på de indsattes børn* (Copenhagen: The Danish Institute for Human Rights, 2012).
22. See "Aftale om kriminalforsorgens økonomi i 2013–2016". Available in Danish at http://www.justitsministeriet.dk/sites/default/files/media/Pressemeddelelser/pdf/2012/Aftaletekst-KRF.pdf (accessed 22 November 2012).
23. Alison Liebling, "Whose Side are We On. Theory, Practice and Allegiances in Prisons Research", *British Journal of Criminology* 41, no. 3 (2001).
24. Liebling, 2001, 472.
25. Liebling, 2001, 481 and 482.

3 Prison and Society

1. Smith (2003 62 f.).
2. William Crawford, "Report of William Crawford, Esq. on the Penitentiaries of the United States Addressed to his Majesty's Principal Secretary of State for the Home Department", in *British Parliamentary Papers. Crime and Punishment – PRISONS*, no. 2, Session 1834, 12.
3. Smith (2004a); Peter Scharff Smith "The Effects of Solitary Confinement on Prison Inmates: A Brief History and Review of the Literature", in *Crime and Justice: A Review of Research*, vol. 34, ed. Michael Tonry (Chicago: University of Chicago Press, 2006), 441–528. See also Michel Foucault, *Discipline and Punish: The Birth of the Prison* (New York: Vintage Books, 1995), and Michael Ignatieff, *A Just Measure of Pain: The Penitentiary in the Industrial Revolution, 1750–1850* (London: Macmillan, 1978).
4. Crawford et al. (1838, 8).
5. Hans Christian Andersen quoted from Smith (2004a, 209 f.).
6. See, for example, Norman Johnston, *Forms of Constraint: A History of Prison Architecture* (Urbana: University of Illinois Press, 2000), chapters 4–6; Ricardo Salvatore and Carlos Aguirre (ed.) *The Birth of the Penitentiary in Latin America: Essays on Criminology, Prison Reform, and Social Control 1830–1940* (Austin: University of Texas Press, 1996), chapter 1.

7. See Peter Scharff Smith, "Solitary Confinement – History, Practice, and Human Rights Standards", *Prison Service Journal*, no. 181 (January 2009), 3–11.
8. Peter Scharff Smith, "Isolation and Mental Illness in Vridsløselille 1859–1873 – A New Perspective on the Breakthrough of the Modern Penitentiary", *Scandinavian Journal of History* 29, no. 1 (2004), 1–25.
9. Herman Franke, "The Rise and Decline of Solitary Confinement: Socio-Historical Explanations of Long-Term Penal Changes", *British Journal of Criminology* 32, no. 2 (1992), 128; Smith (2006a); Francis Gray, *Prison Discipline in America* (Boston: Charles C. Little and James Brown, 1847), 181. See also Smith (2004b).
10. Smith (2003, 192).
11. Smith (2006a, 467).
12. Bill Forsythe, "Loneliness and Cellular Confinement in English Prisons 1878–1921", *British Journal of Criminology* 44, no. 5 (2004), 761; Ignatieff (1978, 3); Smith (2006a).
13. N. Johnsen, *En fanges dag paa Vridsløselille* [A Prisoner's Day at Vridsløselille], unpublished manuscript, 1929.
14. Johnsen (1929).
15. See Nilsson, R. (1999), *En välbyggd maskin, en mardröm för själen: Det svenska fängelsesystemet under 1800-talet*. Lund: Lund University Press, and Ann-Christine Petersson Hjelm, *Fängelset som välfärdsbygge* (Stockholm: Institutet för rättshistorisk forskning, 2011).
16. Hjelm (2011, 222).
17. Ben Raikes and Kelly Lockwood, "Mothering from the Inside. A Small-Scale Evaluation of Acorn House, an Overnight Child Contact Facility at HMP Askham Grange", *Prison Service Journal* 194 (2011), 22.
18. Raikes and Lockwood (2011, 22). Some UK prisons allow special child-centred visits and have family days, but access to these can be linked to whether prisoners "behave well" in prison, which is problematic from a children's rights point of view. See Marie Hutton, "A Labour of Love: The Impact of the Children's Play Project on Family Contact at HMP Doncaster", forthcoming.
19. See Smith (2003).
20. Quoted from Peter Scharff Smith, "Sindssyge bag tremmer", in *Det forrykte menneske. Den psykisk syge i historien*, ed. Edith Mandrup Rønn and Inger Hartby (Ebeltoft: Skippershoved, 2006b), 229.
21. Simo Køppe, *Neurosens opståen og udvikling i 1800-tallet* [*The Emergence and Development of Neurosis in the 17th Century*] (Copenhagen: Frydenlund, 2004), 132 f.
22. Michael H. Stone, *Healing the Mind: A History of Psychiatry from Antiquity to the Present* (NewYork: W. W. Norten & Co., 1998), 114.
23. Knud Waaben, *Retspsykiatri og strafferet i historiens lys* [*Forensic Psychiatry and Criminal Law in the Light of History*] (Copenhagen: Janssen-Cilag, 1997), 96.
24. Christian Borch, *Kriminalitet og magt: Kriminalitetsopfattelser i det 20. århundrede* (Copenhagen: Politisk Regy, 2005), 35.
25. Stephen Jay Gould, *The Mismeasure of Man* (New York: Penguin Books1992), 123 ff.
26. Borch (2005, 35 f.).
27. Borch (2005, 40).

28. Gould (1992, 158 ff.).
29. Gould (1992, 161).
30. Gould (1992, 160 f.).
31. Gould (1992, 164).
32. K. K. Steincke, *Fremtidens Forsørgelsesvæsen: Oversigt over og Kritik af den samlede Forsørgelseslovgivning samt Betænkning og motiverede Forslag til en systematisk Nyordning* (Copenhagen: Stultz, 1920), 237.
33. Gunnar Myrdal and Alva Myrdal, *Krise i befolkningsspørgsmaalet* (Copenhagen: Martin, 1935), 179.
34. Hjelm (2011, 219 and 239). With regard to discussions on biological theories and their application on criminals and prisoners in Norway, see E. Schaanning, *Menneskelaboratoriet. Botsfengslets historie* (Oslo: Scandinavian Academic Press, 2007).
35. Rachel Condry, *Families Shamed: The Consequences of Crime for Relatives of Serious Offenders* (Cullompton, UK: Willan Publishing, 2007), 66.
36. See, for example, Robert Anderson, "A Blessing in Disguise: Attention Deficit Hyperactivity Disorder Diagnoses and Swedish Correctional Treatment Policy in the 21st Century", in Ugelvik, T., and Dallum, J. (eds) (2011), *Penal Exceptionalism? Nordic Prison Policy and Practice*. New York: Routledge.
37. George Schrøder, *Fængselspsychoser og Psychoser i Fængslet* [*Prison Psychoses and Psychoses in Prison*] (Copenhagen: J. Lund, 1913), 22.
38. Schrøder (1913, 139).
39. Harald Selmer: *Statistiske Meddelelser og Undersøgelser fra Sindssygeanstalten ved Aarhus I dens første 25 Aar* [*Statistical Notifications and Surveys from the Mental Illness Institution by Aarhus in its First 25 Years*] (Copenhagen: C.A. Reitzel1879), 147.
40. Borch (2005, 38).
41. Most well known is Emilie Durkheim. see Borch (2005, 41).
42. See, for example, Gresham Sykes, *The Society of Captives: A Study of a Maximum Security Prison* (Princeton, NJ: Princeton University Press, 1974), originally published in 1958, as well as Stanley Cohen and Laurie Taylor, *Psychological Survival. The Experience of Long-term Imprisonment* (New York: Vintage Books, 1974). For a more recent example, see Adrian Ground's "Understanding the Effects of Wrongful Imprisonment", in *Crime and Justice: A Review of Research*, ed. Michael Tonry (Chicago: University of Chicago Press, 2005). See also Ben Crewe, "Depth, Weight, Tightness: Revisiting the Pains of Imprisonment", *Punishment & Society* 13, no. 5 (December 2011), 509–529, and Ben Crewe, "The Sociology of Imprisonment", *Handbook on Prisons*, ed. Y. Jewkes (Cullompton, UK: Willan Publishing, 2009), 123 ff.
43. See Liebling and Maruna (2005, 10 f.).
44. James Bonta and Paul Gendrau, "Re-examining the Cruel and Unusual Punishment of Prison Life", in *Long-term Imprisonment: Policy, Science, and Correctional Practice*, ed. Timothy Flanagan (Thousand Oaks: SAGE 1995), 76.
45. See Henrik Steen Andersen, "Mental Health in Prison Populations", *Acta Psychiatrica Scandinavica* 110, supplement to no. 424 (2004), 39.
46. Liebling and Maruna (2005, 12 f.).
47. Hans Toch, *Living in Prison: The Ecology of Survival* (Easton: American Psychological Association, 2002), xv.

48. Craig Haney, "The Contextual Revolution in a Psychology and the Question of Prison Effects", in *The Effects of Imprisonment*, ed. A. Liebling and S. Maruna (Cullompton, UK: Willan Publishing 2005), 78.
49. Bengt Holmgren, Thomas Frisell and Bo Runeson, *Psykisk hälsa hos häktade med restriktioner* (Norrköping: Kriminalvårdens Utvecklingsenhet, 2011).
50. Raikes and Lockwood (2011, 19). Raikes and Lockwood refer to Pat Carlen and Anne Worrall,: *Analysing Women's Imprisonment*, 2004; and Tuerk, E. H. and Loper, A.B. (2006) "Contact between Incarcerated Mothers and Their Children: Assessing Parenting Stress", *Journal of Offender Rehabilitation* 43, no. 1, 23–43.
51. Tuerk, E. H. and Loper, A.B. (2006); Raikes and Lockwood (2011, 19 and 21).
52. Christopher Wildeman and Bruce Western, "Incarceration in Fragile Families", *The Future of Children* 20, no. 2 (2010), 167.
53. See, for example, Donald Braman, *Doing Time on the Outside: Incarceration and Family Life in Urban America* (Ann Arbor: University of Michigan Press, 2004), 3. See also Hagan, J. and Dinovitzer, R., "Collateral Consequences of Imprisonment for Children, Communities, and Prisoners", in Tonry, M.H. (ed.), *Crime and Justice: A Review of Research*. Chicago: University of Chicago Press.
54. See http://www.prisonstudies.org/info/worldbrief/ (visited on 21 December 2013). The rate is based on two figures from two different dates: US Bureau of Justice Statistics – 735,601 in local jails on 30 June 2011, and 1,504,150 in state or federal prisons on 31 December 2011.
55. See http://www.prisonstudies.org/info/worldbrief/ (visited on 21 December 2013).
56. David Garland, "Introduction: The Meaning of Mass Imprisonment", in *Mass Imprisonment: Social Causes and Consequences*, ed. David Garland (London: Sage, 2001a), 2.
57. Nils Christie, *Crime Control as Industry: Towards Gulags, Western Style* (New York: Routledge 2001), 97.
58. Robert Johnson, "Brave New Prisons: The Growing Social Isolation of Modern Penal Institutions", in *The Effects of Imprisonment*, ed. A. Liebling and S. Maruna (Cullompton, UK: Willan Publishing, 2005), 255.
59. C. Larsen et al. *Forbryderen og samfundet: Livsvilkår og uformel straf* [*The Criminal and Society: Conditions of Life and Informal Punishment*] (Copenhagen: Gyldendal, 2008).
60. See C. Larsen et al. (2008). Regarding imprisonment taking a toll on family resources by decreasing family income and increasing expenses, see Wildeman and Western (2010, 166).
61. See Smith (2003, 38).
62. Crewe (2009, 130). Crewe refers to Christie (1981).
63. Garland (2001, 184).
64. See Smith and Jakobsen (2010), and Helen Codd, *In the Shadow of Prison: Families, Imprisonment and Criminal Justice* (Cullompton, UK: Willan Publishing, 2008), 47. See also Chapter 13 in this book.
65. Quoted according to Liebling and Maruna (2005, 13).
66. Wildeman and Western (2010, 157).
67. Codd (2008, 47 ff.).
68. Candace Kruttschnitt, "Is the Devil in the Details? Crafting Policy to Mitigate the Collateral Consequences of Parental Incarceration", *Criminology & Public*

Policy 10, no. 3 (2011), 831. Hagan and Dinovitzer operate with three very similar categories: strain (economic hardship), socialization (loss of parental support etc.) and stigmatization. See Hagan, J. and Dinovitzer, R., "Collateral Consequences of Imprisonment for Children, Communities, and Prisoners", in Tonry, M.H. (ed.), *Crime and Justice: A Review of Research*. Chicago: University of Chicago Press (123).
69. Codd (2008, 49).
70. See Linda Kjær Minke, *Fængslets indre liv*, Ph.D. dissertation, University of Copenhagen, 2010.
71. Susanne Clausen, *Klientundersøgelsen 2011*, Direktoratet for Kriminalforsorgen (2013, 74 and 123).
72. Clausen (2013, 75 and 124).
73. Codd (2008, 49).
74. Gwyneth Boswell and Peter Wedge, *Imprisoned Fathers and Their Children* (London: Jessica Kingsley Publishers, 2007), 52. Boswell and Wedge's survey builds on interviews of 25 children of prisoners from age 3–19 (the two 19-year-olds were both under 18 when their fathers were imprisoned). Additionally, it includes interviews of 181 imprisoned fathers and 127 adult relatives (often the children's mothers).
75. Jeremy Travis and Michelle Waul, *Prisoners Once Removed: The Impact of Incarceration and Re-entry on Children, Families, and Communities* (Washington, DC: The Urban Institute, 2003), 8. See also Liz Ayre, Kate Philbrick and Marielle Reiss (eds), *Children of Imprisoned Parents: European Perspectives on Good Practice* (Montrouge: Eurochips, 2006), 10.
76. Travis and Waul (2003, 9).
77. Grounds (2005, 35). Grounds's study concerns innocent prisoners, but he argues convincingly that the effects he traces are first and foremost due to long-term imprisonment.
78. Grounds (2005, 41).
79. Quoted according to Grøfthauge (2004, 60 f.).
80. Kruttschnitt (2011, 833).

4 Children of Imprisoned Parents in Numbers

1. Gill Pugh, *Sentenced Families: Signs of Change for Children with a Parent in Prison* (Ipswich: Ormiston Children and Families Trust, 2004), 15.
2. See Smith and Jakobsen (2010, 27). Somewhat similar procedures are underway in Denmark in connection with streamlining prisoner reception practices.
3. There seems to be different practices in terms of how comprehensively prisoners are asked and how they are helped. See Smith and Jakobsen (2010, 27 and 273). See also *Straffa inte barnet*, report from Children's Ombudsman, BR2004:01: http://www.barnombudsmannen.se/publikationer/bestall-och-ladda-ner/straffa-inte-barnet-2004/ (assessed 26 November 2012). Internal attempts by the Swedish Prison Service to use this information statistically have been abandoned as it was discovered that the parental status of the prisoners and the number of children they have is sometimes recorded sloppily in the Swedish prisons (information obtained at a meeting with representatives of the Swedish prison service and the NGO "Bryggan", 22 May 2013, Stockholm).

4. Hoffmann, Byrd and Kightlinger "Prison Programs and Services for Incarcerated Parents and Their Underage Children: Results From a National Survey of Correctional Facilities", in *The Prison Journal*, 90(4), 2010, 397.
5. See Joseph Murray et al. *Effects of Parental Imprisonment on Child Antisocial Behaviour and Mental Health: A Systematic Review* (Oslo: Campbell Collaboration, 2009), 9.
6. Rodriguez, N., Smith, H., and Zatz, M. S. (2009), "Youth is Enmeshed in a Highly Dysfunctional Family System: Exploring the Relationship Among Dysfunctional Families, Parental Incarceration, and Juvenile Court Decision Making", *Criminology* 47, no. 1, (2009), 181.
7. See surveys referred to in Sandra Enos, *Mothering from the Inside: Parenting in a Women's Prison* (Albany: State University of New York Press, 2001), 3.
8. Williams, Papadopoulou and Booth (2012, iii). The overall sample was 3,849 prisoners, but the results were mostly based on "sample 1" that counted 1,435 prisoners.
9. Williams, Papadopoulou and Booth (2012, 16 f.).
10. See Smith and Jakobsen (2010, 28).
11. See *Straffa inte barnet*, 13. Current Swedish estimates used by the NGO Bryggan are much higher (information obtained at a meeting with representatives of the Swedish prison service and Bryggan, 22 May 2013, Stockholm).
12. http://www.kriminalvarden.se/sv/Press/Almedalsveckan/Seminarier/Barn-i-brottets-skugga/ (viewed 5 September 2013). It is not clear what the basis for this estimate is or how it has been calculated.
13. Estimate by Eurochips.
14. See Ayre, Philbrick and Reiss (2006, 7).
15. The Council of Crime Prevention, *Fængsledes børn – en udsat gruppe* [Prisoners' Children – A Vulnerable Group], (Copenhagen, February 2005, 8.
16. Minke (2010); Rikke Olsen, *Invisible Consequences of Punishment: Parental Imprisonment and Child Outcomes*, Ph.D. thesis, Aarhus University, 2013.
17. Minke (2010).
18. See Murray et al. (2009, 9).
19. Clausen (2013, 75 and 124).
20. Private correspondence with Linda Kjær Minke, who designed the interview survey.
21. See Hendriksen, Jakobsen and Smith (2012, 11 and 121).
22. See Rikke Fuglsang Olsen, "Forældres fængsling – en stratificerende livsbegivenhed?", forthcoming, 13. The article is part of Rikke Olsen's Ph.D. thesis (Olsen 2013).
23. Jilliam J. Turanovic, Nancy Rodriguez and Travis C. Pratt, "The Collateral Consequences of Incarceration Revisited: A Qualitative Analysis of the Effects on Caregivers of Children of Incarecrated Parents", *Criminology* 50, no. 4 (2012), 914.
24. Statistics Denmark, *Børns Familier* [Children's Families] 2008, 193.
25. Williams, Papadopoulou and Booth (2012, 16 f. and 19).
26. See surveys referred to in Enos (2001, 3).
27. Williams, Papadopoulou and Booth (2012, 19).
28. Minke (2010) and Clausen (2013).
29. Minke 2010. In the EU coping study, the vast majority of the participating children visited their parents, but this was a result of the selection process,

which primarily identified children with an important connection to the imprisoned parent. See Jones and Wainaina-Woźna (eds) (2013, 57 and 254 f.). In the Danish study used here (Minke 2010), the participating prisoners represented a broad and representative selection of all categories of prisoners in the Danish prison system.
30. Quoted from Rodriguez, Smith and Zatz (2009, 181).
31. See, for example, Turanovic, Rodriguez and Pratt (2012, 916).
32. Wildeman, C., "Parental Imprisonment, the Prison Boom, and the Concentration of Childhood Disadvantage", *Demography* 46, no. 2 (2009), 266.

5 The Problems and Reactions of Prisoners' Children: A Review of Research

1. See Megan Comfort, *Doing Time Together. Love and Family in the Shadow of the Prison* (Chicago: University of Chicago Press, 2008).
2. See, for example, Christopher Wildemann, "Paternal Incarceration and Children's Physically Aggressive Behaviors: Evidence from the Fragile Families and Child Wellbeing Study", *Social Forces* 89, no. 1 (2010), 287. See also Rodriguez, Smith and Zatz (2009, 182).
3. Hagan, J. and Dinovitzer, R., "Collateral Consequences of Imprisonment for Children, Communities, and Prisoners", in Tonry, M.H. (ed.), *Crime and Justice: A Review of Research*. Chicago: University of Chicago Press (1999, 122).
4. Christensen (1999, 23).
5. Liebling and Maruna (2005, 16).
6. Murray and Farrington (2008, 133).
7. Murray et al. (2009, 57).
8. Wildeman and Western (2010, 157 f.).
9. Joseph Murray, David P. Farrington and Ivana Sekol, "Children's Antisocial Behavior, Mental Health, Drug Use, and Educational Performance after Parental Incarceration: A Systematic Review and Meta-Analysis", *Psychological Bulletin* 138, no. 2 (2012), 190.
10. The COPING study is based on data collected from 737 children, age 7–17, of imprisoned parents, as well as on 349 interviews with children and their parents in Sweden, Romania, Germany and the United Kingdom. See Jones and Wainaina-Woźna (eds) (2013).
11. Murray and Farrington (2008, 133). See also Murray and Farrington (2009, 57).
12. Wakefield and Wildeman (2011, 794).
13. See Susan D. Phillips et al. "Disentangling the Risks: Parent Criminal Justice Involvement and Children's Exposure to Family Risks", *Criminology & Public Policy* 5, no. 6 (2006), 680; and Joseph Murray and David P. Farrington, "Evidence-based Programs for Children of Prisoners", *Criminology & Public Policy* 5, no. 4 (2006), 723 and 726.
14. See also Codd (2008, 63).
15. The two quotes are from Murray and Farrington (2008, 187), and from Sytske Besemer et al. "The Relationship between Parental Imprisonment

and Offspring Offending in England and the Netherlands", *British Journal of Criminology* 51, no. 2 (2011), 422.
16. Joseph Murray, *Parental imprisonment: Effects on Children's Antisocial Behaviour and Mental Health through the Life-course*, dissertation University of Cambridge, February 2006, 184. See also Besemer et al. (2011).
17. Rikke Fuglsang Olsen, "Parental Imprisonment: Apredictor of Danish Children's Criminal Convictions as Young Adults?", forthcoming, unpublished version September 2012, 18.
18. Olsen (2012, 18).
19. Olsen (forthcoming, 16, 18 and 19).
20. Sara Wakefield and Christopher Wildeman, "Mass Imprisonment and Childhood Behavior Problems", *American Society of Criminology* 10, no. 3 (2011), 800 and 799.
21. Sara Wakefield and Christopher Wildeman, *Children of the Prison Boom. Mass Incarecration and the Future of American Inequality*, Oxford University Press: New York, 2014, 154 f.
22. Comfort (2008, 15).
23. Christensen (1999, 100).
24. See, for example, Christensen 1999 and Annelie Björkhagen Tureson, *Mor i fängelse – mödrer och barn berätter. En analys av ungdomars resiliensprocess*, doctoral thesis, University of Gothenburg, 2009.
25. See Smith and Jakobsen (2010).
26. Murray, Farrington and Sekol (2012, 190 f.).
27. Murray, Farrington and Sekol (2012, 192).
28. Hagan and Dinovitzer also mention "the importance of knowing the prior relationship between an offender and his family that predates imprisonment". See Hagan and Dinovitzer (1999, 125).
29. See Chapter 4.
30. This has not been adequately explained or researched so far. For some of the existing discussions on this, see Besemer et al. (2011). On the other hand, the (alleged) positive aspects of penal practice in the Scandinavian welfare states are sometimes taken for granted and the less positive sides overlooked. See, for example, Smith (2011c).
31. Interview in Avisen, Denmark, http://avisen.dk/, 12 April 2007.
32. Boswell and Wedge (2007, 79); Smith and Jakobsen (2010).
33. Seena Fazel and John Danesh; "Serious Mental Disorder in 23,000 Prisoners: A Systematic Review of 62 Surveys", *The Lancet* 359, no. 9306 (2002), 548.
34. Henrik Steen Andersen, "Mental Health in Prison Populations: A Review – With Special Emphasis on a Study of Danish Prisoners on Remand", *Acta Psychiatrica Scandinavica Supplementum* 110, no. 424 (2004), 27.
35. Andersen (2004, 27).
36. Andersen (2004, 20–21).
37. See Smith (2006a).
38. Quoted from Sasha Abramsky and Jamie Fellner, *Ill-Equipped: U.S. Prisons and Offenders with Mental Illness* (New York: Human Rights Watch, 2003), 17.
39. Arditti (2012, 29). Arditti refers to Mumola (2000).
40. Olsen (forthcoming).
41. See, for example, Arditti (2012, 26). See also Wildeman and Western (2010, 158).

42. Mette Ejrnæs, Morten Ejrnæs and Signe Fredriksen, "Anbringelser uden for hjemmet", in *Når man anbringer et barn. Baggrund, stabilitet i anbringelsen og det videre liv*, ed. Signe Hald Andersen (Odense: University Press of Southern Denmark, 2010), 103.
43. Anette Molbech, *Children of Prisoners. A Story about the Engelsborg Family House* (Copenhagen: The Danish Prison and Probation Service, 2009), 26.
44. Molbech (2009, 26).
45. See, for example, Arditti (2012, 17 and 27).
46. See Turesson (2009, 22 f.).
47. See Turesson (2009, 24).
48. See Turesson (2009, 24).
49. Wildeman (2010, 287).
50. Besemer et al. (2011, 430). They refer to Murray and Farrington (2008).
51. Arditti (2012, 6).
52. See Smith in Ugelvik and Dullum (2011).
53. Smith (2006a).
54. Christensen (1999, 45).
55. See Murray and Farrington (2006, 724 f.); Bjercke et al. (1994, 18).
56. See Murray and Farrington (2006, 724). See also Boswell and Wedge (2007, 22).
57. Interview with psychologist Marie Gammeltoft.
58. Bjercke et al. (1994, 16). Psychologist Marie Gammeltoft also highlights that the experience for the child is connected, to a high degree, to how close the child is to the parent who is to be imprisoned.
59. Interview with psychologist Marie Gammeltoft.
60. Boswell and Wedge (2007, 72).
61. See Smith and Jakobsen (2010, 45 f.).
62. Turesson (2009, 17).
63. See Murray and Farrington (2006, 725).
64. See Boswell and Wedge (2007, 61 f.).
65. Carl Mazza, "And Then the World Fell Apart: The Children of Incarcerated Fathers", *Families in Society: The Journal of Contemporary Services* 83, no. 5/6 (2000), 522. See also Boswell and Wedge (2007, 62).
66. Charlotte, 18 years old, quoted from the website: http://www.elbecks.dk/minfarifaengsel/. The website is developed by Dorte Høeg Brask, who is also behind the documentary "Et hul i himlen – når mor og far er i fængsel" ["A Hole in the Sky – When Mum and Dad are in Prison"] from 2007. The site addresses older children and youngsters who have a parent in prison and, among other things, contains various accounts from children and youngsters who have a parent in prison.
67. See Chapter 6 about the arrest of parents.
68. Codd (2008, 65).
69. See Boswell and Wedge (2007, 62).
70. Boswell and Wedge (2007, 62).
71. Murray and Farrington (2006, 726).
72. Bjercke et al. (1994, 23).
73. Bjercke et al. (1994, 24 f.).
74. Codd (2008, 71).
75. See Wildeman (2010, 287); Rodriguez, Smith and Zatz (2009, 182).

76. Phillips et al. (2006, 679).
77. Brian Lund Andreasen, former deputy chairman of the Danish association SAVN for children and relatives of prisoners.
78. Dennis, former prisoner (Dennis is not his real name).
79. Boswell and Wedge (2007, 40).
80. Danish prisoner quoted from Christensen (1999, 62).
81. Marie, whose ex-husband is serving a sentence of 14 years.
82. See, for example, (Smith and Jakobsen 2010); Wildeman and Western (2010, 166).
83. Phillips et al. (2006, 728).
84. See also Murray and Farrington (2006, 728).
85. See Murray and Farrington (2006, 728).
86. Murray and Farrington (2006, 728); Phillips et al. (2006, 679); Hagan and Dinovitzer (1999, 136–137).
87. Torben Tranæs, "Den uformelle straf og velfærdsstaten", *Nordisk Tidsskrift for Kriminalvidenskab* 95, no. 3 (2008), 240.
88. Tranæs (2008, 240).
89. See, for example, J. A. Arditti, *Parental Incarceration and the Family: Psychological and Social Effects of Imprisonment on Children, Parents, and Caregivers* (New York: New York University Press, 2012), 32; Condry (2007b). See also Murray and Farrington (2008, 275).
90. Extracts of the taped interview from the website "Min far i Fængsel" ["My Father in Prison"]: http://www.elbecks.dk/minfarifaengsel/. The website was compiled by three journalism students at the Danish School of Journalism and Media in 2005, and belongs to the Danish Red Cross. See also Smith and Jakobsen (2010).
91. Extracts of the taped interview from the website "Min far i Fængsel": http://www.elbecks.dk/minfarifaengsel/
92. M. Grøftehauge, *Fangebørn* (Århus: CDR-Forlag, 2004), 104 ff.
93. Regarding abuse problems, see Mazza (2002, 525).
94. Boswell and Wedge (2007, 73).
95. Boswell and Wedge (2007, 65).
96. See Jones and Wainaina-Woźna (2013, 347 f.).
97. The boy, Jakob, is quoted from the website: http://www.elbecks.dk/minfarifaengsel/.
98. Boswell and Wedge (2007, 65).
99. Christina Søgaard. Christina's father was in prison when she was a child. Christina told her story at a think tank meeting on alternative forms of imprisonment.
100. Rikke Betak, family therapist in the Family House in Halfway House Engelsborg.
101. See, for example, Murray and Farrington (2006, 728).
102. Bjarne Møller, senior consultant for the SUS.
103. Social Development Centre, *Børn som pårørende* [*Children as Relatives*] (Copenhagen, Social Development Centre, 2004), 6. Subsequently, SUS has expanded the booklet (*When Children are Relatives*, 2006), which contains a separate chapter about prisoners' children.
104. See Boswell and Wedge (2007, 26).
105. See Boswell and Wedge (2007, 22).

106. Ayre, Philbrick and Reiss (2006, 9).
107. Christensen (1999, 14).
108. Christensen (1999, 39).
109. Christensen (1999, 50).
110. Grøftehauge (2004, 85).
111. Grøftehauge (2004, 24 f.).
112. See Jones and Wainaina-Woźna (2013, 65).
113. Rikke Betak, family therapist in the Family House in Halfway House Engelsborg.
114. See Boswell and Wedge (2007, 61).
115. Christensen (1999, 39).
116. See also Robertson (2012, 6).
117. Pugh (2004, 34).
118. Rita Christensen, the Swedish Prison and Probation Service.
119. Elisabeth Toft Rasmussen, former employee of the Danish Red Cross, where she worked for 10 years with children of prisoners.
120. As explained by, for example, Line Dahl Krabsen, chairperson of the association SAVN and Rikke Betak, family therapist at the Halfway House Engelsborg.
121. Psychologist Marie Gammeltoft.
122. Christina Søgaard. Christina's father was in prison when she was a child. Christina told her story at a think tank meeting on alternative forms of imprisonment.
123. Warden at a children's home where prisoners' children have lived.
124. Christensen (1999, 12).
125. Trine is quoted from the website: http://www.elbecks.dk/minfarifaengsel/.
126. Turesson (2009, 249).
127. Turesson (2009, 249).
128. Condry (2007b, 65, 66 and 68).
129. Condry (2007b, 66 f.).
130. Condry (2007b, 67).
131. Quoted from Anne Nesmith and Ebony Ruhland, "Children of Incarcerated Parents: Challenges and Resiliency, in Their Own Words", *Children and Youth Services Review* 30, no. 10 (2008), 1125.
132. See, for example, Christensen (1999); Smith and Jakobsen (2011); Murray and Farrington (2006, 722).
133. See, for example, Turesson (2009); Murray and Farrington (2006, 722); Boswell and Wedge (2007, 61).
134. See, among others, Grøftehauge (2004, 26); Pugh (2004, 36 f.); Murray and Farrington (2006, 722).
135. Boswell and Wedge (2007, 64).
136. See Boswell and Wedge (2007, 61).
137. Murray and Farrington (2006, 726); Phillips et al. (2006, 693); Boswell and Wedge (2007, 61 f.).
138. Boswell and Wedge (2007, 26); Grøftehauge (2004, 26).
139. Richard Steinhoff and Anne H. Berman, "Children's Experiences of Having a Parent in Prison – We Look at the Moon and Then We Feel Close to Each Other", *Sociologie Si Asistenta Sociala* 5, no. 2 (2012), 77.
140. Steinhoff and Berman (2012, 90).
141. See Jones and Wainaina-Woźna (2013, 63 f.).

142. Murray and Farrington (2008, 161).
143. Murray, Farrington and Sekol (2012).
144. According to "Summary of Findings from COPING: The Characteristics of Children with Imprisoned Parents, Their Resilience, and Their Vulnerability to Mental Health Problems". Leaflet distributed at the final EU COPING conference in Brussels, November 2012. See also Jones and Wainaina-Woźna (2013, 340 ff.).
145. Grøftehauge (2004, 26).
146. Molbech (2009, 25).
147. Extract of the taped interview with Jesper from the website "Min far i Fængsel ["My Father in Prison"]: http://www.el-becks.dk/minfarifaengsel/.
148. Forum for children and youngsters on SAVN's website, www.savn.dk. Written/published on the website on 23 February 2009.
149. Rikke Betak, family therapist in the Family House in Halfway House Engelsborg.
150. Warden at a children's home where prisoners' children have lived.
151. Grøftehauge (2004, 26).
152. Boswell and Wedge (2007, 72).
153. Quoted from Nesmith and Ruhland (2008, 1129).
154. Rikke Betak, family therapist in the Family House in Halfway House Engelsborg.
155. Boswell and Wedge (2007, 73).
156. Christina Søgaard. Christina's father was in prison when she was a child. Christina told her story at a think tank meeting on alternative forms of imprisonment.
157. Mazza (2000, 525).
158. Psychologist Line Schnettler who has worked with dialogue groups for children in the Danish Red Cross.
159. *Bladet Kriminalforsorgen*, thematic issue on the family and the Prison and Probation Service, September 2009. According to the father, it helped his daughter to "calm her nerves", that he was in the special family unit in the state prison in Horsens where she had the possibility of living with him on the weekends.
160. Line Dahl Krabsen, chairperson of SAVN; Sanne Graffe, former chairperson for the association Balance i Frihed. Today only SAVN is still operating.
161. Shaw (1987, 41).
162. Murray and Farrington (2006, 722 f.); Murray and Farrington (2008, 161); Murray, Farrington and Sekol (2012); Jones and Wainaina-Woźna (2013).
163. See Phillips et al. (2006, 679); Murray and Farrington (2006, 726).
164. Boswell and Wedge (2007, 13). See also Ayre, Philbrick and Reiss (2006, 8 f.); Smith and Jakobsen (2010).
165. See The Council of Crime Prevention, *Fængsledes børn – en udsat gruppe* (Copenhagen: The Council of Crime Prevention, 2005), 3.
166. Murray and Farrington (2008, 152).
167. Murray et al. 56.
168. Murray, Farrington and Sekol (2012, 191).
169. Joseph Murray, *Parental Imprisonment: Effects on Children's Antisocial Behaviour and Mental Health through the Life-course*, Ph.D. dissertation, University of Cambridge, February 2006, 184. See also Besemer et al. (2011).
170. Olsen (September 2012, 18).

171. Wildeman (2010, see the abstract).
172. Statistic Denmark's *Børns Familier (Children's Families)*, 2008, 204 (table 12.6.2).
173. Murray and Farrington (2006, 723).
174. Wildeman (2010, 285).
175. John Irwin and Barbara Owen, "Harm and the Contemporary Prison", in *The Effects of Imprisonment*, ed. Alison Liebling and Shadd Maruna (Cullompton, UK: Willan Publishing, 2005), 94.
176. Crewe, (2009, 132 f.).
177. Beth Grothe Nielsen, *Straf. Hvad ellers?* [*Punishment: What Else?*] (Copenhagen: Tiderne Skifter, 2006), 117. In the quoted context, Nielsen refers to Paul Leer-Salvesen, *Menneske og straf* [*Human Beings and Punishment*] (Oslo: Universitetsforlaget, 1991).
178. Shadd Maruna, "After Prison, What? The Ex-prisoner's Struggle to Desist from Crime", in *Handbook on Prisons*, ed. Y. Jewkes (Cullompton, UK: Willan Publishing, 2009), 661.
179. See also Arditti (2012, 35).
180. Smith and Jakobsen (2010).
181. Arditti (2012, 34 ff.).
182. Christensen (1999, 14 f.).
183. Kristin Turney, Christopher Wildeman and Jason Schnittker "As Fathers and Felons: Explaining the Effects of Current and Recent Incarceration on Major Depression", *Journal of Health and Social Behavior* 53, no. 4 (2012), 13. See also Minke (2012) on prisonization and parenthood.
184. Holmgren, Frisell and Runeson (2007, 17, 21 and 23).
185. Raikes and Lockwood (2011, 19). See also Pat Carlen and Anne Worrall, *Analysing Women's Imprisonment* (Cullompton, UK: Willan Publishing, 2004), 64.
186. Raikes and Lockwood (2011, 19 and 21).
187. Haney (2002), quoted from Arditti (2012, 38).
188. See also Ria Wolleswinkel, "Children of Imprisoned Parents", in *Developmental and Autonomy Rights of Children: Empowering Children, Caregivers and Communities*, ed. Jan Willems (Antwerpen: Intersentia, 2002), 203.
189. Christensen (1999, 67). See also Smith and Jakobsen (2010).
190. See Boswell and Wedge (2007, 61).
191. Boswell and Wedge (2007, 79); Ayre, Philbrick and Reiss (2006, 47). See also Murray (2005, 455), regarding studies that report both positive and negative effects of visits. See also Chapter 10.
192. Regarding the importance of prison regimes and prison practices, see Arditti (2012, 31).
193. Jesper Ryberg, *Retsfølelsen. En bog om straf og etik* (Frederiksberg: Roskilde Universitetsforlag, 2006), 10–11 and 25. Regarding Danes' sense of justice, see Flemming Balvig: *Danskernes syn på straf* [*Danes' View of Punishment*] (Copenhagen: Advokatsamfundet, 2006).
194. Hans Jørgen Engbo, "Ret og etik i straffuldbyrdelsen", in *Straffens menneskelige ansigt? En antologi om etik, ret og religion i fængslet*, ed. Lene Kühle and Carl Lomholt (Frederiksberg: ANIS 2006), 58.
195. See Balvig (2006).
196. Quoted from Grøftehauge (2004, 86).

197. Christensen (1999, 38).
198. Presentation by Alain Bouregba on 12 May 2006 at the conference "Children of Imprisoned Parents: European Perspectives" held by Eurochips in Paris.
199. Translated from Danish. See Tobias Møller, *Den fængsledes børn. Forslag til forbedring af vilkårene for børn af fængslede* [*Prisoners' Children. Proposal for Improvement of the Terms for Children of Prisoners*], unpublished text, presented at a round table held by the Danish Institute for Human Rights on 9 February 2006.
200. Murray (2006, 208).

6 Children of Imprisoned Parents and Their Human Rights

1. Norval Morris, "The Contemporary Prison: 1965–Present", in *The Oxford History of the Prison: The Practice of Punishment in Western Society*, ed. Norval Morris and David J. Rothman (New York: Oxford University Press, 1998), 219.
2. Peter Scharff Smith, "Fængsler og menneskerettigheder internationalt og i Danmark", in *Ret og samfund*, ed. Jacob Sejer Pedersen (Copenhagen: Frydenlund, 2007).
3. "The heyday of the prisoners' rights movement roughly spanned the period from 1960 to 1980." See James B. Jacobs, *Stateville. The Penitentiary in Mass Society* (Chicago: University of Chicago Press, 2004), 183. Regarding the United States, see Edgardo Rotman, "The Failure of Reform: United States, 1865–1965", and Norval Morris, "The Contemporary Prison: 1965–Present", in *The Oxford History of the Prison*, ed. Norval Morris and David J. Rothman (New York: Oxford University Press, 1998). Regarding Germany, see L. Lazarus, *Contrasting Prisoners' Rights: A Comparative Examination of Germany and England* (Oxford: Oxford University Press, 2004), 34.
4. *Wolff v. McDonnell* (1974).
5. *R. v. Institutional Head of Beaver Creek Correctional Camp* (1969).
6. Quoted from Vivien Stern, *A Sin Against the Future: Imprisonment in the World* (Boston: Northeastern University Press, 1998), 197.
7. Dirk van Zyl Smit and Sonja Snacken, *Principles of European Prison Law and Policy: Penology and Human Rights* (Oxford: Oxford University Press, 2009), 10.
8. Smit and Snacken (2009, 11).
9. Dato' Param Cumaraswamy and Manfred Nowak, "Human Rights in Criminal Justice Systems", seminar report, Strasbourg, France, 18–20 February 2009, 5. Available at http://www.asef.org/index.php?option=com_project&task=view&id=504.
10. See http://www.quno.org/humanrights/women-in-prison/womenPrisonLinks.htm#QUNOPUB.
11. See Smith and Gampell (2011, 235).
12. Committee on the Rights of the Child, 30 September 2011. Report and recommendations of the day of general discussions on "Children of Incarcerated Parents", § 31. Regarding the DGD on prisoners children, see also Robertson (2012).

13. Anette Faye Jacobsen, *Børn i alle lande: Om det internationale arbejde for børns rettigheder* [Children in All Countries: About the International Work for Children's Rights] (Copenhagen: The Danish Centre for Human Rights, 1994), 6.
14. See the preamble to the UN's Convention on the Rights of the Child.
15. UN's Convention on the Rights of the Child, articles 1–54.
16. UN's Convention on the Rights of the Child, article 7.
17. See H. J. Engbo and P. S. Smith, *Fængsler og menneskerettigheder* (Copenhagen: Jurist- og Økonomforbundets Forlag, 2012).
18. Stephanie Lagoutte, "The Human Rights Framework", in *Children of Imprisoned Parents*, ed. P. S. Smith and L. Gampell (Copenhagen: Danish Institute for Human Rights, Eurochips and University of Ulster, 2011), 34 ff.
19. For a discussion of article 3 and the exact wording – and the implications of this – see Jean Tomkin, *Orphans of Justice. In Search of the Best Interests of the Child When a Parent is Imprisoned: A Legal Analysis* (Geneva: Quaker United Nations Office, August 2009), 20 f.
20. See, for example, Boswell and Wedge (2007, 149); Wolleswinkel (2002, 192 f.).
21. GC General Comment no. 12 (2009), "The Right of the Child to be Heard" (CRC/C/GC/12), § 26. Here quoted in Lagoutte (2011, 35).
22. See Lagoutte (2011, 38).
23. Ria Wolleswinkel, "The Legal Background", in *Children of Imprisoned Parents: European Perspectives on Good Practice*, ed. Liz Ayre, Kate Philbrick and Marielle Reiss (Montrouge: Eurochips, 2006), 17.
24. The account and interview quote is from Marie Becher Trier, "Jeg græd hele tiden", *Folkeskolen* 24, no. 8 (February 2006), 14 f.
25. Quoted from Nell Bernstein, *All Alone in the World: Children of the Incarcerated* (New York: New Press, 2005), 7.
26. Committee on the Rights of the Child, Rreport and recommendations of the day of general discussions on "Children of Incarcerated Parents", 30 September 2011, § 32.
27. *Klaas v. Germany*, commission report of 21 May 1992, annexed to Klaas judgement, series A.269, § 117. Here quoted in Lagoutte (2011, 39).
28. See Lagoutte (2011, 39).
29. *Gutsanovi v. Bulgaria*, § 125–137.
30. Cf. Administration of Justice Act § 758, section 1.
31. Smith and Gampell (2011, 235).
32. *Sari and Colak v. Turkey* (2006) app. no. 42596/98, 42603/98.
33. See, for example, L. Moore, U. Convery and P. Scraton, "The Northern Ireland Case Study", *Children of Imprisoned Parents*, ed. L. Gampell and P.S. Smith (Copenhagen: Danish Institute for Human Rights, Eurochips and University of Ulster, 2011),133 f.
34. See Smith and Jakobsen (2010).
35. CPT report of 25 September 2002, CPT/Inf (2002) 18, § 16.
36. Circular no. 12154 of 12 June 2001 from the Ministry of Justice to the police and prosecuting authority on notification to relatives, etc.
37. CPT report of 25 September 2008, CPT/Inf (2008) 26, § 15.
38. CPT report of 25 September 2008, CPT/Inf (2008) 26, § 15.
39. CPT report of 25 September 2008, CPT/Inf (2008) 26, § 16.

40. Committee on the Rights of the Child, report and recommendations of the day of general discussions on "Children of Incarcerated Parents", 30 September 2011, § 44.
41. Committee on the Rights of the Child, Forty-first Session, "Concluding observations: Thailand", 17 March 2006, CRC/C/THA/CO/2, para. 48.
42. "Belfast Declaration", adopted at The International Association of Youth and Family Judges and Magistrates XVII World Congress in Belfast, Northern Ireland, 27 August–1 September 2006, see point 9.
43. Committee on the Rights of the Child, Forty-first Session, "Concluding Observations: Thailand", 17 March 2006, CRC/C/THA/CO/2, para. 48.
44. Committee on the Rights of the Child, "Report and Recommendations of the Day of General Discussions on 'Children of Incarcerated Parents'", 30 September 2011, § 30.
45. Quoted from Marlene Alejos, *Babies and Small Children Residing in Prisons* (Geneva: Quaker United Nations Office, 2005), 22.
46. See Lia Sacerdote et al., "The Italian Case Study", in *Children of Imprisoned Parents*, ed. L. Gampell and P. S. Smith (Copenhagen: The Danish Institute for Human Rights, Eurochips and University of Ulster, 2011), 168.
47. See Robertson (2012, 15).
48. Council of Europe Recommendation 1469, "Mothers and Babies in Prison", 2000.
49. "Report to the UN's Committee on the Rights of the Child. Supplementary Report to Denmark's 3rd Periodic Report", Børnerådet (the Children's Council), January 2005, 18 f.
50. See, for example, Public Prosecutor's Notification no. 3/2000, 5.
51. Act no. 1068 of 6 November 2008 on § 82 of the penal code.
52. Administration of Justice Act, U.1985.611H.
53. See Moore, Convery and Scraton (2011, 137 f.).
54. See Moore, Convery and Scraton (2011, 138 f.).
55. See Robertson (2012, 15 f.). For examples from Fiji, see Tomkin (2009, 28).
56. Quoted from Tomkin (2009, 28).
57. The case of S v. M, quoted from Robertson (2012, 15).
58. Robertson (2012, 16).
59. Committee on the Rights of the Child, "Report and Recommendations of the Day of General Discussions on 'Children of Incarcerated Parents'", 30 September 2011, § 43.
60. See Smith and Jakobsen (2010, 100 ff.).
61. Order no. 559 of 21 June 2000 on social security for persons who are in remand custody or imprisoned to serve a sentence in a prison or detention centre, §5, section 1.
62. Order no. 559 of 21 June 2000 on social security for persons who are in remand custody or imprisoned to serve a sentence in a prison or detention centre, § 6, section 1.
63. See Smith and Jakobsen (2010).
64. Committee on the Rights of the Child, Fortieth Session, "Consideration of Reports Submitted by States Parties under Article 44 of The Convention, Concluding observations: Australia", 20 October 2005, CRC/C/15/Add.268, para 41.

65. Committee on the Rights of the Child, "Report and Recommendations of the Day of General Discussions on 'Children of Incarcerated Parents'", 30 September 2011, § 38.
66. Committee on the Rights of the Child, "Report and Recommendations of the Day of General Discussions on 'Children of Incarcerated Parents'", 30 September 2011, § 39.
67. See Smith and Gampell (2011, 236).
68. UN Standard Minimum Rules for the Treatment of Prisoners, rule 37. See also rules 79 and 92.
69. Council of Europe, Committee of Ministers, Rec (2006) 2, the European Prison Rules. See 24.1, 24.2, 24.4, 24.5 and 24.7.
70. Council of Europe, Committee of Ministers, Rec (2006) 2, the European Prison Rules. See 24.4.
71. See, for example, *Messina v. Italy* as well as *Ostrovar v. Moldova*.
72. See *Baginski v. Poland*.
73. *Baginski v. Poland*.
74. *Messina v. Italy*.
75. See, for example, *Sanchez v. France*.
76. *Ciorap v. Moldova*.
77. *Ciorap v. Moldova*.
78. *Estrikh v. Latvia*.
79. *Sabou et Pircalab v. Romania*.
80. *Horych v. Poland*, § 23.
81. *Horych v. Poland*, § 31 ff.
82. *Horych v. Poland*, § 39.
83. *Horych v. Poland*, § 126.
84. *Horych v. Poland*, § 131.
85. *Horych v. Poland*, § 132.
86. *Salahhov and Islyamova v. Ukraine*, § 205.
87. *Salahhov and Islyamova v. Ukraine*, § 202.
88. *Salahhov and Islyamova v. Ukraine*, § 204. The court also noted the importance of "the cynical, indifferent and cruel attitude towards her appeals demonstrated by the authorities both before the first applicant's death and during its subsequent investigation; the fact that the second applicant had to witness the slow death of her son without being able to help him in any way; and, lastly, the duration of her inherent suffering for about three months", § 204.
89. Smith (2012).
90. See Smith and Gampell (2011, 237, recommendation no. 21).
91. See Chapter 10.
92. See Smith and Gampell (2011, 237, recommendation no. 20).
93. "Udgangsbekendtgørelsen", § 31, section 1, no. 1, and "udgangsvejledningen", point 59.
94. "Udgangsbekendtgørelsen", § 31, section 2, no. 1, and "udgangsvejledningen", point 62.
95. Regarding exit in general, see Engbo (2005, 276 ff.).
96. See Smith and Jakobsen (2010, 109 f.).
97. *Golder v. United Kingdom* ruling of 21 February 1975, Application no. 4451/70,.

98. Committee on the Rights of the Child, "Report and Recommendations of the Day of General Discussion on 'Children of Incarcerated Parents'", 30 September 2011, 46.
99. Smith (2012, 478).
100. Lov om gjennomføring av straff mv. (lov-2001-05-18-21) § 3. See also Engbo and Smith (2012, 273).
101. See the remarks to the European Prison Rules (the Committee of Ministers' documents, CM/2005 163 Supplement), the comments to rule 17, https://wcd.coe.int/ViewDoc.jsp?id=924969&Site=CM (assessed 5 March 2013).
102. Committee on the Rights of the Child, "Report and Recommendations of the Day of General Discussions on 'Children of incarcerated parents'", 30 September 2011, § 40.
103. See the Sentence Enforcement Act (the Danish prison law) §§ 78a ff.
104. Alejos (2005, 30).
105. Not counting those who are allowed to visit and stay in special units/visiting apartments during weekends or the children who might be staying in the halfway houses including the so-called Family House. See Smith and Jakobsen 2010 and response from the Danish Institute for Human Rights' questionnaire survey.
106. See Robertson (2012, 5).
107. Natalia D. Tapia and Michael S. Vaughn "Legal Issues Regarding Medical Care for Pregnant Inmates", *The Prison Journal* 90, no. 4 (2010), 438.
108. Robertson (2008, 17).
109. Robertson (2008, 17); Ayre, Philbrick and Reiss (2006, 74).
110. Tarja Pösö, Rosi Enroos and Tarja Vierula "Children Residing in Prison With Their Parents: An Example of Institutional Invisibility", *The Prison Journal* 90, no. 4 (2006), 517.
111. Robertson (2008, 17); Ayre, Philbrick and Reiss (2006, 74).
112. Smith and Jakobsen (2010).
113. Parliamentary Assembly of the Council of Europe, Recommendation 1469 (2000), "Mothers and Babies in Prison".
114. Parliamentary Assembly of the Council of Europe, Recommendation 1469 (2000), "Mothers and Babies in Prison".
115. 10th General Report the Committee for the Prevention of Torture (CPT), 2000 [CPT/Inf. (2000)13 (EN)], chapter on "Women Deprived of their Liberty", pt. 29.
116. Parliamentary Assembly of the Council of Europe's Resolution 1663, "Women in Prison", 28 April 2009, 9.3.
117. Parliamentary Assembly of the Council of Europe's Resolution 1663, "Women in Prison", 28 April 2009, 9.5.
118. European Prison Rules (2006), rule 36.
119. Andrew Coyle, *A Human Rights Approach to Prison Management: Handbook for Prison Staff*, (London: International Centre for Prison Studies, 2002), 134.
120. UN Standard Minimum Rules for the Treatment of Prisoners, rule 23, section 1.
121. UN Standard Minimum Rules for the Treatment of Prisoners, rule 23, section 2.
122. See Alejos (2005, 17).

123. UN Economic and Social Council, Resolution 2010/16, "United Nations Rules for the Treatment of Women Prisoners and Non-custodial Measures for Women Offenders (the Bangkok Rules)".
124. International Centre for Prison Studies, "Guidance Note 13: Reforming Women's prisons", in *Guidance Notes on Prison Reform* (London: International Centre for Prison Studies, 2004), 7 f. See also Wolleswinkel (2002, 196 f.).
125. Robertson (2008, 16).
126. David Ramsbotham, *Prisongate: The Shocking State of Britain's Prisons and the Need for Visionary Change* (London: Free Press, 2003), 18 f.
127. Quote from Wolleswinkel (2002, 197).
128. Se CAT/C/48/Add.3, 35th session, "List of Issues to be Considered during the Examination of the Second Periodic Report of the United States of America", 8 February 2006, point 48. See also CAT/C/ USA/CO/2, 18 May 2006 (advance unedited version), 36th session, point 33.
129. Robertson (2012, 19).
130. Lagoutte (2011, 51). See also Parliamentary Assembly of the Council of Europe's Resolution 1663, "Women in Prison", 28 April 2009, 9.
131. *Togher v. United Kingdom.*
132. *Kleuver v. Norway.*
133. Lagoutte (2011, 46 f.).
134. *M.C. v. Finland.*
135. OE2005. B-3254-05.

7 The Arrest of Parents through the Eyes of Children, Police and Social Services

1. See Smith and Jakobsen (2010, 67).
2. Carolus van Nijnatten, *Detention and Development: Perspectives of Children of Prisoners* (Mönchengladbach: Forum Verlag Godesberg, 1998), 82. Also quoted in Codd (2008, 65).
3. Moore, Convery and Scraton (2011, 133).
4. Moore, Convery and Scraton (2011, 134).
5. Condry 2007b, 52 f.).
6. S. D. Phillips, "Programming for Children of Female Offenders", proceedings from 4th National Head Start Research Conference, Washington, DC, 1998, quoted from The Osborne Association, *A Call to Action: A Report of the New York Initiative for Children of Incarcerated Parents*, May 2011, 17.
7. Bente Boserup, senior counsellor for the children's NGO Børns Vilkår in Denmark.
8. S. D. Phillips and J. Zhao, "The Relationship between Witnessing Arrests and Elevated Symptoms of Posttraumatic Stress: Findings from a National Study of Children Involved in the Child Welfare System", *Children and Youth Services Review* 32, no.10 (2010), 1246–1254. See also Jane A. Siegel, *Disrupted Childhoods: Children of Women in Prison* (New Brunswick, NJ: Rutgers University Press, 2011), 90.
9. Phillips and Zhao (2010, quoted from the article abstract).
10. Siegel (2011, 98).

11. Siegel (2011, 101).
12. Siegel (2011, 101).
13. Siegel (2011, 104).
14. Cherie describes the incident in the film *Et hul i himlen* (2007) by Dorte Høeg Brask. Cherie also tells her story on the DVD: "Far i fængsel" (Dad in Prison) with the Danish Prisoners' choir ("Fangekoret"), the Children's choir and Peter Mygind. See www.fangekoret.dk/ovrige_udgivelser.html.
15. Lars Nicolai Jensen, deputy assistant superintendent and daily leader of The Criminal Preventative Division in Copenhagen Police (now retired).
16. Lars Nicolai Jensen, deputy assistant superintendent and daily leader of The Criminal Preventative Division in Copenhagen Police (now retired).
17. Mogens Lauridsen, chief superintendent at Copenhagen Police (Station City).
18. Rikke Betak, family therapist in the Engelsborg Family House.
19. Christensen (1999, 38).
20. Christensen (1999, 38).
21. According to Charlotte's account on the website: http://www.elbecks.dk/minfarifaengsel/.
22. According to Charlotte's account on the website: http://www.elbecks.dk/minfarifaengsel/.
23. The daily *Information* 02-05-08.
24. The daily *Information* 02-05-08.
25. Lars Nicolai Jensen, deputy assistant superintendent and daily leader of The Criminal Preventative Division in Copenhagen Police (now retired).
26. Eiler Larsen, assistant detective, teacher in police theory at the Police Academy.
27. The Danish Institute for Human Rights' questionnaire survey. See Appendix.
28. Written statements in the Danish Institute for Human Rights' questionnaire survey. See Appendix.
29. Three police officers elaborated that the children's reactions depend on the situation. For example, one police sergeant (Police Sergeant T) wrote: "It is very difficult to give a general answer. Depends entirely on the situation and how 'familiar' they are, that the police come to their home." Six police officers explained in the comment field that the children's reactions are often linked to their ages. The Danish Institute for Human Rights' questionnaire survey. See Appendix.
30. The Danish Institute for Human Rights' questionnaire survey. See Appendix.
31. Along the same lines, Assistant Detective Ø wrote: "Depends greatly on age. Younger children are generally more passive than children over the age of 10." The Danish Institute for Human Rights' questionnaire survey. See Appendix.
32. Police Sergeant S (police), The Danish Institute for Human Rights' questionnaire survey, see Appendix.
33. The Danish Institute for Human Rights' questionnaire survey, see Appendix.
34. The Danish Institute for Human Rights' questionnaire survey, see Appendix. Mogens Lauridsen, chief superintendent at Copenhagen Police (Station City).

35. Eiler Larsen, assistant detective, teacher in police theory at the Police Academy.
36. Tanya Krupat, Elizabeth Gaynes and Yali Lincroft, *A Call to Action: Safeguarding New York's Children of Incarcerated Parents* (New York: The Osborne Association, May 2011), 18.
37. Søren Ravn, deputy assistant superintendent and section leader of PG3 (module 3) at the Police Academy.
38. Søren Ravn, deputy assistant superintendent and section leader of PG3 (module 3) at the Police Academy.
39. Pelle Nigard, psychologist and head of psychology as a subject at the Police Academy.
40. Søren Ravn, deputy assistant superintendent and section leader of PG3 (module 3) at the Police Academy.
41. See the Police Academy's textbook on the subject (psychology): Ibsen Bjarne Frøslee et al., *Politipsykologi: En grundbog* (Copenhagen: Hans Reitzels Forlag, 2008), 105–116. The chapter concerns neglect and assault of children and pages 113–116 discuss specific circumstances for notification of the social authorities. Moreover, the individual teachers use their own teaching materials. In the subject of police theory, the theme is included under different topics: on reports (PG1), domestic disturbances (where the social report is explicitly handled) as well as in Police Theory IV, which concerns children and youngsters. Source: The Police Academy and the Communications Division, National Police.
42. Police Commissioner T (police), see Appendix.
43. Deputy Assistant Commissioner Z (police), see Appendix.
44. Deputy Assistant Commissioner Z (police), see Appendix.
45. Retsplejeloven (Administration of Justice Act) § 758.
46. Lars Nicolai Jensen, deputy assistant superintendent and daily leader of The Criminal Preventative Division in Copenhagen Police (retired).
47. Mogens Lauridsen, chief superintendent at Copenhagen Police (Station City).
48. Police Sergeant W (police), see Appendix.
49. See Chapter 6.
50. The Danish Institute for Human Rights' questionnaire survey.
51. See Smith and Jakobsen (2010).
52. Deputy Assistant Commissioner Z (police), see Appendix.
53. Deputy Assistant Commissioner V (police), see Appendix.
54. Interview with Lis Andersen, mother of three children whose father is in prison: *Avisen*, 12 April 2007.
55. Søren Ravn, deputy assistant superintendent and section leader of PG3 (module 3) at the Police Academy.
56. Smith and Jakobsen (2010).
57. Smith and Jakobsen (2010).
58. Smith and Jakobsen (2010).
59. Police Sergeant V (police), see Appendix.
60. Police Officer S (police), see Appendix.
61. Søren Ravn, deputy assistant superintendent and section leader of PG3 (module 3) at the Police Academy.
62. Eiler Larsen, assistant detective, teacher in police theory at the Police Academy.

Notes 263

63. Deputy Assistant Commissioner Z (police), see Appendix.
64. See Smith and Jakobsen (2010).
65. Assistant Detective U (police), see Appendix.
66. Deputy Assistant Commissioner V (police), see Appendix.
67. Police Sergeant S (police), see Appendix.
68. Police Sergeant U (police), see Appendix.
69. Eiler Larsen, assistant detective, teacher in police theory at the Police Academy.
70. Deputy Assistant Commissioner V (police), see Appendix.
71. Christensen (1999, 42 f.).
72. Christensen (1999, 43 f.).
73. See Smith and Jakobsen (2010).
74. Smith and Jakobsen (2010).
75. Police Sergeant W (police), see Appendix.
76. Detective Assistant V and Detective Assistant Z (police), see Appendix.
77. Detective Assistant T and Police Commissioner T (police), see Appendix.
78. Mogens Lauridsen, chief superintendent at Copenhagen Police (Station City).
79. Smith and Jakobsen (2010).
80. Eiler Larsen, assistant detective, teacher in police theory at the Police Academy; Mogens Lauridsen, chief superintendent at Copenhagen Police (Station City).
81. Regarding CPT's criticism of Denmark, see Chapter 6.
82. Grøftehauge (2004, 19 ff.).
83. Act on Social Service § 153. See also the Service Act § 35.
84. Public employees have a duty to inform social services if they surmise that a child or a youngster under 18 needs special support. Cf. public employees' duty to inform which is established in executive order no. 1336 of 30 November to the duty to inform the municipality according to the Act on Social Service § 1, no. 1. The executive order has legal basis in the Service Act, § 153. See also https://www.retsinformation.dk/Forms/R0710.aspx?id=113910.
85. In the Danish Institute for Human Rights' survey, see Appendix.
86. The Danish Institute for Human Rights' survey, see Appendix.
87. The Danish Institute for Human Rights' survey, see Appendix.
88. Police Sergeant S (police) about an experience with children of arrested persons who have made a particular impression on her, see Appendix.
89. Police Commissioner T (police), see Appendix.
90. Deputy Assistant Commissioner Z (police), see Appendix.
91. Søren Ravn, deputy assistant superintendent and section leader at the Police Academy; Henrik Svindt, deputy assistant superintendent and investigation leader at Copenhagen Police (Station City); B6: Lars Nicolai Jensen, deputy assistant superintendent and daily leader of The Criminal Preventative Division in Copenhagen Police.
92. For example, a Police Commissioner T (police) wrote that when "we involve other persons – the parents come with suggestions themselves (e.g., grandparents) who can come and look after the children. They are not checked as such." See Appendix.
93. Rikke Betak, family therapist in the Engelsborg Family House.
94. *Information*, 2 May 2008.

95. *Information*, 2 May 2008.
96. *Information*, 2 May 2008.
97. Bente Boserup, senior counsellor for Børns Vilkår.
98. *Information*, 2 May 2008.
99. Ten out of 11 comments by participating employees in the social services on this subject are about more information sharing. Some police officers agree, for example, Police Sergeant S and Police Sergeant T. See Appendix.
100. Police Sergeant W (police), see Appendix.
101. Deputy Assistant Commissioner Z (police), see Appendix.
102. Social worker Y (police), see Appendix.
103. Section Leader I (the social authorities), see Appendix.
104. Christensen (1999, 95).
105. Marie, whose ex-husband is serving a 14-year sentence.
106. Søren Ravn, deputy assistant superintendent and section leader of PG3 (module 3) at the Police Academy.
107. In the Danish Institute for Human Rights' survey, see Appendix.
108. Anne Andersen, social worker and vocational leader for Rødovre Municipality's children and family division.
109. Line Dahl Krabsen, chairperson of the association SAVN (At the Institute for Human Rights' Roundtable on inmates' children, on 10 October 2006).

8 Remand Imprisonment: A Stressful Phase of Transition

1. Smith and Jakobsen (2010). See also Boswell and Wedge (2007); Christensen (1999).
2. See, for example, Murray and Farrington (2006, 726).
3. Christensen (1999, 50).
4. See Codd (2008, 52).
5. As previously mentioned, the CPT has found examples of this and has criticised Denmark on that account. See Chapter 6.
6. Siegel (2011, 111).
7. Rachel Condry, "Families Outside: The Difficulties Faced by Relatives of Serious Offenders", *Prison Service Journal* 174, no. 3 (2007a), 4. See also Condry (2007b, 52 ff.).
8. Christensen (1999, 48).
9. Marie, whose ex-husband is serving a 14-year sentence.
10. Kristian, whose father is in prison. Kristian is not the boy's real name.
11. Employee at a children's home where prisoners' children have lived; warden at a children's home where prisoners' children have lived. (Ali is not the boy's real name).
12. Susanne Bjerregaard, prison chaplain in Vridsløselille State Prison (former prison chaplain in Vestre Prison and former chairperson for the Prison Chaplains' Association).
13. Dennis, former prisoner. Dennis is not his real name.
14. Anne Karen Ursø, formerly leader of dialogue groups for prisoners' children in the Danish Red Cross.
15. Mazza (2000, 524).

16. See, for example, Robertson (2012); The Osborne Association *A Call to Action: A Report of the New York Initiative for Children of Incarcerated Parents*, May 2011; Smith and Jakobsen (2010).
17. Quoted from *Socialrådgiveren* no. 4, 22 February 2006.
18. Line Dahl Krabsen, chairperson of SAVN.
19. See report from the Danish Ministry of Justice: http://www.justitsministeriet.dk/sites/default/files/media/Arbejdsomraader/Forskning/Forskningsrapporter/Varetaegtsfaengslinger_2010.pdf (assessed 16 March 2013).
20. Roy Walmsley, *World Prison Population List*, 9th ed. (London: International Centre for Prison Studies, 2011); D. Berry and P. English, *The Socioeconomic Impact of Pretrial Detention* (New York: Open Society Foundations, 2011), 15.
21. Berry and English (2011, 15).

9 After the Sentence: The Family's Way of Dealing with the Children and the Surroundings

1. Christensen (1999, 51).
2. Condry (2007b, 53).
3. Condry (2007b, 53 ff.).
4. Leavens (2007, 4).
5. See, for example, (Christensen 1999, 52 and 54).
6. See, for example, (Christensen 1999, 52).
7. Turesson (2009, 187).
8. Marie, whose ex-husband is serving a 14-year sentence.
9. Interview with Marie.
10. Interview with Marie.
11. Turesson 2009, 176.
12. Line Dahl Krabsen, chairperson of SAVN.
13. Rikke Betak, family therapist in the Engelsborg Family House.
14. Sanne Graffe, former chairperson for Balance i Frihed (Balance in Freedom).
15. Interview with Marie.
16. Interview with Marie.
17. Kristian, whose father is in prison.
18. Grøftehauge 2004, 27 (interview with psychologist Else Christensen).
19. Kristian, whose father is in prison.
20. Boswell and Wedge (2007, 74). ("Head" is slang for "headmaster").
21. Boswell and Wedge (2007, 74).
22. Rikke Betak, family therapist in the Engelsborg Family House.
23. Mazza (2000, 525).
24. Psychologist Line Schnettler who has worked with dialogue groups for children in the Danish Red Cross.
25. Child psychologist Poul Erik Jørgensen, taped interview available at http://www.elbecks.dk/minfarifaengsel/.
26. Line Dahl Krabsen, chairperson of SAVN.
27. Psychologist Line Schnettler, who has worked with dialogue groups for children in the Danish Red Cross.
28. Birgitte Nygaard, family counsellor for SAVN.

10 Visiting in Prisons: Staff, Children, Conditions and Practice

1. J. Murray, "The Effects of Imprisonment on Families and Children of Prisoners", in *The Effects of Imprisonment*, ed. A. Liebling and S. Maruna (Cullompton, UK: Willan Publishing, 2005, 445.
2. Arditti (2012, 31).
3. Murray (2005, 455).
4. Boswell and Wedge (2007, 61).
5. Liebling (2004, 325 ff.). See also Murray (2005, 454).
6. See Jones and Wainaina-Woźna (2013, 58).
7. Raikes and Lockwood (2011, 22).
8. See ICPS World Prison Brief, available at http://www.kcl.ac.uk/depsta/law/research/icps/worldbrief/wpb_country.php?country=134.
9. *Kriminalforsorgens Statistik 2012* (the yearly statistical publication from the Danish prison service).
10. See also B. Crewe and A. Liebling, "Are Liberal Humanitarian Penal Values and Practices Exceptional?", in *Penal Exceptionalism? Nordic Prison Policy and Practice*, ed. T. Ugelvik and J. Dullum (London: Routledge, 2010).
11. Manfred Nowak, report on Denmark, A/HRC/10/44/Add.2, 18 February 2009.
12. See Smith (2011).
13. M. D. Evans and R. Morgan, *Preventing Torture: A Study for the Prevention of Torture and Inhuman and Degrading Treatment* (Oxford: Clarendon Press, 1998). The authors characterise pre-trial solitary confinement as a "peculiarly Scandinavian phenomenon", p. 247. Iceland has also received the same criticism. See CPT, Visit Report, Iceland. Visit 1998, Section 15/49. See also report from the 1993 visit in Iceland.
14. Barnombudsmannen, *Från Insidan. Barn och ungdomar om tillvaron I arrest och häkte* (Stockholm: Barnombudsmannen, 2013).
15. Christensen (1999).
16. Remand prison officer K (detention), see Appendix.
17. *Far i fængsel* (*Dad in Prison*), Danish Prisoners' Choir, Children's Choir and Peter Mygind.
18. Kristian whose father is in prison.
19. *Nyt fra Kriminalforsorgen*, September 2009. The children's quotes (Dennis) are from family therapist Rikke Betak's interviews with prisoners' children.
20. Christensen (1999).
21. Statement from child (p. 5) in compilation of Bosch and Fjord's children's workshop, 27 September 2007, held at the Egmont Foundation. Nine prisoners' children participated in the workshop, which aimed "to obtain inspiration to improve the visiting facilities at Vridsløselille State Prison. To 'hear' the children's needs and experiences in order to be able to design at children's level."
22. Line is quoted from the website: http://www.elbecks.dk/minfarifaengsel/.
23. Taped interview on the website: http://www.elbecks.dk/minfarifaengsel/.
24. Child of prisoner, see Christensen (1999).
25. Prison officer M (detention), prison worker Æ (detention), prison worker T (detention), prison worker J (detention). See Appendix.

26. Prison officer M (detention), prison worker Æ (detention), prison worker T (detention), prison worker J (detention). See Appendix.
27. Prison officer S (detention), see Appendix.
28. Social worker K (the social authorities), see Appendix.
29. Christensen (1999).
30. Barnombudsmannen (2013, 49 f.).
31. Figures emailed from the Danish Prison and Probation Service to the Danish Institute for Human Rights on 21 June 2013.
32. Police Sergeant S (police), see Appendix.
33. Several of the participants marked more than one option.
34. Several of the participants marked more than one option.
35. Mai Alexandersen, police sergeant in the detainee section Copenhagen Police (Station City).
36. Hans Erik Kronborg, remand prison supervisor in Køge Remand Prison.
37. Police Sergeant S (police), see Appendix.
38. The Danish Institute for Human Rights' questionnaire survey to employees in the prisons, see Appendix.
39. For example, prison officer Y, social work consultant W and therapy consultant X. See Appendix.
40. Bosch and Fjord's children's workshop, held on 27 September 2007, 10.
41. Lissi Sørensen, prison officer in Køge Remand Prison.
42. Child of a prisoner, Christensen (1999).
43. Mogens Lauridsen, chief superintendent at Copenhagen Police (Station City).
44. Prison officer K (detention), see Appendix.
45. Hans Erik Kronborg, remand prison supervisor in Køge Remand Prison.
46. See Engbo and Smith (2012, 155).
47. Treatment consultant W (prison), see Appendix.
48. Prices checked on www.dsb.dk on 2 August 2013. Currency rates checked on the same day.
49. Former treatment consultant in Østjylland State Prison.
50. Vibeke Blinn, treatment advisor in Vridsløselille State Prison.
51. Survey in the open prisons by the directorate for the Prison and Probation Service. See The Directorate for the Prison and Probation Service, Sentence Enforcement Office, "Rapport om status på området de indsattes børn i Kriminalforsorgen" ("Report on the Status in the Area of Prisoners' Children with Regard to the Prison and Probation Service), Copenhagen, 30 November 2009. Drawn up in continuation of the parliaments (Folketinget) Legal Committee's processing of proposal for parliamentary resolution no. B 74 on improved conditions for children of prisoners. (see p. 2 of the report on open prisons).
52. Dennis, former prisoner.
53. Grøftehauge (2004, 48).
54. Christensen (1999, 66).
55. Bosch and Fjord's children's workshop, held on 27 September 2007, 11.
56. Remand officer J (detention), see Appendix.
57. Prison officer I (detention), see Appendix.
58. Prison officer Å (detention), see Appendix.
59. Remand officer K (detention), see Appendix.

60. Remand prison manager K (detention), see Appendix.
61. Prison officer V (detention), see Appendix.
62. Prison officer X (prison), see Appendix.
63. Council of Europe, Committee of Ministers, Rec (2006) 2, the European Prison Rules, see rule 24.4. See also Engbo and Smith (2012, 277).
64. Directorate for the Prison and Probation Service, Sentence Enforcement Office, "Rapport om status på området de indsattes børn i Kriminalforsorgen", Copenhagen, 30 November 2009, see 2.
65. Lindberg 2010. The quote is not included in the report from the Nation Council for Children, but appears in the unpublished version of the entire interview, which Stine Lindberg has allowed the Danish Institute for Human Rights to use (see appendix). Maja is not the real name of the girl.
66. Troels Bloch, prison governor of Jyderup State Prison, email correspondence, 28 December 2009. Visits indoors typically take place in the prisoners' own rooms (blocks) and, for example, visitors do not have access to the prison's production workshops.
67. Hans Jørgen Engbo, *Straffuldbyrdelsesret* (Copenhagen: Jurist- og Økonomforbundet, 2005), 44. See also the European Prison Rules, 24.4. Concerning progressive conditions in the open prison Møgelkjær, see Smith and Jakobsen (2010, 144 f.).
68. Visit to Vridsløselille State Prison, 6 October 2009.
69. There are no statistics on how frequently the visiting apartments are used, but according to Hannah Hagerup in the directorate of the Prison and Probation Service, they are used a great deal and often by families with children.
70. Visit to Østjylland State Prison, 18 September 2007.
71. Annelise Brok, prison chaplain in Østjylland State Prison.
72. The two visiting apartments have a large communal courtyard, but this is actually not used. A "playground group" has been formed to assess how the courtyard can be adapted so that the families can use it – according to Hannah Hagerup in the directorate of the Prison and Probation Service.
73. Former treatment consultant in Østjylland State Prison.
74. Hoffmann, Byrd and Kightlinger (2010, 404 f.).; Raikes and Lockwood (2011). I have seen such a unit in Halden Prison in Norway. In Sweden, some prisoners are also allowed to bring their children on a vacation in a special prison.
75. See Hendriksen, Jakobsen and Smith (2012).
76. I have visited both Ringe Prison and Blegdamsvejens Prison several times in recent years.
77. Remand prison manager J (detention), see Appendix.
78. Social worker J (the social authorities), see Appendix.
79. Information obtained at a meeting with representatives of the Swedish Prison Service and the NGO Bryggan, Stockholm, 22 May 2013.
80. "Vridsløselille Infonyt", 15 July 2009 (email bulletin that prisoner spokespersons were allowed to send out for a while).
81. Marianne Secher, deputy prison governor in Vridsløselille State Prison. This is regarding prisoners in the general prison population. In addition, prisoners in special blocks also hold events in their block.
82. Directorate for the Prison and Probation Service, Sentence Enforcement Office, "Rapport om status på området de indsattes børn i Kriminalforsorgen", Copenhagen, 30 November 2009, 5.

83. Directorate for the Prison and Probation Service, Sentence Enforcement Office, "Rapport om status på området de indsattes børn i Kriminalforsorgen", Copenhagen, 30 November 2009.
84. Susanne Bjerregaard, prison chaplain in Vridsløselille State Prison (former prison chaplain in Vestre Prison and former chairperson for the Prison Chaplains' Association). See also the Directorate for the Prison and Probation Service, Sentence Enforcement Office, "Rapport om status på området de indsattes børn i Kriminalforsorgen", Copenhagen, 30 November 2009, 5.
85. With reference to English prisons and through the use of two particular prisoner interviews, Ben Crewe highlights how it is still often a golden rule never to "grass" on other inmates and never to side with an officer above another prisoner. But he also quotes a prisoner saying that "it has become much more acceptable for prisoners to socialize in friendly ways with prison staff". See Ben Crewe, "Prison Culture and the Prisoner Society", in *The Prisoner*, ed. B. Crewe and J. Bennete (New York: Routledge, 2012), 34. Another important factor is local prison cultures, which can vary significantly. Regarding prison culture and "them" and "us" dynamics, see also Minke (2012, 142 ff.).
86. Hendriksen, Jakobsen and Smith 2012. See also "Revideret implementeringsplan og succeskriterier, februar 2013" and "Projektstatus til Egmont Fonden 20 Nov. 2012", unpublished internal reports received at a project board meeting, 25 February 2013.
87. A. Liebling and H. Arnold,*Prisons and Their Moral Performance: A Study of Values, Quality, and Prison Life* (Oxford: Oxford University Press, 2004), 469.
88. Liebling (2004, 235).
89. Liebling (2004, 470).
90. See also Jones and Wainaina-Woźna (2013, 61).
91. Line Dahl Krabsen, founder and chairperson of SAVN.
92. Kristian, whose father is in prison.
93. Interview with Marie.
94. Interview with Marie.
95. Custodial manager J (detention), see Appendix.
96. Rikke Betak, family therapist in the Engelsborg Family House.
97. Employee in the Central Division of Copenhagen Prisons.
98. John Michael Steinmüller, area manager and formerly responsible for the visiting unit in Vestre Prison.
99. Kristian, whose father is in prison.
100. Kristian, whose father is in prison.
101. Mads told his story in the daily *MetroXpress*, 16 October 2006.
102. Prison officer Z (prison), see Appendix.
103. Marie, whose ex-husband is serving a 14-year sentence.
104. Stine Lindberg, *Helst skal man have en god barndom – 40 børns fortællinger om et liv med særlige vilkår* (København: Børnerådet, 2000), 33. Maja is not the girl's real name. The first lines of the quote are not included in the rapport from the National Council for Children but stated in the printing of the entire interview, which Stine Lindberg has allowed the Danish Institute for Human Rights to use (see Appendix).

105. Figures emailed from the Danish Prison and Probation Service to the Danish Institute for Human Rights on 21 June 2013.
106. The visits took place in December 2012 and February 2013. The prison governor is Peter Vesterheden.
107. Police Sergeant X (police), see Appendix.
108. Deputy Assistant Commissioner Z (police), see Appendix.
109. Police Commissioner T (police), see Appendix.
110. Police Sergeant S (police), see Appendix.
111. Assistant detective Å (police), see Appendix.
112. The Danish Institute for Human Rights questionnaire survey, see Appendix.
113. Rikke Betak, family therapist in the Engelsborg Family House.
114. Kristian, whose father is in prison.
115. Peter Scharff Smith, Thomas Horn, Johannes F. Nilsen and Marte Rua, "Isolation i Skandinaviske fængsler", *Social Kritik*, no. 136 (December 2013), 13.
116. See Smith (2006, 503). See also Smith, "The Effects of Solitary Confinement, Commentary on *One Year Longitudinal Study of the Psychological Effects of Administrative Segregation*", in *Corrections and Mental Health* (2011).
117. For a summary of the many possible negative effects, see Smith (2006).
118. Report to the Danish Government on the visit to Denmark carried out by the European Committee for the Prevention of Torture and Inhuman or Degrading Treatment or Punishment (CPT) from 29 September to 9 October 1996, 27.
119. Bent Volf, criminal police superintendent in 2006 and employed in South and Southern Jutland Police in 2010, telephone interviews, June 2006 and January 2010; Steffen Steffensen, detective inspector at Copenhagen Police, telephone interviews June 2006 and January 2010. None of them could come up with instances when visiting permission had been rejected for children of solitary confined remand prisoners. See Smith and Jakobsen (2010).
120. Christensen (1999, 44).
121. Christensen (1999).
122. Christensen (1999, 45).
123. Christensen (1999, 45).
124. Christensen (1999, 45).

11 Home Leave and Other Ways of Maintaining Contact

1. Smith and Gampell (2011, 237).
2. Christensen (1999, 68).
3. Christensen (1999, 68).
4. See Engbo (2005, 276).
5. Engbo (2005, 277).
6. Kristian, whose father is in prison.
7. Marie, whose ex-husband is serving a 14-year sentence.
8. Lindberg (2010, 33). It is not clear whether it is a police officer or a prison officer.

9. Engbo (2005, 277 ff.).
10. See Smith and Jakobsen (2010, 170 and 296).
11. See "Vedrørende fremtidig praksis i visse typer sager der er begrundet i hensynet til indsattes mindreårige Børn", Direktoratet for Kriminalforsorgen, 10 July 2000, Journal nr. 2.k. gr. 104.
12. Grøftehauge (2004, 58).
13. See "Beskrivelse af praksis i visse typer sager der er begrundet i hensynet til indsattes mindreårige Børn", Direktoratet for Kriminalforsorgen, J.nr.: Klientkontoret gr. 104, 14 November 2000.
14. See "Supplerende beskrivelse af praksis i visse typer af sager der er begrundet i hensyn til indsattesmindreårige børn", Direktoratet for Kriminalforsorgen, J.nr.: GR 104, 16 April 2002.
15. Helle Riisberg, treatment consultant at Sønder Omme Prison.
16. Directorate for the Prison and Probation Service, Sentence Enforcement Office, "Rapport om status på området de indsattes børn i Kriminalforsorgen", Copenhagen, 30 November 2009, 6.
17. *Kriminalforsorgens statistik 2010.*
18. See the Ministry of Justice, "Besvarelse af spørgsmål nr. S 1799 fra medlem af Folketinget VillySøvndal (SF)" (SF being the Socialist People's Party), Lovafdelingen (Legal Division) 2005-790-0008, Doc. LOJ40011.
19. Former treatment consultant in Østjylland State Prison.
20. Mogens Lauridsen, chief superintendent at Copenhagen Police (Station City).
21. Police Superintendent V (police), see Appendix.
22. The Danish Institute for Human Rights' questionnaire survey, see Appendix.
23. Police Superintendent T (police), see Appendix.
24. Police Sergeant U (police), see Appendix.
25. Peter Koudal "Indsatte i danske fængsler. Uddannelse og uddannelsesønsker", Danmarks pædagogiske universitet, 2007, 4.
26. Boswell and Wedge (2007, 77).
27. In the Danish Institute for Human Rights' questionnaire survey, see Appendix.
28. Excerpt of taped interview from the website: "Min far i Fængsel" ("My Dad in Prison"): http://www.elbecks.dk/min-farifaengsel/.
29. Engbo (2005, 304 ff.).
30. Christensen (1999, 62).
31. Christensen (1999, 62).
32. Visit leader W (prison), prison officer W (prison), see Appendix.
33. Prison inspector W (prison), prison officer Z (prison), prison officer Æ (prison), see Appendix.
34. Section leader W (prison), see Appendix.
35. Engbo (2005, 304 f.).
36. Prison officer K (remand), see Appendix.
37. Prison officer K (remand), Prison officer Q (remand), see Appendix.
38. Prison officer W (remand), see Appendix.
39. Prisoner officer Æ (remand), prison officer J (remand), prison officer K (remand), prison officer X (remand), Manager I (remand), see Appendix.
40. Quoted: Prison officer Y (remand). See also comments by prison officer Z, N, R and I (remand), see appendix.

41. Manager K (remand), prison officer T, see Appendix.
42. Christensen (1999, 49).
43. Christensen (1999, 46).
44. Mazza (2002, 524).
45. Ina Eliasen, office manager, Sentence Enforcement Office, The Directorate of the Prison Service.
46. Susanne Bjerregaard, prison chaplain in Vridsløselille State Prison (former prison chaplain in Vestre Prison and former chairperson for the Prison Chaplains' Association).
47. Hannah Hagerup, Sentence Enforcement Office, The Directorate of the Prison Service; Susanne Bjerregaard, prison chaplain in Vridsløselille State Prison (former prison chaplain in Vestre Prison and former chairperson for the Prison Chaplains' Association).
48. Smith (2012).
49. See the FFP Newsletter, December 2013 (FFP "Nyhetsbrev julen 2013").
50. See Direktoratet for Kriminalforsorgen (The Directorate of the Prison Service), Straffuldbyrdelseskontoret "Indsattes internetadgang", Note of 21 March 2012, Journal 10-040-0036; See also Justitsministeriet (The Ministry of Justice), Direktoratet for Kriminalforsorgen, "Vedrørende brug af internet i undervisningen", 11 April 2000, UK, Journal 97-3413-9.
51. See *Direktoratet for Kriminalforsorgen*, "Internetadgang, 21 March 2012".
52. *Kriminalforsorgens Statistik 2009*, 9 and 19.
53. Information supplied at a meeting held with Ina Eliasen (head of office) in the Directorate of the Prison Service, 10 May 2012. The agenda was Internet access in Danish prisons.
54. See *Direktoratet for Kriminalforsorgen*, "Internetadgang 21 March 2012"; See also Justitsministeriet "Vedrørende brug af internet i undervisningen".
55. See Direktoratet for Kriminalforsorgen (The Directorate of the Prison Service), Straffuldbyrdelseskontoret, "Indsattes internetadgang", 16 April 2012, Journal 10-040-0036.
56. See *Direktoratet for Kriminalforsorgen*, "Internetadgang", 16 April 2012 (n. 20).
57. *Direktoratet for Kriminalforsorgen*, "Internetadgang", 21 March 2012"; *Direktoratet for Kriminalforsorgen*, "Internetadgang", 16 April 2012.
58. *Kriminalforsorgens statistik 2010*.

12 When Visits Do Not Take Place: Opting Out of Visits and Discontinuing Contact

1. Hairston, quoted in Boswell and Wedge (2007, 26).
2. Boswell and Wedge (2007, 37).
3. See Jones and Wainaina-Woźna (2013, 57 and 254 f.).
4. Siegel (2011, 173).
5. In the Danish Institute for Human Rights' questionnaire survey, 75% of the remand prison staff, 56% of the police officers and 66% of the prison staff estimated that the remand prisoners often had poor or no contact with their children when at the time of imprisonment. See Appendix.

6. See Smith and Jakobsen (2010).
7. Prison officer T (remand), see Appendix.
8. "Lack of job title" I (remand), see Appendix.
9. Treatment consultant W (prison), see Appendix.
10. Mogens Lauridsen, chief superintendent at Copenhagen Police (Station City).
11. L. K. Minke, *Fængslets indre liv* (Copenhagen: Jurist- og Økonomforbundet, 2012), 241.
12. Minke (2012, 242 f.).
13. Boswell and Wedge (2007, 39).
14. Boswell and Wedge (2007, 38).
15. Rikke Betak, family therapist in the Family House in Halfway House Engelsborg.
16. Gresham Sykes: *The Society of Captives*, New Jersey 1974.
17. Prison staff Z (prison), see appendix.
18. Louise Berg Petersen and Iben Bjørgulf Antonsen, "Børnene straffes når mor ryger i fængsel", unpublished article, University of Århus, 2013.
19. Kari Middelthon, unpublished manuscript given as a speech at the 20th anniversary for FFP in Oslo, Norway, 13 June 2013.
20. Boswell and Wedge (2007, 37).
21. Line Dahl Krabsen, chairperson of SAVN.
22. Hanne Ziebe, secretariat manager in the national association KRIM.
23. Psychologist Marie Gammeltoft.
24. Social worker I (the social authorities), see Appendix.
25. Marianne Secher, deputy prison governor in Vridsløselille State Prison; Elisabeth Toft Rasmussen, former employee of the Danish Red Cross; Brian Lund Andreasen, former deputy chairman of SAVN; Sanne Graffe, former chairperson for Balance i Frihed.
26. Brian Lund Andreasen, former deputy chairman of SAVN.
27. Christensen (1999, 50).
28. Elisabeth Toft Rasmussen, former employee of the Danish Red Cross.
29. Birgitta Persson, responsible for the questions regarding prisoners' parentship, the Swedish Prison and Probation Service's head office in Norrköping.
30. Boswell and Wedge (2007, 52).
31. Boswell and Wedge (2007, 53).
32. Boswell and Wedge (2007, 50).
33. Quoted from Minke (2012, 238).
34. J. Travis and M. Waul, *Prisoners Once Removed: The Impact of Incarceration and Reentry on Children, Families, and Communities* (Washington, DC: The Urban Institute, 2003), 8. See also Ayre, Philbrick and Reiss (2006, 10).
35. Travis and Waul (2003, 9).

13 When Contact Is Undesirable

1. Lindberg (2010, 36).
2. See, for example, Boswell and Wedge (2007, 29).
3. Christensen (1999, 100).
4. Fazel and Danesh (2002, 548).

274 *Notes*

5. Peter Kramp, "Registerundersøgelsen" ("The Register Survey") 1993, unpublished.
6. See H. S. Andersen, "Mental Health in Prison Populations. A Review – with Special Emphasis on a Study of Danish Prisoners on Remand", *Acta Psychiatrica Scandinavica. Supplementum* 424 (2004).
7. Mette Lindgaard Adamsen, *Screeningsprojektet for psykisk sygdom* (Copenhagen: Direktoratet for Kriminalforsorgen, 2013), 11.
8. Andersen (2004, 27).
9. Molbech (2009, 26).
10. Psychologist Marie Gammeltoft. Marie has personally warned against contact twice out of approximately 10 cases of prisoners' children.
11. Psychologist Marie Gammeltoft.
12. Psychologist Marie Gammeltoft.
13. Psychologist Marie Gammeltoft.
14. Prison officer Æ (prison), see Appendix.
15. Police Sergeant S (police), see Appendix.
16. Deputy Assistant Commissioner Æ (police), see Appendix.
17. Prison officer Z (prison), see appendix.
18. Deputy Governor Å (halfway house), see Appendix.
19. Social worker I (the social authorities), see Appendix.
20. Karsten Sivgaard, remand prison supervisor in Roskilde Remand Prison from 1981–2008.
21. Karsten Sivgaard, remand prison officer in Roskilde Remand Prison from 1981–2008.
22. Prison officer I (remand), see Appendix.
23. Prison officer P (remand), see Appendix.
24. Prison manager J (remand), see Appendix.
25. Lissi Sørensen, prison officer in Køge Remand Prison.
26. Prison manager J (remand), see Appendix.

14 When Dad or Mum Returns: Re-entry and Release

1. "Kriminalforsorgen – Kort og godt", 10 (updated August 2009). Downloaded from www.kriminalforsorgen.dk.
2. *Kriminalforsorgens statistik 2012*, 50.
3. *Kriminalforsorgens statistik 2012*, 50.
4. See Andrew Coyle, *Understanding Prisons: Key Issues in Policy and Practice* (Maidenhead: Open University Press, 2005), 16.
5. See UK Ministry of Justice, "Proven Re-offending Statistics, Quarterly Bulletin – July 2010 to June 2011, England and Wales", *Statistics Bulletin*, London, April 2013, 7.
6. See UK Ministry of Justice 2013, 8.
7. Shadd Maruna, "After Prison, What? The Ex-prisoner's Struggle to Desist from Crime", in *Handbook on Prisons*, ed. Y. Jewkes (Cullompton: Willan Publishing, 2009), 651.
8. T. Tranæs, "Den uformelle straf og velfærdsstaten", *Nordisk Tidsskrift for Kriminalvidenskab* 95, no. 3 (2008), 29.
9. Tranæs (2008, 136).

10. Tranæs (2008, 137).
11. Crewe (2007, 132 f.).
12. Jamieson and Grounds (2005, 37).
13. Condry (2007, 48). See also Arditti (2012, 110).
14. Psychologist Marie Gammeltoft.
15. Sanne Graffe, former chairperson for "Balance i Frihed".
16. Line Dahl Krabsen, chairperson of SAVN.
17. Quoted from Maruna (2009, 661).
18. Rikke Betak, family therapist in the Engelsborg Family House.
19. Psychologist Marie Gammeltoft.
20. Psychologist Marie Gammeltoft.
21. Engbo (2005, 344).
22. According to the action plan which the Prison and Probation Service in Freedom works from (supplied to the Danish Institute for Human Rights on 10 October 2007).
23. Nete Jørgensen, social worker for the Prison and Probation Service; Anne-Marie Tingrupp, head of welfare section in the Prison and Probation Service.
24. Nete Jørgensen, social worker for the Prison and Probation Service.
25. Engbo (2005, 353 f.).
26. As explained by Bari, ex-prisoner and former resident in the Engelsborg Family House; see Molbech (2009, 30).
27. Leavens (2007, 12 f.).
28. See the Prison and Probation Service's website on halfway houses: www.pensionerne.dk.
29. "På vej til frihed", a re-entry programme at the Prison and Probation Service's Halfway Houses.
30. See the Prison and Probation Service's website on halfway houses: www.pensionerne.dk. See also Chapter 15.
31. The Danish Institute for Human Rights' questionnaire survey – halfway houses in the Prison and Probation Service. See Appendix.
32. See Engelsborg's Newsletter no. 2, June 2005.
33. Rikke Betak, family therapist in the Engelsborg Family House.
34. Rikke Betak, family therapist in the Engelsborg Family House.
35. Rikke Betak, family therapist in the Engelsborg Family House; Kirsten Neiman, governor at Engelsborg Family House.
36. Rikke Betak, family therapist in the Engelsborg Family House.
37. Rikke Betak, family therapist in the Engelsborg Family House.
38. See also Molbech (2009). For another practice with a "family-centred" approach, see the description of the "La Bodega" model in Arditti 2012, 179.

15 With Mum or Dad in Prison: Children Who Live with Their Imprisoned Parent

1. See Alejos (2005, 34 f.); Robertson (2012, 5); Smith and Jakobsen (2010, 201 ff.); Sacerdote et al. (2011, 184); Pösö, Enroos and Vierula (2010); Hoffmann, Byrd and Kightlinger (2010).

2. Smith and Jakobsen (2010, 204).
3. Nijnatten (1998, 117 ff.).
4. Robertson (2008, 17); Ayre, Philbrick and Reiss (2006, 74). See also Pösö, Enroos and Vierula (2010).
5. Robertson (2008, 17); Ayre, Philbrick and Reiss (2006, 74).
6. Hannah Hagerup, The Directorate of the Prison Service.
7. Family therapist at Engelsborg, Rikke Betak, estimates that about 40% of the Family House's adult residents are fathers. In some cases, both mother and father live in the Family House (where both or the one is serving) and in other cases, mother or father who is serving, lives along with his or her child or children.
8. Alejos (2005, 30).
9. See Chapter 6.
10. Hannah Hagerup, The Directorate of the Prison Service – and responses to the Danish Institute for Human Rights' questionnaire survey. Here, 17 out of the 18 Danish prisons and prison divisions in Denmark, corresponding to 94%, to participate and among these, 20% had experienced having children live in the prison in the course of the last five years. According to the survey, this concerned 2 children in the one prison, 3 children in the second and approx. 15 children in the third, respectively. See appendix.
11. Hoffmann, Byrd and Kightlinger (2010, 404 f.).
12. Pösö, Enroos and Vierula (2010, 528).
13. Pösö, Enroos and Vierula (2010, 521).
14. Robertson (2008, 7 and 43) (appendices).
15. Sentence Enforcement Act § 54. See *Indstilling fra arbejdsgruppen vedrørende indsattes børn*, Kriminalforsorgen, October 2012, 25.
16. Hannah Hagerup, The Directorate of the Prison Service (quoting a legal response to the Danish parliament).
17. Governor in Ringe State Prison, Bodil Phillip, Fyens Stiftstidende on 3 August 2009.
18. Fyens Stiftstidende on 4 August 2009. The age limit was raised in 2001.
19. Directorate for the Prison and Probation Service, Sentence Enforcement Office, "Report on the Status of the Area, Inmates' Children, in the Prison and Probation Service", Copenhagen, 30 November 2009, 5.
20. *Indstilling fra arbejdsgruppen vedrørende indsattes børn*, Kriminalforsorgen, October 2012, 26.
21. *Indstilling fra arbejdsgruppen vedrørende indsattes børn*, Kriminalforsorgen, October 2012, 26.
22. Hannah Hagerup, The Directorate of the Prison Service.
23. Directorate for the Prison and Probation Service, Sentence Enforcement Office, "Report on the Status of the Area, Inmates' Children, in the Prison and Probation Service", Copenhagen, 30 November 2009, 5.
24. Inge Halmø, "Resocialisering med familiebehandling i utraditionelle og hidtil uprøvede rammer" ["Resocialising with Family Therapy in Untraditional and So-far Untried Settings"] (Copenhagen, Danish Prison and Probation Service, 2008), 8.
25. Alejos (2005, 4).
26. Robertson (2008, 1).
27. Tue Toft from Psykologhuset in Odense, in the daily *Fyens Stiftstidende*, 3 August 2009.

28. Psychologist Marie Gammeltoft.
29. Psychologist Marie Gammeltoft.
30. Jakob Ørbjerg in the daily *Fyens Stiftstidende*, 19 August 2009.
31. Robertson (2008, 8).
32. Alejos (2005, 71).
33. See, for example, Ramsbotham (2003, 9 ff.).
34. Robertson (2008, 21).
35. Education manager at Askham Grange.
36. Robertson (2008, 12).
37. Se Raikes and Lockwood (2011).
38. Hannah Hagerup, The Directorate of the Prison Service; Directorate for the Prison and Probation Service, Sentence Enforcement Office, "Report on the Status of the Area, Inmates' Children, in the Prison and Probation Service", Copenhagen, 30 November 2009, 5.
39. Directorate for the Prison and Probation Service, Sentence Enforcement Office, "Report on the Status of the Area, Inmates' Children, in the Prison and Probation Service", Copenhagen 30 November 2009, 5.
40. These are the contract halfway house on Funen, Halfway House Skejby, Halfway House Lynge and Halfway House Engelsborg.
41. Hannah Hagerup, The Directorate of the Prison Service.
42. Hannah Hagerup, The Directorate of the Prison Service.
43. Hannah Hagerup, The Directorate of the Prison Service.
44. Molbech (2009, 110).
45. Prison inspector W (prison), see Appendix.
46. Prison worker Å (prison), see Appendix.
47. Section leader W (prison), see Appendix.
48. Robertson (2008, 11).
49. Robertson (2008, 29). Another age limit can in special (exceptional) cases be approved by "the Deputy Commissioner" (source: Alejos 2005, 35).
50. Robertson 2008, 29, citing Jane Woodrow, *Mothers in Prison: The Problem of Dependent Children* (Cambridge: Cambridge University, 1992), 280, originally from "Alliance 44 of NGOs on Crime Prevention and Criminal Justice", 1987.
51. See Sacerdote et al. (2011, 184).
52. Directorate for the Prison and Probation Service, Sentence Enforcement Office, "Report on the Status of the Area, Inmates' Children, in the Prison and Probation Service", Copenhagen, 30 November 2009, 5.
53. Rikke Betak, family therapist in the Engelsborg Family House.
54. Rikke Betak, family therapist in the Engelsborg Family House. See also Halmø (2008, 16).
55. Rikke Betak, family therapist in the Engelsborg Family House.
56. See Turesson (2009) and Enos (2001).
57. Molbech (2009, 31).
58. Molbech (2009, 33).
59. Molbech (2009, 35).
60. Molbech (2009, 35).
61. Halmø (2008, 29).
62. Prison governor in the Prison and Probation Service.
63. Pösö, Enroos and Vierula (2010, 525).
64. Dan Bøgedal, former treatment consultant (until September 2009) in Ringe State Prison.

65. Prison Governor W (prison), see Appendix.
66. Prison Governor W (prison), see Appendix.
67. The prison governor at Ringe State Prison, Bodil Phillip, has on several occasions given numerous accounts of such problems (for example, at a course for children's officers held at the Danish Institute for Human Rights in 2010).
68. Prison manager J (remand), see Appendix.
69. Social worker Z (halfway house), see Appendix.
70. Social worker Æ (halfway house), see Appendix.
71. Prison officer Å (prison), see Appendix.
72. Social worker Z (halfway house), see Appendix.
73. Deputy warden Ø (halfway house), see Appendix.
74. Social worker Ø (the social authorities), see Appendix.
75. Ex-secretary/deputy manager (the social authorities), see Appendix.
76. Social worker I (the social authorities), see Appendix.
77. Ingolf Farvin, retired prison officer.
78. Robertson (2008, 28).
79. Robertson (2008, 28). Robertson is citing Woodrow (1992).
80. Pösö, Enroos and Vierula 2010, 528.

16 Penal Populism and Children of Imprisoned Parents

1. See, for example, Smith 2003; David Garland *Punishment and Welfare: A History of Penal Strategies* (Aldershot: Gower, 2001).
2. Garland (2001); Pratt (2007); Tonry (2004).
3. See Ugelvik and Dullum (2011); Pratt (2008); Pratt and Eriksson (2013).
4. Quoted from Smith (2009, 101).
5. Quoted from Smith (2009, 101).
6. V. Greve, "Retten og samfundet", *Nordisk tidsskrift for Kriminalvidenskab*, May 2010, 98.
7. See, for example, "Får eller Ulve", *Tidskrift utgiven av Juridiska Föreningen i Finland* 3–4 (2004); Greve 2010; B. G. Nielsen, *Straf – hvad ellers?* (Copenhagen: Tiderne Skifter, 2006); Smith and Jakobsen (2010, chapter 17).
8. "DJØF bladet" no. 7, 2002.
9. Interview in *Jyllandsposten*, 23 February 2010.
10. See Mette Mayli Albæk and Neils Schack Nørgaard, "Danskerne siger nei til mobiler og kys i Fængsler", Denmark, 21 December 2011, http://politiken.dk/indland/ECE1485771/danskerne-sigernej-til-mobiler-og-kys-i-faengsler/; Ritzau, "Minister afviser mobiler i fængsler", DR Nyheder, 10 December 2011, http://www.dr.dk/Nyheder/Indland/2011/12/10/083339.htm?rss=true; Michael Ørtz Christiansen, "Kæmper videre for mobiler i lukkede fængsler", BT, 21 September 2012, http://www.bt.dk/politik/kaemper-videre-for-mobiler-i-lukkede-faengsler; Ritzau, "Indsatte i lukkede fængsler får telefoner", Fyens.dk, 7 December 2011, http://www.fyens.dk/article/1984491:Indland-Fyn – Indsatte-i-lukkede-faengsler-faar-telefoner (all links in this footnote accessed 8 November 2012).
11. *Politiken*, 17 September 2008, http://politiken.dk/politik/article568728.ece.
12. Greve (2010).
13. Concerning the various bullet points, see Greve (2010).
14. Greve (2010).

15. W. Rentzmann et al., *Straffuldbyrdelsesloven med kommentarer* (Copenhagen: Jurist- og Økonomforbundets Forlag, 2002), 59; Engbo (2005, 128).
16. The law on Execution of Punishment, § 59, para. 2.
17. Smith (2007); Engbo and Smith (2012).
18. Engbo (2005, 249).
19. Smith 2006 B.
20. *Kriminalforsorgens statistik 2011*, 15.
21. F. Balvig, *Danskernes syn på straf* (Copenhagen: Advokatsamfundet, 2006), 52.
22. Balvig (2006, 309 ff.).
23. Balvig (2006, 323).
24. Balvig (2006, 320).
25. See, for example, Sara Wakefield and Christopher Wildeman, *Children of the Prison Boom: Mass Incarceration and the Future of American Inequality* (New York: Oxford University Press, 2013).
26. Talk given by Hans Jørgen Engbo in connection with hearings at Christiansborg (the Danish parliament) about penal measures and prisons, 16 May 2005. See also Tokkesdal and Lund (2004, 31).
27. Prison governor Bodil Philip, "Set indefra – vilkår under afsoning", *Social Politik* no. 1, (2007).
28. Prison governor Bodil Philip, "Set indefra – vilkår under afsoning", *Social Politik* no. 1, (2007), 27.
29. *Kriminalforsorgens statistik 2010*, 44.
30. Prison governor Bodil Philip, "Set indefra – vilkår under afsoning", *Social Politik* no. 1, 2007.
31. Mikkel Thastum, "Hård kurs mod strafpjækkeri", *Jyllands-Posten*, 1 November 2005.
32. Proposal from Peter Skaarup, Danish People's Party, see Thastum (2005).
33. See proposal B 57, presented 2 December, debate 19 February 2009; proposal B 74, presented 18 December 2008, debate 19 February 2009; proposal B 104, presented 17 February 2009, debate 17 April 2009.
34. Brian Mikkelsen (KF), B.57, 19 February 2009.
35. Mikkelsen, B.57, 19 February 2009.
36. Mikkelsen, B.74, debate 19 February 2009.
37. Mikkelsen, B.57, 19 February 2009.

Appendix: Prison Visits, Interviews and National Surveys

1. See also Smith and Jakobsen 2010.
2. Excerpts from these interviews have been published in Danish (Lindberg 2010), but the entire interviews have been read and used in this study as well as in Jakobsen and Smith 2011.
3. A "children's workshop" made in 2007 in connection with the construction of a new visiting area in Vridsløselile Prison, by "Bosch og Fjord".
4. Documentary "Et hul i Himlen – Når mor og far er i fængsel", made by Dorthe Høeg Brask in 2007.
5. http://www.elbecks.dk/minfarifaengsel/.
6. See Hendriksen, Jakobsen and Smith 2011, 12 and 125.
7. See Smith and Jakobsen 2010, 257.

Bibliography

Books and articles

Abramsky, S., and Fellner, J. (2003), *Ill-equipped: U.S. Prisons and Offenders with Mental Illness*. New York: Human Rights Watch.

Adamsen, M. L. (2013), *Screeningsprojektet for psykisk sygdom*. Direktoratet for Kriminalforsorgen.

Alejos, M. (2005), *Babies and Small Children Residing in Prisons*. Geneva: Quaker United Nations Office.

Andersen, H. S. (2004), "Mental Health in Prison Populations. A review – with Special Emphasis on a Study of Danish Prisoners on Remand", *Acta Psychiatrica Scandinavica. Supplementum* 424, 5–59.

Andersen, S. H. (2010), *Når man anbringer et barn: Baggrund, stabilitet i anbringelsen og det videre liv*. Odense: Syddansk Universitetsforlag.

Andersson, R. (2012), "A Blessing in Disguise: Attention Deficit Hyperactivity Disorder Diagnosis and Swedish Correctional Treatment Policy in the Twenty-first Century", in Ugelvik, T., and Dullum, J. (eds), *Penal Exceptionalism? Nordic Prison Policy and Practice*. Oxon: Routledge.

Arditti, J. A. (2012), *Parental Incarceration and the Family: Psychological and Social Effects of Imprisonment on Children, Parents, and Caregivers*. New York: New York University Press.

Ayre, L., Philbrick, K., and Reiss, M. (2006), *Children of Imprisoned Parents: European Perspectives on Good Practice*. Montrouge: Eurochips.

Balvig, F. (2006), *Danskernes syn på straf*. Copenhagen: Advokatsamfundet.

Barnombudsmannen (2004), *Straffa inte barnet!: En studie av barnperspektivet inom kriminalvården*. Stockholm: Barnombudsmannen.

Barnombudsmannen (2013), *Från Insidan. Barn och ungdomar om tillvaron I arrest och häkte*. Stockholm: Barnombudsmannen.

Bernstein, N. (2005), *All Alone in the World: Children of the Incarcerated*. New York: New Press.

Berry, D., and English, P. (2011), *The Socioeconomic Impact of Pretrial Detention*. New York: Open Society Foundations.

Besemer, S., van der Geest, V., Murray, J., Bijleveld, C. C. J. H., and Farrington, D. P. (2011), "The Relationship between Parental Imprisonment and Offspring Offending in England and the Netherlands", *British Journal of Criminology* 51, no. 2, 413–437.

Bjercke, E. C. (1994), *Arbeidsgruppen som skal utrede forholdene for barn med foreldre i fengsel*. Oslo: Ministry of Justice.

Bonta, J., and Gendrau, P. (1995), "Re-examining the Cruel and Unusual Punishment of Prison Life", in Flanagan, T. J. (ed.), *Long-term Imprisonment: Policy, Science, and Correctional practice*. Thousand Oaks: Sage Publications.

Borch, C. (2005), *Kriminalitet og magt: Kriminalitetsopfattelser i det 20. århundrede*. Copenhagen: Politisk Revy.

Boswell, G., and Wedge, P. (2007), *Imprisoned Fathers and Their Children*. London: Jessica Kingsley Publishers.
Braman, D. (2004), *Doing Time on the Outside: Incarceration and Family Life in Urban America*. Ann Arbor: University of Michigan Press.
Carlen, P., and Worrall, A. (2004), *Analysing Women's Imprisonment*. Cullompton, UK: Willan Publishing.
Christensen, E. (1999), *Forældre i fængsel: En undersøgelse af børns og forældres erfaringer*. Copenhagen: Danish National Centre for Social Research.
Christie, N. (2001), *Crime Control as Industry: Towards Gulags, Western Style*. New York: Routledge.
Codd, H. (2008), *In the Shadow of Prison: Families, Imprisonment and Criminal Justice*. Cullompton, UK: Willan Publishing.
Cohen, S., and Taylor, L. (1974), *Psychological Survival: The Experience of Long-term Imprisonment*. New York: Vintage Books.
Comfort, M. (2008), *Doing Time Together: Love and Family in the Shadow of the Prison*. Chicago: University of Chicago Press.
Condry, R. (2007a), "Families Outside: The Difficulties Faced by Relatives of Serious Offenders", *Prison Service Journal* 174, 3–10.
Condry, R. (2007b), *Families Shamed: The Consequences of Crime for Relatives of Serious Offenders*. Cullompton, UK: Willan Publishing
The Council of Crime Prevention (2005), *Fængsledes børn: En udsat gruppe*. Copenhagen.
Coyle, A. (2002), *A Human Rights Approach to Prison Management: Handbook for Prison Staff*. London: International Centre for Prison Studies.
Coyle, A. (2005), *Understanding Prisons: Key Issues in Policy and Practice*. Maidenhead: Open University Press.
Crawford, W. (1834), "Report of William Crawford, Esq. on the Penitentiaries of the United States Addressed to His Majesty's Principal Secretary of State for the Home Department", *British Parliamentary Papers. Crime and Punishment – PRISONS*. No. 2, Session 1834.
Crewe, B. (2009), "The Sociology of Imprisonment", in Jewkes, Y. (ed.), *Handbook on Prisons*. Cullompton, UK: Willan Publishing.
Crewe, B. (2011), "Depth, Weight, Tightness: Revisiting the Pains of Imprisonment", *Punishment & Society* 13, no. 5, 509–529.
Crewe, B. (2012), "Prison Culture and the Prisoner Society", in Crewe, B., and Bennett, J. (eds.), *The Prisoner*. New York: Routledge.
Crewe, B., and Bennett, J. (2012), *The Prisoner*. New York: Routledge.
Crewe, B., and Liebling, A. (2011), "Are Liberal Humanitarian Penal Values and Practices Exceptional?", in Ugelvik, T., and Dallum, J. (eds), *Penal Exceptionalism? Nordic Prison Policy and Practice*. Oxon: Routledge.
Cumaraswamy, D. P., and Nowak, M. (2009), *Human Rights in Criminal Justice Systems*. Seminar report, Strasbourg, France, 18–20 February 2009.
Danish Ministry of Justice (2011), *Langvarige varetægtsfængslinger 2010*. Copenhagen: Justitsministeriets Forskningskontor.
Ejrnæs, M., Ejrnæs, M., and Fredriksen, S. (2010), "Anbringelser uden for hjemmet", in Andersen, S. H. (ed.), *Når man anbringer et barn: Baggrund, stabilitet i anbringelsen og det videre liv*. Odense: University Press of Southern Denmark.
Engbo, H. J. (2005), *Straffuldbyrdelsesret*. Copenhagen: Jurist- og Økonomforbundet.

Engbo, H. J. (2006), "Ret og etik i straffuldbyrdelsen", in Lomholt, C., and Kühle, L. (eds), *Straffens menneskelige ansigt?: En antologi om etik, ret og religion i fængslet*. Frederiksberg: Anis.

Engbo, H. J., and Smith, P. S. (2012), *Fængsler og menneskerettigheder*. Copenhagen: Jurist- og Økonomforbundets Forlag.

Enos, S. (2001), *Mothering from the Inside: Parenting in a Women's Prison*. Albany: State University of New York Press.

Evans, M. D., and Morgan, R. (1998), *Preventing Torture: A Study of the European Convention for the Prevention of Torture and Inhuman or Degrading Treatment or Punishment*. Oxford: Clarendon Press.

Eyben, B. V., Pedersen, J., and Rørdam, T. (2007), *Karnovs lovsamling: Retspleje og strafferet*. Copenhagen: Thomson.

Faye, J. A. (1993), *Børn i alle lande!: Om det internationale arbejde for børns rettigheder*. Copenhagen: Det Danske Center for Menneskerettigheder.

Fazel, S., and Danesh, J. (2002), "Serious Mental Disorder in 23,000 Prisoners: A Systematic Review of 62 Surveys", *The Lancet* 359, no. 9306, 545–550.

Flanagan, T. J. (1995), *Long-term Imprisonment: Policy, Science, and Correctional Practice*. Thousands Oaks: Sage Publications.

Foreningen for Fangers Pårørende (FFP), "Jeg må få snakke med pappa når jeg har noe å si, Høringsuttalelse fra en gruppe ungdom", http://www.ffp.no/filestore/FFP_filer/Tekst_brosjyrer_og_dokumenter/BarnehringFFP.pdf.

Forsythe, B. (2004), "Loneliness and Cellular Confinement in English Prisons 1878–1921", *The British Journal of Criminology* 44, no. 5, 759–770.

Foucault, M. (1988), *Madness and Civilization: A History of Insanity in the Age of Reason*. New York: Vintage Books.

Foucault, M. (1995), *Discipline and Punish: The Birth of the Prison*. New York: Vintage Books.

Franke, H. (1992), "The Rise and Decline of Solitary Confinement: Socio-Historical Explanations of Long-Term Penal Changes", *British Journal of Criminology* 32, no. 2.

Frøslee, I. B. (2008), *Politipsykologi: En grundbog*. Copenhagen: Hans Reitzels Forlag.

Gampell, L., and Smith, P. S. (2011), *Children of Imprisoned Parents*. Copenhagen: The Danish Institute for Human Rights, Eurochips and University of Ulster.

Garland, D. (1985), *Punishment and Welfare: A History of Penal Strategies*. Aldershot: Gower.

Garland, D. (2001a), *The Culture of Control: Crime and Social Order in Contemporary Society*. Oxford: Oxford University Press.

Garland, D. (ed.) (2001b), *Mass Imprisonment: Social Causes and Consequences*. London: SAGE.

Gould, S. J. (1992), *The Mismeasure of Man*. New York: Penguin Books.

Gray, F. C. (1847), *Prison Discipline in America*. Boston: Charles C. Little and James Brown.

Greve V. (2004), "Får eller Ulve", *Tidskrift utgiven av Juridiska Föreningen i Finland* 3–4.

Greve V. (2010), "Retten og samfundet", *Nordisk tidsskrift for Kriminalvidenskab* 98.

Grøftehauge, M. (2004), *Fangebørn*. Århus: CDR-Forlag.

Grounds, A. (2005), "Understanding the Effects of Wrongful Imprisonment", in Tonry, M. H. (ed.), *Crime and Justice: A Review of Research*. Chicago: University of Chicago Press.

Hagan, J. and Dinovitzer, R., "Collateral Consequences of Imprisonment for Children, Communities, and Prisoners", in Tonry, M.H. (ed.), *Crime and Justice: A Review of Research*. Chicago: University of Chicago Press.

Halmø, I. (2009), "Resocialisering med familiebehandling i utraditionelle og hidtil uprøvede rammer. Afrapportering over erfaringerne med implementering af Familiebehandling i Kriminalforsorgen i perioden 1. juni 2005–1. juni 2008". Copenhagen: The Danish Prison and Probation Service, Engelsborg Halfway House.

Haney, C. (2005), "The Contextual Revolution in a Psychology and the Question of Prison Effects", in Liebling, A., and Maruna, S. (eds), *The Effects of Imprisonment*. Cullompton, UK: Willan Publishing.

Hendriksen, L. G., Jakobsen, J., and Smith, P. S. (2012), "Børneansvarlige I Kriminalforsorgen – Fokus på de indsattes børn". Copenhagen: The Danish Institute for Human Rights.

Hjelm, A.-C. Pettersson (2011), *Fängelset: som välfärdsbygge*. Stockholm: Institutet för rättshistorisk forskning.

Hoffmann, H. C., Byrd, A. L., and Kightlinger, A. M. (2010), "Prison Programs and Services for Incarcerated Parents and Their Underage Children: Results From a National Survey of Correctional Facilities", *The Prison Journal* 90, no. 4, 397–416.

Holmgren, B., Frisell, T., and Runeson, B. (2011), *Psykisk hälsa hos häktade med restriktioner*. Norrköping: Kriminalvårdens Utvecklingsenhet.

Hontoria, T. E., and Loper, A. (2006), "Contact Between Incarcerated Mothers and Their Children: Assessing Parenting Stress", *Journal of Offender Rehabilitation* 43, no. 1, 23–43.

Hutton, M. (forthcoming), "A Labour of Love: The impact of the Children's Play Project on Family Contact at HMP Doncaster".

Ignatieff, M. (1978), *A Just Measure of Pain: The Penitentiary in the Industrial Revolution, 1750–1850*. London: Macmillan.

International Centre for Prison Studies (2004), "Guidance Note 13: Reforming Women's Prisons", *Guidance Notes on Prison Reform*. London: International Centre for Prison Studies.

Irwin, J., and Owen, B. (2005), "Harm and the Contemporary Prison", in Liebling, A., and Maruna, S. (eds), *The Effects of Imprisonment*. Cullompton, UK: Willan Publishing.

Jacobs, J. B. (1977), *Stateville: The Penitentiary in Mass Society*. Chicago: University of Chicago Press.

Jamieson, R., and Grounds, A. (2005), "Release and Adjustment: Perspectives from Studies of Wrongly Convicted and Politically Motivated Prisoners", in Liebling, A., and Maruna, S. (eds), *The Effects of Imprisonment*. Cullompton, UK: Willan Publishing.

Jewkes, Y. (2007), *Handbook on Prisons*. Cullompton, UK: Willan Publishing.

Johnsen, N. (1929), "En fanges dag paa Vridsløselille", handwritten unpublished manuscript. Copenhagen: ABA (Arbejderbevægelsens Arkiv).

Johnson, R. (2005), "Brave New Prisons: The Growing Social Isolation of Modern Penal Institutions", in Liebling, A., and Maruna, S. (eds), *The Effects of Imprisonment*. Cullompton, UK: Willan Publishing.

Johnston, N. B. (2000), *Forms of Constraint: A History of Prison Architecture*. Urbana: University of Illinois Press.

Jones, A. D., and Wainaina-Woźna, A. E. (eds) (2013), *Children of Prisoners. Interventions and Mitigations*. Huddersfield: University of Huddersfield.

Jonson-Reid, M. (2006), "Prisoners Once Removed: The Impact of Incarceration and Re-entry on Children, Families and Communities", *Children and Youth Services Review* 28, no. 5, 585–587.
Køppe, S. (2004), *Neurosens opståen og udvikling i 1800tallet*. Copenhagen: Frydenlund.
Koudahl, P. (2007), *Indsatte i danske fængsler: Uddannelse og uddannelsesønsker*. Copenhagen: Danmarks Pædagogiske Universitet.
Kramp, P. (1993), "Registerundersøgelsen" (unpublished).
Krupat, T., Gaynes, E., and Lincroft, Y. (2011), *A Call to Action: Safeguarding New York's Children of Incarcerated Parents*. New York: New York Initiative for Children of Incarcerated Parents, The Osborne Association.
Kruttschnitt, C. (2011), "Is the Devil in the Details? Crafting Policy to Mitigate the Collateral Consequences of Parental Incarceration", *Criminology & Public Policy* 10, no. 3, 829–837.
Lagoutte, S. (2011), "The Human Rights Framework", in Gampell, L., and Smith, P. S. (eds), *Children of Imprisoned Parents*. Copenhagen: Danish Institute for Human Rights, Eurochips and University of Ulster.
Larsen, C., Svarer, M., Imai, S., Pico, G. L., and Tranæs, T. (2008), *Forbryderen og samfundet: Livsvilkår og uformel straf*. Copenhagen: Gyldendal.
Lazarus, L. (2004), *Contrasting Prisoners' Rights: A Comparative Examination of Germany and England*. Oxford: Oxford University Press.
Leavens, Anja (2007), *Fra afsoner til borger – en praksisbaseret beskrivelse af afsoningskonsekvenser*, Kriminalforsorgen.
Leer-Salvesen, P. (1991), *Menneske og straff: En refleksjon om skyld og straff som et bidrag til arbeidet med straffens etikk*. Oslo: Universitetsforlaget.
Liebling, A. (2000), "Whose Side are We On? Theory, Practice and Allegiances in Prisons Research", *British Journal of Criminology* 41, no. 3, 472.
Liebling, A., and Arnold, H. (2004), *Prisons and their Moral Performance: A Study of Values, Quality, and Prison Life*. Oxford: Oxford University Press.
Liebling, A., and Maruna, S. (2005), "Introduction: The Effects of Imprisonment Revisited", in Liebling, A., and Maruna, S. (eds), *The Effects of Imprisonment*. Cullompton, UK: Willan Publishing.
Lindberg, S. (2010), *Helst skal man have en god barndom – 40 børns fortællinger om et liv med særlige vilkår*. København: Børnerådet.
Lomholt, C., and Kühle, L. (2006), *Straffens menneskelige ansigt?: En antologi om etik, ret og religion i fængslet*. Frederiksberg: Anis.
Maruna, S. (2007), "After Prison, What? The Ex-prisoner's Struggle to Desist from Crime", in Jewkes, Y. (ed.), *Handbook on Prisons*. Cullompton, UK: Willan Publishing.
Mazza, C. (2002), "And Then the World Fell Apart: The Children of Incarcerated Fathers", *Families in Society: The Journal of Contemporary Social Services* 83, no. 5, 521–529.
Middelthon, K. (2012), Unpublished manuscript given as a speech at the 20th anniversary for FFP in Oslo, Norway, 13 June 2013.
Minke, L. K. (2010), *Fængslets indre liv* (unpublished Ph.D. thesis).
Minke, L. K. (2012), *Fængslets indre liv*. Copenhagen: Jurist- og Økonomforbundet.
Molbech, A. (ed.) (2009), *Children of Prisoners: A Story about the Engelsborg Family House*. Copenhagen: The Danish Prison and Probation Service, Engelsborg Halfway House.

Møller, T. (2006), *Den fængsledes børn. Forslag til forbedring af vilkårene for børn af fængslede*. Unpublished text, presented at a roundtable held by the Danish Institute for Human Rights on 9 February 2006.

Moore, L., Convery, U., and Scraton, P. (2011), "The Northern Ireland Case Study", in Gampell, L., and Smith, P. S. (eds), *Children of Imprisoned Parents*. Copenhagen: Danish Institute for Human Rights, Eurochips and University of Ulster.

Morris, N. (1995), "The Contemporary Prison: 1965–Present", in Morris, N., and Rothman, D. J. (eds), *The Oxford History of the Prison: The Practice of Punishment in Western Society*. New York: Oxford University Press.

Morris, N., and Rothman, D. J. (1995), *The Oxford History of the Prison: The Practice of Punishment in Western Society*. New York: Oxford University Press.

Mumola, C. J. (2000), *Incarcerated Parents and Their Children*. Washington, DC: US Dept. of Justice, Office of Justice Programs, Bureau of Justice Statistics.

Murray, J. (2005), "The Effects of Imprisonment on Families and Children of Prisoners", in Liebling, A., and Maruna, S. (eds), *The Effects of Imprisonment*. Cullompton, UK: Willan Publishing.

Murray, J. (2006), *Parental Imprisonment: Effects on Children's Antisocial Behaviour and Mental Health through the Life-course*, dissertation submitted for the Degree of Doctor of Philosophy, Institute of Criminology, University of Cambridge.

Murray, J., and Farrington, D. P. (2006), "Evidence-based Programs for Children of Prisoners", *Criminology & Public Policy* 5, no. 4, 721–735. Murray, J., and Farrington, D. P. (2008), "Parental Imprisonment: Long-lasting Effects on boys' Internalizing Problems through the Life Course", *Development and Psychopathology* 20, no. 1, 273–290.

Murray, J., Farrington, D. P., and Sekol, I. (2012), "Children's Antisocial Behavior, Mental Health, Drug Use, and Educational Performance after Parental Incarceration: A Systematic Review and Meta-Analysis", *Psychological Bulletin* 138, no. 2, 175–210.

Murray, J., Farrington, D. P., Sekol, I., and Olsen, R. F. (2009), *Effects of Parental Imprisonment on Child Antisocial Behaviour and Mental Health: A Systematic Review*. Oslo: Campbell Collaboration.

Myrdal, A., and Myrdal, G. (1935), *Krise i Befolkningsspørgsmaalet*. Copenhagen: Martin.

Nesmith, A., and Ruhland, E. (2008), "Children of Incarcerated Parents: Challenges and Resiliency, in Their Own Words", *Children and Youth Services Review* 30, no. 10, 1119–1130.

Nielsen, B. G. (2006), *Straf – hvad ellers?* Copenhagen: Tiderne Skifter.

Nijnatten, C. (1998), *Detention and Development: Perspectives of Children of Prisoners*. Mönchengladbach: Forum Verlag Godesberg.

Nilsson, R. (1999), *En välbyggd maskin, en mardröm för själen: Det svenska fängelsesystemet under 1800-talet*. Lund: Lund University Press.

Olsen, R. F. (2013), *Invisible Consequences of Punishment: Parental Imprisonment and Child Outcomes*, Ph.D. dissertation. Aarhus: Forlaget Politica.

Olsen, R. F. (forthcoming), "Forældres fængsling – en stratificerende livsbegivenhed?"

Olsen, R. F. (forthcoming), (September 2012), "Parental Imprisonment: A Predictor of Danish Children's Criminal Convictions as Young Adults (unpublished version).

Pedersen, J. S. (2007), *Ret og samfund*. Copenhagen: Frydenlund.

Petersen, L. B., and Antonsen,I. B., "Børnene straffes når mor ryger i fængsel", unpublished article researched and written as an assignment at the University of Århus, Denmark.
Philip, B. (2007), "Set indefra – vilkår under afsoning", *Social Politik* 1, 26–29.
Phillips, S. D. (1998), "Programming for Children of Female Offenders", Proceedings from *4th National Head Start Research Conference*. Washington, DC.
Phillips, S. D., and Zhao, J. (2010), "The rRlationship between Witnessing Arrests and Elevated Symptoms of Posttraumatic Stress: Findings from a National Study of Children Involved in the Child Welfare System", *Children and Youth Services Review* 32, no. 10, 1246–1254.
Phillips, S. D., Erkanli, A., Keeler, G. P., Costello, E. J., and Angold, A. (2006), "Disentangling the Risks: Parent Criminal Justice Involvement and Children's Exposure to Family Risks", *Criminology & Public Policy* 5, no. 4, 677–702.
Pratt, J. (2007), *Penal Populism*. London: Routledge.
Pratt, J. (2008), "Scandinavian Exceptionalism in an Era of Penal Excess. Part I: The Nature and Roots of Scandinavian Exceptionalism", *British Journal of Criminology* 48.
Pratt, J., and Eriksson, A. (2013), *Contrasts in Punishment. An Explanation of Anglophone Excess and Nordic Exceptionalism*. London: Routledge.
Pösö, T., Enroos, R., and Vierula, T. (2010), "Children Residing in Prison with Their Parents: An Example of Institutional Invisibility", *The Prison Journal* 90, no. 4, 516–533.
Pugh, G. (2004), *Sentenced Families: Signs of Change for Children with a Parent in Prison*. Ipswich: Ormiston Children & Families Trust.
Raikes, B., and Lockwood, K. (2011), "'Mothering from the Inside' – A Small-scale Evaluation of Acorn House, an Overnight Child Contact Facility at HMP Askham Grange", *Prison Service Journal* 194, 19–26.
Ramsbotham, D. (2003), *Prisongate: The Shocking State of Britain's Prisons and the Need for Visionary Change*. London: Free Press.
Rentzmann, W., Esdorf A., and Kruse Mikkelsen, J. (2002), *Straffuldbyrdelsesloven med kommentarer*. København: Jurist- og Økonomforbundets Forlag.
Robertson, O. (2008), *Children Imprisoned by Circumstance*. Geneva: Quaker United Nations Office.
Robertson, O. (2012), *Collateral Convicts: Children of Incarcerated Parents. Recommendations and Good Practice from the UN Committee on the Rights of the Child, Day of General Discussion 2011*. Geneva: Quaker United Nations Office.
Rodriguez, N., Smith, H., and Zatz, M. S. (2009), "Youth is Enmeshed in a Highly Dysfunctional Family System: Exploring the Relationship Among Dysfunctional Families, Parental Incarceration, and Juvenile Court Decision Making", *Criminology* 47, no. 1, 177–208.
Rønn, R. M., and Hartby, I. (eds) (2006), *Det forrykte menneske: Den psykisk syge i historien*. Ebeltoft: Skippershoved.
Rotman, E. (1995), "The Failure of Reform: United States, 1865–1965", in Morris, N., and Rothman, D. J. (eds), *The Oxford History of the Prison: The Practice of Punishment in Western Society*. New York: Oxford University Press.
Ryberg, J. (2006), *Retsfølelsen: En bog om straf og etik*. Frederiksberg: Roskilde Universitetsforlag.
Sacerdote, L., Battevi, F., Fleischner, E., Gaspari, V., and Piccione, M. (2011), "The Italian Case Study", in Gampell, L., and Smith, P. S. (eds), *Children of Imprisoned*

Parents. Copenhagen: The Danish Institute for Human Rights, Eurochips and University of Ulster.

Salvatore, R. D., and Aguirre, C. (1996), *The Birth of the Penitentiary in Latin America: Essays on Criminology, Prison Reform, and Social Control, 1830–1940*. Austin: University of Texas Press.

Sampson, R. J. (2011), "The Incarceration Ledger. Toward a New Era in Assessing Societal Consequences", *Criminology & Public Policy* 10, no. 3, 819–828.

Schaanning, E. (2007), *Menneskelaboratoriet. Botsfengslets historie*. Oslo: Scandinavian Academic Press.

Schrøder, G. E. (1913), *Fængselspsychoser og psychoser i fængslet*. Copenhagen: J. Lund.

Selmer, H. (1879), *Statistiske Meddelelser og Undersøgelser fra Sindssygeanstalten ved Aarhus i dens første 25 Aar (1852–77)*, Copenhagen: C.A. Reitzel.

Shaw, R. (1987), *Children of Imprisoned Fathers*. London: Hodder and Stoughton.

Siegel, J. A. (2011), *Disrupted Childhoods: Children of Women in Prison*. New Brunswick, NJ: Rutgers University Press.

Smith, P. S. (2003), *Moralske hospitaler. Det moderne fængselsvæsens gennembrud 1770–1870*. Copenhagen: Forum.

Smith, P. S. (2004a), "A Religious Technology of the Self – Rationality and Religion in the Rise of the Modern Penitentiary", *Punishment & Society* 6, no. 2, 195–220.

Smith, P. S. (2004b), "Isolation and Mental Illness in Vridsløselille 1859–1873 – A New Perspective on the Breakthrough of the Modern Penitentiary", in *Scandinavian Journal of History* 29, no. 1, 1–25.

Smith, P. S. (2006a), "The Effects of Solitary Confinement on Prison Inmates: A Brief History and Review of the Literature", in Tonry, M. H. (ed.), *Crime and Justice: A Review of Research – vol. 34*. Chicago: University of Chicago Press.

Smith, P. S. (2006b), "Sindssyge bag tremmer", in Rønn, E. M., and Hartby, I. (eds), *Det forrykte menneske. Den psykisk syge i historien* : Ebeltoft: Skippershoved.

Smith, P. S. (2007), "Fængsler og menneskerettigheder internationalt og i Danmark", in Pedersen, J. S. (ed.), *Ret og samfund*. Copenhagen: Frydenlund.

Smith, P. S. (2009). "Solitary Confinement – History, Practice, and Human Rights Standards", *Prison Service Journal* 181, 3–11.

Smith, P. S. (2011a), "The Effects of Solitary Confinement, Commentary on *One Year Longitudinal Study of the Psychological Effects of Administrative Segregation*", in *Corrections and Mental Health*, http://community.nicic.gov/blogs/mentalhealth/archive/2011/06/21/the-effects-of-solitary-confinement-commentary-on-one-year-longitudinal-study-of-the-psychological-effects-of-administrative-segregation.aspx

Smith, P. S. (2011b), "A Critical look at Scandinavian Exceptionalism. Welfare State Theories, Penal Populism, and Prison Conditions in Denmark and Scandinavia", in Ugelvik, T., and Dallum, J. (eds), *Penal Exceptionalism? Nordic Prison Policy and Practice*. Oxon: Routledge.

Smith, P. S. (2012), "Imprisonment and Internet-Access: Human Rights, the Principle of Normalization and the Question of Prisoners Access to Digital Communications Technology", *Nordic Journal of Human Rights* 30, no. 4, 454–482.

Smith, P. S., Horn, T., Nilsen, J. F., and Rua, M. (2013), "Isolation i Skandinaviske fængsler", in *Social Kritik* 136.

Smith, P. S., and Jakobsen, J. (2010), *Når straffen rammer uskyldige: Børn af fængslede i Danmark*. Copenhagen: Gyldendal.

Smith, P. S., and Jakobsen, J. (2011), *Børn af fængslede: En informations- og undervisningsbog*. Frederiksberg: Samfundslitteratur.

Socialt Udviklingscenter (2004), *Børn som pårørende*. Copenhagen: Socialt Udviklingscenter (SUS).

Socialt Udviklingscenter (2006), *Når børn er pårørende*. Copenhagen: Socialt Udviklingscenter (SUS).

Statistics Denmark (2008), *Børns familier*. Copenhagen: Statistics Denmark.

Steincke, K. K. (1920), *Fremtidens Forsørgelsesvæsen: Oversigt over og Kritik af den samlede Forsørgelseslovgivning samt Betænkning og motiverede Forslag til en systematisk Nyordning*. Copenhagen: Schultz.

Steinhoff, R. and Berman, A. H. (2012), "Children's Experiences of Having a Parent in Prison – 'We Look at the Moon and Then We Feel Close to Each Other'", *Sociologie Si Asistenta Sociala* 5, no. 2, 77–96.

Stern, V. (1998), *A sin against the Future: Imprisonment in the World*. Boston: Northeastern University Press.

Stone, M. H. (1997), *Healing the Mind: A History of Psychiatry from Antiquity to the Present*. New York: W. W. Norton & Co.

Sykes, G. M. (1974), *The Society of Captives: A Study of a Maximum Security Prison*. Princeton, NJ: Princeton University Press.

Tapia, N., and Vaughn, M. (2010), "Legal Issues Regarding Medical Care for Pregnant Inmates", *The Prison Journal* 90, no. 4, 417–446.

Toch, H. (2002), *Living in Prison: The Ecology of Survival*. Easton: American Psychological Association.

Tokkesdal, L., and Lund, U. (2004), *Prøveløsladelsesinstituttets historiske udvikling*. Master thesis, faculty of law, University of Copenhagen.

Tomkin, J. (2009), *Orphans of Justice. In Search of the Best Interests of the Child When a Parent is Imprisoned: A Legal Analysis*. Geneva: Quaker United Nations Office.

Tonry, M. H. (2004), *Thinking about Crime: Sense and Sensibility in American Penal Culture*. New York: Oxford University Press.

Trænæs, T. (2008), "Den uformelle straf og velfærdsstaten", *Nordisk Tidsskrift for Kriminalvidenskab* 95, no. 3, 225–242.

Travis, J., and Waul, M. (2003), *Prisoners Once Removed: The Impact of Incarceration and Reentry on Children, Families, and Communities*. Washington DC: The Urban Institute.

Trier, M. B. (2006), "Jeg græd hele tiden", *Folkeskolen* 24, no. 8.

Tuerk, E. H. and Loper, A.B. (2006) "Contact between Incarcerated Mothers and Their Children: Assessing Parenting Stress", *Journal of Offender Rehabilitation* 43, no. 1, 23–43.

Turanovic, J. J., Rodriguez, N., and Pratt, T. C. (2012), "The Collateral Consequences of Incarceration Revisited: A Qualitative Analysis of the Effects on Caregivers of Children of Incarcerated Parents", *Criminology* 50, no. 4, 919–959.

Turesson, A. B. (2009), *Mor i fängelse – mödrar och barn berättar: En analys av ungdomars resiliensprocess*. Doctoral thesis, University of Gothenberg.

Turney, K. (2013), "The Intergenerational Consequences of Mass Incarceration: Implications for Children's Contact with Grandparents", Working Paper WP13-07, Princeton, NJ: Princeton University, Woodrow Wilson School of Public and International Affairs, Center for Research on Child Wellbeing.

Turney, K., Wildeman, C., and Schnittker, J. (2012), "As Fathers and Felons: Explaining the Effects of Current and Recent Incarceration on Major Depression", in *Journal of Health and Social Behavior* 53, no. 4, 465–481.

Ugelvik, T., and Dullum, J. (eds) (2011), *Penal Exceptionalism? Nordic Prison Policy and Practice*. New York: Routledge.

UK Ministry of Justice (2013), "Proven Re-offending Statistics, Quarterly Bulletin – July 2010 to June 2011, England and Wales", *Statistics Bulletin*. London: Ministry of Justice.

Van, Z. S. D., and Snacken, S. (2009), *Principles of European Prison Law and Policy: Penology and Human Rights*. Oxford: Oxford University Press.

Waaben, K. (1997), *Retspsykiatri og strafferet i historiens lys*. Copenhagen: Janssen-Cilag.

Wakefield, S., and Wildeman, C. (2011), "Mass Imprisonment and Racial Disparities in Childhood Behavioral Problems", *Criminology & Public Policy* 10, no. 3, 793–817.

Wakefield, S., amd Wildeman, C. J. (2011), "Mass Imprisonment and Childhood Behavior Problems", *American Society of Criminology* 10, no. 3.

Wakefield, S., and Wildeman, C. J. (2013), *Children of the Prison Boom: Mass Incarceration and the Future of American Inequality*. New York: Oxford University Press.

Walmsley, R. (2012), *World Prison Population List*, 9th edition. London: International Centre for Prison Studies.

Wildeman, C. (2010), "Paternal Incarceration and Children's Physically Aggressive Behaviors: Evidence from the Fragile Families and Child Wellbeing Study", *Social Forces* 89, no. 1, 285–309.

Wildeman, C., and Western, B. (2010), "Incarceration in Fragile Families", *Future of Children* 20, no. 2, 157–177.

Wildeman, C. (2009), "Parental Imprisonment, the Prison Boom, and the Concentration of Childhood Disadvantage", *Demography* 46, no. 2, 265–280.

Wildeman, C., and Bruce, W. S. (2010), "Incarceration in Fragile Families", *The Future of Children* 20, no. 2, 157–177.

Willems, J. C. M. (2002), *Developmental and Autonomy Rights of Children: Empowering Children, Caregivers and Communities*. Antwerpen: Intersentia.

Williams, K., Papadopoulou, V., and Booth, N. (2012), *Prisoners' Childhood and Family Backgrounds. Results from the Surveying Prisoner Crime Reduction (SPCR) Longitudinal Cohort Study of Prisoners*, Ministry of Justice Research Series 4/12. London: Ministry of Justice.

Wolleswinkel, R. (2002), "Children of Imprisoned Parents", in Willems, J. C. M. (ed.), *Developmental and Autonomy Rights of Children: Empowering Children, Caregivers and Communities*. Antwerpen: Intersentia.

Wolleswinkel, R. (2006), "The Legal Background", in Ayre, L., Philbrick, K., and Reiss, M. (eds), *Children of Imprisoned Parents: European Perspectives on Good Practice*. Montrouge: Eurochips.

Woodrow, J. (1992), *Mothers in Prison: The Problem of Dependent Children*. Cambridge: University of Cambridge.

Newspaper articles

Avisen.dk, "Far er i fængsel", 12 April 2007.

Bladet Kriminalforsorgen, September 2009 (thematic issue on the family and the Prison and Probation Service).

BT, "Kæmper videre for mobiler i lukkede fængsler", 21 September 2012.

"DJØF bladet" no. 7, 2002 (Interview with Minister of Justice Lene Espersen).
DR Nyheder, "Minister afviser mobiler i fængsler", 10 December 2011.
Engelsborg's Newsletter, no. 2, June 2005.
Fyens.dk, "Indsatte i lukkede fængsler får telefoner", 7 December 2011.
Fyens Stiftstidende, 3 August 2009.
Fyens Stiftstidende, 4 August 2009.
Fyens Stiftstidende, 19 August 2009.
Information, "Når uskyldige bliver straffet", 2 May 2008.
Jyllandsposten, "Hård kurs mod strafpjækkeri", 1 November 2005.
Jyllandsposten, 23 February 2010, interview with Minister of Justice Brian Mikkelsen.
MetroXpress, 16 October 2006.
Politiken, "Danskerne siger nei til mobiler og kys i Fængsler", 21 December 2011.
Politiken, "Søren Pind: Tredje gang skal straffes hårdt", 17 September 2008.
Socialrådgiveren, "Pårørende til kriminelle svigtes", no. 4, 22 February 2006.
Vridsløselille Infonyt, 15 July 2009.

Court rulings

Baginski *v.* Poland, 11 January 2006 (app. no. 37444/97).
Ciorap *v.* Moldova, ruling of 13 September 2005 (app. no. 35207/03).
Ciorap *v.* Moldova, ruling of 19 Juen 2007 (app. no. 1206602).
Estrikh *v.* Latvia, ruling of 18 January 2007 (app. no. 73819/01).
Golder *v.* The United Kingdom, ruling of 21 February 1975 (app. no. 4451/70).
Gutsanovi *v.* Bulgaria, ruling of 15 October 2013 (app. no. 34529/10).
Horych *v.* Poland, ruling of 17 April 2012 (app. no. 13621/08).
Klass *v.* Germany, ruling of 6 September 1978 (app. no. 5029/71).
Kleuver *v.* Norway, admissibility ruling of 30 April 2002 (app. no. 45837/99).
M.C. *v.* Finland, admissibility ruling of 25 January 2001 (app. no. 28460/95).
Messina *v.* Italy, ruling of 2 Sep 2000 (app. no. 25498/94).
Ostrovar *v.* Moldova, ruling of 13 September 2005 (app. no. 35207/03).
R. *v.* Institutional Head of Beaver Creek Correctional Camp (1969).
Rhode *v.* Denmark, ruling of 21 July 2005 (app. no. 69332/01).
Sabou et Pircalab *v.* Romania, ruling of 28 September 2004 (app. no. 46572/99).
Salahhov and Islyamova *v.* Ukraine, ruling of 14 Jun 2013, (app. no. 28005/08).
Sanchez *v.* France, ruling of 27 January 2005 (app. no. 59450/00). Grand Chamber judgement, 4 July 2006.
Sari and Colak *v.* Turkey, ruling of 4 April 2006 (app. no. 42596/98; 42603/98).
Togher *v.* the United Kingdom, report dated 25 October 1999 (app. no. 28555/95).
Wolff *v.* McDonnell (1974).

Human rights sources, reports and recommendations

10th General Report the Committee for the Prevention of Torture (CPT), 2000 [CPT/Inf.(2000)13 (EN)], chapter on "Women Deprived of their Liberty".

Belfast Declaration, adopted at The International Association of Youth and Family Judges and Magistrates XVII World Congress in Belfast, Northern Ireland, 27 August–1 September 2006.

CAT/C/48/Add.3, 35th session "List of issues to be considered during the examination of the second periodic report of the United States of America", 8/2 2006.

CAT/C/USA/CO/2, 18 May 2006 (advance unedited version), 36th session.

Committee on the Rights of the Child: "General Comment no. 12 (2009). The right of the child to be heard", CRC/C/GC/12, Fifty-first session, Geneva, 25 May–12 June 2009.

Committee on the Rights of the Child (2011). "Report and Recommendations of the day of general discussions on 'Children of incarcerated parents'".

Committee on the Rights of the Child, Forty-first session, Concluding observations: Thailand, 17/3/2006 CRC/C/THA/CO/2.

Committee on the Rights of the child, Fortieth session, CRC/C/15/Add.268, 20 October 2005, Consideration of reports submitted by States Parties under Article 44 of The Convention, Concluding observations: Australia.

Council of Europe Recommendation 1469 (2000) "Mothers and babies in prison".

Council of Europe, Committee of Ministers, Rec. (2006) 2 "The European Prison Rules".

CPT report of 25 September 2002, CPT/Inf (2002) 18, § 16.

CPT report of 25 September 2008, CPT/Inf (2008) 26, § 15.

CPT, Visit Report, Iceland. Visit 1998, Section 15/49.

Parliamentary Assembly of the Council of Europe's Resolution 1663 (2009) of 28 April 2009 on Women in Prison.

Report to the Danish Government on the visit to Denmark carried out by the European Committee for the Prevention of Torture and Inhuman or Degrading Treatment or Punishment (CPT) from 29 September to 9 October 1996.

UN Economic and Social Council, Resolution 2010/16 "United Nations Rules for the Treatment of Women Prisoners and Non-custodial Measures for Women Offenders (the Bangkok Rules)".

UN Standard Minimum Rules for the Treatment of Prisoners.

UN Special Rapporteur on torture, report on Denmark, A/HRC/10/44/Add.2, 18 February 2009.

Other media

Brask, D. H. (2007), "Et hul i himlen – når mor og far er i fængsel". Documentary Film.

"Far i fængsel" ("Dad in Prison") with the Danish Prisoners' Choir ("Fangekoret"), the Children's choir and Peter Mygind.

Index

antisocial behaviour, 7, 49–51, 53, 60, 66, 74–76, 221
anxiety
  and the effects of imprisonment on children, 7, 60, 117, 119, 135, 142, 181, 192
  and the effects of imprisonment on mothers, 78
  and the Engelsborg "family house", 59, 189
  and mental disorders in prison populations, 58
  and solitary confinement, 61, 167
arrest
  and the aim of the study, 18–19
  and CRC recommendations, 85
  and its effects on children, 3–5, 48, 56, 62, 80, 228
  and the experiences of children, police and social services, 115–132
  and informing the social authorities, 97–98
  and the placement of children in foster care, 184–185
  and the rights of the child, 90–96
  and solitary confinement, 168
  and special house arrest for mothers with young children, 98
  and visiting, 149, 166
Auburn model, 22–23

Bambinisenzabarre, 15, 16
Bangkok Rules (UN Rules for the Treatment of Women Prisoners and Non-custodial Measures for Women offenders), 110
bedtime stories, 16
Belfast Declaration (adopted at the International Association of Youth and Family Judges and Magistrates 2006), 97
biology, 27–32, 74

Bouregba, Alain, 81
Bowlby, John, 61
Bryggan (association for prisoners relatives, Sweden), 69, 237

Cherry Hill (prison), 22
Children's Council (Børnerådet), 98, 147
children's ombudsman (Sweden), 43, 146, 150
children's rights, 10–11, 16, 19, 85–107, 232–233
Children's Welfare (Børns vilkår), 130
Christensen, Else, 50, 52, 67–68, 77, 126, 141, 150, 168, 169, 176, 187, 223
closed prisons
  and children in prisons, 109, 111, 202–213
  and children making prison visits, 145, 155, 190
  and the Children's Officer project, 16
  and communication, 79, 175–179
  and the Danish prison system, 145–147, 203
  and home leave, 170
  and safety considerations, 147
  and the transport times, 154
  and visiting facilities, 155–159
  and visiting regimes, 26
Committee for the Prevention of Torture, CPT, 94, 95, 110, 127, 146, 168
conjugal visits, 26, 146
Convention Against Torture and Other Cruel, Inhuman or Degrading Treatment or Punishment, 83
Convention on the Rights of the Child (CRC), 10, 11, 85–89, 91, 96, 101, 102, 106, 112, 170, 233
Convery, Una, 15

correspondence, and correspondence control, 167, 174, 176
  and the birth of the modern prison, 24, 25
  and contact between children and parents, 47, 174
  and human rights, 87, 89, 102, 106
  and remand prisoners, 106, 176
  and statistics on Denmark, 165
  and visiting during remand in custody, 136, 150, 151, 152
Covenant (convention) on Civil and Political Rights (ICCPR), 83, 85, 87, 89
Coyle, Andrew, 110
criminal behaviour, 28, 48, 49, 60, 74–76
criminology, 19, 20, 27, 30, 36, 37

degeneration, degenerate, 28, 30, 31
depression
  and the effects of imprisonment on children, 60, 69, 71
  and the effects of imprisonment on parents, 77
  and the Engelsborg "family house", 59
  and mental disorders among prisoners, 57–58, 188, 189
  and solitary confinement, 61, 167
deterrence, 8, 214
divorce, 38, 46, 47, 58, 60, 73, 184, 185, 212
dogs, 62, 118, 163
drugs, drug abuse
  and arrest, 3, 5, 91, 111, 118, 119, 126, 128
  and the effect on prisoners' children, 48, 50, 53, 74
  and the Engelsborg "family house", 189
  and home leave, 174
  and the involvement of the social authorities, 128
  and parents who use the children to gain something, 69, 192
  and prison health, 57, 58, 59, 188
  and visits, 190, 191
  and zero-tolerance policy in Danish prisons, 218, 219, 222

effects of imprisonment, 9, 10, 50, 182, 227–233
  and effects of mothers on babies, 109
  and effects on the family, 36–39, 50, 134
  and effects on the parent, 49, 76–78, 109
  and effects on the surrounding society, 34–36
  and historical discussions, 8, 27
  from the 19th century until today, 31–34
electronic tag, 108, 213, 223
Engelsborg family house, 118, 129, 142, 167, 189, 199, 201, 203, 205, 208, 210
England, 8, 23, 26, 44, 51, 62, 63, 81, 159, 161, 195, 202, 204, 206, 215, 219
Espersen, Lene, 12, 215, 216, 217, 222
Eugenics, 29, 30
EUROCHIPS (now called COPE: Children Of Prisoners Europe), 8, 15, 16
European Convention on Human Rights and Fundamental Freedoms, ECHR, 84, 92, 94, 102, 154
European Court of Human Rights, ECtHR, 11, 84, 90, 92, 94, 102, 103, 104, 105, 106, 111, 112
European Prison Rules, 89, 102, 107, 109, 153, 157
exclusion, 34, 36, 49, 79–81, 195

Farrington, David, 50
fear, 7, 62, 92, 117, 126, 142, 182
FFP (association for prisoners relatives, Norway), 43, 44, 237
financial problems, financial assurance, financial help, 49, 64, 81, 100
foster care, 47, 58, 59, 112, 134, 180, 184, 190
Foucault, Michel, 9, 10

Garland, David, 35, 36
Germany, 23, 66, 71, 72, 98, 127, 145, 204
Goddard, H. H., 29, 30
Greenland, 146, 154
guilt, 49, 69–70, 79, 142, 191, 212, 229

halfway house
  and children living with their parents in prison, 109, 200, 203, 205, 207, 208, 209, 211, 212
  and the Danish prison system, 146
  and the halfway house Engelsborg, 72, 118, 129, 199
  and re-entry, 198–200
  in relation to home leave, 172, 173
  and response rate in research project, 14
  and visiting facilities, 155
handcuffs, 62, 110, 115, 116, 118, 119, 121, 124, 129, 171
Hendriksen, Lise Garkier, 16
history, 20–27, 82, 167, 194, 231
home leave, 12, 47, 77, 78, 101, 105, 106, 139, 170–179, 187, 221, 222

India, 108, 202, 203
infants, 52, 109, 110, 111, 203, 206
internet, 79, 105, 106, 177–179
isolation
  and the birth of the modern prison, 22–27, 82, 227
  and the effects of imprisonment on children, 81
  and penal populism, 218
  and remand regimes, 138, 147
  and solitary confinement, 167, 168
Italy, 14, 15, 16, 18, 26, 27, 98, 102, 202, 208

Jakobsen, Janne, 13, 16, 52
Johnson, Robert, 35

Kjærum, Morten, 11, 12

Lagoutte, Stephanie, 15, 87, 111
letters, 91, 101, 105, 106, 165, 174, 176

Liebling, Alison, 9, 17, 50, 161
lies, lying, 49, 127
Lombroso, Cesare, 28, 29, 32
loss
  of autonomy, 182, 183, 230
  of contact, 61
  and the experience of loss, 7, 34, 56, 63, 70, 81, 133, 193

marginalisation, marginalised, 17, 50, 64, 195, 223
Maruna, Shadd, 9, 50
mass imprisonment, 10, 34–36, 55, 60, 76
media, 43, 66, 70, 81, 217
mental health
  and the effects of parental imprisonment on children, 7, 49, 50, 51, 53, 58, 70–74, 112
  and health problems in Pennsylvania-model prisons, 23
  and the mental health of prisoners, 188–189
  and mental health problems of parents, 67
mentally ill, 31, 32, 33, 36, 67, 188, 189, 223
methodology, 14–18, 48
mobile phones, 106, 175–177, 217, 223
Moore, Linda, 15
Murray, Joseph, 50, 81

non-custodial sentence, Non-custodial sanction, 98, 99, 206, 229
normalisation, 146, 147, 158, 159, 219
Norway, 18, 23, 24, 27, 43, 44, 61, 96, 107, 108, 111, 138, 146, 151, 155, 159, 167, 177, 202, 214, 233

open prisons, 79, 138, 145–146
  and access to the internet, 105, 178
  and children who live with their parents in prison, 203, 207
  and home leave, 170, 174
  and mobile phones, 175, 177
  and visiting facilities, 155, 157

panoptic, panoptical, 23, 25
parole, 80, 197–198, 219
penal populism, 12, 36, 79, 80, 214–226, 231, 232
Pennsylvania model, 22, 23
police
   and the methodology and aim of this study, 14–15, 17–20
   and arrest, 2–6, 62, 91–93, 115–132
   and home leave, 170, 172, 174
   and informing the children, 94–95
   and informing the social authorities, 96
   and penal populism, 12
   as perceived by children of imprisoned parents, 80–81, 115–132
   in relation to shame and stigmatisation, 135
   and restrictions on communication, 61, 106
   and solitary confinement in police detention, 147
   and visits during remand, 149–153, 165–167
   and visits during solitary confinement, 168
prisonization, 48, 52, 78
private life, 87, 89, 92
psychiatry/psychiatric, 27, 28, 30, 33, 36, 57, 59, 92, 188
psychology, psychological
   and psychological effects of solitary confinement, 28, 31, 61, 77, 167–169
   and psychological problems in prison populations, 57, 188, 189
   and psychological problems of prisoners' children, 8, 48, 59, 66, 71, 74, 88, 91, 182
   and psychological research on the effects of imprisonment, 32, 33
punitive, 24, 36, 80, 167, 215, 216, 217, 220, 221, 222

qualitative (methodology), 7, 8, 16, 38, 49, 50, 52, 53, 54, 55, 70, 71, 74, 115, 116, 133

quantitative (methodology), 7, 32, 50, 51, 52, 53, 54, 55, 59, 70, 74, 134, 228

race, racial, 30
recidivism, 30, 35, 38, 186, 194, 195
regime, 145–147, 219
   and contact with the imprisoned parent, 78
   and the historical development of prison regimes, 21–27
   and the impact of different prison regimes, 54
   and the remand regime, 138, 151, 229
   and security risks, 103–105
   and visiting regimes, 61, 155, 158, 165–166
rehabilitation, 8, 24, 153, 171, 194, 214, 215, 217, 222
release, 194–201
   and the different stages in the criminal justice process, 18–19, 228–230
   and release data, 139
   and release on parole, 219
   and release on probation, 172
   and the situation after release, 35, 38, 39, 47, 76, 78, 185, 186, 193
remand prisons, 14, 16, 32, 33, 145, 147, 188
   and the aim of the study, 18–19
   and children living with their parents in prison, 203–205, 209–211
   and communication, 54, 79, 108, 175–179
   and home leave, 170, 174
   and remand prisoner(s), 38, 45, 135, 137
   and solitary confinement, 168
   and visits, 54, 56, 78, 106, 147, 149, 150–153, 155–156, 159–164, 165–167, 223, 229
restrictions (during remand), 106, 136–137, 152, 229
retribution, 214, 215
risk factors, 7, 49, 51, 59, 75, 76

SAVN (association for prisoners relatives, Denmark), 74, 131, 136, 139, 142, 147, 161, 183, 184, 196
Scandinavia, Scandinavian, 26, 29, 47, 55, 61, 99, 146, 151, 167, 195, 214, 215, 229
school, 3–4
 and children living in prison with their parents, 208, 209
 and childrens' rights, 86
 and the educational backgrounds of imprisoned parents, 58
 and the effects on children of parental imprisonment, 8, 50, 71, 72, 101
 and home leave on the first school day, 170, 172
 and informing children, 127
 and informing the school, 134, 141, 142, 143
 and parents involvement in children's school work, 64, 77, 156
 and prison school, 23, 25
 and visiting, 166, 228
Scraton, Phil, 16
secondary prisonization, 48, 52
secrecy, secrets, 49, 67–69, 142
security
 and children living in prison with their parents, 207, 208
 and closed prisons, 146, 147, 155
 and the effects of imprisonment, 68, 135
 and home leave, 171, 173, 174
 and human rights, 82, 89, 90
 and penal populism, 218, 219, 232
 and remand prisons, 155, 159
 and restrictions in communication, 106
 and risk, 103, 104
 and the security checking of children, 163–165
 and the security function of prison in society, 81
 and solitary confinement, 167
 and visiting in prisons, 27, 54
sense of justice, 12, 80, 216, 219–220, 222

sentence, 3–6, 99–100, 221
 after the sentence, 138–143, 194–201
 and the Danes' perception of justice, 219–220
 and death sentence, 82
 and the different stages of the criminal justice process, 18–19, 229
 and the effects of long sentences, 64
 and informing social authorities, 96
 and penal populism, 79–80, 215–219, 232
 and sentencing parents and the rights of the child, 97–99
 and serving a sentence with children in prison, 202–213
 and short sentences and electronic tagging, 108
shame, 30, 49, 66, 69–70, 135, 142, 229
sleeping problems, 71
social services, social authorities, 3–5, 12–14, 191, 209
 and the arrest of parents through the eyes of social services, 115–132
 and children placed in foster care, 58
 and cooperation with the police, 127, 128
 and the different stages of the criminal justice process, 228
 and informing social authorities, 96–97
 and involvement of the social authorities, 128–131
social worker(s), 5, 15, 18–19, 81, 131, 136, 159, 166, 184
 and children living in prisons, 212
 and cooperation with the police, 130
sociology, 20, 30, 32
solitary confinement, 167–169
 and the birth of the modern prison, 23–25, 28
 and children living in prison with their parents, 211

solitary confinement – *continued*
  and the effects of imprisonment on the prisoner, 31–34, 229
  and health problems of parents in, 77
  and rise in the use of, 146–147
  and use during remand period, 61
  and visits, 151
South Africa, 99
stigmatisation, 65–69
  and penal populism, 222, 232
  stigmatisation of prisoners and their families, 8, 27–31, 36, 37, 48, 195, 220
supervised visits, 147, 148, 152, 165–167
Sweden, 3, 14, 18, 23, 24, 27, 43, 44, 61, 66, 69, 71, 72, 75, 96, 135, 138, 145, 146, 150, 159, 160, 167, 185, 202, 214, 233

taboo, 48, 49, 65–66, 67, 81, 139
telephone contact, 106, 107, 229

UK, 26, 72, 145, *see also* England
UN Committee on the Rights of the Child, 85, 91, 97, 100, 102
UN prison rules, Standard Minimum Rules for the Treatment of Prisoners, 83, 110
Universal Declaration of Human Rights, 25, 84, 87, 89
USA, US, 24, 47, 58, 75, 83, 117, 133, 144, 181

violence
  and children's rights, 86, 92
  and the Danes' sense of justice, 220
  and domestic violence, 36, 37, 62, 78, 117, 190
  and the effects of parental imprisonment on children, 51, 116, 117
  and violent arrests, 115
visits/visiting (in prisons), 14–19, 56, 78, 144–169, 187–188, 191
  and the birth of the modern prison, 23–25
  and changing visiting regimes, 26–27, 231
  and children's rights, 89, 101–107, 232
  compared to home leaves, 171
  and ECtHR court cases, 102–106
  and the family situation and prison visits, 45–47
  and parents who handle visits badly, 190–191, 193
  and prisoners' experiences of, 63–64, 172
  and qualitative research, 52
  and remand imprisonment, 61, 79, 80, 99, 136, 143, 229
  and statistics on visits, 39, 228
  and telling the truth, 140
  and transport, 100
  and visiting control, 174, 176
  and when visits do not take place, 180–186
  and zero-tolerance policy against drugs, 222
Vridsløselille (penitentiary), 23, 24, 158, 160, 161, 177

Wakefield, Sara, 50, 52
welfare state, 10, 29, 30, 55, 151, 195, 204, 214
Wildeman, Christopher, 50, 52

Printed in Great Britain
by Amazon